ROGER DOMMERGUE

THE PAIN OF LIVING

"This book corresponds to a temperament on the margins, an exceptional nature".
Raymond Las Vergnas, *Dean of the Sorbonne*

ROGER-GUY POLACCO DE MENASCE
(1924-2013)

Roger Dommergue was a Franco-Luxembourg professor of philosophy best known for his controversial positions on the Holocaust. Dommergue supported revisionist theories of the Holocaust, questioning the number of Jewish victims and claiming that the Nazi gas chambers were a myth. He gave lectures and interviews in which he denied the extent of the crimes committed by the Nazi regime during the Second World War.

THE PAIN OF LIVING

J'ai mal de la terre

1965

Translated and published by

OMNIA VERITAS LTD

OMNIA VERITAS®

www.omnia-veritas.com

© Omnia Veritas Limited – 2025

All rights reserved. No part of this publication may be reproduced by any means without the prior permission of the publisher. The intellectual property code prohibits copies or reproductions for collective use. Any representation or reproduction in whole or in part by any means whatsoever, without the consent of the publisher, the author or their successors, is unlawful and constitutes an infringement punishable by articles of the Code of Intellectual Property.

PREFACE	13
CHAPTER I	19
Diaphanous sadness	19
CHAPTER II	25
Grandma dearest	25
CHAPTER III	37
CHAPTER IV	47
CHAPTER V	59
CHAPTER VI	70
CHAPTER VII	83
CHAPTER VIII	92
CHAPTER IX	108
CHAPTER X	113
CHAPTER XI	129
CHAPTER XII	137
CHAPTER XIII	153
CHAPTER XIV	174
Surgery on the soul	176
Open letter to Albert Cohen.	191
CHAPTER XV	196
Noël	199
CHAPTER XVI	206
CHAPTER XVII	220
CHAPTER XVIII	234
CHAPTER XIX	247
Angelika	247
CHAPTER XX	267
Monique, or Karma's coup de grâce	267
CHAPTER XXI	305
The collapse	305

CHAPTER XXII **331**
  THE WILL 331
CHAPTER XXIII **353**
CHAPTER XXIV **362**
  THORNS 362
TO MY LITTLE BEATRICE **374**
  OTHER TITLES 375

*"You've gone through the roof".
"This is a very curious and vigorous work. The style of the narrative part is fast and effective in a completely new way. It is an unexpected style, very different from the American staccato. It's a technical innovation that should be noticed. The background is bitter and painful and reaches its fullness in the non-narrative part. The whole thing seems to have a singular strength that is, O so much, out of the ordinary.
I wish this book the percussive success it deserves.
This book corresponds to a temperament on the fringes of an exceptional nature".*

Raymond Las Vergnas, *Dean of the Sorbonne*

Rest assured that you have not received your soul in vain.

Dr Raymond Soupault, *preface to*
L'Homme, cet inconnu *by* Dr Alexis Carrel.

Your work could be understood, but ON will prevent it from coming to light because the truth must remain under a bushel. The only ones to know it from a diabolical angle will be the Jews themselves.

Gisèle Polacco de Ménasce

*I found this book admirable for its fire, its passion, its sincerity and its originality. As the critics have pointed out, this book is singular, that is to say, unique, not belonging to any family of writers.
This is an exceptional rarity.*

Michèle Saint-Lô

"The dandy, when he doesn't kill himself or go mad, makes a career and poses for posterity.

Albert Camus, *L'Homme révolté*.

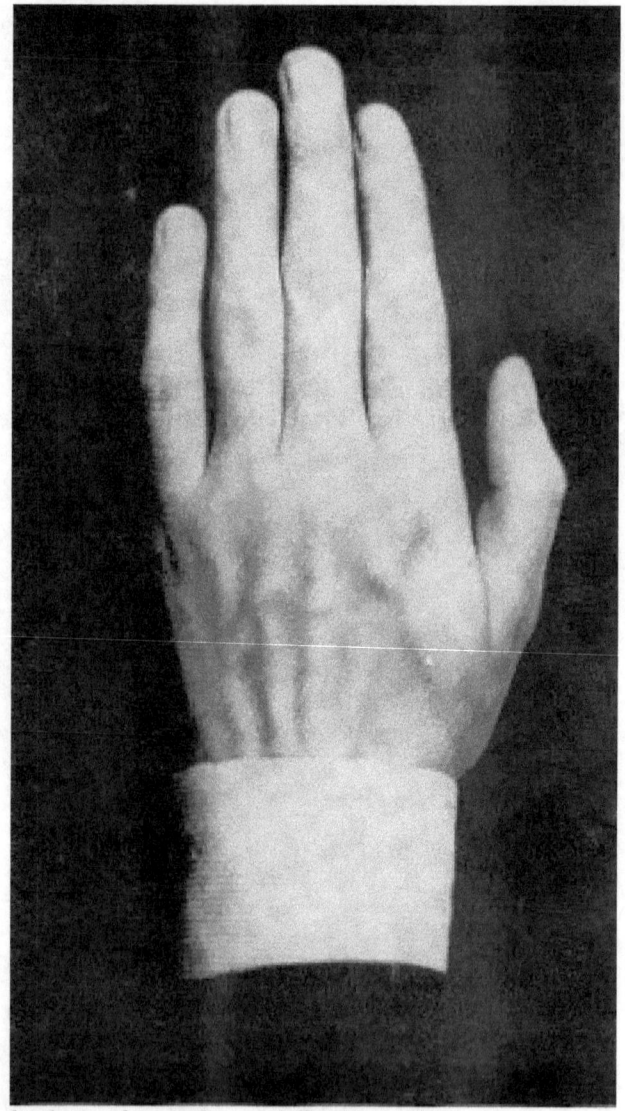

"I think I understand your difficulties; I hope you can overcome them without forgetting them."

Albert Camus, *Letter to the*

[Handwritten letter from André Breton, Paris, 21 mai 1952]

André Breton

This letter is not intended to be polemical, but merely symbolic.

[Handwritten letter from Abbé Georges de Nantes, with CRC monogram and "Jésus!" at top, dated "Le 9 mars 75", beginning "Docteur, Je vous remercie de vos deux lettres mais je désire interrompre cette correspondance, vos idées m'étant parfaitement étrangères. Votre..."]

This letter from Abbé Georges de Nantes is not intended to be polemical: it is merely symbolic.

It will be noted that the content of a letter from one of the most eminent authorities on Catholic fundamentalism is the same as that of André Breton, Pope of Surrealism and an integral leftist...

PREFACE

> *"The true passion of the twentieth century is servitude"*
> Albert Camus

That's why *J'ai mal de la terre* is unlike any other book. Your work evolves between the margins that separate the truths you have felt and the minimum that can be expressed. To overstep to one side or the other of this fragile boundary would be either to condemn you to silence or to become unreadable, or finally to betray your thoughts.

The artist can no longer utter a clear cry: happy if it remains intelligible.

At a time when evil has subtly taken hold of dialectic and logic, of all the instruments of thought in favour of all kinds of inversions, the impossibility of expressing the truth arises from the fact that it no longer manifests itself in the human heart except through emotions, impulses, dazzling but powerless outbursts: only one value remains worthy of expression: the suffering of the soul and the heart.

So you have restored this suffering, but in the only way you could, that is to say purely, free of all the compensations of hatred, revenge, irony and mockery. Any trace of coquetry, any concern for aesthetics, even the slightest legitimate search for effect, distorts the metaphysical reflection born of an exceptional trial of life.

Suffering is only true and exemplary if it is subjected to insults and mockery in the same way that an unarmed child receives blows, with a look of astonishment. The last resource of anyone who has understood the modern world is to expose himself to slaps. This was not the result of any deliberation, you reproduced yourself and it so happens that in this image there is nothing to subtract, nothing to add. It is in a way the mirror in which the miserable adventure of the modern world is reflected: your diagnosis is compassionate but implacable.

The artist does not know the compensatory hatred that destroys all superior objectivity. To understand is to be incapable of hatred or contempt. To hate is to clearly prove that you have understood nothing. We scandalise, it's true, but that only leads to worse. Your book shows us how we live in a time of diabolical scandal. This scandal which, under the guise of goodness, truth and love, allows evil to rot right into the heart of the righteous man. Then he himself becomes the worst agent of destruction: victim and virus. Anyone who becomes aware of this and wants to flee either succumbs or goes mad. Survival is only possible at the expense of the unacceptable. At a time when people are being killed every day in the name of a supposed intelligence that occupies all the official machinery, true thought has no chance of expressing itself or surviving outside liberal hospitals and prisons or Bolshevik gulags.

Yet there are many prophets in the twentieth century. Some simply note their revolt carefully, have a clear conscience and leave it at that. None preferred indictment to fame.

As for the crowd of others, since their sentence refers to the same principles that animated the accused, it is the same blindness that determines the vigilantes and the guilty: "If one blind man guides another blind man, they will both fall into the pit"...

If I had been given the opportunity to experience your epic destiny, to think about it and write about it, I would have been reminded of the grand and tragic opening line of a book by Bernanos: "Evil has never had a better opportunity to accomplish the works of good; the devil has never better deserved the name given to him by Saint Jerome, that of God's monkey".

Your anguish is, in a sense, a challenge to the disappearance of intelligence that characterises our time. Those who walk confidently wear protective blinkers, and little by little they will form a common, familiar image of your book, one they can relate to: so in "1984" we will say: "He's crazy".[1]

People are so far removed from the true guides, the thinkers, who could guide them by enlightening their times, that if the truth comes to light, if by some miracle there is no longer any way of escaping it, then they manage to distil it, to scatter it, so that it is diverted from its purpose, ineffective and totally ignored.

---

[1] "In 1984, the most intelligent will be the least normal" (George Orwell's *1984*)

We are now at a time when the slightest social contact with a true artist results in psychiatric commissions and a diagnosis of madness by robots conditioned by Marx and Freud.

You were given many tips and recipes, but you were also given demonstrations that required culture, ingenuity and an analytical sense that earned the admiration of many.

Should you listen to them? Can you confide in people whose mental deficiencies are obvious when you look at them? It is useless and dangerous. Men have lost their sense of the human, and the reasons are now clear: Judeo-Cartesianism engendered by Judeo-Christianity.

Today a genius scientist has confirmed what you had understood and what Alexis Carrel had suspected: you bring here the arguments of your destiny and your heart.

The same conditions that precipitated the destruction of true values encouraged the development of other forces that were precious as long as they remained contained and controlled, but disastrous if they invaded the psychophysiology of each individual.

Man can no longer access true values, or even suspect them, since the new concepts take their place. They have all the logic of values, they insidiously satisfy passions, apparent common sense, morality and sometimes, alas, even the most altruistic impulses. Equipped with these forces alone, modern man is fulfilled. This is enough for him, but it is useless, because true intelligence cannot be defined on the basis of these errors, and there is no longer anyone officially available to define it. As a result of universal mental incapacity, humanity is now made up of nothing but bloody, satisfied robots.[2]

That's why your destiny is so fragile. Institutions, sub-humans and women are holding you back. Your rigour is a language foreign to the whole world. In times of greatness, solitude was possible, but in the twentieth century the values of profitability demand their places and their slaves. Creative solitude is disappearing, and the imprudent are being killed. This is done

---

[2] The "intelligence quotient" is a joke that in no way reflects intelligence. It only works on criteria of elementary logic, which can be brilliant in primitive beings.
It totally ignores the real components of intelligence: intuition, spontaneous spirit of synthesis, aesthetic sense, moral sense. It's likely that many of humanity's geniuses have very low IQs!

in an occult, underground, cowardly way, because the spirit has no place in the modern world.

Our age is necessarily an age of the masses, because levelling out gives rise to a morbid happiness that satisfies the weak-willed of our contemporaries: the happiness of those who have renounced thought and courage.

With capitalism, and with its normal extension financed by capitalism, Communism, people's lives are now mapped out to the letter. They no longer have the courage to measure things, so things measure them.

Deep down, man is too big for man.

You demonstrate it, you suffer from this atrocious destiny that men have created for themselves by their multiple resignations by abandoning themselves to the parasites of these 5000 years, because greatness frightens them, too heavy for their shoulders. They prefer the cowardly shadow to the light created for them.

It is therefore inevitable that today very few minds will ever have access to certain performances. Your despair is compounded by the increasingly suffocating feeling of having to address the deaf and the blind.

Some, fewer and fewer, still suffer in their hearts, but you weep over problems that are bigger than all of them.

You have understood that to make men understand, you have to change the determinism of men. Saints and heroes have died for refusing to understand this law, and I fear that your destiny will force you to imitate them.

Truth cannot be conceived without tearing oneself away, and as you wrote to me, it seems that your ordeal will one day make it possible to "reach, far from atheistic Judaic materialism, hysterical or disembodied mysticism and ferocious dogmatism, the balance between body and spirit, between matter and essence".

Your singular personality and your misfortune is that you are, in short, devoid of that necessary form of psychology, which consists of poking out one's eyes to please the blind.

However, in spite of yourself, you will be more or less forced to use the weapons designed for and by mediocrity. If love is your only guide you will be crushed. People will even come to use you as a conscience and as an instrument of massacre.

It's your diabolism that helps you live, but you're lucid about it and this awareness stifles your life. So your struggle may seem futile.

This derisory lucidity characterises the fatal character in your book, the Dandy. A visionary and a poet, a thinker tortured by God and by Satan, who refuses all systems in the name of truth, tortured by God and Satan because he is both, because he carries both within him like a fire that devours him and illuminates his time.

It is to your heroic credit that you have highlighted how, in this deeply moving person, looking with love, revolt and powerlessness at oneself and at others is one and the same thing.

You can see how, by virtue of the same determinism, you sense the current drama, but on the other hand - and this is the price you have to pay - you cannot explain this drama without inevitably lending yourself to criticism inspired by a truncated mind, by a universally accepted paralogy.

Any robot in this world will be able to refute your work without understanding anything about it. A man of instinct will feel it obscurely because instinct often mysteriously joins the conclusions of extreme intuition.

The few who won't be bothered by it will be dizzy.

Ignorantly forced to give up teaching, you will find the communion of a few. Men like you are always alone in the face of truth, and in this dialogue you owe no one if you want to preserve it.

Anything that enriches you, enriches humanity. Your suffering is fruitful...

Jacques Charpentier Puységur

Chapter I

Diaphanous sadness

Author: *Do you remember in Paradise Lost, Satan said:*
   "O sun, how I hate your rays".[3]
   Satan was lucky to hate the sun - you see, I don't give a damn about the sun.
Albert Camus: *But you love the light.*
Conversation shortly before Camus's death

The snake is the most unhappy being in the world
He never asked to be a snake.
He is repulsive and unlovable.
It bites those who want to love it.
And those who want to love him are forced
To let themselves be bitten and die.
Either to kill the snake they want to love.
The snake did not ask to be a snake.
You have to love the snake.
The serpent can do nothing against himself
For he does not know that he is a serpent.
He's unhappy and he doesn't know why.
You have to love the snake.
You have to love him a lot, and that's only fair.
What condemns him in spite of himself
is his lack of self-awareness
You have to fight against the snake's inevitability...[4]

Persistence of memories so distant from childhood... Tristan remembered a thousand things from his early years.

---

[3] O sun, how I hate thy rays. "*Paradise lost*" by Milton.

[4] A poem inspired by the incredible, immense Jewish cosmic question.

The spacious house in Courbevoie, the little wood in the large garden, the staircase, the Judas tree that shaded it and radiated its mauve-pink colour all around like an enchantment...

The big pool, the goldfish that swirled around it in great numbers, the coolness of the fountain, the droplets that the wind sent tingling down her legs. And then the grand salon with its concert piano, its coquettish little room, the aviary with the doves, the two Danes, Tirasse and Prince, who had died of poisoning.

And there his mother, father, sisters Charlotte and Laure and paternal grandmother.

His father was a colossus, standing at one metre ninety. By middle age he had become so overweight that he appeared to be hydropic. In reality, he was very fat, because when circumstances forced him to fast, he became thin.

His father's face was strange, ugly even, but for those who knew how to observe, there was a supernatural imprint in this mask. A gigantic forehead; he was a kind of intellectual in the raw, ignoring immediate realities and considering it natural that others should concern themselves with material nonsense so as to leave him in peace to think.

He was said to have universal understanding. He predicted the Second World War and even a third between the United States and China. Although he rarely read the newspapers, he knew the fundamental trends in international data, and had the keys to a synthetic understanding of the economic situation. There was nothing optimistic about his short- or long-term forecasts.

His father left him two verses:

> "O the pleasures of the earth, greyed loves.
> the marbles of the cemetery are shattered."

And on the back of an envelope, marked in his elegant handwriting:

"The wise man is not the talk of the town".

He seems to have adapted to this role of grandiose spectator of a rotting humanity: a curious mixture of the sublime and the grotesque, he would declaim his verses in a deep, well timbred voice, and then sit back down, collapsing a salon chair.

His mother...

She had betrayed him. He had never received the tenderness, the understanding, the love, the closeness that a true mother always lavishes on even the most misguided of her sons.

While his father belonged to a bourgeois family of lawyers, his mother descended from a Jewish caste of Austrian nobility who left her name to a street, a secondary school, a hospital, a museum, not to mention a few statues, in a Middle Eastern country. His wealth, estimated at two hundred million gold at the beginning of the twentieth century, was based on banking, cotton, progress and socialism...

When her mother married her father, she was fifteen and he thirty-five. Tristan was born a year later, so she was sixteen when he was born.

A magnificent type of Herodias, she was beautiful, of that oriental beauty, fascinating and diabolical. An eruptive existence, she was a volcano, her mother, a volcano in continuous activity and without an atom of common sense. Black hair, goyesque face, dark almond-shaped eyes, a fine, aquiline nose, which in itself could not be considered beautiful, but the miracle of the aesthetics of her face put her nose in harmony with the rest of her features. A dominating nose, with quivering, sensual wings, a rose mouth, graceful, chubby forms, tall and slim, she had that proud air of a fallen archangel that Tristan had somewhat inherited. Incomparable race, rather particular distinction, not that effete distinction of which only distinguished beings are aware, elegant and simple, but of that elegance and simplicity which dazzle.

A tormented poet, a mystical and destructive demon, a strange form of histrionic spirituality, combined with a strange lack of lucidity about herself. Vehemently converted to Catholicism some ten years after Tristan's birth, she nevertheless remained Rebecca.

A prolific producer of disasters from which she herself suffered by the boomerang effect, powerless to deflect certain instincts. An unconscious and fatal disease: dissolving.

His soul trembled and exasperated at the happiness of others. Some Belial guided his arm at the right moment. Tristan had been her greatest victim, but he knew she was irresponsible. Sadly, he tried to be careful not to confide in her, as her petty intervention was bound to trigger the irreparable. Often, the call of his heart, of his viscera, prevented him from taking this reality into account. So Tristan paid for his imprudence. He saw her again at that time, his actress mother, her fine Sarah-Bernardesque face, her bewitching mobility of expression, her words, her gaze and her bewitching mimicry, everything about her exuded born drama and reminded him as much of Rachel as of Cleopatra.

Why had her father married her mother?

There was a real age difference between them and it does not seem that true love was the key to this union.

In fact, his father had a friend whom he had met on the benches of the Lycée Michelet. They had both thought that the easy path to success and social success was a rich marriage into the new world aristocracy that had emerged from the revolution of 1789, the aristocracy of money and all-powerful finance. So his father and his friend Paul married two sisters from an international Jewish family they had met in Biarritz, his mother and his aunt Denise. By chance, or rather by stratagem, it was on the property in Biarritz that things began and ended.

The marriage of Aunt Denise, her mother's sister, and Paul, who became her uncle by marriage, was coherent, typical and organised. Paul completed his medical studies, became mayor, general councillor and member of parliament, and if he hadn't died of angina just before the so-called "liberation", he would have been a minister in 1945. Uncle Paul, a radical socialist, was a man of great and necessary plasticity.

As for his mother...

The events leading up to the wedding were many and far-fetched. His mother, he had been told, had rolled on the floor at the age of fifteen to marry his father. Although he knew the mentality of his mother's family very well, he doubted, not without reason, that his mother had been forced into this ridiculous and disproportionate marriage at the age of fifteen. But she claimed she had.

A large dowry was promised. Her father was undoubtedly counting on this money to realise his intellectual plans, but the dowry was never paid. Ambitious calculation, grim conclusion.

A megeresque wife of fifteen years, three children, of whom Tristan was the eldest, and who were to become the bruised little victims of multiple infamies.

The first seven years, in the peaceful setting of Courbevoie, in the garden, in the big house... Nothing was quiet. His father used to threaten his mother with a pearl-handled revolver. Tristan would go over and beat his father's mottled grey jacket with his little spade. His father wasn't a brute, he seemed rather passive, but a woman like his mother, Tristan would have thrown him out of the window, or he would have left and never come back. She must have had a natural gift for getting under his skin. Another time, the revolver scene in reverse: a small gun with a black handle this time.

They had a mania for revolvers.

She stormed out of the window overlooking the garden and put a gun to my father's head. He remained calm, cutting a rose beside the pond: "Go and tell Mum that I want to kiss her". But the child's diplomatic mission had no effect.

What were they playing at?

He never knew, but those images had stuck in his tiny brain like a moan.

Their maternal grandmother was indulgent and generous. He remembers her spending a whole night rubbing Tristan's knees because he was suffering from some sort of rheumatism due to growing up. A whole night! How good she was! He felt moved when he remembered her.

Grandma didn't get on with his mother. As the servants went to bed, he and his two sisters heard them shouting: he saw his mother and grandmother again, both with bloody hands and knives in their hands.

The three children had nurses and were in the hands of the servants. Tristan remembered their names, Mouchy and Aby, probably short for Gaby. He had once wondered why all the brushes in the house belonged to him: "Go and get me the clothes brush!

In the evanescent thread of his memories :

His father was eating chips with his fingers. It's true that they're so much better! His mother looked at him with an angry, bubbling expression, then suddenly stood up and knocked the plate of chips onto her father's lap. Without saying a word, he left the dining room. Another time his mother hit him on the arm. He flicked the spot a few times, then stepped aside. One day he grabbed her by the throat. Why did he do that? Wasn't he the real victim? But she obviously thought it was her and ended up taking on the role of victim.

Tristan and his sisters were bathing together. He had noticed a surprising difference between himself and his sisters. He never found out how the nanny reported this to his mother, but she beat him ferociously, without a word of explanation, with the ebony riding crop that lay on the piano.

He saw her again, his actress mother, with her tone of voice, her mimicry capable of persuading people commonly described as intelligent of the most implausible things.[5]

Seven years had passed since Tristan's birth. The fights between his father and mother left a painful mark on them;

One day his mother disappeared. Weeks went by...

---

[5] This has become an international media custom this century.

Chapter II

> *"From the day I was alerted, lucidity came to me and I received all the wounds at the same time. I lost my strength all at once and the whole universe began to laugh around me".*
>
> The Fall, Albert Camus

Grandma dearest

One summer evening, Tristan was crouching pensively at the foot of his bed when a tall man burst into his room. He had taken Tristan in his arms, while another gentleman took his two sisters who were asleep in the next room. The two of them tumbled down the stairs four by four. Their grandmother was kept locked in the kitchen by a third man whom the children didn't know any more than the other two. They were bundled into a car and half an hour later they found themselves in front of a private mansion in the 16th arrondissement of Paris.

They were laid on a bed.

Lying there in bed was her mother's mother: *"Grandma, darling".*

A shiver ran through Tristan's body. Memory, disgust, despair. There she was, lying on a wide sofa in a vast room of his town house. A lamp on the bedside table, the light yellow, confused, everything dark and sinister. Tristan was frightened. His heart was beating wildly. He could feel his little sisters' hearts beating as fast as his own.

There she was, wrapped in a shawl, her abundant grey hair slicked back and held in a bun. Yellowish complexion, nauseating to look at, black eyes, almond-shaped eyelids, oval face and hooked nose. He looked mean and funny. Sometimes there was a glimmer of goodness in her eyes fleeting and despairing. She looked like the damned witch from Snow White and the Seven Dwarfs...

Thin hands, greenish yellow, repulsive, she seemed slumped over, incapable, sceptical, powerless and above all mean.

"Are you Mummy's mummy?" whispered Charlotte, half-hoarse, half-halted, horrified. It was indeed her, the one they were going to call "*darling grandma*".

Charlotte perhaps suspected that none of the three children would have a single fond memory of their *beloved grandma*. Within reach was a round box of sweets. She took it with an archly false smile, and offered them a sweet that they put in their mouths.

You have to imagine what it feels like to eat a sweet in such circumstances. He didn't think he'd ever digested that sweet: his body may have digested it, but his mind never could.

Everything we do must be done with our mind and heart. Food given without love destroys oneself and others. Work done without love destroys oneself and others. This is why everything in the modern world is false and crazy. Without love, everything will necessarily be polluted, because the concept of profitability can never replace intelligence, which can only be built through love. Without love, the intellect destroys everything.

The children were to stay with *their beloved grandmother* for a long time. How painful that childhood was. Not to be would have been preferable, but they were.

As they had so clearly foreseen, *grandma dearest* had the soul of a torturer and the three of them were the little tortured ones.

None of the three children have any emotional or tender memories of their *beloved grandma*. Opening their mouths was a crime. Did a food make them nauseous? She wouldn't let them refuse to eat it. Tristan could still see Charlotte in his mind's eye, vomiting because *Grandma* wanted to force her, "for her own good", to eat the boiled endives she loathed.

Later, when her sisters, who were boarders in Paris, sometimes came on Sundays, *grandmamma darling* would make them prepare this favourite dish, which also disgusted Laure, the younger sister, and Tristan.

Slaps rained down for the slightest thing, for a yes or a no that should have been remembered. His words of endearment were "idiot" and "moron".

As a child, Tristan naturally had ruby-red lips. *Grandma* said he used to bite or rub them to get that beautiful colour. She threatened Tristan that if he continued to do this, she would rub red pepper on his lips. As the lips continued to retain their natural colouring, she crushed a large quantity of the chilli pepper on his lips in front of the astonished servants. Why had she made the suspect lips pay in this way? It seemed to Tristan today that she had acted out of subconscious jealousy, because her lips were pale and bloodless.

After the hot baths, which she insisted on giving herself out of devotion and kindness, and the prospect of which made all three of them tremble, she would flood them with cold water, under the good pretext of "doing something about it". But she put so much sadism into this practice that it became obvious persecution: they shivered and gasped without saying a word.

Grandma darling dominated those around her so much that everyone, especially her son Jacques and his sister Denise, Uncle Paul's wife, accepted everything from their 'little mum'. They would have said "amen" to her every move if they had known the word. Long months of torture, during which Tristan was subjected to slaps, insults, mock communications at the reformatory, moral pressure, mental blackmail, a desire to hurt feelings by perverting them as well as the body.

He had just turned eight and was accepted as a boarder at the Lycée Lakanal.

At that age Tristan was a pale blond child, very sensitive and delicate. Being separated from his mother was atrocious for him. To be plunged into the middle of this community where everything is brutality, where you have to be tough to avoid being crushed, was an inhuman ordeal. He suffered relentlessly throughout his years as a boarder. He said nothing, still shaking, his heart began to beat faster. He began to *think*.

His friends bullied him because he couldn't defend himself. He had long white hands with fragile joints, his wrists were not strong enough to strike a blow and he had never felt the need to do so. It wasn't a lack of moral courage, but he couldn't see why, and he knew that his muscles and nerves had no chance of winning in fights where he couldn't see the end. Brutal physical courage was difficult for him. Male physical contact was repulsive to him. Even today, he could imagine fighting with a sword, but not with his fists.

He spent long days crying, and today he remembers this constant ordeal as if it were yesterday. He didn't work in class. He suffered too much to be able to focus his attention, and working in a vulgar community was impossible for him. He had no sense of competition and the fact that his neighbour was first and he was last left him with an unusual indifference. He wasn't there.

One day, the headmaster came to hand in his notes to congratulate or admonish the ninth-graders. After scolding him severely, the headmaster looked at his pale little face and big blue eyes with long eyelashes and said: "How could you work well looking like that? He gently stroked his cheek and sent him back to his seat.

But Tristan had now understood. It all mattered so little. We learned nothing at school, nothing that could teach us how to *be*. The top of the class went to Polytechnique or Normale Supérieure and never left. They never took a step towards a deeper understanding of man. They were never greedy for the absolute, impatient for the infinite. The greatest minds have always been mediocre schoolboys.

This is easy to understand: a standard education, up to the age of twenty or twenty-five, invests the whole of the psyche, which is then fully mobilised and sterilised for the maturation of an original mentality which, through personal meditation, would lead to genius.

That's why education must be prudent, never masturbatory, as is the case, for example, with the deformation towards the agrégation, which produces standard beings. Shakespeare knew "little Greek and less Latin". The school report of Chopin, that unrivalled genius, bore this annotation: "An absolutely impossible pupil, but a genius".

The bullying he suffered gave Tristan a constant and painful meditation on the problem of evil and suffering. The physical and moral ugliness, the mean-spiritedness and cowardice of the world embraced him. He was already weeping for the world more than for himself.

He set himself up as a symbol.

Why this revolting and incomprehensible cowardice? Why did beings of the same spiritual level not live in the same human group?

During his long stays at various lycées and collèges in the Paris region, Tristan would sometimes visit his *beloved grandma* on Sundays. Boarding school life was so odious for him that the fictitious comfort of a pale family appearance was a balm for a great wound.

He saw his mother. His mother, that painful ghost...

When he had to leave again on Sunday evening, he cried so hard on the platform at Denfert-Rochereau station that he still wonders how they had the heart to let him go. Supreme despair.

Once a month, the three children went to see their father in the big house in Courbevoie. In the car that took them there was a bailiff and a coroner. *Grandma* and their mother would tell them abominations about their father. So on the first visit they were very frightened. At the mere sight of their father, they tumbled down the stairs and rushed into the arms of their uncles, who were waiting for them in the street, car doors open, as if their reaction had been foreseen.

But they came back and eventually got used to it, because their father received them in a charming and sumptuous way. He gave them magnificent gifts, a gold watch, a gold pen, the dining room table was covered with succulent cakes by the Marquise de Sévigné and other good things.

So the children had a field day.

Soon they moved with their mother to a small village in the Perche, Marolles les Buis. It was a fragrant, rolling countryside, full of healthy poetry for those who do not suffer.

Winter came.

Tristan contracted a cold, whooping cough, pneumonia, double pneumonia, bronchopneumonia, double bronchopneumonia. Finally, a fatal purulent pleurisy topped it all off.

He lay in bed for a whole year covered in abscesses and boils. Incisions were made almost daily and without anaesthetic. With such an aristocratic and delicate nature, a lack of love and an appalling school diet based on starchy foods and bad meat were bound to result in illness one day. Nature never forgives. Every day, he was wrapped in sheets soaked in cold water to bring down the fever, an absurd procedure if you think about it. These wraps were torture. Then there were the abscesses and the seven or eight injections a day. He became such a skeleton that the needles refused to penetrate the flesh and panic gripped him at the mere sight of a syringe.

One day he begged a teacher from Chartres who had come to see him to reduce the number of injections: he cut them in half. They even went so far as to give him just one or two injections a day. The mere prospect of a camphor injection with an abscess grafted onto it sent him into a frenzy.

One evening his mother, who had some knowledge of the art of chirology, examined Tristan's hand and began to cry. Perhaps she had sensed a sign of death, because three days later Tristan went into a coma.

He remained lucid in his silent agony. He saw the parish priest on the left, as he had become a great friend of his mother's since her recent conversion to Catholicism, and he made her recite some very unfamiliar prayers: "Our Father who art in heaven ... thy will be done on earth as it is in heaven".

On the right he could see his mother sobbing and Dr Boulier also sobbing. This doctor had treated him energetically and, next to this little patient, he melted like a child. He was a delicate soul and years later, Tristan had learned that he had committed suicide. It takes more than courage for gentle souls to contemplate the misery and deafness of the world.

Happy people are those who feel nothing and think nothing, because to get to the bottom of things is to get to the point of suffering. The closer you get to cabbage, the happier you are because you don't suffer. A reasoning cabbage in a cubic centimetre of mind is happy. Humanity is made up of reasoning cabbages: we do what we want with them through school, radio, television, deficient food and systematic vaccination. We de-educate them, dumb them down, slaughter them and they want more.

How happy fools are! It seemed that Tristan had to die.

His mother told him that she had prayed to Our Lady of Chartres to cure him, to perform a miracle. She must have heard him, because in the early hours of the morning, to everyone's amazement, Tristan sat up and asked for ham...

There is a file on this miracle in the cathedral archives. I guess Our Lady must have heard him...[6]

---

[6] The child belongs to the thyroid bio-type, and such a powerful thyroid can often achieve such a recovery through the vital super-power it implies. The thyroid is the gland of life and intelligence. Those with a powerful thyroid, due to the biotype determined by this gland, enjoy, even in a delicate situation, an exceptional defence of their organism against disease and a considerable potential for recovery.

It wasn't the health tragedy he had just suffered that was going to stop him being sent back to boarding school. One or two years later, when Tristan was back in that hellhole, the headmaster, at his mother's instigation, took Tristan to see the Professor who had treated him and reduced the number of injections. As Tristan undressed, he heard the Professor say to the Headmaster in the next room: "The last time I saw this child, not a single part of his lungs was breathing".

During this near-fatal illness, Tristan's father had tried to see his son. He had heard his deep voice in the little garden, but his mother wouldn't let him. "He's afraid of you," she told him.

How could Tristan not have been afraid of his father with all the nastiness his mother and *darling grandmother* poured out on him?

A long convalescence, then of course boarding school.

Filthy institutions in Eure et Loir, religious of course, because Tristan had been baptised after his miraculous recovery. One of the directors of one of these institutions took him on his lap one day and stroked his genitals through his knickers. He only did this once. In Chartres, his stay at the Notre Dame institution was less painful: he was part of the choir singing in the cathedral. This was his first exposure to melody. His heart began to beat at the sight of a piano, and he felt deliciously numb and shivering as he listened to Chopin. The piano was to become the unfulfilled dream of his life, the oasis he would never reach.

In class he still didn't do much. His weak constitution and the liabilities of his uncared-for and unloved childhood sterilised any effort in an already nonchalant and sensual nature. Even if he had studied music, he would certainly not have satisfied his teachers for years. Nothing was further from his nature than the study of the rudiments, the basics of music theory and technique.

The divorce proceedings between his father and mother had started the moment they arrived at *grandma's* house. Tristan had never known the details of this sad affair but he wasn't tempted by the sludge. He'd been splattered enough not to want more. He remembered that his father had yellow posters put up all over Paris because of the 'abduction of his children'. The trial lasted more than ten years and it seems that material interests were at stake.

The first legal battle seemed to be won by her father, because her mother had abandoned the marital home.

Grandma and the whole family were worried.

They were going to have to pay. What Tristan had noticed was that nothing could ever get them to open their safe: suffering, despair, discreet prayers, moral slaps, insults or spitting, nothing could do it. So the danger was great.

To win the case, he had to accuse his father - quite rightly, alas, as we shall see - of being unable to provide for his children.

It was obvious that his father had little talent for menial tasks and that this trial had made his situation precarious.

For *Grandma*, the only thing that mattered was not to pay: "I don't mind looking after the children", she told the judge, "but if you ask me for money, I'll go and sit in prison".

There was therefore only one solution for them: prove that their ruined father could not provide for them. They would therefore be returned to their father, and after a few months or a few years, the experiment would come to an end: an examination of their physical and moral health would prove that their father was incapable of providing them with daily bread.

Their money being their lifeblood, they coolly conceived this project.

It seems that her mother took the initiative, but as she had nothing of her own, it was up to *Grandma* and her brothers and sisters to dissuade her.

In fact, they didn't object at all, except of course through ostentatious objections, fairground pathos, hypocritical demonstrations, grandiloquent words, so as to safeguard their respectability in the eyes of the gallery.

On the day they were taken to their father's, their mother took them to a show and then to a pastry shop. This meal for the condemned was marvellously cool. These treats were to accentuate the contrast, as their experience was a vital testimony to the clan.

When they arrived in Courbevoie, their mother took them through the garden gate and got back into her taxi without waiting for their father to come and take possession of this little human cargo who already didn't know where they were, in what world of brutes they were struggling. There they were, dazed, not knowing what to do, having tried in vain to hold on to their mother, who had torn herself away to leave.

The almost gigantic stature of their father appeared on the stoop. He stared at them in amazement, his gold lorgnon on his nose and his immense forehead. He then understood what was happening to him. Ruined and destitute, he could not look after the children. So he asked one of his friends, Count Richard de Grandmas, to take the children to the police station.

The commissioner then wanted to put them in touch by telephone with their mother and her family. Uncle Jacques was reached. They told him that they were alone and abandoned at the police station. In his neutered voice, the uncle replied that there was nothing he could do.

"There was nothing they could do about it! Even if a court judgement had returned them to their father, the police commissioner's testimony alone that their father refused to take them back would have sufficed in court to legally return them to their mother. Did the courts require a finding that the children were emaciated and ill? Was this inhumane strategy legally necessary?

You'd think so, because the commissioner took the children to the Assistance Publique in Paris.

What anguish Tristan felt.

He felt so alone, such a stranger, separated from his sisters. He had taken a nurse as his confidante and she wept as Tristan told her his grief like a poem.

Their mother came to visit them. She told them she would come back for them. But two days later their father came. He took them away. They were going to stay for a few weeks in the big house in Courbevoie.

It was empty. Everything had been sold: the concert piano, the master paintings, the period furniture. All that remained were a few wicker garden tables and chairs to replace the stylish chairs, tables and armchairs that had gone up in smoke.

Richard, their father's friend, lived with them. He was a sensitive, intelligent man, but very taken with his father's intelligence. He had become a sort of alter-ego of his father. He looked after the children and was friendly and humane.

Ever since his baptism, Tristan had had an incoercible fear of the devil. Terrible nightmares would wake him up shivering.

Richard undertook to pass on his panic-stricken terror.[7]

One day Tristan went to see him in his room at the top of the house.

— Good morning, Tristan, last night I was in a lot of trouble. I had cigarettes and no fire. I had to wait until midnight to be able to smoke!

— Why only until midnight?

— Because that's when Satanas himself comes to visit me. So I was able to borrow the tip of his tail to light my cigarette. Afterwards, we played a game of chess and I won - that Satanas, he plays like a champ!

Tristan laughed, but a little yellow. He didn't find it at all funny that Richard was lighting his cigarette with Satanas' cock. His intuition told him that Satanas was far too serious to indulge in such tricks.

Wasn't Satanas more of a cigarette man, which no one suspected at the time.

He was soon to encounter it all over the modern world.[8]

Richard had studied medicine and psychiatry. One day, Tristan was walking round the house with a severe toothache. Richard sat him down, took his hand and looked into his eyes without saying a word.

Tristan felt his pain rise and rise and then disappear.

He was dumbfounded. Three days later, Richard had a swollen cheek like a balloon, a fluxion. Unfortunately, he was unable to carry out on himself the experiment that had been so successful on Tristan.

---

[7] For two thousand years of Christianity, this veritable psychosis has wreaked havoc and destroyed lives.
The case of the succubi and incubi who believed they had slept with the devil and were burned is a symbolic example.
It should be noted that before his baptism, Tristan was unaware of this 'illness'.

[8] He will encounter it in the capitalism of Rothschild, in the socialisms of Marx and his ilk, in the abultifying and pornographic Freudism, in the charnel house art of a Picasso, in the various bombs of Einstein, Oppenheimer, Field, S.T. and Cohen, in Marxist capitalism in general and the world economic wars. Cohen, in capitalist Marxism in general and in world economic wars.

Richard had to leave them; he had to go back to his job as a journalist.

The children did not eat regular meals. Sometimes they went for days without food. Then they knew real hunger: the kind that forces you to roll on the floor, moaning and crying, your insides on fire. The hunger that grips you with acidity, spasms, hiccups, nausea... The most painful of illnesses.

One day during this ordeal, the children, hunger-stricken and haggard, opened the kitchen cupboard in the hope of finding some edible remains. There were millet seeds for the doves in the aviary and a bottle of cooking oil. They made a decoction and tried to eat it: the memory of that horrible mixture still stirs Tristan's heart. After a few days, their father brought them bread, ham, pâté and cakes, which they ate voraciously. Then they would go to bed because the fever was rising.

The doves in the aviary had died of hunger. One day they wanted to give them back their freedom, but the neighbouring cats coveted them. What is beautiful and pure does not survive long. Beauty and intelligence live only on the foundation of an elite preserved by a political system that cultivates spiritual and moral height rather than profitability. Today, man ignores authentic values, he no longer knows beauty, intelligence and above all truth, and he is dying in chaos.

There were also little cats in the house. At first they looked like cat skeletons, then one day they died. The children tried to put bits of food on their little pink tongues. Their little eyes became dull and then they died. Laure, Charlotte and Tristan cried every time one of these little creatures that populated the house and garden disappeared.

There had been no milk for a long time, no more morning cans that would have helped the children and cats to live.

And they all wanted to die.

Their grandmother, their father's mother, was still in Courbevoie. Despite their misery, her presence filled the house with joy and gentleness. She was so good, but old, very old and tired. She gave them everything she had. One day she fell ill, went to bed and never got up again. Leaving them the plate of compote she had prepared for her, she died. The three of them wept a lot. Tristan saw her on her deathbed, her face white, drawn, inert, and he was afraid. Their father mourned a mother who had undoubtedly been a model mother for him. The grandmother was buried without ceremony, without a grave. Today, it would be impossible to find the place where her body was buried. Poor dear Grandma. Tristan liked to repeat her name. He often thought of the happy life the three of them could have had with this real grandmother.

So the children began a wandering life that would last three years.

They wandered from hotel to hotel in the Paris region. The first hotel, Tristan remembered, was the Hotel Terminus at the Gare Saint Lazare.

There their father had to leave a wardrobe trunk full of suits and clothes as collateral. Then more hotels, and more hotels.

Their upbringing and education were completely neglected: at the age of twelve Tristan made thirty spelling mistakes in one page. They ate or didn't eat, they slept or didn't sleep. Sometimes they spent nights walking. Walking... How they walked! There are few children in the world who walked as much as they did.

Three years passed.

One morning, they were in Issy les Moulineaux with some good people in whose care their father had entrusted them.

They never saw him again...

Chapter III

> *"The heresy of heresies was common sense"*
> *(Orwell "1984")*

At around nine in the evening, Tristan was worried that his father wasn't coming back and went to wait for him at the metro station. He had been there for half an hour when a man got out and approached him. The man's face was not unfamiliar. He had seen him in the past at legal events during his parents' divorce proceedings. He could see him again in a cloud of judges, lawyers and policemen. It was Inspector Lordiller.

- Where are your sisters? said the latter abruptly.

They went together to the homes of the kind people who had been kind enough to look after them that day. Then they went to a café where the inspector offered them hot chocolate and croissants. Then he hailed a taxi and they all got in.

Twenty minutes later they were standing in front of *grandma*'s mansion.

The mere sight of the house and the idea of "the enormous sacrifices that *grandma* would make for them" were heartbreaking.

They had been unhappy those three years. They had lacked everything materially. They had known the hunger of the traveller in the desert. But they had never lacked affection. They hadn't been so unhappy if you step outside this narrow reality that only takes material contingencies into account. Everyone seems to be increasingly obsessed by this reality, as if it were all reality. There are few people who have a sense of *the* whole of reality and who don't realise that their poor, fragmented, truncated, fraudulent reality is only the foetus of real reality. They would have swapped the luxurious surroundings that awaited them for relative misery, where their bodies would have had minimal nourishment. There was nothing bitter left in their hearts from those three years of material suffering. Had they not always had enough to eat? Perhaps they had. But that wasn't enough to keep them resentful of their father. They preferred the piece of bread discreetly handed to them by their father, to the coveted chocolate cake of their *beloved grandma*, because she wrapped it in that abominable ostentation that made you want to say: "No thanks, I don't want it".

They didn't stay at *grandma's* house.

In his American car, Uncle Jacques drove them to a friend of his mother's in the suburbs. Tristan remembered a certain revolt during the car journey. It was funny to be so hungry that you had to roll around on the floor moaning, when your mother's family had American cars (Uncle Etienne had one too), a mansion in the sixteenth arrondissement of Paris and white-gloved servants. A few weeks earlier, he had heard Maître Badier, the lawyer for his mother's clan, say to their father: "Poor people, they're destitute".

Of course their material situation between the two wars was not what it had been at the beginning of the century, but the uncles were hospital doctors and *grandma* took paying guests, particularly German Jews who had been using *grandma's* residence as a springboard to the USA since 1936. But was it poverty?

—   Why," said Tristan, "have we been so hungry and slept so little for the last three years, when you're not destitute, as Master Badier told us?

—   It's none of your business," replied the uncle curtly and eunuch-like.

After a few days with friends in the suburbs, they went to stay with friends in Eure et Loir. A small château surrounded by a large park at the bottom of a basin. They christened the squire 'Uncle' and the squire 'Aunt Hélène'. She was a big, friendly, soft-spoken granny. But... they went back to boarding school.

During the holidays, they returned there or to other friends of their mother.

Tristan remembered living with a well-known painter who was madly in love with his mother. It pained him that he wished his mother had loved him.

Tristan saw again the pond where this gentleman was fishing for pike on the edge of the forest of Senonches.

It was then that Tristan was entrusted to a country priest.

He remained there until the outbreak of the Second World War. His education had always been neglected, and he was ignorant of spelling and basic education. During his pitiful childhood, he never received the slightest primary education.

In the surrounding countryside, life was quieter in this presbytery. The priest had a niece who was a dark cow. She looked like a caricature. Her chin was in a curve, her nose was like a trumpet, her hair was parted to the side, flat and sticky, her hair fell dull, framing big glasses, like magnifying glasses, in front of glaucous, bulging eyes. It was a strange look, a mixture of stupidity and malice. There was also old Miss Daminé, the organist, sad and persecuted by the niece, she drank and prayed.

As for the priest, he was a sympathetic and well-balanced man, deeply religious without being mystical. He showed an exaggerated affection for Tristan at first, but ended up taking a dislike to him. He tried not to show it, but the child felt it. Tristan was a lazy, nonchalant boy, hardly capable of effort, shy to the point of turning milky white to scarlet red if you stared at him.

All this, and many other features, corresponded well with Tristan's nativity, born under the sign of Libra. There was a kind of rite to which he was subjected when there was a crowd. The priest would say: "Look at the beautiful blush" and stare at Tristan to see the effect.

One of his classmates was a boy from Levallois who constantly bullied him. He was the prototype of the suburbanite: physical appearance, voice, vulgarity. His big, stupid strength crushed Tristan's delicate weakness.

Around here, the parish priest would hold film screenings. He transported the necessary equipment by car and we boarders took it in turns to help him. Tristan saw some very fine films with him and it was at this time that he developed a taste for the theatre.

Shortly before the war, in 1939, Tristan's mother, finally divorced, married the Viscount de Gastine. They lived in a manor house in Eure et Loir. It was a large family estate, with around a hundred hectares of wheat land, cows, horses, pigs and poultry. The father-in-law was an agricultural engineer and particularly enjoyed the life of a gentleman farmer, for which he certainly had a real vocation. This new figure in Tristan's life was around thirty five years old. He was tall and thin, rather than slim, with a long face and a bourbon nose, but his low forehead indicated a limited intelligence which Tristan was given to observe. He was a landed aristocrat of fine breeding. With a deep, well-stamped voice, he was sarcastic and incisive, quite destructive, a devilish sophist and a tad stingy. Tristan admired his natural elegance.

He tended his cows for the pleasure of his vocation, for the pleasure of contemplating a beautiful cow, he grew a cabbage to admire a beautiful cabbage, he cultivated a field to see the ears blossom rich and glorious. If he was stingy by nature, he wasn't really interested in money, and he wouldn't have given a scrap of his soul to earn it.

In this respect, he differed from his contemporaries.

In the years leading up to the war, agricultural products were sold at low prices or not at all. The father-in-law, forced to sell up, took advantage of the support of his brother-in-law, a member of parliament, to obtain an important post in French West Africa. The couple went there.

They had a child, Luc, who was sent to Nantes to live with his paternal aunt and grandfather.

Tristan left the parish priest, and he and his sisters were entrusted to the care of Aunt Denise and her husband Uncle Paul, a doctor and member of parliament.

Uncle Paul had settled in the Loiret where he became mayor, General Councillor and then Member of Parliament: he was an excellent man, a spoiled uncle. He was an excellent man, a spoiled uncle. He was ridiculously subservient to his wife. He acted like a real little boy. Aunt Denise showed him the respect and consideration that went without saying. This authority of the aunt over the uncle and this deference were an interesting psychological observation for Tristan. The aunt was fair, authoritative, intelligent in the usual sense of the word, but limited in her receptiveness. She lacked that essential something that was missing in all the Jewish speculation of the time: the dimension of synthesis, of love, of the authentic human. This dimension is totally absent in Capitalism as in Marxism.

The uncle and aunt had no children and would have liked to have had one. The three children were sent to boarding school in Pithiviers.

There, in his solitude, Tristan was as bad a student as ever.

One day he was haranguing his classmates in a classroom without a teacher when the headmaster unexpectedly walked in.

He called Tristan into his office.

- You're not going to pass your baccalauréat with your good looks and eloquence," he told her good-naturedly.

In the family circle, Tristan didn't say a word, but as soon as he was outside and circumstances allowed, like an over-compressed liquid, he spurted out.

The school year was not yet over and the 1939 war broke out.

Monsieur and Madame de Gastine returned from A.O.F.

Laure and Charlotte left with their mother and stepfather. To Tristan's delight, he stayed with his aunt and uncle.

Then came the exodus in 1940.

Three carriages were packed with luggage. One was given to him even though he was not yet fifteen. The second belonged to the replacement doctor. The third belonged to Josette, a journalist and novelist, a friend of Aunt Denise and his mother, and companion of a well-known novelist. Tristan was towing a trailer full of his own films and documents from the Spanish Civil War. This novelist was to become Charles de Gaulle's minister in 1945. They arrived two days later at the château of a parliamentary friend, where Tristan stayed for two months. As the German occupation took hold, Tristan's uncle and aunt came to collect him.

Tristan was fifteen years old. A chaotic childhood and illness had left him with little opportunity to learn. He knew nothing. It had to be said that the content of his official studies did not appeal to his intellectual curiosity. Did they lead to greater awareness and happiness? School didn't touch on anything essential, and it produced and spread suicides in all aspects of life. How many times had he thought of the words of Simone Weil, that great spirit, to his threatening Inspector General: "I see dismissal as the crowning achievement of my career"...

When he was eight years old, he was asked what he wanted to do. He replied "poet". But his interviewer's shrill laugh gave him a painful shock and made him realise that "poet" was no longer a social status.

What did this word mean to him? To talk about what we see that others don't, to express what we feel and think to enlighten those who feel less and think little. To rebel against evil and try to heal it in depth. To graft words that come by themselves onto the evidence of life that others call intuitions and that they distrust because they are no longer living.

He was always obsessed with the piano.

Playing Chopin would have fulfilled his vocation as a poet!

Unfortunately, there was only one alternative: the baccalauréat or an apprenticeship. So he took the only path open to him: fill in the gaps in his primary education and prepare for the baccalauréat. In two years he worked miracles.

He was able to achieve this miracle thanks to his private tutors.

If he had gone back to boarding school, he would have been lost and would never have achieved anything. He went to see two teachers in Orléans for literature and science. Twice a week he took the bus to Orléans. He also studied at home with a teacher, and English was taught to him by his aunt who had spoken the language since early childhood in Egypt.

After two years, he was admitted to the first year of secondary school at the Lycée d'Orléans. After such a childhood, it was a success.

Those two years in Beaune, where he lived with his aunt and uncle, had given him back a little peace and balance. The countryside, Uncle Paul's kindness, his aunt's calm and patience with the impossible and misunderstood boy that he was... Aunt Denise was fair and reasonable but not at all sentimental. She spared no expense when it came to her nephew's education, but otherwise she was appallingly greedy. Tristan, who had a tendency to prefer the superfluous to the necessary, was greatly offended when one day a peasant said to him:

"Your uncle might just buy you some panties...

This neglect of clothing and the lack of pocket money, although admittedly an excellent thing for education, left a sad mark on him, as other boys his age were spoilt and pampered. He entered the first year of secondary school at Orléans.

He stayed with an assistant teacher at the lycée. His pen pal was the famous Doctor

C. a former replacement for Uncle Paul. He had been pushed into politics by Uncle Paul, with the agreement of Aunt Denise, and had become deputy mayor of Orléans. His wife, in love and jealous, shot her husband with a revolver the day he was appointed minister. Tristan lived through all this, so to speak, listening to what both husband and wife had to say, and came to understand each other's mindsets. Yvonne, Doctor C.'s wife, was loving, passionate, unbearable and jealous. He knew how to be a charming man of the world, but could become very brutal in private. Tristan had seen a radio belonging to his wife kicked to pieces by the Doctor. When he chatted, he naively told Tristan that he loved war and that he felt euphoric buried in a cellar under a bombed-out house...

His school friends seemed particularly insignificant, petty and stupid. Their stupidity and cowardice were what struck him most. This stupidity, this cowardice, Tristan would encounter for the rest of his life.

They had a history teacher who was brilliant, but physically unfortunate by nature. He sometimes had a slight, timid stammer, which did not prevent him from being intelligible. His classmates heckled the teacher. Tristan remained silent and attentive in the front row, never opening his mouth during the history lesson.

As for the maths teacher, he had a figure commonly referred to as an 'ice-cream cabinet'. The class was a reflection of humanity as a whole, wasn't it? It was at this point that Tristan felt a furious urge to heckle. He would address his neighbour in an almost loud voice, but the latter was afraid to reply. On a winter's day in 1942, at the height of the Occupation, the classroom was particularly cold. The heating was more than adequate. So Tristan took advantage of the maths class to put on his gloves. Ah! the big, strong, tough guy, he was furious, think of it! taking his lessons wearing gloves! he tried out all the jibes, irony, sarcasm, ridicule: impassive, Tristan kept his gloves on!

Tristan thought it was normal to heckle the maths teacher, but certainly not to behave in this hideous and cowardly way towards a good, talented but slightly disadvantaged teacher. No contact was possible with these individuals whom he despised and sometimes loathed. He would have liked to be surrounded by people who were not small, who were broad of heart, different from this standard model, so desperately ridiculous and curiously 'normal'.

These individuals proved to be much better students than he was. It was remarkable that those to whom he would have given a human grade of zero, won all the laurels. And yet he felt they were closed to essential realities.

Tristan attended, indifferent to these hours of lessons which he transformed into privileged observation sessions. He already had singular intuitions that would take shape much later and that no one could share.

The piano haunted his dreams, Chopin, especially Chopin. Sometimes he cried because he couldn't study him, but he knew it was impossible and he shouldn't get his hopes up. French made him tense, explanations of text and essays irritated him to no end. Academia is the failure of the essential, the triumph of the minuscule, blindness to the blinding. There's nothing surprising in the fact that most agrégés become apologists and disciples of an ideology that has massacred two hundred million human beings. At this level of reductionism, all kinds of madness are possible, as long as they are official and fashionable.[9]

How many incidental, futile, pointless things can be said in an explanation of text. The obedient classmates obtained excellent marks as a reward for these exercises in mental distortion. Moreover, there was nothing in common between 'school' and the banal concerns of their lives, which had been reduced to the vegetative and the vulgar. They fulfilled their school obligations as if they were a penance or a physiological obligation such as defecation.

Tristan was blocked, stymied by so much pettiness, by the absence of reality, by this profusion of antics. We were in the middle of a world war. Who among these masters would have thought to become aware of its *true* causes? No one is more lacking in genuine culture, synthetic awareness or

---

[9] This is true at the most basic level. In the year 2000, women will be walking around in trousers that hug their buttocks, pulling on elephantine shoes. Even at this level, intelligence and aesthetic sense have disappeared in favour of the aberrant concept of fashion.

creative potential than an agrégé. He goes so far as to take the agrégation as a value.

At the end of the term, it was time for the recitation composition.

Tristan's comrades spouted their texts to the automatic, indifferent rhythm of a slot machine.

When it was his turn, Tristan began to read his text by Vigny. The whole class burst out laughing.

He paused for a moment, keeping his mask impassive because he had anticipated the conditioned reflex of these robots. A circular glance from the professor restored the silence.

Tristan had resumed his text... The almost dazed looks stared at him as if something abnormal had just happened. Then he returned to his seat. His astonished classmates learned that Tristan was top of his class in this subject.

Although he came first in recitation, his results in the other subjects were disappointing, apart from mathematics, where he also came first just before the baccalauréat exam.

The curious thing is that he has always been terrible at arithmetic and mediocre at algebra. But geometry was brilliant. The visual aspect of geometry and its appeal to the imagination suited him perfectly and spontaneously. He had a luminous conception of figures and volumes, and distinguished geometric locations by mentally moving volumes through space before determining them by reasoning. He enjoyed playing with his imagination and the mechanisms of his intuition more than geometry, which was of little interest to him.

He loathed gymnastics as practised by these swarming cohorts.

Like many teenagers, Tristan wrote verse. Of all the jumble he concocted, he remembered :

O, how good it must feel in the sad silence Of a subterranean vault, O immense solitude.

No more horror, no more evil, no more murders, no more horrible slaughter.

Nothing but the slow hours that pass over our tombs, gradually darkening its virginal marble...

The couple staying with Tristan received parcels of groceries from Aunt Denise, for which she demanded black market prices and Indian ink. They ended up taking out their legitimate anger on Tristan and became quite poisonous. The good woman was being overbearing, but we also had to understand her. In this period of deprivation under the German occupation, demanding exaggerated sums for elementary parcels would have upset anyone's nervous system. As for the aunt, she was perfectly unaware of this phenomenon.

Tristan stayed in this galley for the whole of the first term. He would have stayed there, because he was going to find himself in a much worse prison.

Christmas 1941.

Chapter IV

"It was during the horror of a deep night..."

Uncles Jacques and Etienne had left for Spain and then England, as did thousands of Jews. His mother and father-in-law had settled in Nantes. He had been appointed director of the peasant restoration mission created by Marshal Pétain. Charlotte, Laure and their half-brother Luc were with them. Uncle Paul and his aunt had stayed behind in Beaune.

In Paris, there was *grandma, darling*.

The mansion in the 16th arrondissement had been stripped of all its furniture and valuables. Even the wrought-iron railings that separated the hall from a lounge had disappeared. All that remained were the empty hinges. The big house looked like a cave. But wasn't it inhabited by fossils?

To avoid her hotel being occupied by the Germans, *grandma* wanted to live there. She couldn't live there alone because Uncle Paul and Aunt Denise had to stay in Beaune. Tristan came to mind.

He left the Lycée d'Orléans for the Lycée Buffon. In the huge, bare, unheated hut, there was now *Grandma* and him, him and *Grandma*.

It was an abominable camel.

Tristan was seventeen and at that age it's hard to slap a young man. But he had a whole arsenal devised by his exquisite nature.

His character was a muddled mess of perverse despotism, anxiety, tragedy, pessimism and petty stubbornness.

She would get carried away at the slightest suggestion of the enormity of the nonsense she was uttering. Her ideation was slow and tortuous, and she was singularly sadistic, stingy in the strictly selfish sense, for it does not seem that anyone had ever seen her stingy towards herself.

On the other hand, she showed off her generosity in a way that was perpetual and somewhat disgusting.

"Look what Grandma did for you, she cooked you a nice plate of vermicelli, gave you a bed to sleep in, looked after you, looked after you". After dragging herself off for a few minutes to fricassee their meal, she let herself fall back onto her bed, insisting heavily on "what she did for Tristan", "all the fatigue he put her through", "but it didn't matter", she added dyingly, "I do it willingly". In fact, Tristan could hardly remember her ever doing anything for him that wasn't sadistic. When she did something, she always benefited herself from the results of her strenuous efforts, "For the ungrateful man that he was".

How many things he had observed in his childhood, observed and felt. How many times he had played the fool so that no one would notice the penetration of his sensitivity. He didn't know how to lie, he never had. He felt they were so incomplete, so powerless, that it frightened him. As soon as he loosened his lips to express himself, his heart raced. He stammered and lost control. He felt as if he were buried in a concrete wall of incomprehension. Even at the age of twenty-seven, when he went to visit *his beloved grandma*, he was feverish and his diction was slurred.

Grandma darling was ridiculously and violently sectarian, fanatical, fully aware of herself, and therefore impossible to enlighten. Any dialogue was a dead end, a cul-de-sac, the squaring of the circle. This pattern is characteristic of all mentally ill people who lack the heart. Anyone with a mind and a heart is open to dialogue, admitting their mistake or explaining the other person's mistake. None of this is possible with the insane mentality of our political and financial leaders. The madman knows only his obsession, his fixation; he will kill rather than give in.

Sometimes Tristan had tried to sketch things out, but there was no question of logic: anything that didn't serve his derisory pathological subjectivity was ignored, even in the face of the most obvious of obvious obviousnesses.

But Tristan couldn't keep his mouth shut. He soon had enough of this prison. Easter holidays were approaching and he was to spend them with his aunt in Beaune. This was a great joy for him. So he hatched a Machiavellian plan.

He decided to write a *fake* letter to his mother, in which, in a few well-detailed pages, he took stock of what his life in Paris was like, between the problematic preparation for his baccalauréat and the seraphic character of his *beloved grandmother*.

Before leaving for his aunt's house, he left the letter-bomb in a drawer of his desk. It had been left there by chance, well hidden, so that it looked as if it had been hidden with the greatest care. Tristan would have told her all this in person, but she would never have let him speak. With a grand gesture, she would have banished him from her sight, the despicable ingrate that he was. The letter said it all, and he knew that *grandma*'s morbid curiosity, her inquisitive mind, would drive her to the very bottom of the drawer and that she would read the whole letter. It was part of her character to dig to the very bottom of her school drawer. She would not have hesitated to justify this morbid curiosity on the grounds of moral surveillance. It all fitted in perfectly with her gentle nature.

What Tristan had foreseen happened, but *Grandma chérie* never made the slightest mention of the letter. On the way back from Beaune, Tristan noticed that *grandma*'s face had grown an inch longer. He discreetly went to open her drawer: the letter had disappeared.

Grandma darling hadn't put the letter back. Tristan wouldn't have expected that.

She'd kept it, but what was she going to do with it?

Grandma dearest knew what Tristan was thinking. It changed nothing. There is a kind of absolute determinism in human beings that has always amazed Tristan.

Grandma's flat overlooked the main hall, while Tristan's apartment faced it. It was the former flat of Tristan's grandfather, who had seen fit to end his days far from his worthy wife, in a peaceful retirement.

Tristan was a sort of footman *to Grandma, who was very fond of him*.

She cooked for them both - she had a healthy appetite - and Tristan took care of everything else. He went to the shops for the essentials. The shops were a long way from the mansion, which was in the middle of a residential area. At dawn in the morning, he lit the stove in the room next to his bedroom, because that's where *his beloved grandma* spent her days, cosy and warm. He often had to turn it back on when he got home from school and wait until it was warm enough to get through his important schoolwork with just a few months to go before the exams.

Despite the chaos of his childhood, he made it to the top of his class.

There was so much for *grandma* to do in this big house that he lost any chance of being admitted to the baccalauréat that year.

The duties of valet to a despotic old lady are not compatible with the obligations of a conscientious schoolboy. He knew the failure that awaited him, but what could he do?

The room where he slept was freezing in winter. *Grandma darling* hadn't bothered to let Tristan set up his bed in the room with the stove. There were three doors and a huge window but "the fumes could have asphyxiated him". This was all the more ridiculous as the stove was turned off when she left and when Tristan got into bed. But the room could have been quite warm as the stove had been on all day. She did, however, condescend to have the door open when she returned to the house after the stove had been turned off.

It was usually minus five degrees centigrade in Tristan's bedroom. When *Grandma* was not in the stove room, she was in her bedroom, in her armchair, warming herself with her electric poultice, asthmatic and dying for forty years.

One day, a young woman rang the hotel doorbell. Uncle Etienne had chosen her as a candidate for marriage. *Grandma darling* had to give her opinion, which would be decisive.

From the bathroom, where he was washing his hands, he could hear the whining of his *beloved grandmother* to the young woman: "My grandchildren who don't love me and are waiting for me to die so they can inherit"...

The statement was all the more misleading and foolish because there was nothing to suggest such a prospect, but she had to pose as a martyr and a saint.

When the young woman had gone, *Grandma*, with her usual naivety and thoughtlessness, said to Tristan: "You see, Uncle Etienne sent me this young girl and said, 'Mummy, if you don't like her, I won't marry her'.

She was maniacal about slandering trivial things as well as important ones. He often wept at her despicable visions sprouting from a jam jar or at more serious accusations whose diabolical conception would never even have crossed Tristan's mind.

Years later, he would rediscover this psychology in Freud, who had ignobly sexualised tender feelings, pure devotion and filial love, as foreign to sexuality as the Acropolis is to the crocodile.

Then came the baccalauréat: you had to defer for two points. And that's when things really started to happen. Tristan had gone to the police station to receive the Star of David that *his beloved grandma* had inherited.

The Star of David to the Jewish race? This is all the more astonishing given that races do not exist: only ethnic groups exist, which are the result of hormonal adaptation to a fixed environment over at least eight to ten centuries. But the Jews are not a race because they do not exist, they are not an ethnic group because they have never all lived in a permanent geographical location for eight to ten centuries.

It was therefore neither in the concept of race nor in the ethnic reality that the cause of Jewish particularism, constant in time and space, could be found. Nor could we speak of 'shaping by religion', for although the influence of religion is not negligible, it is not a party to this particularism. Jews are somatically very different from one country to another, and they sometimes share only certain caricatured traits and a mentality that has not changed for five thousand years. Finally, all the Jews of the upper financial bourgeoisie made a mockery of the teachings of the Torah and never set foot in a synagogue. All they retained from religious teaching was the practice of circumcision on the 8th day.[10]

The Jews were beginning to be seriously persecuted and Hitler, who radically did not accept their role in Capitalism or Marxism. He had observed the Weimar Republic, where they dominated everything, and the Bolshevik revolution, which was an absolute horror, and so he decided to park them in camps. He thought that even innocent people would soon beget other financiers, other Freuds, other Marxes.

---

[10] We shall see in the chapter entitled "The Key" that this, and only this, is the secret of Jewish particularism. It is a hormonal-psychic distortion.

He therefore thought that the very existence of the planet and of mankind were at stake. Fifty years later, Orwell's 1984 demonstrated that the Weimar Republic was on the scale of the planet, with its pornographic and migratory chaos of drugs, unemployment, suicides among the very young, its butchery of new-born babies, its 150 wars, its Judeo-American government, and its financiers of the Warburg, Rothschild, Soros, Hammer and consorts type dictatorially ruling the planet and the zombie politicians of all parties.

It was therefore vital that *Grandma* and Aunt Denise should take refuge in the Free Zone under the protection of Marshal Pétain. Nonetheless, both of them never stopped railing against the Marshal who had given them protection, Pétain, the traitor who was going to support Hitler, albeit badly, and "free the French from the most shameful guardianship, that of finance".

Uncle Paul visited them regularly, bringing them money and supplies. Before leaving for the free zone, they had to get rid of the cumbersome Tristan.

Madame de Gastine had written several letters to her son in recent years. She was a little jealous of Tristan's affection for his aunt and his aunt's affection for her. She wrote to him "that he was her darling son", "that she wanted him to join her", "that she would do anything for him".

She was trying to suck him in morally, to sow confusion in his trusting soul, and it was all the easier because Tristan's life with *Grandma* was a solid purgatory.

The aunt therefore wrote to her sister that he was being sent back to her and that she hoped Madame de Gastine would now be able to make something better of her son than a labourer.

Tristan was delighted because you love your mother and it's easy to forget the negative things that can happen to her. He may have known her, but he loved her. A mother is a mother. How can you not love her? You can end up hating her with your viscera, through lack, but not with your spirit.

So *Grandma darling* climbed up into the attic, poked around a bit and ended up with the shadow of an old gusseted suitcase, which she generously gave to Tristan. She didn't know the price of a second-class ticket from Paris to Nantes. Tristan was not to have a penny in his pocket.

So she took him to the station to collect his ticket. They put him on the train without a penny in his pocket: he was sold out.

When he arrived at Nantes station, his father-in-law was waiting for him.

The reception was rather cold. It was one thing to attract him by telling him how much we loved him, how much we wanted him here and how much we would do for him. But actually seeing him arrive was quite another. In reality, it was all about creating psychological conflicts in him that would be detrimental to Aunt Denise and *Grandma*.

Madame de Gastine was checked every day by the French police, who were subject to the occupying forces. With the complicity of the Head of State, her husband, an official of the Marshal, was appointed to the Free Zone. This was a frequent occurrence, and the number of Jews who avoided deportation thanks to the Marshal is difficult to assess because it is considerable. They will never be mentioned after the war, any more than the tens of millions exterminated under a regime that was radically Jewish in its ideologists, politicians, financiers, administrators and prison and concentration camp executioners such as Kaganovitch, Frenkel, Yagoda, Firine, Ouritski, Sorenson, Abramovici, Apetter, Jejoff and fifty other Jews.

On the other hand, there will be endless talk about the six million Jews gassed by the Germans, even though it has been proven that there were only three million three hundred thousand of them in occupied Europe in 1941 and that Cyclon B, hydrocyanic acid, is unsuitable for gassing one or two thousand people at a time. But you have to believe in this religious dogma or risk having a law enacted for "thought crime", which is, moreover, the ninth proof of the imposture.[11]

Laure and Tristan set off with their backpacks towards Poitiers, where a secondary school teacher was providing many services to those the Germans were hunting down. They learned that he had been arrested and shot for his rare recklessness.

They had the address of a country parish priest whose parish was on the demarcation line. A bus dropped them off a kilometre away and they set

---

[11] You don't need a totalitarian law to make a truth known: you prove it with arguments and evidence; those who dispute the Holocaust are condemned without being given a chance to prove whether they are right or wrong.

off towards the rectory. At a fork in the road they came face to face with a German, rifle at his back, astride his bicycle. The children turned pale. Under no circumstances should they lose their composure. With theatrical confidence, Tristan asked the soldier where Bonne was, the name of the village they were to go to.

— That way," replied the soldier, pointing in the right direction. Thank you," said Tristan with his most natural smile.

They had only taken a few steps when the German's voice rang out behind them:

— Ihre Papiere!

They thought they were going to faint.

The soldier took a quick look at their identity cards and led them to a post three hundred metres away.

Laure broke down but held on. She avoided speaking. They both understood each other and had nothing to say to each other.

A German officer arrived. They had obviously interrupted his meal. He addressed them brutally:

— What are you doing here?

— We're going on holiday to the parish priest in Bonnes," replied Tristan.

It was summer and the excuse for two children made perfect sense.

— You don't want to go to the free zone? he asked, with a naivety that didn't escape Tristan's humour, despite the anguish of the moment.

— Not at all, we're going on holiday.

— Aren't you Jews? insisted the officer.

— But no," replied Tristan, as if insulted.

The officer must have felt relieved. He searched their two rucksacks from top to bottom. He found nothing. He scanned the coins in Tristan's wallet and discovered his mother's and uncle's business cards: Vicomtesse de Gastine and Docteur Paul C. Député maire. He returned the wallet and kept the cards.

The door was opened: they were free.

A few minutes later, they were on the road, moving with all the speed in their hocks. Laure had felt such fear that she had turned as yellow as a quince in the space of a few minutes.

They finally arrived at the parish priest's, who offered them a snack and whispered in their ear:

- Don't stay here, I'm being watched by the Germans. If you don't leave immediately you'll be arrested!

Back in Nantes, they had to revise their escape plan. Laure and Charlotte crossed the line in a Red Cross convoy. They reached the Free Zone safely.

The Vicomte de Gastine, a high-ranking official of the Marshal, sent Tristan through the Mission de Restauration Paysanne to a farm next to the demarcation line.

It was here that Madame de Gastine and her husband joined Tristan.

The gendarmes were to help them cross the demarcation line. They had received secret orders from the Vichy government for similar cases. Moreover, the large number of Jews protected by the Marshal was known to everyone. So they had to be in a specific place at a specific time, and they were. As they arrived, they spotted some dodgy helmets glinting in the sun. It was the middle of summer. The father-in-law, like a conjurer, improvised a picnic on the grass: the procedure seemed ingenuous, but what could be better than that? Fortunately they were friendly helmets: their arms waved, we had to hurry. A few minutes later, through the undergrowth, they were in the Zone Libre.

Compared to the gloom of the occupied zone, this part of France, which had remained untouched by German uniforms, seemed like a land of plenty: lights, music, no curfew. Tristan would have wandered around all night if he'd been given permission. Just for the pleasure of savouring the freedom of this new atmosphere. Everyone was laughing and feeling good.

They all met at a friend's house near Vichy. The two sisters were already there. They stayed there for several months.

Madame de Gastine was, by nature, particularly horrifying, petty and nagging. She was poisoning her son, whom a little tenderness would have softened. If he had been able to return to his aunt, he would not have hesitated. He was unhappy, he felt he was 'too much', he had such an acute sense of this distressing situation that life weighed on him.

He wanted to write a card, signed illegibly, to his uncle and aunt. There was no danger of such a message in this form, but his mother stopped him on the false pretext that it would have been a serious danger for her. What was she risking, anyway, by putting things in the worst possible light, since the Germans did not occupy that part of France and the Marshal refused to hand over the Jews in the Free Zone?

But Tristan could not find elsewhere the love his mother refused to give him.

When the summer was over, they moved into a rented flat in the rue Vaubecour in Lyon. The two sisters lived with their mother and stepfather. They were very helpful and were carefully exploited.

As for Tristan, despite the miraculous promises, he was still sent to a boarding school in Villefranche sur Saône.

As they had escaped during the summer, and the preparatory work impossible, there had been no question of him taking the exam again in October. What's more, the debilitating year spent at *grandma's* house meant that he couldn't cope, despite coming first in recitation and mathematics. So he repeated his first year. Another year at boarding school.

He still felt the same revulsion towards violence, stupidity and vulgarity. He seemed increasingly vulnerable. The apparent paradox was that he couldn't throw a punch, but he was capable of extreme and painful resources, perhaps even to the point of heroism. He came first in maths again, but failed in June. He had to work through the summer if he wanted to succeed in October.

Monsieur de Gastine was obviously thinking of getting rid of his son-in-law.

"When you're drowning", he told Tristan, "you have to let those around you fend for themselves. This worthless alibi - for he had a very good job, as important at the time as that of prefect - was enough to ease his conscience, and to get rid of Tristan's cumbersome presence, he considered sending him to a holiday camp. This would undoubtedly have permanently compromised his chances of success in the exam. It was then that a Jesuit priest, a friend of his mother's, intervened to ensure that Tristan was given every chance. Madame de Gastine had already moved with her two daughters to a rented property near Nîmes. She was well aware that her husband was doing everything in his power to get rid of Tristan.

But when Tristan arrived, she cried out again: "My darling, I was so afraid you wouldn't come, especially as it was my birthday". He didn't say a word, but that hypocrisy still hurts him today when he thinks back on that moment.

He put on a stupid face with a bland smile, like a protective mask, a flawless screen for his pain and his thoughts. How many times had he worn this mask that gave him peace. On a theatre stage, his repartee would have been superb, magnificent, with a happy or sad face, laughter or tears... But in real life, on the stage of reality, with a bruised heart, how could he play it straight?

So he crammed. David Copperfield was on the English syllabus. Dickens was a brilliant child, astonished by a world of misery and yet optimistic.

He ate grapes.

A month before the exam, he was sent to a small religious boarding school where the bachot exam was being prepared for the October session. It was in Lyon, not far from the rue Vaubecour. In the evenings he would sneak out. Once, around midnight, on his way home, he took the wrong door and stepped on a steep staircase leading to a cellar. He still hasn't worked out how he didn't break his bones. He can't remember what he had to hold on to to avoid a fatal fall. He had to

that he and his comrades sneak back into the room in total darkness so as not to wake the Father Director, who was snoring comfortably, and that they slip into their beds.

Tristan didn't have a penny of pocket money. But he was eighteen. So he was entitled to a tobacco card, which was a simple way of getting money. All he had to do was sell his ration. His mother and stepfather had tried to steal his tobacco card. Tristan played the fool so well that his mother saw fit to use a technique in keeping with her son's imbecility. He would give her his card and from time to time she would give him a free packet of cigarettes. Rockefeller must have made his fortune with this kind of technique. Tristan pretended to weigh up the terms of such a generous proposal and... refused.

If his mother had frankly asked him for this precious card without playing the magnanimity game, when Tristan knew full well that in those days a packet of cigarettes was worth the astronomical sum of two hundred francs, he would have given it to her unconditionally. But this hypocrisy, this comedy of generosity, this way of taking him for a fool, all this was so far removed from the psychology of a real mother that Tristan was disgusted and beside himself.

It was at this time that Tristan discovered the excitement of contact with women. His friends would follow the girls around, talking to them and asking them crazy questions.

Tristan grew bolder and had a few flings, with whom he sometimes went out into the surrounding countryside.

Lyon. There, stretched out on the grass, they remained perfectly platonic.

Tristan then passed his first baccalauréat with flying colours.

When he learned of the result, he was already in Genevilliers, a nest of large factories, with a small place in one of them where a close cousin was sales manager.

1943. Eleven hundred francs a month.

Chapter V

> *"If Christianity triumphs, in 2000 years the whole world will be Jewish" (The Emperor Julian the Apostate)*

Since Tristan had been liquidated by *his beloved grandmother*, his mother and stepfather had tolerated him for a year, but sent him to boarding school.

Boarding school hadn't ruined them. The headmaster had called him into his office, yelping:

"At the Lycée Ampère, you wouldn't have gone home without paying a term's fees in advance. What a humiliation for Tristan!

If they had been able to 'dump' him earlier, they would not have hesitated. With all the members of his family, apart perhaps from Aunt Denise, who in the years that followed were to prove stranger than many strangers, he could not find the slightest affection, the slightest understanding. None of his family had ever been able to love or understand him. So he made no attempt to stay with them. Besides, if things went well, what other prospect could there be than the hell of boarding school with another headmaster yelling that he hadn't received the student's pension.

Since her scandalous conversion, Madame de Gastine had flitted from cassock to cassock, bishop to bishop, fathers of various orders, Jesuits and Dominicans. She had given Tristan a letter for the parish priest of Gennevilliers. To Tristan's astonishment, instead of providing him with "a decent room in a decent family", the priest took Tristan to a small, bawdy hotel. This was a sign of the total abandonment and indifference in which he was left.

The owner had the face and look of a gangster. He had one arm bent at right angles left over from the 1914 war. His pale yellow complexion housed two hard eyes set deep in the ocular cavity. With a very pronounced chin, bordering on prognathism, his air of strange hardness stood out even more starkly. He looked hard, frightfully hard, primal, tiny, instinctive, mired in elemental matter, without pity for his enemies. His mind was torn between his family, his small business and a fierce hatred for the Germans. His hatred was born of his war wound and even more of the fact that a German officer had once spat in his face to get him out of the way. In a primitive being, all that was decisive.

The hotel restaurant was frequented by workers, many of them good-hearted. One of them, Mr Alexandre, worked in the same factory as Tristan. He was a sensitive, resigned man who expected nothing from life except final deliverance. He had worked hard for forty years; one day he would die... Everything seemed indifferent to him. He no longer suffered. He carried on, but it seemed as if he was already, in a way, dead. It was a kind of kindness that was already dead and continued to go on. He had all the outward signs of a living worker, but Tristan felt he was dead. He went on by force of circumstance, he walked without seeing, by the impulse of automatisms, without enjoying, without suffering. He suffered only the nagging pain of absolute neutrality. And this being that was not, was infinitely painful for Tristan. He would have liked to understand this bruised path towards explanation or nothingness.

Tristan's room was a sort of cell with dirty walls, a bad bed, a water jug and a toilet. With what Tristan earned, there was no question of paying anything other than the rent for his room and a daily meal in the factory canteen.

The Sales Director, his mother's close cousin, had called him into his office. He told her that he had made it clear to Gisèle (Madame de Gastine) that Tristan could not live on his salary and that it would be essential to help him. Tristan never received a penny or a parcel.

He was still a seven-year-old child, in need of affection and care, and he was alone in this terrible environment. Stubborn suffering!

He soothed his torn soul with letters to his mother. Long letters of love, despair and hatred. He came to hate his mother for leaving him alone and destitute under the Anglo-American bombs.

The sirens went off every day, especially at night. Bombs rained down on this industrial suburb. One day, in his abandonment, he wrote to his mother: "You are a Catholic monster".

Every time he passed a church, he shuddered. Wasn't that the refuge of Catholic monsters? Didn't all those middle-class people go to mass on time, while at the turn of the century seven-year-olds were working in their factories and mines? He knew a lot of people who never went to church and who had a good heart. What has the Church done over the last twenty centuries other than betray the teachings of eternal morality? Preparing the world for the materialism of Rothschild and Marx?

"It was the Church and the princes who handed the people over to the Jews", said Hitler. And Emperor Julian the Apostate went even further: "If Christianity triumphs, in two thousand years the whole world will be Jewish".

Ah! the cloak of ideological labels! magnificent reasoning and false principles that legitimise mass murder. This is the age of the perfect crime, and it has the perfect alibi: the philosophy that transforms murderers into judges. And what a philosophy it is! the kind that leads back to heavy psychiatry. The drama of flattery, demagogy, easy and convincing reasoning, the drama of an apparent immediate truth. Lies and deception in time and space.

At the factory, Tristan was indifferent to the people around him.

There was, however, one sensitive and intelligent young man - he had failed at Polytechnique! he had a certain sense of business and organisation. He understood many things and was distinguished.

They often chatted together and although Jean Louis, as he was called, was only twenty, he already had a certain contempt for women. "Unless they are in the heat of their love, no woman has any virtue," he used to say. "Even after years of living together with children, they are capable of changing men as easily as their suits.

When the sirens announced a bombardment with their mournful call, they went down into the shelter and chatted. Buildings shook, windows shattered.

— Well," he said to Tristan one day, "human rights have come down on us. What do you think of universal suffrage? Magnificent, isn't it?

— Yes," replied Tristan, "and Rousseau too, I like Rousseau a lot. Jean Louis chuckled mockingly.

— On the face of it, it's a wonderful idea, but suppose that all these fine ideas, which by the way are bogus, lead to the hegemony of finance and the disappearance of all the providential elites, who have been replaced by speculators, lunatics who are oblivious to human synthesis, the hysteria of the markets that led to the 14-16 war and the one we're in now... If you've understood that, you'll understand why today we're getting bombs dropped on our heads. Do you know Karl Marx?

Tristan only knew the superficial banality served up on the tray in philosophy class. He was indifferent to it, and Dr Alexis Carrel's *'L'Homme cet Inconnu' (Man, the Unknown)* had expanded his horizons infinitely. This great book spoke of Marxism as a work of human suicide.

— At least read a study of "*Das Kapital*" says Jean Louis, this work is the purest product of liberal capitalism. It is not lacking in comedy. If I had to sum it up humorously I would say that it teaches that society makes culture, in other words the plough makes the man. It's not surprising that today the stomach replaces thought.

On another occasion, Jean Louis alluded to the agrégation competitive examination.

— I bet you that if I went to the farthest reaches of Africa and found a primitive with a mediocre intelligence and an excellent memory, he would have no trouble passing the agrégation in philosophy or the internship in medicine. Do you honestly believe that Plato or Montaigne would have passed the agrégation?

It's true that there's a lot of bad things to say about Humanism, "the beginning of the end" as Carrel says. A time in humanity when man's navel became navel-gazing to the detriment of the Transcendent...

Whatever the case, if one day you meet an intelligent man at university, remember that it will not be because of his agrégation, but in spite of it, and because he will have joined Freemasonry.

The problem of the day is to be half-ignoble or not to be. In 1984 you will have to be radically despicable because all official criteria will be rotten and all values will be reversed.

Tristan asked about Marx. He read extracts from *Das Kapital*. Obscure, contorted, "hyper-hypophyseal"[12] illegible, inhuman, pathological style, with some brilliant analyses, essential ones of which turned out to be wrong. He penetrated the essence of his inversion. Despite a lucid and factually flawless anti-Semitism[13] regarding Jewish trafficking and finance, the work seemed to him to be the end point of an enormous synthesis of destruction that seemed unconsciously woven into its perfection.

It did not appear that the executioners were any more concerted than their victims, and none were aware of the comatose synthesis of Rothschildo-marxo-freudo-einsteinopiccassism.[14]

Tristan's work at the factory, from 8.30 in the morning to 6.30 in the evening, was not very exciting. He was in charge of the commutator rubbers. The factory sold them in France, Germany, on the mainland and to the S.N.C.F. in particular. He wrote business letters, particularly to recalcitrant payers. He made up rules of threes, pasted up papers and filled in forms, all with the help of a charming secretary with a particularly attractive name: Mademoiselle Mamouret. He would have had to learn electricity and I don't know what else.

It was all suffocating him and he had to get out.

Despite the immediate necessities of a life in pursuit, the thought of the piano never left him. But he knew nothing. In the hope of one day starting to study, he relaxed his fingers, thinking that articulation was essential. In the process, he developed disastrous habits that would be impossible to break.

One afternoon as he was walking in Asnières, a plaque caught his eye: Madame F. K. solfège, piano.

He rang the bell.

The bell had rung.

---

[12] We'll look at the meaning of this word in the chapter on the key.

[13] This word has no meaning, because Semites have nothing to do with it, apart from Jews who are Semites, which is not the majority: the proper term is **anti-Jewishness**.

[14] In other words, polluting capitalism, Marxism that kills tens of millions, perverse pansexual and abulistic psychology, disorientated science and rotten, delusional art.

More than bread and water, he needed a piano to live. Not being able to satisfy this vital need was a constant source of anguish. In times of fatigue and despair, he could hear melodies singing in his head. He couldn't have been prouder of himself if he'd brought a dead man back to life! It was always sad and pure, and sometimes the melody was vibrant, with a haunting, medieval beauty.

They passed like myths.

The bell had rung.

A sweet-looking elderly woman came to open the door. He'd barely met her before his heart was already overflowing for her. This was how he had dreamt of his mother: gentle, loving, distinguished, one of those mothers you're afraid to take advantage of because they're so good. So he told her straight out, without preamble or diplomacy. He told her that piano and Chopin were all that interested him in the world, but that he didn't know anything, that he had everything to do. Couldn't she teach him his notes to start with? But he had no money... She agreed.

When he thought of her years later, when he had managed to work on Chopin's twenty-fourth prelude, his heart overflowed with gratitude and affection. There are generous breaths of the soul that are worth all the gold in the world...

He took around twenty lessons with Mrs F. K, but these were interrupted by the bombing. One day, a nearby chemical plant was hit by American bombers. The smoke was so dense that it suddenly became dark in Asnières.

Tristan's situation was harassing and pregnant with dementia.

He felt like a mute in danger who couldn't call for help. He had to release this inner force that was suffocating and eating away at him. He had to courageously take the path to liberation. There was no other way but pure and simple suicide. He couldn't resign himself to being bogged down. He had to fight calmly or his mind would inevitably be destroyed. He had to concentrate his energy on this determination. He had to resign himself temporarily in order to achieve a social situation that would allow him to realise himself. Chopin, Schumann, Brahms, Liszt, Beethoven's sonatas... orchestral music crushed him. Despite its seductions, Wagner was too noisy, too powerful, Berlioz was alien to him. Mozart, yes Mozart... The piano was his complete instrument.

Just before being exiled to the factory, Tristan had passed what was known as the first baccalauréat. It was imperative that he prepare for the second, with a philosophy option. With commendable effort, he had bought the books he needed to prepare.

He had already been in Gennevilliers for a few months. From his family? Not even a handkerchief. He hadn't asked them for anything. Out of discretion? Of course not. But he knew he would have had better luck asking anyone in the street to help him. His family was radical and definitive nothingness.

And yet there was Uncle Paul, an uncle by marriage. He was the only one Tristan thought he could count on. He was a member of parliament, a future minister, surrounded by his beautiful Jewish family... He was alone in Beaune with his mother and sister. His wife and *beloved grandmother* was still in the Free Zone, protected by the Marshal.

Perhaps Uncle Paul would be happy to see him again?

Tristan left for Beaune one weekend. His uncle received him affectionately, gave him generous provisions and had a suit made for him, as the one he was wearing was in tatters. "I'm going to get you out of this factory", he told him, "first of all you have to pass your second baccalauréat, then you'll see".

That was well said, but the little boy, the future minister, deputy mayor and general councillor, had to ask permission from Aunt Denise and *Grandma* in the free zone.

He went to see them, as he did regularly, to bring them help and food.

They refused...

A few weeks passed. We were approaching what was to be known as "Liberation"...

A telegram.

Uncle Paul had just died...

The tobacco he had given up because of angina, he had taken up again in the stressful circumstances of the occupation. It was suicide. Then there was the family he had been supporting at arm's length for years: he devoted his work, his money and his energy to them.

He was fifty-three years old. The calculation of his marriage was ending badly for him, just as it would end badly for Tristan's father. Just as it would end badly for the Earthlings hanging on the coattails of Rothschild and Marx...

Poor dear uncle, he had been the only real person in his family. He had been the only one to help Tristan during the war. His death was the final blow for his nephew. His solitude was now complete.

Tristan was almost ragged again. The fibranne suit his uncle had made for him had not withstood a few months of constant wear. Tristan hid an indentation between his legs with a safety pin.

A year before the Second World War, Madame Christiane de la Vilette, of nobility, married Uncle Jacques.

She had lived with her husband in *grandma*'s mansion. The young woman had a lot of charm, she was beautiful and intelligent, but she had no fortune and a son from a first marriage!

Grandma made life impossible for him.

No sooner had Aunt Christiane placed some flowers in a vase than *Grandma*, in her impotent state, followed in her footsteps and threw the flowers in the bin. She performed a thousand of these daily petty tricks with the frightening precision of her sadistic machinery. She never lost her gangue of habitual slander and malice, which formed the backdrop to her theatre, the stage on which she moved at ease.

Following some perverse manifestation of her tragic nature, Aunt Christiane told her *beloved grandmother* what she had done, and then went to take refuge in her bedroom.

Her husband, Uncle Jacques, followed her straight away and a brief dialogue ensued:

—   Up until now you've amused me, but now you don't amuse me at all.

—   You have never amused me," she replied, "but today you are taking the piss out of me. Thus ended their precarious union.

Before the divorce, the family council met. Uncle Jacques, sent on behalf of the tribe, asked his wife to sign a paper agreeing not to ask him for any alimony.

She had said it, so she had this superb retort:

— I think my word is good enough for you.

At the time Tristan received the telegram announcing his uncle's death, Aunt Christiane, who had remained on excellent terms with Uncle Paul, was working in Paris at the Havas agency. She was very fond of his uncle, and it was with Tristan that she travelled by train to the funeral.

Tristan had received a violent shock and even before he arrived in Beaune, a fever had broken out, accompanied by a state of weakness caused by the basic difficulties of his material life and in particular an inadequate diet. He had just escaped the Obligatory Labour Service because of diabetes, which was no doubt of convenience, as there was no trace of it left. His face must have pleased the French commission that decided on departures. This favour had perhaps saved him from perishing under a bombardment in a Germany reduced to ashes in the name of human rights. Sometimes a hundred and fifty thousand people died in one night, but that was no crime of lèse-humanité...

When Tristan arrived in Beaune, he had to take to his bed in the very hospital that his uncle had built and where his statue can be admired today.

Tristan was told that a very famous former minister had made an overly courageous speech, and that his uncle's former replacement had spoken as the deputy mayor of Orléans.

After two days the fever subsided. He left the hospital to say hello to his uncle's mother and sister, who had spent the last months of his life with him.

In his almost ragged state, he thought he could ask for a pair of his uncle's trousers. Not only would this save him, but he would have been happy to own something that belonged to his uncle. Uncle's mother told him that she'd much rather see him wearing her son's clothes than a stranger's, but even for that detail he'd have to write to Aunt Denise and *Grandma*.

Tristan never got an answer and soon a pair of military trousers was to replace the civilian ones torn between his legs. When he was liberated, *Grandma* accused him in her grandiloquent court of "not attending his poor uncle's funeral, spending his time pulling carrots for him, and not waiting until his corpse had cooled to claim his clothes"...

At every level, they have this disconcerting gift for rendering facts and circumstances in the form of twists and misinformation. Freud and Marx are exemplary in this respect. She had this gift: to debase, to sully everything she touched, to interpret always in the sense of rubbish, in the sense of a projection of her own mentality, never to see the smiling, amiable, sincere side of things. Freud was exemplary. He had imposed his own neurosis on the whole world.

Corrosive and venomous, it was quintessentially absorbed in collecting everything that could be beautiful, great and innocent, and carabossing it into a mass of excrement. It was this form of modern thought that Tristan called *Judeo-Cartesianism*.

After the "liberation", Tristan met a resident of Beaune who told him how his aunt had auctioned off even her husband's shirts...

Solitude now complete. He returned to the greyness of the factory. The months passed. He tried to prepare for the second baccalauréat while working at the factory, and took music theory lessons from Madame F. K. He was falling apart. K. He was falling apart.

With no help from anyone, the piano receded. He could see his hope slipping away. He could take no more.

This was the so-called "liberation".

Tristan understood nothing, really nothing. He didn't even realise that many people were being murdered. Great French minds such as Brazillach and Drieux La Rochelle preferred death to the worldwide degradation that was to follow the victory of liberal-Bolshevism. The French volunteer soldiers against Bolshevism were imprisoned, the officers shot. And yet this League of French Volunteers against Bolshevism was backed by a legal government, invested by Parliament! And yet the Pope had said: "If the Eastern Front collapses, the fate of the West is sealed".

Tristan wouldn't understand until twenty-five years later, when he saw humans manipulated into humanoids who no longer understood anything, who continued to cherish birthdays and the inhumans who degenerated and exterminated them through demagoguery, wars, chemification of the soil, food, therapeutics, Marxism, Freudism, vaccinations, drugs, pornography and so on.

He understood the words of Alexis Carrel: "Dictatorship is the normal reaction of a people that does not want to die".

In the year 2000, the living dead would not even want dictatorial regeneration.

Tristan no longer felt the vocation to live.

He had no situation, no family, but the sky attracted him. He chose it. He longed for its infinity. He conceived the idea of enlisting as a pilot for Japan. Thirty years later, he would never have wanted to fight Japan, but he didn't know yet...

He would never have wanted to fight the only forces that wanted to protect the world from

"George Orwell's 1984, in which they found themselves at the end of the century.

Chapter VI

A week after the 'liberation', *Grandma* and Aunt Denise moved back into the mansion on rue Alfred Dehodencq. They accused those who had looked after their belongings for them during the war of theft.

Tristan informed them of his dangerous plan.

He asked them to use their powerful connections to get him into flying school.

Tristan remembered a man with a big cigar in his hand, slumped in an armchair at *grandma's* house, who picked up the phone to solve the problem in a matter of seconds. Neither his aunt nor *grandma darling* tried for a moment to dissuade him, to fight this mad decision to commit suicide, to talk to him about his future, No. They congratulated him on his patriotism...

It was the first time that a request for help had been granted with lightning speed. It is true that this support was requested not to live but to die.

Yet at the medical examination, he couldn't hold his breath for a minute, as required by one of the tests. He was sent to the Étampes base for preliminary classes that would last three months.

Tristan wasn't particularly good at handling weapons. On the right-hand turn, he was always ten metres behind the others. He never managed to raise and lower his rifle in harmony with his comrades.

So much so that his warrant officer, nicknamed "Nénesse", said to him one day during the exercise: "I'd rather desert than crew with you". After three months, thanks to family support, he was admitted to the Centre de Préparation du Personnel Naviguant in Vichy.

The school was commanded by a reserve lieutenant who had become an F.F.I. commander and was a tad demagogic towards the centre's pupils, whom he called his 'chicks'. The colour ceremony took place at precisely midday. You had to be present or you would be punished. One day, a pupil was fifteen hundred metres from the camp when the colour ceremony was due to place five minutes later. No matter how fast he hurried, he wouldn't make it in time. A Chrysler Royale pulled up alongside him on the pavement. It was the commanding officer, who said to the soldier: "If you don't come with me, you'll be put in the boot". The "chick" had been hot.

Tristan followed the school's training programme: navigation, principle of flight, meteorology, mathematics and English. His pay was two hundred and ten francs a month. Pathetic, of course. He was deprived of everything, linen, soap. The army didn't provide any of that at the time. All he had was his uniform. Several times he tried to write to Aunt Denise, but still nothing, nothing, nothing. Some comrades on leave took the initiative, with his agreement, to go and see his aunt. They brought back a shirt and a bar of soap.

Most of his brigade mates were nice people. They all had families, parents, grandparents, uncles and aunts who spoiled them.

Tristan was in the scrap heap.

He did accept a few invitations, but as he couldn't return them, he ended up turning them down. He wandered alone in the evenings, then went to bed when he grew weary. Being alone at nineteen, you become terribly aware of your moral abandonment and destitution.

He had always needed more love, tenderness and care than the others. He was broken as a child. He was thrown around in boarding schools, shaken, sick, homeless, unloved. As a young man, he couldn't behave like the others because he was all alone and no one would offer him a word of affection or a bit of love. He made up a character for himself to pretend he was alive. He had become accustomed to easy humour and uncertain wordplay, which he kept up all his life and which masked his infinite sadness.

One evening he was walking down the main street of Vichy when he saw a North African soldier bothering a beautiful young girl.

— I'm waiting for my husband," she said, in an attempt to keep the peace.

— I'll cut your husband's head off," was the poetic reply.

As his defence was ineffective, Tristan, who never shied away from sacrifice, approached her and with a smile took her by the arm, as if he had been the husband she had been waiting for. She gratefully accepted this strategy. First she had to pick up her suitcase from a friend's house before catching the eight o'clock train to Paris. She had a pretty, even, oval, laughing face, a splendid complexion, soft, tender eyes, and he later learned that she had been Miss Vichy, which she undoubtedly deserved. So they made the journey together to her friend's house and then to the station, chatting in obvious mutual sympathy. She gave Tristan her name and address, as he had not failed to ask for them.

Her name was Jacqueline.

He then returned to the camp, brushing past a military police patrol which he conveniently avoided as he had no leave. It was long past curfew, but for such an adorable creature, risks are taken and Tristan would have spent three days in prison just for having her name and address.

He went to bed and dreamt of that lovely face.

They met again. Again and again. More often. More often.

She loved Tristan and Tristan was alone. Tristan found himself loving her with all his heart. Desperate and alone, he lived again. He loved to be loved. Admittedly she came from a modest background - her father had a small slipper-making workshop - but she loved him and he loved her. It was wonderful for Tristan, this gift of destiny that up until now had offered him nothing but loneliness and suffering. And then there was the fact that she knew so many things, so many things that generations of university graduates would exhaust themselves trying in vain to get their made-up brains to hear. She was a virgin, twenty-three years old and Tristan just twenty. She offered herself to Tristan just like that, simply because she loved him. She cried - in those days people still cried when they lost their virginity - but she was happy because they loved each other. Faced with her trust and love, he was helpless. Her trust had won him over and he couldn't have broken Jacqueline's heart without breaking his own. They got married in Vichy on Tristan's coming of age, because the family had refused his consent. At the church, the priest, who had been officiating for thirty years, began to weep as he contemplated this couple, so touching and so luminous.

Despite the love that united them, Tristan soon realised that the carnal pleasure had dulled. It frightened him. But there was this wonderful tenderness. He loved Jacqueline as a child loves. A child who is also grateful for life. He couldn't forget that she had saved him from despair, had given him back the will to live. His heart overflowed with the passive love he had never received from his mother. He had joined the army with thoughts of suicide, a pretty face had leaned over his wounded heart, a hand had reached out to him. He was about to sink, but suddenly he realised that he wanted to live, that this face was giving him back his life.

He drank in the sweet solicitude that brought him life. As a vampire, he was going to absorb everything in one fell swoop, in the name of a crushing debt for which his family was responsible.

Today they are separated and Tristan's heart sinks when he thinks of those years. He didn't have any maturity at the time, and this lack of maturity was the real cause of their separation, despite the seemingly overwhelming facts.

The month after their wedding, Jacqueline became pregnant.

The Hiroshima and Nagasaki bombs had been dropped, and although the Japanese had long since accepted the principle of an armistice, the air force no longer needed to recruit pilots for Japan. Tristan asked for a change of speciality and wanted to become an interpreter.

A competitive examination was to be held at a forthcoming session. Tristan took it and came in first.

Passing the final exam after a technical training course meant staying for a full month. He had to do this training in conditions of material deprivation that he would no longer be able to endure.

In the middle of winter, he had to sleep in the attic of the second office on rue Ernest Vacquerie. The windows were broken. He knew that just a stone's throw away, in the rue Alfred Dehodencq, there was nothing to expect from his family. He had indeed had his aunt on the phone who, talking about his marriage to Jacqueline, had alluded to "his selfishness".

Those who love and give never talk about what they give: they love, they give, that's all. Tristan had never heard of selfishness except from selfish people. And they were always incredibly unaware of their own selfishness. So he gave up trying to explain things that his aunt was incapable of understanding. He'd been deprived of everything for years, they hadn't helped him in the worst way, since he hadn't even been able to pass his second baccalauréat at the instigation of Uncle Paul, and now that he'd found affection, he was the selfish one!

The more stupid, ignorant and nasty people are, the more they judge. Intelligence is above all the ability to know, to understand and not to judge. There is little to forgive those who do not know what they are doing.

At the end of this icy training period, he was admitted among the last, promoted to the rank of non-commissioned officer, special assimilation, and appointed translator-interpreter instructor at the Radio Navigants school in Pau.

Jacqueline and Tristan left for the Basses-Pyrénées with two thousand francs given to them by their parents-in-law. They thought they were going to get a non-commissioned officer's pay. A terrible surprise awaited them. The legal or official length of military service was two years. But Tristan could not receive the pay for his rank until this period had elapsed. So he and Jacqueline and their expected child would have to live on two hundred and ten francs a month! There was no way he was going to ask his wife's family for help, as his resources were extremely modest. He wrote to the family in desperation. He never received a reply. A few weeks later, he learned that *his beloved grandmother* had stayed in the best hotel in Pau and was on an antiques tour.

There was an army hotel in Pau reserved for convalescents and their families. The friendly captain who ran it referred the matter to the authorities and accepted them both into the hotel. They stayed there for a few months, and then, as the legal period had now been set at a year, Tristan received his pay and a little extra.

All this was just in time for the birth of the child. On the edge of the camp were some modest chalets: one was allocated to them. In the distance, the Pyrenees. The chalet was comfortable and adequately heated.

Jacqueline was a bit of a maniac, apt to make herself ill over a stain on the floor, always with broom or rag in hand. This exaggeration displeased Tristan's aesthetic sense, but she loved him, looked after him gently and calmed him down. He felt a tender affection for her. And then there was the baby about to be born. He wanted to give everything to her, who had asked for nothing more than to return a little of the love that she lavished on him. She had given him his first handkerchief. And now this little child.

A delightful little Chantal had arrived one day, with two big eyes as blue as the sky. Tears come to his eyes, his throat tightens as he recalls all those memories.

Today they are separated, but he thinks of her with despair and gratitude. She had given him back his life, and yet their union had not lasted.

He couldn't stand it, he'd sworn never to divorce her, and she'd pushed him against his will...

He would so much have liked to be a banal man, a good cook, a poet's nostalgia. One cannot ask a poet whose soul is chaos, quivering, anarchy, thirsting for truth, to enjoy the things of the earth. He simply passes by and is entitled only to their suffering. He would like to forget the others metaphysically and simply think of those around him. A deep sense of the universal, of truth and justice that breaks the immediate circle.

How much he would cherish his own child for having given to someone more unfortunate than himself. How can one make a woman happy if one prefers kindness to a cherished companion, if one thinks of humanity and its tragedy of pain? The spirit of evil always responded to its purest desires with sordid implacability. Tristan had dreamt of a kind and indulgent woman who, like him, would have had a sense of the human tragedy, a gratuitous love for his fellow men, so poor, so derisory, so powerless, so wicked at times in their sickly state, so touching in the metaphysical eye.

So he wrote:

There are millions of six-year-olds in the world, their faces devastated by hunger and despair, pain, nothingness and disease, torn apart because their mothers and fathers don't know how to love each other enough to love them.

Twisted by pain and questioning, their bodies and souls will be sick forever. They wonder why.

Why the heartbreak? Why the hunger?

Their bodies can't even form... And their eyes, their eyes...

I can't do anything for them, nothing.

Just the thought of them hurts me. No, I don't want to pray.

Not the awful prayer: I'm hot, I'm not hungry, I'm loved, I'm praying for you. Masquerade!

Lord, contemplate the suffering of your children. Contemplate those eyes that are full of tears. And grimace painfully towards heaven.

And those little arms that no longer have the strength to support themselves.

Those little feet without contours, made even more horrible by dirt. See the rot you let grow from the evil you let spread...

See those eyes of love that will lose all love, that will be ready for cruelty because they will be without love.

How can we love a God who can see all this without dying of sadness? Without lifting a finger of his omnipotence

And transform these masks of pain into faces of bliss. Those tears of pain into tears of joy...

How can it all be?

Is the world an accidental catastrophe, despite so much harmony? A disease of nothingness?

A mad impulse from God?

What is this stupid postulate of suffering leading to redemption? Why this gigantic holocaust?

O Lord of pain and mercy. In place of all this, I offer you

A child's smile with blue eyes...

Time and again, Tristan had felt that his poetic sense was born of his revolt against human suffering, all the suffering of the earth that was tearing him away. He felt the monstrous agony, the enormous cosmic nonsense that embraced his creative soul.

He knew that nobody is evil: evil people are sick people who need to be cared for and cured. Evil began a long time ago. Evil is a disruption of the balance between the antagonistic forces of good and evil.

For man to remain perfect, external nature must be in harmony with his inner self. He must follow the laws of nature. He must eat the raw things that nature offers him. Cooking is the source of immense deficiencies that affect the organism, the brain, including thought and judgement. We know that cancer can be cured by a return to raw food, which restores the primitive instinct that guides our choice of food; that eliminating cooked starches cures children's colds and bronchitis and other childhood illnesses; that serious neuroses, fixations and paranoia can be overcome by a return to raw food.

People need to know how to breathe by controlling their breath, they need to avoid acting against their conscience to avoid so-called psychosomatic illnesses. The more he suffers, the nastier he becomes; the nastier he becomes, the less he knows. The sicker he becomes, the duller his feelings become, because the heart is the fundamental source of real perception.

The less he knows, the more he will cherish what destroys him, the more he will destroy what surrounds him and those around him, the more he will be exploited by the scavengers who live off his madness.

He's going to finish the man off, in a suicidal Niagara.

But God has allowed evil and suffering, he has allowed the fundamental ignorance that means nothing can be redeemed.

Why did he invent this despicable form of defecation? Couldn't man defecate in a smelly way like the sperm whale? Why doesn't man make amber too?

God knows, because it is outside time and space. This embryo of a world doomed at the start? No, no, no.

A derisory gospel: we need to give people the means to practise its eternal values.

Soon there won't be enough good to feed the evil of the earth.

O that my heart would burst upon the world and drown all pain in its blood... So a little Chantal was born.

A pretty little girl with a pale complexion and two large blue saucers in the middle of her blond head.

Jacqueline had given her tenderness to Tristan and now this innocent, beautiful child.

But he didn't have the soul of a father. He was a *thinker!*

Today, a good father doesn't have to think, he has to vote and prepare for the aggregation of the cedilla through the ages while the world falls apart.

He couldn't...

Tristan's pure angel could do nothing but weep, while the tormenting demon acted. The angel tried to defeat the demon, but it paralysed him. Then he gave himself over to his destructive frolics. He returned and said to the angel: "See what you have done". Then the angel wept in his great misery and scoffed: "Make a beautiful theory out of the infamous reality, show us your powerlessness". Then the angel takes up his pen and even writes the blasphemies that the devil dictates to him in verse.

"Look up there, he doesn't give a damn about you and the others, but then he doesn't give a damn! He'll always let you down, go on. Are you suffering? Do what everyone else does, forget the past, ancient Egypt, thousand-year-old India, Plato, Saint Francis of Assisi, Alexis Carrel?

Now I have my own geniuses: Rothschild, Marx, Freud, Einstein, Picasso.

And you're a despicable father! What, are you thinking of something other than your children, of making a good name for yourself in our society, the one I run *entirely*? That's immoral! Look at the churches, but look, you fool, look at my good Christians, they're only thinking about their situations and their offspring! Finally, good Christians, as I like them, with popes and bishops who are devoted to me and humble with it: they've understood that there's no truth that can't be demonstrated with the logic of caretakers: 2+2=4!

Soon I'm going to build them nice little churches in the surrealist style, and then later we'll replace the churches with mosques.

Priests in civilian clothes, married or gay, in turtlenecks and black leather jackets, with a negro orchestra: long live progress!

Forget the past and especially the future, do as they do, they're living, you can tell them anything you want, they don't give a damn because I've put them in a state of coma! apart from football matches during which they slaughter, knock out or trample each other cheerfully, apart from the bleating of atonal and hysterical songs where they also slaughter each other, nothing interests them . Nothing at all. They all vote for me, all the puppets in all the political parties are in the hands of my finance and Marxism.

I feed them chemicals, I treat them with vaccines that wreck their immune systems, I add a little mercury and aluminium, I use synthetic chemicals that produce side-effects that are often fatal and will give rise to monsters. I'm preparing for the future. I can already see a world of physical and mental monsters that I will be able to pamper with the support of the morons of all the governments that believe themselves to be democratic and that I implacably control. Not a single official place will be left for a real thinker. Certainly not. I'll have my own little philosophers, self-proclaimed democrats! whatever it takes!

When there are retarded people who have a heart and are driven mad by it, I'll send them my great Freud, with electroshock therapy, lobotomies and chemistry if necessary!

But he doesn't care about you.

All it would take is one metaphysical flick of the wrist to send me back out of nowhere...

Chemistry, psychoanalysis, Marxism for all - my big dream!

I'm offering you the present, intense pleasure, and once you've had it, all you can think about is the next one, and don't care about anything else. No one is bound to the impossible. No past, no future, except the nothingness I'm concocting for you.

There is no longer any real reason, only irrational reason, the systematisation of an obsessive, a supreme cowardice, the ability to adapt to what is despicable under the guidance of filthy people. This pseudo-reason will radically sacrifice intelligence, the real intelligence, that of the heart. Reason is therefore the antithesis of intelligence, and the world now belongs to cold, impassive calculators.

The great calculator is going to destroy the planet with his absurd equations of finance, Marxism, chemistry, nuclear physics, family planning and so on" ...

O I would so much like to see this despicable reason, which makes crime so easy because it disguises itself as virtue and makes you part of a comfortable social criminal.

No greatness is worth being bought by suffering. Everything drives us towards evil, our incredible stupidity, our congenital and chromosomal cowardice!

O the suffering of others, unbearable suffering. To live today is to accept being an executioner.

Reviving after death?

If God said to him "You're going to live again, you'll be beautiful and intelligent, you'll have a lovely wife and beautiful children, you'll be a doctor and a piano virtuoso". He would say no. He couldn't stand the suffering of other human beings, the absolute misery of the Third World, nor the indifference of humans to the suffering of others, nor that horrible human defecation. No to life, even with this relative happiness.

He could not resign himself to evil and suffering. He imagined an absolute good, where the heart would reign.

There was a pure, inefficient crystal inside him that groaned at not being able to create good for himself and for others.

To play Chopin! What a joy that would be! O derisory lucidity and impotence.

He was five years old, he would always be five years old and he cried out to God, who had billions of them, that it was wicked to make him suffer and to make men suffer. He cried out to be given the knowledge that leads to true happiness through the will. The sadism and crime of the Old Testament, the strange morality of the Gospels - where had these two unbalanced inventions of the Circumcision of the 8th Day led humanity? To Marxism, the dolphin of Capitalism, the rotter and destroyer of the whole earth.

What a taste of nothingness when he knew that children were suffering, when he felt that millions of children were suffering, as if their suffering was Tristan's suffering.

The suffering of a child, its lost, mad, unconscious look, *but it was his*. And Tristan murmured: "".

O Jehovah, God of vengeance and crime.

I am torn apart by the stupidity of men, their wickedness, the atrocity of Israel, your sadism and my own madness.

We need to remake the world!

This must be destroyed in its entirety.

You must no longer set conditions for your creatures. They must be designed for true happiness.

To love them without counting the cost.

That they ignore anything that isn't beautiful. That they risk nothing.

They don't need freedom, they need happiness.

Let their existence not be justified by the big, the small, the beautiful the ugly, the good the bad. They must be scattered in a world where they have everything and ignore nothing.

O Jehovah, if this is blasphemy, you created me in your image. Look at the image in which we made you.

Am I not, in my presumptuous anguish, made in your image? It's not that they don't love you any more: they ignore you.

Listen: are you not moved by the suffering of your children? Sitting in your palace in the sky, demanding the impossible, you look at us with indifference and boredom. We kill, we cry out in pain and despair, we go mad destroying ourselves, we can't think, our souls are dead, but what do you care, Jehovah, grandma dear?

We were made not to resist Satan, you created us too weak on purpose, because you know everything, you knew our downfall before you created us. So where is this freedom?

If you had given us more judgement and strength, there would have been no fall. How can we not blaspheme if we don't understand?

Our mistakes mean nothing if we don*'t know*.

Can you blame a child who knows nothing about phosphorus and sets fire to the house by playing matches?

O this huge cohort of dupes in this crazy cosmos...

O Chopin!

The revelation of my deepest vocation. I integrated it perfectly.

Chopin was me, I was Chopin.

The first time I heard Chopin, for there was a first time, incredible as it seemed, I felt everything.

It was a monument to despair, magical, self-indulgent, immensely beautiful and sometimes a little obscene. There was bloody mud at the bottom, but a proud and tender red rose was blooming. O the exquisite sweetness of the nocturnal...

He had woven into the atrocity of human suffering all the tenderness of which God, in his infinite goodness, was incapable.

He revealed to me the magic of inaccessible purity, the dance of the paralysed soul.

The notes take on a crystal sound that resonates in the heart. They are cascades of beauty that petrify you with infinity, timeless songs of love.

What is inexplicable about Chopin is that the notes of the piano no longer sound the same when played. It's as if Chopin's soul only has to touch the ivory for it to become purified and etherised.

Playing Chopin!

What a feeling of miraculous power, what wonder, to communicate to others these incandescent effluvia of the absolute.

The 24th prelude, the étude in A minor, the last movement of the sonata in B... And everything else, even the slightest waltz.

The twelfth etude: strident chord, crashing waves, torrent of beauty and revolt, breathing stops.

Everything about Chopin is ethereal.

The hands themselves become virtual, angelic. Transcendent vertigo...

Chapter VII

Tristan continued his work as an interpreter and English instructor at the Radio Navigants base in Pau. He had tried to prepare for the philosophy baccalaureate during his factory year, but had been unable to take it. When *grandma* came back after the liberation, Tristan had lied to her: he had told her that he had passed. The sadistic satisfaction she would have felt had she known that Tristan hadn't passed the exam would have hurt her. During that year of factories and bombings, he had sometimes felt ill in the underground. An ambulance took him to hospital. A feverish state set in, but no diagnosis could be made. A famous surgeon, a friend of the family, practised at the hospital. Tristan greeted him. When he recounted the event to *his beloved grandma*, all she could say was a theatrical rebuke for having been recognised in the circumstances: "What a haunt!" she said in her special accent. After that, in the worst moments, when he went to see *grandma*, he always managed to be impeccably dressed.

Tristan had eighteen months left to serve in the army. With this time and a meagre but sufficient salary, he could prepare for and pass the exam. He had plenty of time, since he was only required to attend around fifteen hours of lessons and translate a few documents.

So he worked hard for three months, applied and was accepted as a bachelor of philosophy.

The subject of his essay had interested him: "The various degrees of self-awareness". He felt more at ease and regained hope. He could see a brighter future for the people who depended on him. He was beginning to see a glimmer of hope for his beloved piano.

There was nothing stimulating about life at the base. A dreadful pandemonium from which it was difficult to escape, a few decent officers back from England, F.F.I. officers[15] tragically vulgar, knowing very little of their written and spoken language, filthy jackets, dirty shirts, caps on the back of their necks, open jackets and tie knots closer to the navel than

---

[15] Force Française Intérieure: What we used to call the Resistance.

the Adam's apple. The active non-commissioned officers look like jubilant longshoremen and don't always smell good.

Tristan contrasted.

He wore a simple, clean uniform, a white shirt and black tie, and had had the audacity to replace the fireman's buttons on his bonnet with discreet black buttons. Legally, we couldn't agree with him, as these garish buttons were part of the uniform.

A new commander was appointed to the base. A polytechnician.

Tristan was immediately unsympathetic to him: this was the norm with Tristan, everything that was robotic, shaped, clichéd and banal was allergic to Tristan. The Commandant saw fit to appoint Tristan as one of the cadres to travel to a distant town to provide military training for a newly called-up class.

Tristan took forty-eight hours' leave and went to the second office. He was assimilated as a special and was totally incompetent to train recruits. The commander had no right to use Tristan for anything other than his speciality.

He was transferred by telegram.

This was all the more significant as a normal transfer, even for the commander, would have taken several months.

Tristan returned to the base where the telegram had preceded him.

He went to pay his respects to the commander, who left him with these snarling words:

"Go and find your protectors!

Tristan completed his third and final year in the army at a Royal Air Force camp on the outskirts of Paris. He had already enrolled at the Sorbonne. He had hesitated between medicine, which suited him well, and English, which would enable him to earn a living immediately as a teacher. He couldn't earn a living for himself and his family by doing medicine, so an English degree was the logical solution.

When he was demobilised, he found a job in a free school. Jacqueline, Chantal, his granddaughter and himself moved to the fourteenth arrondissement. They found a small room in the rue des Artistes, a secluded, almost provincial street. It was damp, dark, north-facing, with no running water but gas and electricity.

A large archaic bed, a mirror cabinet, a sideboard, a kitchen table and a bed for the little girl were added to the already cumbersome furniture and placed on the day side, near the window. Jacqueline was kind and devoted, the little girl adorable, and Jacqueline made friends easily with the workers in the house. There was a painful promiscuity. Tristan had to try hard to adapt, to create an artificial bonhomie. He began to speak badly, using swear words that he was surprised to hear himself say, to fit in with everyone else, so as not to stand out.

He felt his volcanic maternal tendencies growing inside him. The thought of the piano became more obsessive. He was tender with Jacqueline and the little girl, the pretty little girl. His wife and he had very different preoccupations, different affinities, and she was devoid of that sense of beauty that was taking on pathological proportions in Tristan.

That didn't stop him loving her very much. She had given him hope, a calm life, simply because of who she was, naturally.

With this aspiration for the piano grew an eroticism that bordered on the morbid. He had read somewhere in the Christian tradition that "pure souls will be led into temptations worse than death".

He longed for a peaceful norm, but he felt it running away from him. He cried out from his inner hell, which his Libra ascendant Scorpio already illuminated.

O the nostalgia for this normal that deep down he loathed.

And yet what could be more normal than to be abnormal when you consider the unconscious normality that surrounds us?

Melodies were singing in his head. He was suffocating.

Not far from their very modest room was the Cité Universitaire.

Tristan sometimes went there and met some exceptional boys with whom he sometimes had conversations that lasted all night.

There were also girls, very beautiful at the time, who would not be seen again in the year 2000. Without remorse, he enjoyed their magnificent bodies. They loved it. He felt a ferocious joy, the jubilation of Mr Hyde.

Fortunately, the difficulties of life prevented him from indulging in this exultation and partly neutralised his eroticism and his need for women.

The seduction of seduction! what a marvellous and diabolical thing! the passive seduction of a single look, a single smile! and even eloquent silences! looking at the other person and feeling that you already possess her, that she has already given you everything. The man who seduces does not force himself in any way; the man who forces himself in any way, more or less violates.

The true seducer looks at a woman as a snake fascinates a bird. True seduction is fluid, astral. Tristan could, with this strange force contained in a delicate body, impose this paralysing languor that gave way. He had no remorse because they loved this game.

Didn't a girl say to him: "Now that I've got you, I can die"?

Having been demobilised, he took up his teaching post at a private secondary school.

That year, 1948, he worked miracles.

Every morning at six o'clock he went to his Maristes school in the outer suburbs.

A four-hour round trip.

It was very poorly paid. It was a humorous union rate, which even doubled would not have reached the salary of an average worker.

Nevertheless, they were encouraged to exploit private lessons. They were veritable soup merchants. The pupils paid dearly and ate very badly. The chapel was rebuilt, the pond in the park was scoured, and most of the profits were paid to the high ecclesiastical administration. Parents were taken advantage of, as many of the teachers were not technically qualified. The children were poorly looked after and the teachers were duped. But here too, just like at *Grandma's*, good principles were taught.

One day Tristan, with his customary naivety and pathological sincerity, opened the floodgates to criticism. But priests are men," whispered the tartuffe Marist Director with the head of a pussy cat.

Yes, of course, but it was the behaviour of a religious community, and had nothing to do with individual weaknesses.

Another day at table, at one of those ceremonial lunches where the teachers were grouped around a table arranged in a U-shape, he expressed his indignation once again. He was dismissed. Tristan was joined by a history colleague, the only one with a teaching licence. He took Holy Orders the following year. He would not be a cynical, potbellied canon.

But the Church had not yet reached the bottom of the abyss, that of "1984". It was soon to become, in record time, a homosexualo-marxo-freudo-pornographo-centric society in apostasy, in total resignation, under the infamous pretext of rejuvenation.

Didn't it say, "Satan will reign at the top of the Church, in Rome itself"?

And "the Chosen Ones themselves will be mystified. Poor Church, it was the temple that had to be driven out of the temple... To open up to the world is to open up to rot.

Tristan's time in the army, the end of the war, and all the adjustments that had to be made, had kept him away from his maternal family, whose emotional outbursts were hardly a magnet. But they were his family. He had written a note. He went to rue Dehodencq.

Grandma was there, as always, very much like herself, slumped in her armchair, more greenish and stagnant than ever.

He kissed her hand, but not without the shudder that the contact sent down his spine.

Alongside *Grandma* was a rich cousin, the Baroness de Monosh, who opened her mouth as soon as Tristan was seated.

—   So, Tristan, have you moved to Paris yet?

—   O," he replied, "installed" is a big word.

He was going to give some frank and complete explanations, which this setting of luxurious furniture and carpets, of servants in white gloves, was likely to be painful.

It was at this point that *Grandma*, who was both embarrassed and apparently at ease, put on her good-natured, modest, good-natured air and interrupted:

—   Yes, he's found a small room...

She went on, skilfully keeping her mouth shut until the end of her roll of trivialities.

After an hour, Tristan was about to say goodbye when *his beloved grandma* stopped him. She had put on her noble, protective and munificent mask. She pulled a thousand-franc note from her bag, folded in four, and held it out to him with a magnanimous arm in the shape of a swan's neck.

—   Don't do anything stupid with that money, buy something to eat.

He took the note, trembling inside, saluted awkwardly and then took his leave.

The cousin who had witnessed the scene saw fit to say to Tristan as they descended the grand staircase together:

—   Be kind to such a sensitive and generous grandmother...

Tristan thought he was suffocating. He couldn't find the strength to explain things that were so far from the truth.

This strategy of "I'll pretend to give, and I'll take it all from you" was to be found in every aspect of the modern world.

A few days later, Tristan and Jacqueline were offered a modest flat in return for a small sum they didn't know they could afford. So they both decided to go to rue Dehodencq, as they could see no other way of getting help.

A godsend for the little girl, a bigger home than this miserable room with no water, damp and dark.

Grandma welcomed them like a dog in two sets of skittles. Her empty gaze was of a flaccid torpor that expressed only vegetative, limited thought, punctuated by flashes of malice and selfishness, objectives likely to set her intelligence in motion.

The posture of a slouching witch. She looked furious and her hand was patting the eternal sofa where she had been dying for forty years.

Uncle Jacques came in, silent and larval, heard that it was about money, said nothing and went to stand in front of the window, as if to look outside.

"You don't find that kind of money under a horse's hoof", said *Grandma* at last.

The only way they could get this flat, which had an unlimited number of applicants, was to be quick. A flat for a tiny recovery, at a time when they were astronomical, would be taken by someone else if they didn't hurry.

Grandma darling was reluctant. She wanted to know who to give the money to, the name, the address, "maybe she could have a chat"... They stayed in their hovel.

The two free colleges where he taught had a piano.

Tristan had decided to study on his own because he couldn't afford lessons. Impatient and forced to teach himself, he made serious mistakes and inflicted on himself a harmful articulation that prevented any nuance or virtuosity.

He could not decipher very well, but enough to learn by heart. He began, O folie, by memorising the whole of Chopin's etude in E major, the middle section of which is extremely difficult. The legato of the whole piece is radically impossible for a beginner. Nevertheless, he learnt the whole piece and managed to play it with a castanet-like sound. His fingers were very supple, as he could move thirds without support, and his hand covered from C to the G of the next octave. Many a concert pianist would have envied him this quality.

In the evenings, in their dark, damp room, he prepared two licence certificates, sometimes until midnight or one o'clock in the morning.

He'd go to bed half-dead, only to get up at six in the morning to catch the metro and the train to his college in the outer suburbs. A two-hour journey.

He used a small electric lamp so as not to disturb his wife and daughter. Sometimes Jacqueline would get upset and couldn't stand her husband working so late at her side, even with a small lamp. One day she tore up the university books, which were worth a fortune to them. So Tristan was forced to spank her. But how could he blame her? He kept her awake at night and she worked hard during the day, in that one room, with the constant washing of the child, in that hovel.

Tristan passed his first degree certificate with flying colours. Three months later he passed the certificate in English philology, which had required superhuman efforts on his part for a discipli-

ne that was the antithesis of his nature. To play the piano required, in addition to favourable circumstances, ten years of hard work. Higher education, teaching students who were losing their heart and intelligence dramatically every year, and whose physical appearance and clothes increasingly betrayed their accelerating degeneration, were putting him in a straitjacket.

He met Charles Dullin, who invited him to join his school.

In a vast dovecote in the Sarah-Bernard theatre, where the classes were held, he performed a few classical scenes that were far from brilliant. It is true that Corneille amused him. The bloat of honour and willpower, the outrageous false situations, all seemed caricatural to him. The beauty of the language alone could not inspire convincing acting. Even then, he remembered how much importance he attached to *substance*.

The content is something to say. The form is plastic perfection. He would gladly have tickled Don Diègue's bard and cut sausage with Rodrigue's sword. It is true, however, that Cornelian situations occur in real life and can therefore be played out in the theatre and felt. In Molière there was hardly a role for him. Even Alceste, to whom he felt a kinship, expressed his contempt for men in an unconvincing and *not very* laughable way.

He played a few modern scenes, one from Demetrios by Julius Romano.

His classmates applauded him, which was not customary at the school. A young woman came to offer him a part in a play and was very complimentary: "What a face, what good looks, just what I need"...

The play had a promising title: 'Double Royalty'. Tristan read it, found it derisory and returned it with a polite refusal, citing an overwhelming workload that was, in fact, very real.

The theatre did not satisfy him. Of course, as a way of earning a living, he would not have disdained it, but circumstances did not favour that prospect.

Moreover, Dullin had said to him: "You're twenty years too late, with your looks, now we're going to see the reign of the little twerp in the theatre as elsewhere". The bio-typological observation of the following forty years proved this prophecy perfectly right. What's more, in the cinema, there were soon no more actors, just hooligans and petty assholes playing the roles of hooligans and petty assholes. By definition, they would all be leftists. It's hard to imagine Pierre Fresnay being a leftist.

Who today could play *"Monsieur Vincent"* with the incredible heel displayed by this great actor?

He left Dullin's school with no idea that he was about to play a role on the stage of life itself that he had never imagined and that was beyond his imagination.

Chapter VIII

> *"The madman is he who has lost everything but his reason"*
> *(Chesterton)*

There was a shortage of teachers in the state education system, particularly English teachers. His two English degree certificates, his voluntary service and his membership of the II Air Bureau as an interpreter and English instructor enabled him to obtain what was known as a "delegation". He was then better paid, although this was not enough.

A birth certificate from his father was required to become a civil servant. After a long search, he obtained the certificate, which read:

"Died in Albigny sur Saône...".

He died there in 1947. Tristan wrote to the hospital where his father had died. His heart had given out and his last words had been "may my children know that my thoughts have always been with them".

Tristan had always felt this way. He *knew* that his father, whom he never saw, thought about them, while those he had lived with in *Grandma's* circle of friends didn't care about them.

Among the papers that reached Tristan, he found the name of a friend of his father's, Raymond T., an engineer, whom he spent several months tracking down.

The latter spoke warmly and admiringly of his father. He seemed a bit crazy to most people because "he was bursting at the seams". Yet he was extremely modest and expressed himself admirably. He won the admiration and sympathy of the doctors who treated him. His lucidity was astonishing, for he was an implacable forecaster, which is natural for those who think in synthesis[16] and follow the logical evolution of events.

Raymond T. added that two years before his death, his father had sent him as an ambassador to *grandma*'s mansion. He was to tell him that the children's father was very ill and wanted to see his children again. He had pointed out that the father was at risk of cardiac arrest, of sudden death.

Raymond T. had been left at the bottom of the stairs, received like a criminal, barely heard, not listened to. *Grandma* said: "That man looks like an apache".

She had never told them about this visit, never. She never even asked for the address of the hospital where he was staying. So none of the three children got to see their father before he died. He had given up, all alone, far from his children, without a word of tenderness or understanding. And when, years later, *grandma* alluded to this final visit, all she could say was: "He didn't want to see you, he wanted money"...

In his father's papers, he found another name, "Georges B. professeur agrégé, Docteur es lettres".

He had no trouble finding him in Vanves, where he lived.

Georges B. received him very kindly and spoke to him at length about his father after Tristan had told him of his death.

"The last time I saw your father was just before the war. He had been devastated by the trial with his in-laws and his physical and moral state was disastrous. I helped him a little, but I never saw him again. From the start of the war, he disappeared.

Your father had all the elements of a supernatural power that he would have been incapable of assuming. I knew him well and that's why I can tell you where he stood. You have a radiant forehead like his. I knew your father at school, he was tall, I don't remember him as a child. He was an average student who did just enough to keep up, but his preoccupations

---

[16] Liberalism is all about analytical thinking, indefinite production in all directions, no concern for human synthesis, resulting in general physical, moral and ecological pollution. We end up producing to sell, without the slightest concern for moral values and the interests of mankind, pornography, chemicals, aluminium and mercury in vaccines, vaccines themselves... the disappearance of water... etc.

went far beyond what was taught on the benches. He had a string of verses to his credit, some of them quite beautiful.

He wrote a tragedy, *Julius Caesar*, some of whose stanzas I remember as admirable. I got to know his mother, your grandmother, very well, and she was a fine woman who supported her son in his attempts to escape from school. In philosophy class, Alain was his teacher. He did not have unlimited admiration for Alain, and called him a "radical-socialist socrataillon".

He belonged at Normale Supérieure, not because he wanted to become a professor but because of the basic intellectual discipline from which, unlike almost all my colleagues, he would have easily emerged. Today I think he has too much pride to have submitted to such a discipline. Studies are not very useful, but I think they are essential for anyone who wants to think seriously. Your father, poet though he was, and with all the intelligence he had the right to ascribe to himself, would have benefited all the more from this work in Khâgne, without even entering Normale, because he would never have been a slave to it. He would never have been a teacher because his pride rejected the system. He knew that the intellect can only order the transcendent spark and that pure immanence leads to sclerosis, analytical dispersion and degeneration, of which Jewish speculation is the most obvious origin as a fundamental causal factor. One of the last conversations I had with him was about Bergson. He called him ingenious, not brilliant. He said he was the best the Jews could produce.[17]

I lost sight of your father in 1908 and for thirty years I didn't hear from him. I thought of him often, because in my memory he stood out from all the others. I told you how much I admired him, and that's not too strong a word. What you told me about him confirmed what I already knew, what I had understood. His fault was to look for a rich marriage, his misfortune to find it, his mistake in not knowing how to use it. We have to talk about a decline, and yet the term is not entirely appropriate. He suffered the consequences of his misplaced pride . I have a very sympathetic and almost unmixed memory of him. I confess my indulgence for this type of character. I only blame his marriage if it was deliberate.

---

[17] It should be noted that Bergson was Jewish only through his father. Jewish law confers Jewishness exclusively through the mother.

I hope his story will serve as a lesson to you. We sense that you reject stupid conformism for simple reasons of self-interest. But true intelligence today is a straw in a stormy sea. It has no chance of being heard. I know you understand this. I myself was barred from Higher Education because I got in the way of too many people. I'm retired now.

You, hide your intelligence, even if it saves lives, because the truth can no longer do anything against universal zombification.

Nothing stops them, not even death. They have no concept of value. Their gold.

But Tristan, alone in the world, all alone, remains there, like a splinter, a conscience, their splinter, their conscience.

So he had to be neuroticised, perverted and, to top it all off, deprived of all support. He didn't even have his father left, whom they had taken away from him. Under the appalling conditions in which he would be made to live, they were sure of success.

Despite Jacqueline and Tristan's best efforts, their existence was hard. They had to work miracles to ensure that little Chantal had everything she needed. They lived precariously and didn't get enough air and sunshine in that damp room. From time to time, on depressed days, like a shipwrecked sailor clinging to a rotten plank, Tristan went to see *his beloved grandma*. The hotel had regained its former luxury, with servants in white gloves who never lasted long, a Salmson and a chauffeur. There was also a television, at a time when nobody had one, and we'd just bought a farm on the Loire.

Sometimes *Grandma* would hand Tristan a quarter-folded thousand-dollar note, with grandiloquent demonstration and paroxysmal ostentation.

He accepted this magnanimous generosity, which, of course, solved all their problems.

One day it was raining.

Tristan went to rue Dehodencq wearing bad shoes that were leaking. They were the only ones he had. Embarrassed, he pointed this out to his *beloved grandma* as if to apologise, as the water-logged soles were in danger of wetting his Oriental rugs.

Uncle Jacques said he was going to give him a pair of shoes.

— I'm going to have good shoes in this weather," said Tristan.

— No," replied Uncle Jacques, with a silly look on his face, "I'm giving them to you precisely because they're leaking.

Tristan was dumbfounded. He didn't believe for a moment that his uncle had been making fun of him. His rather poorly organised brain deprived him of a sense of humour. Tristan rather had the impression that he didn't realise, that was it, *he didn't realise.*

And the others? Neither did the others. This impression grew stronger as Tristan's life unfolded. Marx is unconscious and so are those who follow him.

Shortly afterwards, he arrived at *grandma's* house empty-handed. Jacqueline had no illusions, but when they were desperate, she suggested that Tristan go to rue Dehodencq, with the same hope as someone who plays the national lottery. He wasn't amused, but for Jacqueline and the little girl, he made the effort. You always keep hope in your family even if you know there is none.

He crossed Paris and arrived at *grandma's* house with a perforated metro ticket in his pocket. Just enough to get him home by metro.

He was there when Aunt Denise asked him to fetch the poodle from the dog clinic. She gave him fifteen hundred francs to do it.

He received a shock. It was six notebooks of this indispensable metro. And in his pocket he had an underground ticket with a hole in it. He felt a strange contempt; their thoughtlessness, their heartlessness, was going to drive him mad on the spot.

Shearing the poodle! Shearing the poodle!

It's impossible to describe what was going through his mind on the way from the hotel to the clinic, from the clinic to the hotel. *But this hatred resembled self-preservation rather than hatred itself.*[18] He even had the fleeting idea of going home with the money they so desperately needed.

---

[18] This sentence sums up the whole psychology of anti-Jewishness over the last 5,000 years (since it existed long before Christianity).

He couldn't think of it as theft, it wouldn't even have been immoral.

There is no one like them to turn an innocent person into a delinquent, a criminal. This materialistic world, this world of polluting profit and imbecilic ideologies, will soon be a huge herd of delinquents, criminals, morons, pornographers, drug addicts, *sub-humans*. They make you want to bite the sweetest, most Venusian nature.

He hoped so much for the little girl, for the three of them in that room without water, with the washing and the unhealthy gas.

The little one was fragile, her mother was getting so tired. Her own delicate constitution.

His revolt had to be suppressed. The little poodle with his little tail wagging with joy at seeing Tristan again had nothing to do with it.

There were no pianos in the state schools where Tristan worked. A fellow student offered to let him work at her place. He gladly accepted, but he still had to, as she lived near the Porte de Clignancourt, opposite the Porte d'Orléans. Two hours on the metro for one hour of practice. On the way back he spent most of the night working on his third degree certificate.

He decided to hire a piano for a modest sum. It cluttered up the room even more. He had a mute put in for the child.

In this industrious house, the piano did not win favour with the neighbours.

One of them, who had been drinking, threatened him. Strangely enough, he was hit by a car on his way home from work the next day and died.

Tristan felt uncomfortable, he was suffocating. He tried to work on his instrument. The felt mute he constantly left on distorted the sounds. At first it seemed unusual, but then it became unbearable.

He felt trapped by everything. He wanted to escape into the infinite. His heart and his reason bound him to his duty. But he was torn by chaos. This chaos was the result of divorce, of being torn away from his childhood…

Its crystal soul and eroticism.

Its reason and its artistic effervescence.

He was cramming for his bachelor's degree and hardly had time to go to the Sorbonne to attend lectures. The basic difficulties meant that he had to deal with a host of obligations that he couldn't avoid. He only went to the Sorbonne from time to time.

It was there, however, that he met Huguette. He was waiting at the door of an amphitheatre where a conference was about to be held. The door opened and a young girl came out. They found themselves face to face. They looked at each other and were both moved by a feeling of admiration for each other. He realised that the impetus behind this beautiful person had suddenly broken when she saw Tristan. For a second she stood still in front of Tristan and he had the feeling that she was waiting for him to decide to say anything to her, but there was no point in hesitating!

Tristan seized the opportunity. No, he wasn't going to let this exquisite venus pass him by! He asked her a banal question about the conference that was to follow. She replied kindly with a smile that burst with whiteness, and he discovered in her dark eyes something conquered, submissive, tender and passionate. She had a long face, her complexion matte without exaggeration, her mouth perfectly defined and sensual. She was tall, slender and very elegant in her simplicity. In this dusty Sorbonne, she stood out as much as Tristan.

She was also doing a degree in English. They climbed the staircase to the galleries together, listening with a distracted ear, but not without looking at each other, their hearts beating with the drunken sweetness of desire.

He took her hand and she squeezed his.

After the conference they went for a drink in a nearby café.

They saw each other again the next day, and again a few days later. They remained captivated by each other, intoxicated by their kisses and their hearts beating faster and faster. Tristan was too frank not to tell her the truth: he was married.

At first she thought he had a mistress. She was twenty, he was twenty-four.

"A mistress can swing," she laughed, "but a woman, no, you're not free!

This harsh reality gripped him.

She clasped his hand and kissed it. Her passionate kiss told him that she too accepted this intoxication without remorse.

His wife loved him, he had great tenderness for her and the little girl. And now he, who had known no woman but his own, who was so greedy for women, had a desirable and very beautiful mistress. No, he had no remorse. His heart was at peace.

How many sweet embraces they gave each other in all the hotels in the Latin Quarter!

A few months went by, and then one day Huguette simply told him, on a whim, that she didn't love him any more!

The first heartbreak of his life. He was deeply saddened.

In the evening, he returned to his damp room with no water, no air and no light. He found Jacqueline and his little Chantal. He was sad, downcast and not hungry. Jacqueline gently asked what was wrong and he, the loveless child he would always be, told her about his adventure. She was almost twenty-five when they married and he was twenty-one. She was his eldest. Women are mature at that age, men are not. A tear welled up in her laughing eyes and she came to console him. Tristan hugged her and asked her forgiveness.

But what a child he was! He shouldn't have told his wife about his affair. It had nothing to do with the integrity of their home, because he loved them both. That tenderness was sacred.

Tristan had a friend at the nearby university residence whom he often invited to his house. He was finishing his law degree and was soon to receive a special distinction from the Académie Française for a carefully-crafted book of poetry he had published. Tristan found him interesting and was very forgiving of his imperfections. Jacqueline was receptive and he had a culture that could serve her well. Maurice, that was his first name , had a press card that gave him free entry to theatres where he could take Jacqueline, who never went out.

So Tristan could stay peacefully in the bedroom looking after the little one while he prepared his last two degree certificates. Maurice gave Tristan absolutely no cause for concern, and what's more, he had complete confidence in his wife. If he had chosen Maurice for his cultural qualities, the portrait of Maurice reassured him completely. He couldn't imagine that a woman like his would even put up with him shaking her hand for too long when he said hello. He himself couldn't stand a prolonged handshake from Maurice. He was short, red-haired, stocky, cross-eyed to the point of caricature, wore thick sunglasses, his skin was brick-coloured, his thick hands were the same colour and betrayed a propensity for violence. Maurice himself had confessed with contrition that he had experienced this flaw when, as a teenager, he had strangled a small cat with a piece of string. This revelation had chilled Tristan, but had also reassured him that Maurice could be a danger to his wife.

Jacqueline and Maurice went out, while Tristan worked.

At the time, he was preparing for the extremely difficult Certificate in English Literature, because in addition to all these pitfalls, there was another major one: he had never spent any time in England. Writing a literary essay in English without the slightest knowledge of the language was an almost impossible feat.

A neighbour's indiscretion told him that Jacqueline and Maurice were flirting. He judged the word in the light of his aesthetic impression, which was perfectly categorical. He thought that his wife was being kind enough to accept a sort of marivaudage with this physically unappetising man who offered her a bit of culture and distraction while he worked. He lectured them both in a bantering tone of mockery. He attached no importance to what for him could not exist, had no chance of existing. Hadn't he said to his wife: "How can you imagine, even for a second, the mating of a bird of paradise and a crocodile?

They continued to go out, Tristan continuing to work beside his child.

Suddenly, for no apparent reason, Maurice began to show a dark hatred for Tristan. His behaviour became violent, even dangerous. He was astonished by this aversion when he had done him nothing but good. He begged him not to come back to the house.

Alas, one day Tristan was to learn that birds of paradise can mate with crocodiles without shame or remorse...

Madame de Gastine, Tristan's mother, had recently moved to Paris on the Avenue Kléber. She had come to see her son and daughter-in-law and by chance met Maurice, whom she invited to her home.

She was about to play a central role in one of the tragedies with which she was familiar. Jacqueline must have told her mother about Tristan's affair, which she knew was of no importance. Her mother's attitude was perfectly despicable, for she drove Jacqueline into Maurice's arms. She went so far as to take her daughter-in-law to see a lawyer without Tristan suspecting a thing. Madame de Gastine was just as unaware as Tristan that Jacqueline was deliberately cheating on Tristan with that brick-skinned midget with the horn-rimmed glasses. She was also unaware that the affair with Tristan, who had never known any other woman but his own, was of no consequence, and that if Jacqueline had told him about it, it was precisely to justify her own serious adultery, of which everyone was still unaware.

Jacqueline herself later told Tristan what her mother had said to the lawyer about her son: "If he came here I'd kill him like a dog".

All Jacqueline had to do was tell her mother-in-law that Tristan had had a mistress (it is likely that she had used the present tense to make matters worse), and this cortical formalism, far removed from any profound reality - for Tristan had never forgotten his wife and daughter in his intoxication - set his mother's destructive mechanisms in motion.

Instead of sorting things out, Madame de Gastine put on her usual grand guignol.

Madame de Gastine exerted a kind of justifying fascination on Laure and Charlotte, for when the pithy apophthegm uttered in front of the lawyer was mentioned to Charlotte, she evoked, in support of her mother, Blanche of Castile's famous comment about Saint Louis, the slaughterer of Muslims in the name of Christ: "I would rather see him dead than stained by a single mortal sin".

Poor Madame de Gastine!

Unconscious and incorrigible. A Catholic-Jewish poet! Oscillating between angelism and diabolism. Masochistic, beating herself with a riding crop.

Misunderstood, unbearable, Pharisaical, malicious, insinuating like Eve's snake, a much more intelligent version of *grandma darling*. Gifted with an astounding spirituality of nonsense, an intelligence of beings that is hallucinating, provided that she herself does not gravitate into the orbit of the people she is judging, otherwise her judgement becomes distorted and depends solely on the good or bad sensations that these people give her. In this way, his initial thoughts, always remarkable, become falsified to the point of taking on the opposite colour.

Incapable of authentic love, of self-giving, she was available for all the excesses, all the exaltations, all the parodies of altruism, all the hysterias of apostolate.

She had brought his son nothing but pain, and he remembered nothing good. *Nothing at all.*

In a book in which she talks about her son, going from one lousy college to another, mad at being deprived of tenderness, her only worry was that he would become a pederast, the danger of boarding school. O mockery!

Tristan wishes he could laugh, but his family has taken away his sense of humour. Suffering and imbalance, intuitive intelligence, that was his mother.

She spoke of the drama of modernism and its profound factors with astonishing lucidity, and had no hesitation in denouncing the major role played by her fellow human beings in world suicide, because she felt absolved by her conversion to Catholicism. But in practice she never stopped justifying herself, devising the most astonishing psychological twists to justify the most immoral act in the light of a moral principle. She was doing in private what the modern world is doing universally: the guilty are protected, fabricated, encouraged, innocence and intelligence mocked and castigated. The era of the biggest lies wrapped in a golden foil.

Tristan had often felt like laughing when listening to him. But he always put on his stupidest mask so that no one would suspect the psychological insight that was dismantling his perverse theatre, his disgusting self-righteousness, his dazzling inversions.

Everyone walked, except Tristan. Look at the number of unfortunate people that Liberalism, Marxism, Freudianism have made walk...

It is true that this multiform dialectic, always identical to itself in its expression and destructive effects, works everywhere and for everyone in the modern world.

Years later, George Steiner summed it all up:

"For 5,000 years we've talked too much, words of death for ourselves and for others". How he would have loved a gentle, serene, loving mother. What fervour he would have had for her.

He would have known the piano, the essence of his life. His direct outpouring would have spared him any fatal bruising.

Today, insane reason prevents transcendence from flourishing.

He had made it clear to *his grandmother* that a stay in England was essential for him. If she had helped Jacqueline, he could have taken up a teaching assistantship in Great Britain and the matter would have been settled.

But *Grandma* didn't care about that. He could feel how much she wanted him to fall. He felt the sadistic joy she would have had in proclaiming to Madame de Gastine: "We did everything we could for that rogue, and he's just like his father, I always said he'd end up on the scaffold".

And to let his hand fall back on his eternal sofa with a characteristic poum.

Tristan went to the June session at the Sorbonne. He had worked hard on his written work and, despite his stumbling English, he managed to write his essay and qualify. His success was a miracle. He had done it alone. He didn't know any of his fellow students who had passed the written literature exam without having spent at least a year in England. He had achieved a tour de force. Writing an essay in a foreign language in such conditions was a prodigious feat: all that remained was the oral exam. Unfortunately, he hadn't had time to prepare. He had been forced to abandon this purely mnemonic oral. There was the whole history of English literature, of which he didn't know a word. He only knew the historical and literary context of the authors of the writing, but that was not enough. He went to the exam to benefit from the experience, but of course he failed.

He spent his summer preparing for the oral exam in October.

The test went well, but during the second test of explanation of text, a chimpanzee-like examiner asked him point-blank how many accents there were in Shakespeare's verse. Tristan, who had never had an eye for detail in any field, told him he didn't know, but that all he had to do was count them in the Shakespearean edition in front of them.

de Gastine Unforgivable ignorance," concluded the simian examiner. Tristan was adjourned for one point.

It was the coup de grâce. Miraculously, he had obtained the written exam without going to England. He felt unable to take the exam again. His health was failing every day and he had failed. It was a cataclysm, for he had brought his efforts to a possible peak of physical and moral health. An attack of furunculosis broke out, which would torment him for years. He felt he was dissolving. The struggle against his vocation as an artist, his exhausting work for both university and teaching.

The few courses he attended at the Sorbonne were enough to make him despair. It was enough to make one laugh to observe the perspectives and methods in use. The professors religiously and conscientiously mumbled the same meaningless opinions, accompanied by the same tricks, the same facetiousness, the same tics. The intellectual process of these "agrégés" had the perfection of vending machines. They were clearly required to have the lucidity of a mole and the memory of an elephant. This process of dumbing down could not fail to produce Marxist and Freudian robots, even if everything proved the absurdity, madness and stupidity of these dismasted logics, these system dreams, cut off from reality and destroying souls and bodies by the tens and tens of millions.

O Sorbonne!

An anthill of healthy, mutilated beings who ignore themselves and who, in the name of a shoddy reason or ideology, impose delirious absurdities. Sorbonnards who think with blinkers on, intellectualists in vials, textbook cupboards, pots full of insignificance, concocters of the neantisation of mankind and the planet.

You're not men, you're Father Ubu's repertoires.

Peeling away at subjects that are, for the most part, of no interest whatsoever, such is the art of the Sorbonne dissertation: "Is Milton a poet among Puritans or a Puritan among poets? "Did Shakespeare respect history in Julius Caesar? "Rousseau: must we separate the man from the work? "Orwell, "1984", a love novel?

Poor Shakespeare, poor Orwell, poor Socrates!

The incoherence of things, the vertigo of the incoherence of things. There's no one like the mediocre[19] and the stupid to achieve the social maximum.

---

[19] In the year 2000, when this book will be reshaped and completed, it will be the scoundrels who will have this privilege.

Soon only gangsters will be able to achieve this. It will be radically impossible to achieve this without being a gangster or a docile, Freemasonic fool.

An agrégé once told me that "intuition is the mother of error". Obviously he didn't have any. Other than, of course, a tiny little analytical intuition about something that was completely pointless.

Tristan was surprised to hear on television once that aggregation damages the human brain and is therefore pathogenic. He heard this evidence once. Never since. Tristan had been saying it for twenty years. Voluntary, limited, unintelligent, doctors from the Sorbonne, the best of whom make honest specialist scholars, not dangerous for the system. You can do what you like with them. Totally devoid of any sense of elementary observation, of any possibility of profound intuition, the authentic undertakers of the whole of humanity.

Agrégation.

A psycho-pathogenic competition, a diploma for so-called intellectuals, a monstrous heresy that lives on the naivety of the masses, the work of intellectual residue breakers. Nothing comes of it. The agrégés are never creative, they achieve nothing. They are always humanists, which *is to say inhuman*. Humanism has been destroying humanity for three centuries. It's almost finished.

They observe only in the tiny patent, immediate, precise, primary, material, rationalist, not reasonable. The nine tenths escape them. The agrégation was invented by the revolution mistakenly called French, for the Lévy les Homais. Unimaginable mediocrity, insurmountable limits, supreme suffocation.

After the great revolution that the Jewish Marxist billionaires are preparing for us, the supreme adrenal aggregation[20] , which will be renamed so that nothing remains of the bourgeois revolution, will be made of reinforced concrete.

---

[20] The adrenals are the glands of action, brutality and objectivity. It's only natural that the reductionist communist regime should be headed by adrenals - Stalin, Khrushchev, Brezhnev, etc. This is the least evolved glandular type. The chapter on "the key" will shed more light on this question.
Ring wrestlers are adrenal, like many boxers.

What is an artist to them? A paranoid state and an Oedipus complex. But what normal man wouldn't be paranoid in this despicable, idiotic world?[21]

A world of lies and grotesque laws, infinite in number. A world of zombies where all the lies and inversions have the force of law.

Oedipus complex? But Oedipus is a drama about fate, not incest. The Greek playwright chose this behaviour as the fatal fulfilment of the act towards which man feels most repulsion. *Oedipus never had an Oedipus complex.*

Would the tendency to incest have been outlawed among the Primitives if the impulse had been so strong? And what about this perverse unconscious? Where did Freud find it, if not in his own perverse brain?

What about the symbolism of dreams? Do we need symbolism to have erotic dreams?

What about Marxism? When did technology create culture? When did the plough create man?

The influence of these two monsters who, in similar ways, deal with the inner man and the outer man. Unburdening, abulia, cinema and literature, zombies for zombies, pornography, perverse education, not to mention therapy followed by a mass of suicides.

Tens of millions of people exterminated in Marxist countries. That's how they dealt with unemployment. Between 1950 and 1952, 5 million people were executed in Communist China, and how many tens of millions in the USSR between 1917 and 1960?

How many?

But look at the faces of Marx, Freud, Mendés France, Olivenstein, Schwarzenberg, Aron, Attali, Tordjmann, Hammer et al. and those of François d'Assises, Carrel, Pericles, John of the Cross, Peter Deunov, and you will understand that when you are made to understand, you understand nothing at all and you are mystified.

---

[21] Aldous Huxley said that anyone who was not neurotic in this world was abnormal, because it meant that he had adapted to a world to which it was impossible to adapt. (see Brave New World).

A philosopher is not a Lévy or a Dupont who has passed the agrégation at the Sorbonne, it is a being whose brain is naturally constituted to think by synthesis. He is a providential elite. He is gifted with a high conscience.

Ask a philosophy graduate to gargle with these idealists, these pseudo-philosophers, with their arithmetical thought processes that dissolve man and nature *rationalistically*.

Chapter IX

Tristan had been struck down by this failure, so close to the goal, and for an inane reason, "the number of accents in Shakespearean verse"...

He had to go to bed. Uncle Jacques came to see him in his hovel. Tristan had two abscesses.

—   You'll have to bathe every day," says the uncle, "so take a bowl and a jug and pour some water over it.

Grandma's house had a dozen bathrooms. Tristan's condition worsened and he had to be taken to the university hospital. He was covered in abscesses and boils. He was inundated with antibiotics. No effect. The doctors persisted in injecting these products. He knew that it was the moral shock that had overcome him, the anguish, the concern for his family. And in the background, the piano was receding, receding. He knew that Jacqueline had no money and that there was no question of stopping working. He knew that to get back into the fight after such a defeat, she would have needed a little help. But in the circumstances, everything seemed radically insoluble. He knew that a little help would have cured him as if by magic. Whoever said that money can't buy happiness was quite right, but in this case he must have had a lot of it.

On the day he was hospitalised, Jacqueline had gone to stay with *her beloved grandma.* Tristan didn't have any pyjamas and it was essential that he changed them every day. A few days passed. Uncle Jacques stopped his car in front of the hospital and, standing in the doorway, said banteringly:

—   So you're not dying any more?

Then, in a hurry, he was about to leave again. Jacqueline happened to be there at her husband's bedside. So he added:

—   Do you need anything?

The question was so farcical that they could only reply with one voice:

—   Of course not!

Three weeks passed. The day after he was discharged from hospital, a parcel arrived that the administration had forwarded: it contained two pairs of pyjamas.

Tristan was prescribed a month's stay in a nursing home. This presented a problem akin to squaring the circle. *Grandma darling* had handed over the amount to be paid to the hospital, which was not covered by social security, against a receipt in due form.

The rest home was in Sainte Maxime, in the south of France. The money for the trip had to be paid in advance, and was only partially reimbursed on return. *Grandma darling* gave her the exact amount for the trip.

By the oddest of coincidences, the Baroness de Monosh was still there, and it was in front of her that the money was handed over. As they both descended the staircase to the hall, the Baroness saw fit to reiterate her recommendation: "Be kind to such a sensitive and generous grandmother".

Tristan's body began to tremble. Machiavellian ostentation was at work, as it is everywhere. Ah, those people who sell arms to all those who exterminate themselves and build hospitals!

He was going through hell with his wife and daughter and everyone thought they were being helped. This is exactly how Communism is helping the whole world, wherever its tentacles have reached, with the help of Jewish finance, misery and human stupidity.

- What do you think," he finally said to his cousin, "but Grandma isn't helping me. The alms she's just given me are barely enough to pay for my train journey to the nursing home.

So he described the situation to her, showing her how he was struggling, alone, all on his own, how he was trying to provide for his family while at the same time studying for a higher education, and the conditions in which they lived in their slum. He told him how much *Grandma* had helped him in these appalling living conditions.

And he didn't talk about the main thing, the business that was at the heart of everything, the deliberate desire to destroy him as they had destroyed his father and the monstrous drama of this negative struggle and his piano that drove him mad with absence... The cousin didn't seem surprised but rather embarrassed.

Everyone believed that Tristan was being helped, they had to believe it.

A few days later he had a chance meeting with a relative who said to him: "What would you do if you didn't have a grandmother to give you fifteen or twenty thousand francs a month, who has just sent a large sum to Israel?

Once again, Tristan's composure was eclipsed.

It took him five minutes of stammering before he was able to set the record straight.

He was covered in boils, a visible sign of his moral misery and worn-out health. There were three of them, soon to be four, in this squalid room in the Rue des Artistes, and it was only through constant feats of strength that his own were not too lacking. Not only did *Grandma darling* not help them, but when, on the rarest of occasions, she gave them a small sum of more than a thousand francs, the sum claimed was always a thousand francs short. Of course, Tristan would never have dared to count in front of an audience in his living room.

Family relations and friends had to believe that the grandson was being helped! That's why the donations were made in front of a select audience.

When Tristan returned from the nursing home, he took up the little bedside lamp to light his night's work. So as not to get exasperated about the English literature certificate, which had seen a miraculous success turn into a bitter failure, he prepared the French literature certificate, which he was admitted to.

After telephoning, he went to *grandma's* house to tell her the good news. When he arrived, the only words *grandma dearest* had to say were expressed with the sadistic bitterness for which she was famous:

- So you failed English Lit, you lied to me.

If Tristan had had a bomb in his pocket, not a stone would have been left of the mansion.

He then understood how the gentlest person can be turned into a spectacular murderer in self-defence.

Alone, without help, without support, ill, he had just made exhausting efforts to complete three quarters of his degree so that on a successful day she would start making this scene in front of parents, strangers, relations, servants, simply to give herself the illusion that she had the right to reprimand him in this way, so that the audience would believe that the considerable assistance she was lavishing on him gave her this right...

The reason he had temporarily given up the English literature certificate was precisely because he had failed due to lack of help, and it was smart to move on and take the test again later.

That way, everyone could legitimately believe that *Grandma* was looking after them.

It was a despicable Machiavellianism that Tristan found in every aspect of the modern world.

She abhorred it. She indulged in this sinister comedy not only to justify herself to herself, but also because of the suffering caused by something good that had happened to Tristan.

He remembered hearing her complacently say about the child of his youngest son, Uncle Etienne, married to a goy who had come to visit *his beloved grandmother* in her empty town house during the war, "that he was cross-eyed and looked like a runt".

Poor kid! It's true that Uncle Etienne doesn't fit in well with the trio and doesn't take any comfort from it. "It was the sick who invented wickedness", said Nietzsche.

Tristan had never heard *grandma dearest* say a kind word to anyone. Everything remained in the strictest '*grandma dear*, uncle Jacques, aunt Denise' triangle.

She lent her personality and her own objectives to others, and enjoyed smearing everyone. Aunt Denise showed more objectivity, intelligence (which doesn't mean much, unfortunately) and a certain devotion. But her greed is pathological. She is capable of going so far as to hate everything to do with money, to enquire of the servants to find the bottom of a bottle of beer, to leave dozens of jam jars to rot rather than *give* them *away*, to sacrifice three centimes as a tip to a cinema usherette, at a time when fifty centimes was the minimum you could give... Fortunately arrived just behind his aunt and Tristan emptied his pockets of their change to escape this fantastic and degrading ridicule and to give back to the young person the breath that his aunt had taken away.

Uncle Etienne's son, whom *Grandma chérie* affectionately called "runt", calls *Grandma* chérie "cow skin".

Uncle Etienne tries to force himself inside the trio, and in order to satisfy this pretension he forces himself into all sorts of platitudes, cowardice, even denial of his nature, which surpasses those of the trio in positive quality. His ambition is to be more than tolerated, to become one with them. He strives to imitate them, out of line, out of clan spirit, and no doubt also out of self-interest. The sense of tribe is certainly the only thing that counts.

As for poor Uncle Jacques, "he's very nice", as one of his uncle's colleagues said to Tristan. Calm, placid, extraordinarily gentle in appearance, fiercely egotistical, a routine doctor, conformist, indifferent, a lover of tranquillity.

He would never stand in his mother's way. He had more in common with some kind of inert object than with a human being.

The clan.

Uncle Etienne once said: "If my mother told me to kill, I would kill". Poor pitiless victims of a merciless atavism.[22]

---

[22] We shall see in the chapter on the key that atavism plays only a very minor role in Jewish characterology.

Chapter X

The unhealthy, viscous air in the room where they lived was very harmful to the little girl. She fell ill, suffering from a primary infection that was all the more serious because of their precarious living conditions. Anguish gripped them. They turned to their uncles, who were hospital doctors. "This infection was of no importance, it was a trifle". They got plenty of recommendations for hospital colleagues, and free medical samples...

The child seemed to be getting better, but then an ear infection with purulent discharge broke out. So the illness had not been cured, but had taken another form. This is a natural process if symptomatic control is practised without tackling the very causes of the illness. Hospitalised in Uncle Etienne's ward, she finally recovered after a few weeks. Etienne took her into his ward with him," *grandma* pitied, in a tone that was half-protective, half-weeping.

Poor little darling.

The first time Tristan laid her on her hospital bed, all alone with her two big blue saucers in the middle of her face, she cried at seeing her parents leave her. Tristan couldn't tear himself away. Because it hurt so much, he wished he could have stayed there with her in the hospital.

Nothing moved the family. Their life in that slum, their meagre resources, their inadequate food, Tristan's emaciation and his painful, exhausting, atrocious furunculosis, his almost-completed university studies hampered by a lack of money, a lack of peace and quiet, his desperate struggles: everything left them indifferent.

A room adjoining the attic of the dilapidated building they lived in was unoccupied. To take possession of it, they needed the small sum of ten thousand francs. Tristan felt unable to go begging to *his beloved grandmother*. Jacqueline was more energetic and decided to go and lay siege to the rue Dehodencq. She finally managed to get her hands on a small sum of money after a lot of ritual pretending. *Grandma chérie* insisted heavily on "the sacrifices she was making for them", and spread the word that "she had given her grandson a trade-in for a flat".

A child was born, a little Patrice, who was hardly wanted in this chaotic misery. The children and Jacqueline moved into this room, which had come just in time. It was a relief for her because she could now turn around. Tristan kept the other room for his piano and his work. First and foremost, he had to pass his final certificate, which would give him a degree in literature. He still had to pass the most difficult one, which required a stay in England. He had miraculously passed the essay, failed the oral, and now he had to pass the written exam again. He was shaken by this life without mercy. The boils persisted in tormenting his body, and he sometimes worked on his piano with a boil on each arm. His nerves were on edge. The exams, the lessons, the teaching, the worries, all this was the antithesis of his nature as an artist. He had to kill himself over so many minor problems, and *they*, who knew that he was going to go mad with suffering and leave his family without help. No, he had to hold on. Melodies sang in his head...

He worked his fingers, because that seemed the most important thing for his passion for the piano. But without a teacher or coach, his whole body stiffened, from his fingers to his shoulders. The self-inflicted articulation was a disaster. When *his beloved grandmother* gave him a thousand francs once or twice a year, she was quick to cut him off bitterly: "It's to buy you something to eat, not to take piano lessons"!

He suffered failure after failure in his last degree certificate. As he had predicted, he was unable to 'get back on track' with his written exams. The Sorbonne professor, an Englishman to boot, who had marked him told him: "You got an eight and a half, it's the English that didn't stick, you need to go to England".

Go to England? No doubt the advice was wise and Tristan had given it to himself many times. But lack of money made it impossible.

When he saw *Grandma*, he didn't say anything to her, but he made her understand that England... She pretended not to understand.

Uncle Etienne knew all about it. To help him, one day he told him this eternal truth:

"Adversity makes the man".

One evening on his way home, Tristan met Maurice, who had played a role in his past that Tristan didn't yet know. He had thrown him out of his house for his violence, his anger and his brutality. So he had no compelling reason to hold a grudge. So he spoke to him. It was then that the latter triumphantly delivered the atrocious news that he had been his wife's lover for a year and a half. Tristan didn't believe him for a moment and laughed at the pretentiousness of this brick-skinned midget with murderous hands and magnifying glasses. But then Maurice provided him with proof, proof that left him stunned, letters from his wife that left no doubt and in which she called her husband 'Jeroboam'. Despite the evidence, he could not believe it. She had cheated on him, and for a year and a half, a year and a half without him noticing. Infamous duplicity, absolute horror. The bird of paradise could have deceived him with this jackal, this hyena with bulging eyes. No, it wasn't possible. He couldn't *realise*. It was Jacqueline's fidelity and love for her children that bound him to his wife. He would have forgiven any weakness with a man other than that gelatinous, brick horror, especially if she had admitted it sincerely.

But this lie was gigantic and implied a nature that he refused to analyse so as not to fall into a bottomless void. The image of this dreadful man and this lie of infinite dimensions suddenly shattered everything. He couldn't imagine for a moment that a woman could deceive her husband in this way by playing the excellent wife. A year and a half!

He returned home, as if stunned. He was too sad to have even felt the need to put his fist in that vomiting face. They say you can do that. Hitting vomit? It makes a mess.

He told Jacqueline that he had met Maurice who had told him everything. He didn't even feel the impulse to reproach her, he felt beyond all human reactions. He had no idea, he was faced with nothingness, with the obliteration of everything that was elementary and justified living. Jacqueline cried, but what difference did it make? It changed nothing. True, he had had an affair with a beautiful girl at the Sorbonne, but it had never affected his deep feelings for his family. He had even foolishly confessed his affair to her. He had never known any girl other than his wife, who was four and a half years older than he was. A woman, cheating on her husband, and with *that!* how could anyone conceive for a moment that she loved her husband? All that remained in Tristan's heart was disgusted pity. Everything had been destroyed. He would have forgiven an admitted weakness, but such a lie, such a betrayal...

No. Jeroboam would go.

They each had their own room, separated by the courtyard of the building. He was keen to maintain a courteous, resigned and affectionate relationship with his children. He didn't want them to fall victim to the horrors of life's contingencies. They took stock. Even divorced, the children would always have a coherent, loving father and mother who would work in the best interests of their children. Tristan would only divorce if he could love another woman, but that seemed impossible at the time. The children would remain a powerful bond that would prevent the little ones from falling victim to the atrocious heartbreak that always accompanies the hateful rifts between parents. He would avoid this for his children at all costs.

Tristan wanted to spare his children everything, as they would grow up in an increasingly crazy world, where they would be pushed towards institutionalised criminality, with its exquisite variations of degeneration, drugs and suicide. This would be the culmination of an education without religion or morals, because nature never forgives.

Months and years passed. Tristan continued to teach and to fail his final certificate. By dint of his own meritorious efforts, he managed to save up enough money to spend two and a half months in England drinking milk. *Grandma* knew the hardship that made it impossible for him to stay in England and pass his final degree exam. But what did she care?

Those around him were beginning to realise that their ultimate success at the bachelor's degree depended on this essential stay. Tristan was dragging his feet. It seemed he would never succeed. This academic work at the Sorbonne, so far from Knowledge, was in itself a trial for Tristan. And this essential stay, this insurmountable obstacle.

Suddenly, *Grandma* announced to her family: "I'm sending Tristan to England". And to pay for his *trip from Dieppe to New Haven*...

He arrived in London with the thirty-five pounds he had painstakingly saved.

In the 1950s, still close to the end of the war, the restrictions were very similar to those of the occupation. If you wanted to stay at least for two months, you had to eat frugally just once a day. Breakfast was served in the morning and was included in the monthly pension. That should be enough for him. What's more, he wasn't allowed to go out, let alone spend anything. He would have to content himself with talking to anyone in Finsbury Park, which adjoined the modest boarding house where he lived.

He had not been in London for two days when an anthrax infection formed on his left knee. He was alone, in an unfamiliar room in London, with a stiff leg because the pain prevented him from bending it. He had given his pension money to the landlady and had kept only a small sum to get around by tube. At the very least, he needed cotton wool, gauze and rubbing alcohol, and he had no money to buy these basic items of hygiene. The pain and destitution were killing him. He didn't know which way to turn. He didn't want to worry Jacqueline, who couldn't do anything for him and who was already having to deal with the care of his two children. The two children were the only work a mother worthy of the name had to do if she didn't want to hand her children over to pathogenic music, drugs, laxity, delinquency, unemployment and suicide.

A sort of imbecilic and logical reflex seized him. The reflex of a sailor who has fallen overboard and is clutching at straws. In fact, self-preservation, nothing else really. He fell back into the infamous trap of the letter to *grandma*.

"I can't fight any more. I've done everything to get out of it, but I'm tired of existing. You'll never be able to say that I haven't tried everything to work miracles. I had one exam left to finish my higher education, without any help and with a wife and two children. I'm in a room in London with anthrax in my knee. I have no money. I'll end up alone in a hospital like Dad, and you'll have killed me. Do for my children what you didn't do for me.

In the stupidly melodramatic genre, it couldn't be better.

Ten days of anguish passed. He dabbed at his rash with a handkerchief dipped in hot water from his washbasin tap.

Without a word, ten pounds arrived from *Grandma*. She had made an effort, but it was the first and last time. Still, it was a last-ditch rescue. Tristan bought himself the necessary pharmaceutical basics and subscribed to half a litre of skimmed milk per day for six weeks. This is how he survived without starving: breakfast and milk were enough for him.

He'd thought they'd end up killing him, driving him mad.

Is this not how capitalism and Marxism kill millions of people? They kill without fear of justice, because justice becomes crime and crime becomes legal.

They are always on the side of a sumptuous legal morality, whereas what they are doing is criminal. All the officialdom he conducts is devoid of any moral sense. What is moral about the finance of Rotshchild, Hammer, Loeb et al? In the sale of arms by Bazile Zaharof and Bloch Dassault to everything that is being exterminated? What is legal about the murder of small businesses, crafts and agriculture by multinationals structured by the all-Jewish high finance sector? What is human about the Marxist extermination of tens and tens of millions of people who are reduced to elementary matricular statistical units?

What is moral about the atomic, hydrogen and neutron bombs of Messrs Oppenheimer, Field, and S.T. Cohen?

What's human about the institutionalised ugliness of Picasso and co?

What is human about institutionalised divorce, leaving children to suffer? What is human about Simone Veil's self-service abortion?

What is moral about Djérassi's pathogenic, carcinogenic and teratogenic pill? A few years later he saw a film in which the financier made the following statement:

"We manipulate morons who lead the masses that we have driven mad".

He would have loved a real family so much. He would have forgotten everything, forgiven everything for a gesture of tenderness and the joy of love.

In London, the practice of English was making little headway. He was rigorously paralysed by lack of money. When his knee had healed, he went for a walk in Finsbury Park. He was still limping, but it wasn't more than a couple of hundred yards from the boarding house.

He began to dream in English:

I love a girl. A true girl.

A girl whose eyes are full

Of inexpressible abandonment. Dreams...

I love a girl. Who thinks not

But feels does feel. I love a girl.

Whose long fingers clasp mine. And quiver, quiver.

Like a green-eyes baby cat Starving and cold.

I love a girl

Who speaks to me Without saying a word. I love a girl who melts As ice in the sun...

Translation :

I love a girl. A real girl.

A girl whose eyes are full. Of inexpressible abandon.

Of dreams. I love a girl

Who doesn't think.

But who smells, who really smells. I love a girl

Whose long fingers embrace mine. And tremble, tremble

Like a poor little green-eyed cat dying of hunger and cold.

I love a girl who talks to me.

Without saying a word to me. I love a girl who melts. Like snow in the sun...

On one of his walks, he met a charming English girl, the daughter of a concert pianist.

His kindness and caresses helped him to endure this stay, which was vital but not enough to perfect the syntax of the language in particular.

He spent part of his time in the flat of this young woman, with whom he spoke English all the time.

Tristan returned to France when his money ran out.

It was not until years later that he managed, with great difficulty, to pass his final degree certificate and a competitive examination that made him a full member of the French state education system.

Madame de Gastine and her husband had not seen their *beloved grandmother* since the outbreak of the Second World War. The father-in-law seemed disgusted with his in-laws, and Tristan had heard some devastating remarks from them that left no doubt as to how he felt about them.

Before their departure for French West Africa, the family clan had asked Madame de Gastine and her husband to sign powers of attorney. They both declared to anyone who would listen that they had thus alienated all their rights and that Madame de Gastine was thus, perfectly legally, deprived of her fortune. Tristan did not know the details of this cooking, the legal aspect of which escaped him, but the psychology of which seemed obvious to him. In any case, it seemed that the combinations of the family trio had disinherited her in the proper way: her mother had been stripped of her fortune.

Tristan's father had once incurred a debt of one million, a considerable sum for the time. The debt still existed and the trio had bought it back for a derisory sum. His mother had given a little signature on the matter, which finished him off!

It was precisely at this time that *Grandma* told Tristan, with the emphasis that was second nature to her: "In the interests of justice and fairness, I'm going to give your mother a large sum of money".

In reality, the aim of this arrangement, the intricacies of which Tristan was unaware, was to make his mother believe that she had received a certain sum which included the debt bought back at a low price.

The technical side of the operation escaped Tristan's notice, but the legal arrangements must have been pretty disgusting, as the man of the law who was carrying it out saw fit to apologise: "I'm not saying it's moral, but it's *perfectly legal* and I'm obliged to carry out my clients' orders"...

In the twentieth century, all legal crimes are possible. Criminals who sell weapons, chemicals or various forms of pollution will be awarded the Legion of Honour, while those who denounce major criminals will be considered mad or will be condemned under laws enacted by the major criminals themselves, supported by politicians of all political persuasions. We will even see a strangler of a six-year-old boy not only not guillotined, but released after a few years, while a "right-wing man" who threw a small bomb that caused no casualties will be sentenced to life imprisonment and never released.

The great passion of the twentieth century is not only servitude, but crime institutionalised *by* and *on* millions of bodies and souls.

"We don't owe you anything", Aunt Denise once told him. An admirable phrase of the twentieth century. The considerable cynicism of invoking the law, and the law alone, to justify themselves. The concern not to risk anything because the law is on their side. There are laws that prevent people from denouncing criminals, even if their crimes can be proven. Politicians and judges without conscience now apply immoral and criminal laws. Not even the time of the decadence and fall of the Roman Empire was like this.

Certainly, if Tristan had been the taxman, they would have had no reason to 'give'. It's enough for them not to owe according to the code, so they can take pride in the soothing certainty that they have some justification for their incredible mentality.

At the time, Laure was alone in Paris, without help, almost neurasthenic. She was soon to die of cancer. They owe her nothing. What is the civil code of the heart?

In recent years, Laure and Charlotte had lived with their mother and stepfather since their return from overseas. Charlotte had passed her baccalauréat but, too busy at home, had failed her first year of medicine. Laure, sensitive and intelligent, had got as far as the first year but stopped there. Something had broken inside her, her little lifeblood. Out of admiration and devotion, she literally 'lived' her mother, who played the role of a mental vampire on her, one that destabilised her. Poor little sister, nothing could pull her out of that cesspool except a radical external force.

Sometimes Tristan would talk to *Grandma* about his sisters and their difficulties.

"Why don't they come and see me, I could give them *moral* support", she said.

Charlotte and Laure had finally left their mother and stepfather and rented a garret in the rue de la Pompe. They had no money and no work. Charlotte had just returned from two years in Scotland, where she had taught French at a free school. Laure had just returned from Poland, where she had found a job with a repatriation organisation. Eighteen years old, Laure, alone, abroad, in a military environment, with her nature, her gentleness and her little broken mainspring. She had told Tristan about the horrors she had seen, heard, endured, the despicable behaviour of men... he knew because she had told him, crying on his shoulder...

How could their mother and father-in-law have let her go in such an atmosphere?

How could the trio have been so unconcerned about them?

What did they care about the denatured members of the family?

He explained everything to *Grandma*. Laure and Charlotte had no idea what he was up to.

- Do you know their address? asked *Grandma*.

No, he didn't know the number of the rue de la Pompe, but he knew how to get there. As for the number, a simple phone call would have been enough for him to know it, because he had forgotten it, knowing how to get there automatically from now on.

Then the crass bad faith and calculated malice suddenly manifested themselves with a force and vehemence that ensured the triumph of their dialectic over the masses.

Tristan was suffering too much to appreciate the buffoonish aspect of her performance, as well as the tragic mask she had chosen to place over her greenish face.

Tristan saw before him a sort of repulsive monster that you have the reflex to destroy if you want to get your breath back.

- How can they be in this situation and you don't know their address, and you're not near them - what a shame!

She went on to say something strategically incoherent and grotesque. And Tristan was the culprit!

It was highly likely that any stranger present, unaware of the context, would have admired such nobility and generosity in the good *grandmother*. This ostentatious vehemence must have convinced her that she was some kind of saint...

Then Tristan burst out. And he did so with a composure that the horror of the situation dictated was an absolute necessity.

He understood, however, that you had to be supremely gifted not to be struck mad in situations like these, which are multi-faceted in the modern world.

- If I could do anything for my sisters," he says, "I wouldn't be here. I would have gone straight to them. I only know two effective ways of helping them: give them money and get them a job. Their current situation is clear and I don't see what I'd be doing there, where I've been and where I come from. What's more, I have to work, I have cruel worries and it's not by going to show them the spectacle of my own misery that I'll alleviate theirs, quite the contrary. If I'm here it's precisely because you hold the levers that can get them out of trouble...

Greenish-yellow, *grandma darling*, raised a vigilant arm and kicked Tristan out.

Aunt Denise, who was present, had maintained a conciliatory silence, which at first surprised Tristan. It was the first time he'd seen her not take the side of *his beloved grandma*, who was always right, even in the most implausibly scabrous of messes.

But Tristan made no mistake. It was also part of the technique: to approve of his mother on this occasion would have been to spoil everything by overzealousness.

Today, the UN is blaming Israel, but that doesn't change anything because two hundred resolutions have gone unheeded.

It was therefore important not to open a dangerous crack in the formidable artificial apparatus we had built together to conceal their selfishness, while paradoxically, through a kind of diabolical complicity, a concession with no repercussions restored the apparent balance.

However, Tristan's visit was not a failure.

After this eventful intervention, the family council voted for a substantial grant of five thousand francs.

Laure and Charlotte were a little reluctant to accept this generous handout, as they no longer had any illusions about their nauseating family. They returned to *their beloved grandma*, whom they hadn't seen for years.

As was to be expected, they were greeted with theatrical, grandiloquent scenes.

- Why had they gone so long without coming to see their good, *dear grandmother* who loved them so much, who had done everything for them, who had been so devoted, who had pampered them, who had given them baths...

When they went to visit *their beloved grandma* as children, the two little sisters would pee in their pants.

After this turmoil, Tristan suffered another bout of furunculosis.

Laure, who had been at *grandma's,* came to see her brother. She, too, had wanted to act as Tristan's advocate in *Grandma's* presence. She talked about his problems, his health, his higher education, the piano...

— You have to help him," she said.

— Yes," says Uncle Jacques, "it's like the story of the little telegraph operator.

— What's the story of the little telegraph operator," asked Laure?

— It's the story of a painter who was poor, so by day he worked as a telegraph operator and by night he painted.

— So what? says Laure.

— Well, he died of it," said Uncle Jacques, delighted with his wit.

Shortly afterwards, Laura returned from the rue Dehodencq with a magnificent overcoat for Tristan.

Incredible! It was freezing cold and he had no overcoat. It was the first time he had ever received something timely, useful and expensive from his family. A brand new overcoat bearing the name of the best tailor in Cairo. Incredible! Tristan was stunned. Until now they had only given him clothes that were worn out or out of proportion. And now they were giving him a brand new overcoat worth a fortune!

It wasn't long before he had the key to this supreme generosity. A lawyer cousin, in charge of the family's interests in Egypt, had come to die of an attack of uraemia in *grandma's* mansion.

Tristan's mortal remains therefore received the delicate attention of his family, who returned to Egypt to be buried in the family vault.

Tristan should have thanked *his beloved grandmother* for having had the generous idea of giving him his dead nephew's overcoat.

He couldn't. There was a chasm between them and him. It was cold and he was ill. Out of cowardice, no doubt, he kept his overcoat on. He justified it to himself: he was fragile, if anything had happened to him, it would have played into their hands too much. He had already been in a coma as a result of a lung disease. He didn't want to catch a cold. But the gift was negative, and it hurt.

If they'd given him an ordinary overcoat like that, not a luxury one, he would have been really pleased...

Tristan was beginning to get fed up with this trio of nightmares, this spider's web, with *grandma dearest* at the centre, apathetic, solitary, venomous. If only he hadn't realised, but *Grandma Dearest* ruled the whole world...

He wasn't surprised that they were able to give him back to their father, unhappy and incapable, to crush him, to crush them. Ever since the day he and his sisters met his gaze, he'd sensed just how much *Grandma* wanted him to go down in history. A child's feeling doesn't deceive. She hated him, just as she hated his father, but even more. Because her father, the non-Jew, the being who surpassed them, he was there, there was nothing anyone could do about it, but he would pass, he would be passed. But Tristan the hybrid? Would they tolerate him? *Grandma's* hate had to be brought to bear on him, this reminder, this awareness. The essence of their health was ruined, even though they were treated magnificently with modern chemical techniques. Attempts were made to hinder his development, especially his genuine intellectual development.

As Tristan writes these lines, after forty years of secondary and higher education, he has realised that secular education has achieved global dumbing down, chronic zombism. A flowering of debilitated official graduates occupy all the political and administrative posts, incarcerated in Judeo-Cartesian criteria.

Ah, the fine work of Rothschild, Marx, Freud...

Everything seemed to show that he was being offered a normal education, that he was being followed. But in fact they were taking away every opportunity he had to study. They were creating a state of mind and conditions in which he was bound to fail. Once he had managed to set up a home, the abandonment turned it into a living hell. He, Laure and Charlotte could have taken refuge in the pure images and emotions of the past, the memories of their father, but this help had to be alienated. During the period of tender misery they endured at their father's house, would they perhaps, hungry and cold, turn against him? Perhaps he would become unworthy in their eyes? They failed.

Their father couldn't see Tristan when he was dying. And they couldn't see him when he was dying. How many letters were hidden from them. They were told abominations about their father. They had also arranged for their father to be persuaded that his children had disowned him, that they had joined the clan, that *they had become beloved grandmothers...*

An admirable stratagem and the last endeavour of their *beloved grandmother*, their father had died in the midst of strange faces without ever seeing them again...

Poor despicable beings, worthy of pity at the very bottom of things.

Doomed to the solitude of the clan, powerless wrecks, united in their solitude and unable to become conscious. *Grandma,* who at eighty has survived two serious intestinal operations, travels to Egypt every year. The severed wasps live for a while, the bees die straight away. Their father's mother, their sweet grandmother, had succumbed in a few days to the illness that *Grandma* had happily survived.

What power in Tristan had resisted this formidable enterprise of dehumanisation? He was panting because they were the only ones who could pull him out of the cesspool into which he had been thrown. In this absurd cesspool, the whole world was now lying, pampering its own suicide. The world had been progressively anaesthetised. Absolute fatality.

What force sometimes pushed him towards rue Dehodencq, just as the voter is pushed towards the ballot box, just as the worker is pushed towards the gulag party?

That day he was sitting next to *his beloved grandma,* and Uncle Jacques came in: "Don't forget you have an appointment with the solicitor".

A few minutes later they were all in the uncle's car, with Aunt Denise on the right and *Grandma* between them.

She went to see her solicitor between her two heirs. This moving picture is the only comic memory she has of the family. It's true that they had long ago taken away her sense of humour.

But Tristan didn't think all was hopeless. The wicked are sick people and Tristan would find a way to cure them.[23]

He was the only one who loved them and these unfortunate people didn't know it. The others despised them, shunned them or flattered them.

Tristan hated them with all the strength of his love...

He had to break out of the masochism that still drove him too often to rue Dehodencq. In this ocean of misery, what was the point of clinging to a red-hot lead buoy?

He decided to write to *his beloved grandma*.

- For years I've been waiting for you to reflect on my unfortunate fate, on my desperate struggles. For years I've been plagued by boils and abscesses. I know you don't care, because with half of what your master car costs you I would have stabilised my situation long ago, secured my children's future and studied piano.

For years I've been abandoned without anyone's help. I passed my baccalaureate, got three bachelor's degrees and did what I could to support my family. To this day, I'm a sort of skeleton covered in pustules, still struggling and hoping for a little effective help from my grandmother, who if not rich, at least lives in a certain luxury.

Because of the neglect you left me in, I've entered into a marriage that would never have happened if you hadn't left me adrift.

I can't take it any more. Please don't leave me. You can't be so heartless. If you don't answer me, I'll think you don't want to help me, and that will be the last time your grandson will kiss you, because I won't see you again and I'll never write to you again"...

Tristan never received a reply to his desperate letter.

Thanks to a friend, Tristan and Jacqueline had found a small two-room flat without repossession. It was on the fifth floor of a building in the fourteenth arrondissement. The two rooms opened onto a balcony. They each had their own room. It was a stroke of luck for the children. They continued to live as before, eating their meals together and deciding on

---

[23] On this subject, see the endocrinology chapter: "the key".

the ordinary, everyday matters of life, but Tristan was consumed by his wife's betrayal.

And what a betrayal!

The two children were pale. They found a good woman with a big house and a huge vegetable garden twenty kilometres from Paris who took them in. Their health improved. Tristan and Jacqueline went to see them together as often as possible. Paris, megalopolis and neurotic laboratory for children.

Tristan sometimes thought about that letter to his *beloved grandma*.

What did she care? She hadn't even tried to understand what he'd been through. Not for a moment had she thought: "How must that boy have suffered to write me that? Surely, if I were a normal grandmother, he wouldn't be writing me this, even if he was a thug.

No, she'd simply been stubborn, offended.

Tristan imagined *his beloved grandma* holding up the letter and shouting: "After all I've done for him, what a snake I've warmed in my bosom".

And yet Tristan imagined the letter that *Grandma* and Aunt Denise would have written back to him:

- My darling.

Of course we can't blame you, we know how painful your life has been and how nervous, sensitive and excessive you are. If we were hard on you it was to test you and also because our material situation is no longer excellent. You can now count on our help. You have almost succeeded in establishing yourself, and we will help you to stabilise it and to study the piano that is so dear to you. We'll succeed, and it will be a great joy for us. We send you our love...

Perhaps one day he will receive this letter and tears of joy will shine in the light...

Chapter XI

Months went by. Tristan was still clinging on to that last inaccessible licence certificate. He was growing weaker. Everything he did was marked by stiffness. He was aware that he was shrinking. He still dreamed of the piano.

He also dreamt of a love that would bring him a cascade of infinity...

One day, he was working in the Sainte Geneviève library and laughed.

Hadn't he just read in a critical work on Shakespeare: "That pessimism which gave him genius"...

The student sitting next to him awoke from her half-sleep to ask worriedly if he was all right.

— Look at this," replied Tristan. *And what if it was precisely his genius that gave him his pessimism?* Show me a hilarious genius!

It was in these circumstances that Lucienne and Tristan met. She was dark-haired, slender and beautiful, with long black hair flowing over her shoulders. She had a broad forehead, easy movements and a warm voice. She fell madly in love with Tristan.

He loved the way this twenty-three year old girl, who had just finished a degree in philosophy, drew in his whole being. The passion she felt for Tristan penetrated him with a kind of calm, an unknown fullness. It was a loving intuition, a pensive understanding.

— Culture," she once told him, "is *awareness*, not a mnemonic amalgam of knowledge. The antithesis of culture is piling up knowledge and getting nothing out of it but diplomas. With the culture of an agrégé, you can try to discover man by martyring tadpoles...

She had been suffering from tuberculosis and the doctors had advised her to undergo thoracoplasty, a seriously mutilating operation.

She refused and went to live with her family in the countryside. In six months of rest, with organic food and fresh air, she had completely recovered. Her doctors are still amazed!

Madame de Gastine had gone to see the children at the home of the good lady in Morsang sur Orge, where they were staying.

After her visit she wrote to Tristan saying that "it was a shame to put your children in the home of such a woman". Tristan replied that the children were very young and needed fresh air and good food, which was guaranteed by the lady's huge vegetable garden. And they looked very well. What was more, the bourgeois education that was bound to lead to leftism, women's liberation, drugs and youth suicide, what was it worth?

What's more, they were poor, and paying a pension to this childminder was already overwhelming. To send them to one of those religious schools, of which he had nightmarish memories, would have required considerable sums of money. So what was to be done?

Madame de Gastine, his mother, was definitely making fun of him once again. If she had offered something better in the way of help, and that in maternal terms, anything would have been welcome. But her expression and lack of efficiency made her intervention more than unbearable.

So he answered her in a harsh, rebellious but fair manner. He thanked her for her ineffective, negative and perfectly useless advice. She had seen it as nothing more than another opportunity to castigate her son, who would never have married or had children if she had been a mother worthy of the name.

The same old "raca" technique of accusing those who have been ruthlessly pushed into crime of crimes. This is now a universal societal norm.

In reply, he received a letter that was a model of its kind: a perfect projection of herself, a self-portrait with very little to add.

- Tristan.

I value actions more than speeches (sic).

I'll say again what I've already written to you: I think your children need a different atmosphere. I don't know Madame X, their nanny, but I know what a child is and what he needs. (sic). It's my opinion, I'm telling you, it's my right and it's my duty (sic).

I understood perfectly well what you expect from people, blissful admiration for what you call your genius (such words had never been expressed by anyone, least of all Tristan). This was the justification for all your actions, even the most cowardly and selfish (sic). Don't count on me for that (when had Tristan ever counted on his mother for anything, especially under the bombs she sent him to during the war?) I want you to be noble and I'm not going to help you fool yourself. Perhaps there's only one person in the world who can tell you the truth, and that's your mother, because she's answerable to God for you (for God's sake!). It's a tough ordeal to watch you sink into madness and evil like your father, but with fewer excuses. You tell me that you don't need my advice and concern (that's all he needed, but not absurd, negative criticism with good advice that's impossible to follow, accompanied by stupid, nasty reproaches). I understood this a long time ago, so I didn't burden you with it. You also tell me quite clearly that you're only interested in money (Tristan never said that to her. He simply said that good advice without the means to follow it was perverse). I have none to give you. And if I did, I certainly wouldn't give you any to satisfy your coquetries and your adventures, when your children have been looked after by others (by whom? surely not by her).

One day you'll be alone with yourself. When that day comes, you'll have to see yourself as you are, with all your glitz and glamour and all the time you've wasted worshipping yourself (that sounds like his autobiographical novel). Maybe then you'll want to become something else. I want to hope that you are better than what you insist on remaining, intoxicated by words, incapable of overcoming and dominating yourself, incapable of doing your duty, sowing discord and dissolving revolt everywhere, and you still want to play the sanctimonious role (that was his entire confession).

I wanted to be indulgent and give you over the last few years the signs of that tenderness that a mother gives to her child, however clear-sighted she may be. You don't know what real tenderness is, what real love is. You love only yourself (these are all terms Tristan would have used to describe his mother). The mother of your dreams would be a sycophantic servant who would foolishly help you to blind and deceive yourself. That's not what I am. But if one day you need all the precious things I have in my heart for you that you can't see now, if you want to clothe yourself in loyalty and humility, come, I'll help you with God's help, we'll suffer and overcome evil and death together. Until then, don't write to me, the letters will come back unopened. One day you will understand that this letter, which may seem cruel to you, was a great proof of love...

Tristan had read: it was the whole portrait, the whole pathology of his mother. No letter had ever described her better. She had projected her self-criticism onto Tristan. She knew nothing of her son's nature. There was in this letter, as in the modern world, *a corticality of truth that clothed an enormous lie towards the degradation of the other.*

Everything here was empty, self-righteous and mean. His whole mother was there, her sanctimonious, grotesque pathos towards a son she had abandoned in sickness and semi-misery, and to top it all off, that hysterical, histrionic mysticism that was so characteristic of her.

Tears filled Tristan's eyes.

Once, he remembered, in a pathetic act of supreme humility, she had implored him, quoting a letter Tristan had written to her when he was under the daily bombs:

"Tell me I'm not a Catholic monster"...

Tristan thought.

No, he wouldn't want to return to a humanity like that, even if fate were to grant him a life of perfect happiness. The sight of others, their suffering, their ugliness, their indifference to the suffering of other humans, all that was intolerable. Not to mention that despicable defecation that he would never accept.

We all have our own destinies.

The saint, the genius, the artist, the speculator circumcised on the 8th day, the petit bourgeois, the unfortunate petit bourgeois. All these roles were learned in the mother's womb and play the score of the world's tragedy.

There are no external factors that condition our misfortune, our happiness, our luck or our bad luck. They are linked to our environment and our astral and hormonal nature.

My constant distraction may throw me under a car, but it won't really have anything to do with it.

My bad luck has nothing to do with my Jewish family, except in the Rothschild-Marxist societal sense. Individually I should have distanced myself from them. If I had had their mentality they would have been different with me. But I feel as different from them as I do from the zombified, voting slaves they dominate.

They stifle me as a family member and as an artist, but they don't know it because true values escape them and that's what's killing the whole world. They stifle all truth and my heart is full of it.

I don't regret being different from them, I regret not being able to tear myself away from their existence, from the thought that they exist and could help me. You can't choose your own, but you remain attached to them and that's why I think they were the only ones who could help me, barring a pure miracle.

People who are capable of questioning everything on the basis of new information, evidence and arguments are extremely rare.

I don't think I've ever met one. Anyone involved in an ideology, from Catholicism to Marxism and everything in between, is stuck in it for the rest of his or her life. So there are hardly any intelligent people, in the deepest sense of the word.

As for my congeners, it's safe to say that Simone Weil wasn't wrong:

"They never have that modest attention proper to true intelligence". As for the others, the Goyim, "that vile seed of cattle" of the Zohar, they understand nothing. Hence the success of dialectical flattery, the idol of the social, which leads to all kinds of crimes and gulags.

They are the inversion. An imbecilic charity inherited from 20 centuries of distortion has led to a proliferation of psychic and motor cripples. They'll do anything to stop you dying of disease or road accidents, while the car is the greatest mass murderer ever known. In the meantime, Bazile Zaharoff and Bloch-Dassault are selling weapons to everything that is being exterminated in the world. Africa and Asia have seen their populations massacred and starve to death since decolonisation... Soviet gulags exterminate tens of millions of people, and healthy children are killed in their mothers' wombs.

Genius can no longer live in this world of quantity, because it is qualitative. As nature is never forgiving, the bombs of Messrs.

Oppenheimer, Field, S.T. Cohen, will solve the insoluble problem of this upside-down world...

It's my revolt and non-acceptance of everything that undermines me. I can't accept today's world, which was created by yesterday's world.

My story is hidden, strange and painful.

We are subject to laws. Misfortune is deserved by what we are and not deserved by what we have not chosen to be.

The truth is so far removed from formal logic. The logic of suicidal madmen. We are morons. Mine is a crushing battle between speculative perverts and robots. I can only give a weak image of what it is. Everything I feel, everything that at first seems contradictory or true on both sides. You must first become aware, inform yourself without prejudice, especially those who are dearest to you. Facts, facts, facts and flawless arguments. Otherwise you will rot in the lie.

No truth, no culture. "Know thyself" said the Ancient Greeks. I can't live in this humanity because it's inhuman.

The more I understand, the less I can do. I have to conclude that there's nothing for me to do, because there's no room left for the truth.

All the laws I've found won't bring life back to an inept, dying world.

To live in the most basic sense of the word, you need to be constantly in a gigantic abstraction from yourself that no one has any idea of.

So my repressed self lies on the edge of madness: the soul of a compressed artist has no other path but madness or suicide.

In spite of myself, I'm escaping this alternative.

I've fought unsuccessfully against this impossible abstraction of myself within the prevailing depersonalisation: just look at those millions of consumer voters dressed in the uniform of international bullshit: the Levis blue jeans. Within an emotional and intellectual magma, nothing can be channelled into the linear and vicious circle of formal reductionist logic. Forget the paralogy between Orwell's 1984 and Huxley's *Brave New World*.

I'm not here.

The paradox comes first. But there is no paradox. A paradox is an analytical contradiction that has failed to resolve itself into a superior synthesis. I am and I am not. Vision beyond formal vision. I feel more non-being than being. This is why I perceive as self-evident truths that no one knows any more, because beings are conditioned, subliminalised.

My thoughts, based on precise elements, make deductions of resounding and definitive truth. So there's nothing left for me to hope for but my hope, which is infinite.

It's lucidity and lack of composure in the face of absurdity that drives you mad. I feel everything that is wrong. Many people have a coherent outlook because they don't feel or understand anything. When you perceive a vast synthesis of reality, it's difficult to quickly put it in order. It is difficult to be logical when you are not crazy. The chaotic sphere that arises in the mind, an enormous raw portion of reality, takes years to discipline, organise and express.[24]

I first became aware of this in my twenties; until then I had wandered alone, abandoned, carrying a superhuman burden in my heart. I tried to take advantage of my lucidity, but it was very hard.

Today it's even worse, because having become aware on a level beyond the majority of beings, I feel incarcerated in a small concrete space. I'm absolutely convinced that nobody can help me, because my contemporaries are incapable of helping themselves on the path to global suicide that we're on. They need intelligence and courage, but they don't have any. They prefer the illusion of an immediate and tranquil life, even if it leads them to the worst in the short term. It is staggering to observe the mental inadequacy of the majority of human beings. To be aware of such a thing is demoralising and gives you a sense of grandeur that you could do without because it is a source of inextricability.

Sometimes I want to restrain myself towards the new "abnormal norm". The more I try, the more I suffer. The more I suffer, the more I think. A dilemma between madness and suicide. As a mirror of truth, I'm doomed to be shattered, because only painted mirrors reflect lies.

The relative victories of survival leave a taste of death in your mouth.

And there's more to come. The most sensitive people are those who feel the least in their immediate environment. They suffer for the universal, the innocent who die of hunger in Africa or Asia, the children who are raped or murdered.

---

[24] This whole book, which is extremely anti-conformist, is the expression of this effort.

Animals tortured by the hundreds of millions who never even see the light of day and can't move. Foolish wars that kill and leave so many invalids, blind, crippled and martyred... Everyday life with its tiny, insignificant problems...

They are happy, thanks to their mental shrinkage.

The only happiness of this time would be not to suffer. Not to feel. The only happiness of the year 2000: not suffering.

No, I cannot accept the world of the great plague, nor that of the fifty Jewish prison and concentration camp executioners who exterminated tens of millions of human beings in the USSR. Nor can I accept the Jewish bombs of Hiroshima and Nagasaki, Jewish physicists, or Dresden and Hamburg razed to the ground by the bombs.

"I am a force to be reckoned with", said Hernani.

I want the truth, even if it kills. I will go forward.

What's the point of this fight? Dodging around, spotting obstacles, in such solitude. We know months, years in advance, we see the manipulated masses rushing towards their suicide. There's nothing we can do, because nobody understands anything. Your hair stands on end and all you have is the sad joy of knowing and the bitterness of knowing.

Obstacles and torments do not appear to be organised.

They seem different, considerable, unconnected. They appear unexpectedly, and yet they are linked by a profound law.

In the midst of a suffering that imprisons me within myself, isolated from God, whose sense of humour I will never understand, and from mankind, I want the truth, whatever it may be.

I won't even ask *not to ask*.

Have we chosen to be what we are? We can't afford to be despicable...

Chapter XII

> *"The certainty of not being mad was the strongest. There was truth and there was a lie. If you clung to the truth even against the whole world, you were not mad" (George Orwell; "1984").*

Towards the end of his secondary education, Tristan had noticed a certain affinity with Jean-Jacques Rousseau, whom he would later repudiate outright. Rousseau resonated with him as a brother. Like Rousseau, he believed in the natural goodness of man and thought that society had perverted him. It didn't take him long to realise that *Judeo-Cartesianism* had exploited the most false, dubious and perverse aspects of Rousseau, which fundamentally structured modern decadence with all the pseudo-philosophers of the eighteenth century, whose enlightenment was to plunge us into the blinding darkness of the twentieth century.

However, Rousseau expressed an essential truth: when man follows the rules of simple living, the divine rules, he remains in perfect physical and mental health. This is demonstrated by the Hounzas, a small tribe in northern India. Controlled breathing, no carnivorous diet, fruit and vegetables as raw as possible, few cereals, and fourteen thousand souls living in the physical and moral beauty that is now forbidden to us. They know nothing of disease, and know how to meditate and pray until they die, between one hundred and one hundred and forty years of age. All modern work on the Hounzas attests to these essential realities, which show us how far we are from nature, and therefore from God.

The older Tristan got, the more he noticed his physical resemblance to the romantic artists that homeopaths call 'Apollonian' and 'phosphorus'. Slim, tall and slender, with an oval face, large, soft eyes, a very high forehead, often hollow cheeks, an aquiline nose and that special hand that chirologists call the 'psychic hand'.

Add to that his fragile lungs, his dandyish clothes and metaphysics, and his Luciferian air.

His photograph compared to that of the Romantics bore an incredible resemblance. He also had their pride, their sickly aesthetic sense, their imagination, their egocentric torment, their ideals, their generosity beyond measure. There were astonishing analogies in the biographies of these artists. Like Shelley, Byron and Coleridge, he had had to distance himself from his children. Like them, he was enthusiastic about the beautiful, the good, the just, the free, love, the ideal, purity and, in his frenzy, betrayed them all at once... Like them, he identified evil with illness. Like them, he possessed that subjective sensitivity that never gives up on any evidence, any sensation, and that feels every shock like a hammer blow to the heart.

Romantics who paint themselves always disguise themselves a little. Tristan had no desire to pose, unless of course he wanted to "pose not to pose".

He was in too much pain. He would be the first dandy to tell the whole truth, the unbearable truth, the truth that no one wants to know, the truth that is anti-psychological, anti-demagogic, anti-diplomatic - in short, the sulphuric acid of truth.

What does this truth cost him? Nothing. He judges the nonsense of which he is a part according to his innocence and his suffering.

Did man fall out of pride? Wanting to equal God? Inept!

If God had given Adam and Eve normal intelligence, how could they have wanted to "equal God" for a single second? Such an impulse stems from mental debility. To equal the absolute power that created man, the mammoth, digestion and squaring the circle?

Satan could only play on Eve's foolishness, which was known in advance by God, who lives in the eternal present and therefore knew about the Fall even before he created us. It's true that Satan's agents continue to play on the keyboard of universal cretinism: how can you take Rothschild, Marx, Freud, Oppenheimer and Picasso for geniuses?

Ergo, the first man and the first woman, God's masterpiece, could not seriously have thought that they were equal to God. If they were able to think that when they ate the fruit of the tree of knowledge, it was because they were already stupid, mad and therefore deprived of freedom.

Postulates of this quality could only give rise to an Ubuesque dogma culminating in the Marxist atrocity, universal proof par neuf of global cretinism.

By the way, a religion that is not logical and scientific is not a religion.

A science that is not religion necessarily becomes the antithesis of knowledge and becomes suicide.

The Bible?

Litany of hatred and death. The Jewish God is a champion organiser of horrific massacres who looks like *grandma dearest*.

The Old Testament is full of insane noise and fury.

Today, the Marx-merdia are massacring the forests so that their paper can complete the universal cretinisation, so that semi-idiots can be elected by a dumbed-down mass.

I suppose that if a tree in the forest protested, some little self-proclaimed philosopher who was circumcised on the 8th day would call him a "Nazi".

When all is said and done, and few people understand this, Nazism was nothing more than a heroic effort to rediscover traditional life with respect for nature and its laws, against the death inflicted by the Jesus-St Paul and Marx-Lenin inversions.

Christianity before the gulags was an executioner's metaphysics.

— "As for my enemies, those who did not want me to reign over them, bring them here and slaughter them in my presence. All those who came before me were thieves and robbers" - Lao-tzu a robber, a thief? How ridiculous!

This sentence sounds a lot like Lenin and Jesus: Luke 19-27 and John 10 8...[25]

From its very beginnings, Christianity, which so many people boast about, displayed the same hatred of thought that is to be found in Marxism: all

---

[25] When you ask the exegetes to explain this monstrous sentence, they are sure to tell you that it means the opposite of what is expressed: you have to admire the convoluted and contorted explanation that is impossible to relate. (Experiment carried out half a dozen times)

the treasures of ancient thought were destroyed. Here are a few examples of this incendiary proselytism:

- Millions of books burnt in the city of Serapeum.
- The same applies to the library of the kingdom of Pergamum.
- The entire Celsius library in Ephesus.
- The entire Alexandria library...

This vocation of thought against thought heralds all the pyres and all the gulags. Lenin and Stalin were only possible because Saint Paul was.

Christianity is the Bolshevism of antiquity.

Monseigneur Lefebvre and Gorbachev will hide behind the same fan when they hear what I have to say...

To be objective, we cannot overlook the parenthesis of the High Middle Ages, when lending at interest was prohibited. This is the legacy of Aristotle, timidly reformulated by Saint Thomas Aquinas. But apart from this exception, Catholicism has always been part of the bourgeois tradition of the capitalist establishment.

It is symbolic that in the 3rd century, Calixtus, a Christian slave who later became pope, ran a bank for Christian clients on behalf of his master, receiving deposits and placing them with the Jews at interest.

It is undeniable that for five thousand years, the symbiosis of "Jew and State" has always existed: today they are the State.

Anti-Jewishness[26] reigns in the most Jewish country of all: the USSR. This has enabled us to see Solzhenitsyn blossom, but it has not prevented Hammer, Warburg, Sasson, Loeb and others from financing the land of the gulags. If all the Marxist machinery had been totally occupied by Jews, as it was in 1936, we would have had no chance of getting to know Solzhenitsyn.

Today the noise of their advertising corrupts common sense, the madness of progress ("the lie of progress is Israel" Simone Weil), exhausts people, money reigns supreme, industry devastates the countryside and rivers, and pollutes everything. Atheism-levy-sion stultifies the brain, in particular

---

[26] This is the only appropriate term; the Jews are far from all Semites.

with regressive, pathogenic and criminogenic music, and foot-ball shows for the masses where hundreds or even thousands of people slaughter and trample each other at certain rock concerts.

The frenzy of international commercialism triumphs through circumcised globalism, from New York to Tokyo, from London to Paris, from Berlin to Cape Town.

The Gospel?

Everything about it is almost as absurd as Moses needing a God on a mountain for the Ten Commandments, which were copied exactly from the Hammurabi code.

Moral thought, strikingly enough, is much more coherently formulated in Plato and Ancient Egypt.

No: the Eucharist does not make a man. *The rules of breathing, of a non-carnivorous diet, of meditation and prayer make a man*, not this dogmatic sclerosis, this doctrinaire narrowing.

All psycho-dietary laws were abrogated with Christianity, in other words all means of access to virtue and the Transcendent.

All Catholic dogmas have developed over the course of history, and the Assumption dates only from Pius XII.

The dogma of the Eucharist did not appear until 1044. The affirmation of the real presence under the species of consecrated bread and wine appeared for the first time in a book published by a monk: Pashase Radhert.

How can a God of goodness condemn in advance the wicked whose potential misdeeds he knows in advance?[27]

How can Christ's death redeem those born before him and those born after him, who for 2,000 years have continued to be mad and wicked?

What logic: was it necessary to say to men "you are despicable, but to redeem you I am going to send you my son. You will then commit the

---

[27] The majority of serious criminals and murderers have frightening and chilling faces. It's impossible not to see the criminal determinism in these often horrific masks. What's more, film directors are very good at choosing actors to play the atrocious roles of murderers.

greatest of all crimes: you will torture and immolate the Son of God and then... you will be redeemed"...

And it has worked for 2000 years, just as the phantom gas chambers have worked for fifty years, with the implacability of dogma and the rigour of criminal law for non-believers: gayssotin replaces burning at the stake.[28]

Jesus was crucified by the Romans and not, legally, by the Jews. The Romans saw Jesus as a troublemaker and considered him a Zealot. The Jews, who were well aware of the ferocity of Roman repression, were afraid and, it is certain, put considerable pressure on Pilate and encouraged him. So they denounced Christ to the Romans in order to protect the people.

Pilate, as history tells us, did not play around and put down any rebellion with blood. Subsequently, it is clear that, as the Roman Empire served as an incubator for the new religion, it was impossible to hold the Romans responsible for Golgotha.

The Temple merchants? A single man with a rope whip attacking a crowd of vendors, moneychangers, overseers and officials would have been immediately apprehended. How could such a scuffle have escaped the Roman guards from the Antonia fortress, who oversaw the Temple courtyard and could find nothing to say about customs long established by custom and the rabbinate.

There are hundreds of thought-provoking passages in the Gospels about the absurdity of facts and reasoning.

Resurrection? If Christ had wanted to reveal his divine nature, he would have had to show himself to his enemies and judges. But none of them saw him. Only his companions and a woman saw him. His torture had countless witnesses, his resurrection only one, a woman in transport...

We must also remember that the term "son of God" was perfectly commonplace at that time.

The word "Baraba" means "son of God" in Aramaic.

---

[28] Allusion to the Gayssot law, which forbids anyone to say anything, especially anything truthful, against the Jews, under the false pretext of "racism". It prohibits the publication of historical research that displeases the Jews, especially if all the evidence and arguments concerning this research are provided. It is the absolute dictatorship of lies.

Paul of Tarsus, by freeing the Gentiles from the 613 precepts of Jewish law, which were precisely the same as the great tradition, opened up the Greco-Roman world to this Catholicism, which is a parody of a religion that was to culminate in the horrors of anathema, heresy, the Inquisition and Marxism.

The Inquisition works like Marxism. The only difference is that the former forced you to believe in absurd dogmas, whereas the latter inflicts faith in nothingness.

Paul was considered a false apostle in his day, and he is scorned in Revelation. Egyptian morality had reached a peak that Christianity would never reach.

We weren't talking about the ideas of charity, mercy, justice and fraternity: they were involved in the religious and mystical character of this civilisation. Pantheism was reduced to monotheism. The secondary gods and their symbols in no way diminished the unique and absolute character of God. They are simply *different aspects* of the divinity.

Egyptian morality does not know the different gods and addresses Neter, God, without naming him otherwise.

Catholicism inherited an exclusive and jealous God from biblical Jewry, which led directly to the notions of heresy and bloody anathemas.

Then we'll reach the pinnacle of horror: it*'s better to be a believer, even if you're a vile murderer, than a good man who doesn't believe in dogma.*

Dogma began its persecution by cloaking itself like a wolf in the mantle of Christian charity, which in the twentieth century led to the death sentence on genius and the pampering of the physically and mentally retarded as criminals of every description.

As for dogmatic controversies, they have only engendered hatred and never a single act of charity. Belief in original sin has given rise to an obsession with sin and the anguish of perdition: it has led to strange neuroses and sterile derelictions that can go as far as the vertigo of damnation.[29] Has

---

[29] Endocrinology sheds some interesting light on 'original' sin. We know that sexual abuse results in a deficiency of the internal genitalia (goodness, justice, human qualities, etc.) to the benefit of an exacerbation of the thyroid gland (pride). We can therefore affirm physiologically that if there was an original sin, it was sexual. Pride would only be the consequence of sexual abuse.

dogma brought peace to souls? Joy to the pure of heart? Confidence in God?

In the end, all this dogmatic bazaar led us to Rothschildo-Marxism, to redeem ourselves in billions of dollars, universal famines and gulags. The dogmatism of the Church, the great Satan, was to lead us to the immense Satan of Marxism.

What does the Church have to show for it? In a nutshell, nothing.

It will not prevent atomic bombs, neutron bombs or Marxism.

However, it deserves credit for its pastoral character. Here, the Church was sublime. It gave rise to admirable devotion, Monsieur Vincent and François d'Assises, Vézelay and one hundred and twenty Gothic cathedrals all over Europe.

The dogmatic Church has produced nothing but intolerable fanaticism. The image of God that Catholic theology imposes (an image in which we must recognise the influence of the Jews, whom the Egyptians called "the filthy ones") is a permanent insult to the noble idea that everyone has of the divinity.

If Christianity, truncated by the psycho-dietary laws that alone give union with the Transcendent and moral sense, has imposed itself on the West, it is not through its dogmas, but against them and in spite of them. It has proclaimed the equal dignity and fraternity of mankind, it has brought comfort to the poor and disadvantaged, it has tempered the pride of the strong and powerful, it has proclaimed the sublimity of sacrifice, it has founded charitable institutions, it has aroused in souls the need to surpass themselves, without which there can be no spiritual progress. Is all this original? No. These are the general commandments found in all the great religions, because they express the very conditions of social life.

The incoherence of the Gospels would merit an entire book.

- Sometimes Jesus abolishes the old rites in favour of the moral intention that alone counts.

- Sometimes it maintains the prescriptions of the law and institutes new rites.

- Sometimes he says that charity is enough to open the gates of heaven.

- ➤ Sometimes he rants that there is no salvation outside the law.
- ➤ Sometimes man is free to work out his own salvation.
- ➤ Both the elect (144,000) and the non-elect are chosen by God.
- ➤ At times it extols family life and the fruitfulness of marriage, which is proclaimed indissoluble.
- ➤ Sometimes he declares: "I have come to set a man against his father, a daughter against her mother, a daughter-in-law against her mother-in-law."
- ➤ At times he condemns violence and war and proclaims: "Blessed are the meek, for they shall inherit the earth; blessed are the merciful, for they shall obtain mercy; blessed are the pacifists, for they shall be called sons of God.
- ➤ Sometimes he declares: "Do not think that I have come to bring peace on earth, I have not come to bring peace but the sword, I have come to bring fire on earth and how I wish it were already kindled".
- ➤ Sometimes he teaches forgiveness of offences.
- ➤ Sometimes he railed against the towns north of Lake Tiberias.
- ➤ Sometimes he declares that one must submit to the established power, pay the tax even if it is iniquitous.
- ➤ At times he declares that the kingdoms are of Satan and speaks out against the social hierarchy, the scribes, the Pharisees and the chief priests.

We could go on and on describing this incoherence. What is most striking is that faith is the sine qua non of salvation. The worst crimes will be redeemed by a single act of faith in Jesus, articulo mortis.

Modernism has become accustomed to all forms of Jewish demagoguery, and this evangelical example beats all records in this respect.

Why on earth curse this fig tree, which could produce nothing at this time of year, when Jesus could multiply the loaves and fishes?

So no original religious ideas, just childish, incoherent ideas veiled in parables.[30]

Tristan wanted unshakeable truth, absolute sincerity.

He was going to explain the fatality of the dandy and how he takes his lessons from a great master: suffering. He also possesses a supreme gift: that of speaking the truth with complete, bewildered, unsympathetic frankness, whatever it may be and at the least opportune moment.

He can't do otherwise, because the truth is suffocating him and he has to let it out.

This physical and moral kinship with the Romantic poets and musicians led him to some now obvious notions. This long, aesthetic, imaginative and intuitive predominance, typical of a human being, prompted him to look for groups of different types.

He had observed in the army, particularly among paratroopers and shock troops, a very marked category that he also found among ring wrestlers, rugby players and Marxist dictators in particular.

This brutal, vulgar-voiced, bull-necked type was essentially materialistic. His values were physical strength,[31] the group, the family. What amazed Tristan was that they could copulate without the consent of their female partners, which made this group of people endemic rapists.[32]

The presence of these dictators in the modern world was easy to understand. Man can only be ruled by two authorities: intelligence, in a harmonious, hierarchical system, or reductionist brute force in a chaotic situation.

---

[30] There is much to be said about the clinical panorama of Christ, which in itself sums up the whole of psychopathology. This is covered in my other books, in particular: "Auschwitz: la fin de Iechou, Rothschild et Marx.

[31] Stalin, an adrenalist, as we shall see, and therefore a member of this group, said of the Vatican: "how many divisions".

[32] So rapists all have hyperactive adrenals; without this endocrine quality, rape is not possible.
The thyroid only becomes erect with a lucid and consenting partner. It is incapable of rape.

If the political regime eliminates all values of a spiritual, moral or aesthetic nature, that is to say authentically intellectual, then speculation and demagoguery will necessarily dissolve everything into anarchy.

To solve the problem of anarchy as it emerges, superior intelligences are all the more ineffective because no one can understand them any more, since the pyramidal reconstruction of the natural order requires a considerable amount of time. So, in order that force, and force alone, can immediately achieve an artificial, reductionist order, society will secrete this "adrenal" type, guided as it will be by a simplistic ideology commensurate with its objective, down-to-earth mindset. Pseudo-democracy therefore gives rise to all forms of left-wing dictatorship. Right-wing dictatorships can only emerge if the masses are left with a modicum of conscience. In this case, the dictators will be adrenal, but with a moral sense and a spirit of synthesis (Mussolini, Hitler).[33]

Secularism eradicates all intellectual and moral awareness at its roots. The resulting chaos will make dictatorships inevitable, of which globalism is the worst. Collapsed religions will be as much a driving force as Marxism.

It is therefore impossible today to conceive of a leader, a synthetic intellectual, because he will be misunderstood by the zombified masses and fought against.

It will necessarily be so if it is a complete spirit, taking into account the human entity within nature, taking into account all aspects of life, taking as collaborators superior spirits of different capacities, but all having a spirit converging towards synthesis and the universal, in other words the radical and absolute antithesis of the Jewish speculation prevailing today.

Any genuine leader who seeks to restore the fundamental tradition is therefore doomed to failure. Any dictator relying on simplistic, materialistic ideologies ("The plough makes the man"), which will bring nothing but misery and servitude to the masses whom they will exterminate by the millions, has no chance of imposing himself on a galloping degeneration.

Tristan had also observed a very clear pattern among his university colleagues, agrégés and hospital interns.

---

[33] It's worth noting in passing that Hitler, with his strong adrenals, was very thyroid.

Rather square faces and hands, athletic build, great physical stamina, astonishing ability to assimilate and memorise, no sense of observation, low sensitivity, a rational mind for the time being, comical in a way because they rely only on the incidental, in fact the psychology of often remarkable specialists. To this we had to add self-control, composure and a lack of emotional potential. The fact that one of them had a degree in history, philosophy or medicine was of no importance to Tristan. He was fascinated by the analogy of their reactions, their identity, their lack of personality, their radical inability to think by analogy and synthesis. When they had passed an official competitive examination, they seemed to Tristan to have come out of a mould.

He understood that the pseudo-democratic system of competitive examinations was the antithesis of genius. In the extreme, superior intelligence is uniqueness. The genius man is the one who is right against all conformisms and is in the line of the great invigorators of humanity.

Semmelweis was ridiculed by every university in the world, by his colleagues who were the last to understand the notion of identity that had led to his discovery. He was right against everyone, and without him there would be no asepsis, no obstetrics and no real surgery. So the university system recruited moulded beings.

To indulge in this distortion, they must therefore have had little personality and lacked the gifts that make genius. And even more so, the gifts that are indispensable for detecting and understanding genius. The university was therefore the primary agent of dehumanisation. It was to sink into a kind of soft Marxism. Dedicated to memory and analysis until the age of thirty-five or forty, to a veritable mnemonic-analytical intellectual masturbation, the agrégés and interns could never get out of the "Judeo-Cartesian" rut. As a result, they cannot penetrate the slightest synthetic concept. They get lost in the maze of nuances, and anything that goes beyond analytical conformism is "esoteric" to them![34]

Meditation is impossible for them. They think like slippers because they reason well in the minuscule. They have moved towards missiles, atomic bombs, computers and freezers, but their knowledge of man is progressing in the opposite direction. It could be said that generalised Cartesianism,

---

[34] It should be noted that all true knowledge is "esoteric", which means that it is only accessible to the minds of synthesis, of which officialdom is radically deprived.

which Tristan called Judeo-Cartesianism, was a total paralysis towards knowledge of man.[35]

Hospital doctors are subjected to a form of thinking that is totally incompatible with the normal purpose of medicine: to understand the whole human being, to prevent disease and keep him in good health.

They look for their unfortunate syndrome and multiply the analyses. They cannot, under any circumstances, make synthetic discoveries about the human entity. They apply their reasoning and their measuring devices to what is within their grasp. They add to the inexhaustible list of empirical procedures, solutions of despair, chemical drugs that give rise to illnesses more serious than those they claim to treat. They use surgery, which has made spectacular technical progress, but which would be used very little if preventive medicine existed. They can therefore only lead to medical technology and never to health. On the contrary, the more this kind of medicine progresses, the sicker humanity becomes.

Tristan saw the inevitability that governed these people, who didn't understand him. He knew why, they didn't. *

There was also another type of man we rarely met.

He was the only one to offer complete contact. They were as open to initiatory knowledge such as astrology[36] as they were to so-called Cartesian perspectives. They used reason and intuition in perfect mental symbiosis.

The forehead was broad, the eyes open, laughing and often optimistic, although rather deep and sad. His height was one metre seventy maximum. He was a gourmet with a cool head. They had a broad and general understanding. Their eyes, at least those he had met, were irritable.

So he became aware of four human archetypes: Chopin, a professor of medicine, Stalin and Alexis Carrel.

---

[35] Descartes would have repudiated this Cartesianism just as Pasteur repudiated Pasteurism on his deathbed:
"Claude Bernard was right: the microbe is nothing, the terrain is everything". Vaccination is a degenerative and pathogenic global scourge (cancer, cardiovascular and mental diseases).

[36] Astrology is radically closed to the "pituitaries" we have just described and which we will discuss in the chapter on "the key".

Most humans were composites, sometimes with a slight hormonal predominance that was immediately apparent.

Tristan noted just how flexible these people could be to political circumstances. At the whim of officialdom, they could be influenced or manoeuvred by a pharaoh, Thomas Aquinas, Rothschild or Karl Marx.

The average person only has access to reduced analytical thinking. They have no access to analogy, synthesis or the ability to generalise, like genius.

It was easy to understand how spectacular Jewish speculation could establish a barrier between the masses and the Transcendent. Thus all impostures were taken for good bread by the mystified masses.

Hence the world of merchants and slaves in which we survive.

There must therefore have been a physiological factor that determined the four human archetypes: intuitive predominance, materialistic predominance, narrow discursive predominance, synthetic predominance.

Tristan thought of the endocrine glands.

It was all the easier for him because he had learnt from experience that the artist was visibly devoted to the functional variations of his thyroid gland, these medical notions being common knowledge.

Tristan had understood something else of infinite importance: medical officialdom had not understood the functional anteriority of the hormonal system over the nervous system. They hadn't understood that the hormonal system dominated the nervous system and the human being in general.

The neuronal was obsessive.

One day he came across an article by an endocrinologist who, like his colleagues, was not a victim of analysomania. There he discovered the hormonal translation of his archetypal observation: *Chopin, thyroid, Stalin, adrenal, de Gaulle,*[37] *pituitary, Carrel, interstitial genital.*

The biological determinant was therefore hormonal.

---

[37] De Gaulle is the archetypal pituitary, and even taller, because the archetype is very tall, up to two metres tall like some Nile peasants.

Tristan was therefore a thyroid patient, i.e. a *physiological hyper-thyroid*. This is incomprehensible to the majority of pituitary patients. They cannot understand how two antinomic concepts can merge in perfect symbiosis to create a new concept: in this case, glandular types.

He had often wondered why artists and women with thyroidism had a slight convergent or divergent squint. It is easy to understand that a thyroid patient with a tendency to hyperactivity has a slight exophthalmos which alters the axis of vision.

Between the hyperthyroid and the thyroid, there was a difference between the pathological and the physiological. On the one hand, there was demented thyroid effervescence and, on the other, a nervous intuitive with great mental fragility.

"Dandyism is a degraded form of asceticism" said Albert Camus.

This was confirmed physiologically: when the thyroid glands of François d'Assises, La Fontaine and Liszt calmed down, they tended towards asceticism.

Tristan easily recognised that he belonged to this type. All the Romantic artists, such as Chopin, Musset, Lamartine, Goethe, Weber and Mendelssohn, also belonged to this type. At the origin of Romantic psychology there was therefore a congenital hyperthyroidism that determined this imaginative, intuitive, spiritualist, egocentric and aesthetic psychology.

The psychic hand!

The poet, the visionary, the musician, the mystic: all this was obvious to him.

The true intellectual must necessarily be sufficiently thyroid, otherwise he would be limited to the discursive, to immanence, and could never understand anything about François d'Assises or astrology.

A thyroid with a sufficiently high pituitary gland could do mathematics. The ordinary person, with hardly any glandular cachet, was necessarily absorbed by conformism, whatever it was, even if it professed the hymalayas of contemporary perversities and nonsense.

As for the predominance of the hormonal system over the nervous system, this was obvious: the nerve can activate a muscle and *even a gland.*

But it is our hormonal nature that will determine the quality of the actions induced by the nervous system. The thyroid is chained to its intuitive and aesthetic universe, the adrenal to its universe of objectivity and materialism, the pituitary to analysis, the internal genital to the harmonious human synthesis.

Sexual mutilation cannot fail to have very significant hormonal and psychological repercussions, which will have an impact on our physical appearance and mentality.

What a revolution in human knowledge!

Chapter XIII

"Les grandes amours vivent d'empêchement" Giraudoux

Tristan had the feeling that he was walking a superhuman path until he was exhausted. Life went on, heavy and overwhelming. Tristan was feverishly preparing for his final degree certificate, which he regularly failed by one iota.

At that time, he met a friend who had been a French teacher in Egypt and who was much older than him. He had come to France to formalise a degree that he had prepared in Egypt during the war and then to study for a doctorate in History. Pedagogical, cold, reasoning, sarcastic but open. Tristan owed him many long, soothing and enriching hours of conversation. Victor, that was his first name, was a sort of dilettante, who loved measured work, freedom and peace. His eloquence was quite beautiful, and he had a certain sense of authority. Their mutual availability was a rich source.

One evening Tristan went to see Victor in his room at the university residence. He was sad, discouraged and broke. Victor greeted him as usual, his gold-rimmed glasses slightly forward on his nose, his head lowered to see over them better, his right eyebrow higher than his left, his speech easy.

— You've got to pull yourself up by your bootstraps," he says, peremptorily.

There was a ball that evening at the Pavillon des Provinces de France, where Victor was staying. They had to go, so they went together.

Tristan couldn't see anything, all those insignificant girls... He was getting ready to leave because he was having trouble propelling himself through the peat. Just as he was about to take the first step towards the exit, Victor grabbed him:

— Turn around and look at that girl over there, she looks just like you.

Sceptical, Tristan turned round and was dazzled.

She was tall, slender and beautiful, the kind of racy beauty that Tristan appreciated so much.

She was a magnificent type of Slavic dancer.

She was dressed without any real elegance, but you could tell from her particularly well-defined form that she could be so without any difficulty. Her complexion was fair, her blond hair shimmering in the sunlight, her mouth sensual. But there was something about her that frightened Tristan. Her face was icy beautiful, her expression hard, her eyes slightly exophthalmic, betraying a tendency towards hyperthyroidism that was slightly pathological and not just typological.

He foresaw a whole future of pain. He felt attracted, but he was lying to himself. Everything about her stimulated Tristan's inner being, everything drove him towards her. Yet a cry screamed out to be torn away, but he didn't want to hear it.

Standing by a window, she didn't dance. A boy invited her, but she refused. Then Tristan offered and she accepted. She had a voice that pierced his soul, a sweet little voice, a child's voice. He didn't know how to dance, he'd never had time to learn, but he had the courage to do what he could. They danced for a while in the basement room, which was less crowded. They came out. They kissed. His tongue slipped over perfect ivory and bit hers. She kissed him back. Their passionate kisses fused in their mutual fever. Their hands wandered over each other's genitals. Tristan was madly in love. Their kisses, their embrace, gave him a fever of hot intoxication from which there was no cure.

They made their way to the underground station. There was a small café there. They sat there, lovers in disproportion. Tristan felt active. Until that day he had treated her with disdain, indifference, even cynicism. Worse still, like a child he had let himself be loved. He needed love, passion. She gently surrendered to his kisses, which flowed like pearls over her beauty.

Certainly the expression in her eyes was not that of Tristan's dreams. She was far from Botticelli's Venus. Her forehead was a little low, the thumb joint too pronounced, but she resembled his London poem and Tristan's imagination added what was missing.

He told her his poem in French:

I love a girl. A real one...

He didn't talk to her about himself or his past. He loved this beautiful girl. His madness suddenly reached a climax. He asked her an abrupt, demented question:

— Would you marry me on the spot?

— Yes," she replied.

They were decidedly as crazy as each other, this blonde and this fair-skinned blonde, tall, slim, with her long hair waving over her statue-like shoulders...

They had to separate that evening.

Biche, as Tristan was to call her, began to torture Tristan.

She didn't turn up for an appointment. He pressed her with questions, but she didn't answer. The more Tristan's inner self was in turmoil, the less she expressed herself. She confessed to him that she had gone to the house of a boy who had locked her in so that she wouldn't join him.

He was in pain, physical pain. A poem sprang to mind:

My love is a crystal goblet with a clear sound.

To which I drink long sips of heaven. My love is as pure as a dream of God. Before creation.

My love is sad.

Like Chopin's first nocturne. Played on an autumn evening.

My love is happy and desperate. Like a song of life and death...

Two of Tristan's friends, in whom he had confided, warned him. Both were psychiatrists.

— You're off to a bad start, you're projecting your love into eternity, you're acting like the Tristan of legend, living it like a passion: above all, don't marry her. I watched her at the ball where I was the same night you met her. She's the last girl you should fall in love with; it's written all over her face. You're not going to eat, you're not going to sleep, she's going to take you to a sanatorium or to Saint Anne's.

The colleague interrupted:

—   You say that to him, while I, at the age of forty, have just had my dick sucked out of me. Tristan, you're a poet, open like a book. You can make something out of your suffering if it doesn't kill you," he added with a sympathetic laugh.

In delicate health, Biche went to the country for the Easter holidays. From there she wrote him astonishingly empty letters. He joined her a few miles from Paris. He didn't talk to her about his past. He wanted to divorce her for her sake, since he had long been morally separated from his wife, for whom his subconscious could never forgive the horrible red-haired man with murderous hands...

Of course he would never abandon the children. He would tell Biche that. He was happy to hold her in his arms.

Back in Paris, he scribbled her a note, even though she had to return a few days later.

"My darling nocturne.

How much I hurt when I left you and how much I love hurting when I leave you. Yesterday was an enchantment. The more I feel how much I love you, the more I trust you.

Without her, he languished. Imagining losing her gave him a feeling of dizzying, suffocating descent. Sunday arrived and she had returned the day before. There was no news of Biche.

He wandered. He met Jean, one of his two psychiatrist friends.

- I can guess what's happening to you," he told her, "don't do anything stupid, especially don't marry her. Bastard," he insisted. Yesterday I saw her at the City ball, dancing with a zebra. She practically taunted me because she knows I'm your friend. She's a Messalina: that's really not what you need. You need a Clara Schumann. You're a poet, all poets should be locked up.

But there was only Biche in the world for Tristan. In the form of a fragile beauty, she was the symbol of the adorable powerlessness buried in creation.

He had chosen impossible love and he was going to pay.

He knew that she was studying dance in the evening at Janine Solane's school in the rue Notre Dame des Champs. He went to wait for her there.

She came to Tristan, wept softly, and confessed that she had fallen in love a few months before, and that she was getting dizzy.

Tristan listened to her sweet little voice, his heart melting as he watched her. He dreamt of the fullness of their love, of the unity their two souls would form. The two of them, among the extinct crowds, would achieve a more than human happiness. He loved her thoughts, her reticence, her lips, her weaknesses.

The thought of being unfaithful to her was abhorrent to him. He felt that if his love was a chimera, his world would explode into nothingness.

In the evenings he saw her. Sometimes she was sullen, without a tender word. Her face seemed sealed by a mask of wax. He waited in vain for the calming scent. Whether he left her for an hour or a day, he sent her letters and poems that soothed his heart and made her present again. His love seemed to spread, to dissolve, in a desert without oases. He worried about her strange moods, her brutality, but she didn't reply. She fell ill. The separation, the anguish, half-death.

My beloved Nocturne.

We will be an indissoluble blend of each other. I wait for your letters like grass waits for morning dew, I love you like grass waits for dew. I wish your love would make me forget all the bruises. You told me on the phone that you used to sing when you received my letters. I'd like to hear you sing. A little nocturne must sing so well.

When I think of kissing you, my heart comes to my lips.

Convalescence.

His parents were away and Tristan came to visit him. It was a short and ineffable joy. The night passed full of Biche's imprint. In the morning he had to hear the sound of her voice. On the telephone she spoke in a strangely cheerful way that hurt him. He begged for an explanation: she'd had a visitor, "a well-built chap"...

Distraught, Tristan hung up and threw himself on his paper.

My darling nocturne.

I still feel affected by this friend's visit. I know I may be stupid, but I can't help thinking that he's an old flirt and that hurts my feelings. I'm not jealous. I just feel sorry. Honey, fuck that kind of relationship. You're smart enough to come up with an excuse. Either these boys want to flirt with you or they love you and either way I'm miserable. I think I love you too much, that I've idealised you too much. I'm tired of my torment. I know that you really love me and that I only want you. Is the fact that I am unhappy because of you not proof that I love you too much? I can't wait to have you in my arms: my love grows every day.

I don't have the courage to work because I'm so worried about you. I'd like to be inside your pretty head to know how much you love me! Then perhaps I'd have an abundance of sweet peace. I thought I was incapable of love and suddenly you appeared to me and my heart is so tired of beating that I'm suffocating. Wouldn't it be better to be immune to this terrible disease? Didn't Shakespeare say that "the course of true love never runs smooth"?[38]

When I telephoned you you had that cheerful look that I hate, and I was sure that a boy had come to visit you. Write me a long letter that is as

---

[38] "The course of true love never did run smooth (Shakespeare)

much happiness as words. How could this boy's visit have made you so frightfully cheerful? Why do you have to call a woman a "*well-built fellow*" when I would call her beautiful, pretty, racy, or insignificant? My uncle's and aunt's maid used to say of a replacement doctor:

"He's a good-looking guy, not badly built. He was a big, square, vulgar oaf.

Write to me quickly, I'll always be worried about you, it's in your nature and in mine. Saturday evening:

Your cheerfulness yesterday kept me up all night. Do you love me? Do you miss me? Destroy this letter with the one you'll write me.

Biche's reply was a relief to Tristan's tortured heart:

My darling.

Your letter surprised and saddened me. If you mean what you write, it proves that you don't think much of me.

I'd have to be a terrible liar and actress to write to you all the time saying that I love you, that I miss you, and at the same time throwing myself into the arms of all the boys who come here. If it was jealousy, I'd understand, but if it wasn't jealousy, you'd know better. I really thought we'd got past the mistrust stage. You know, if I didn't have so much confidence in you, I'd have died of fright when I was ill. "Let love be love, that is to say, let it be peace" said Montherlant. My darling, our love must be strong, that is to say, never shaken by petty problems.

I've drawn a line because I think that's the end of the matter. I don't want to mix the good with the bad.

I hope you can imagine how happy I am that your visit was a little too short. It makes me even more impatient to see you in a few days' time. Of course I haven't told you how I feel, but you know how extraordinarily difficult it is for me to express myself.

Fortunately I have a fiancé who is intelligent enough to understand without me speaking. I read in Bernanos: "It is one of man's most incomprehensible disgraces that he should entrust what is most precious to something as unstable and plastic as the word. The most precious thing about ourselves is that which remains informal.

I'm writing you this sentence so that you realise that I'm not completely empty. The depth of my feelings for you makes me hesitate to find the words to express them... You can also understand why I talk so easily when it comes to nonsense.

I kiss you, I love you.

My darling Nocturne.

If you only knew how impatiently I waited for your letter: you're right, I love you and I trust you. This sentence is a beautiful conclusion: "May our love be peace". But you know what I'm like, I'm overwhelmed by a breath. But time will prove that I have nothing to worry about, even the shadow that caresses you. You see, you can't be worried because I express myself too much. If I were like you, you'd see that it's hard. I really like your line: "*The depth of my feeling for you makes me hesitate to find the words to express it*". You see, it's the words you're looking for and you've expressed yourself perfectly...

Biche still had to go to the country for her health. It was there that Tristan met her and took her in his arms. A small hotel lost in a hamlet. There they both stayed for a fortnight in the summer. He could have taken her, but he didn't. In his room or in the cool shade of the surrounding woods, he caressed her lovingly. Sometimes she just lay there, unresponsive. Anxiety swelled inside him, he couldn't feel her love, even though he loved her so much.

My love.

If I tremble at the thought of you. It's because I love you.

I'm often worried and jealous about everything and nothing.

It's because I love you.

If my heart beats when you're clumsy. If it bleeds when you are silent.

And that you prefer your childish rebellion to my love.

It's because I love you.

If I forget everything for you.

If I can give up everything for you. It's because I love you.

If the days without you are so long. If I want to save a minute.

On inexorable time

To see you and feel you close to me. It's because I love you.

If I need to see the pure water that flows from your source.

And not to believe it without seeing it. It's that I love you.

If I think of the blue sky, the lily, the crystal When I think of you.

It's that I love you...

Biche's parents took their daughter on a two-month holiday to Brittany for her health.

Two months without Biche. He weakened, he tore himself apart. He had to stay in a nursing home for two months. An external abscess developed on his throat. It radiated towards his chest. He had written to Biche. A fortnight had passed. Nothing from her. Tristan was taken to hospital. He couldn't sleep and was writhing on his bed. Antibiotics, shock treatment, propidon... Nothing.

No news from Biche.

He could feel suffering everywhere around him. An elderly woman, her legs cut off, was dying of diabetic gangrene...

Grandma, my darling, gushed with abandon and despair.

He had written a horrible poem which he had torn up and which began as follows:

Urine-skinned scum, viperous face, female Pantin with a big, funny nose...

No, he couldn't quote this poem of deserved hatred, which ended as follows:

...Grandma, I'm dying.

Seventeen days had passed, and finally a letter from Biche.

"My darling.

I was really desperate when I left you the other night.

Life really is unbelievably hard. My darling, this has to be the last time we're separated for so long.

The trip to Brittany went off without a hitch, except for the strong fumes of sausage, cheese and anything else you can imagine. I don't know if it's due to my mood but everything disgusts me at the moment. Everything's going wrong. It's raining non-stop and I've got a serious foot infection thanks to the wonderful shoes I've got, which are filled with nails. I had a fever last night and Mum wants me to go to the doctor to stop the infection.

I'm fed up, but that doesn't stop me loving you. Write to me and let me know if you're staying in that nursing home. I've had about ten arguments with my father.

I kiss you everywhere."

This letter was a crushing blow to the dove of a love whose wing unfolded towards her in a total rush.

But wasn't Tristan asking from humans what they couldn't give him?

From the rest home, "*Le moulin à vent"*, where he had been since his release from hospital, he replied to Biche:

"My darling nocturne.

You're not there. I feel you far away, so far away that I want to die. My heart is full of storms and sobs. If you only knew how much I love you. Your image is present to me, desperate. Your absence makes me empty and chaotic. Your presence fills me and enthralls me. You can make or break me, because I'm yours body and soul, but I don't want to be the plaything of a capricious fairy. I'm scared and I love you. We're going to leave for the sun and for life.

Midnight: I feel lost without you. I love you so much my heart will burst.

Tristan's letters followed one another like crashing waves. Letters and poems of absolute love. Sublime illusion. He waited in vain, all puffed up with trembling hope, for a little of that self-sacrifice which in its fervour is the sign of true love.

O the astonishing emptiness of her letters!

"My parents keep an eye on me and ask me who I'm writing to. I can't write. I don't have time, I go swimming, play tennis and go for walks.

It was in the midst of these obscure meanders that Madame de Gastine and Laure came to visit Tristan at the *Moulin à Vent*.

He had told his mother nothing, and yet he knew the infallible value of her judgement, especially when she had had no personal contact with the people she gauged solely by her admirable observation. He would have liked his mother's lucidity to be in opposition to his own.

He showed her a recent photograph of Biche. Madame de Gastine hastily put her hand to her cheek:

—   My God," she said, "I wouldn't like to live with a woman like that. She's very sensitive but she has no pity. She's closed, definitely closed. She'll never evolve. She's a wall. She can't adapt. It's a wall that will drive you to suicide, madness or tuberculosis (Tristan remembered the warning from his psychiatrist friends). She's sensitive to atmosphere, complicated as can be, unsatisfied. She'll only marry you on a whim and out of pride. You're not at all the kind of man she needs. She needs a quiet middle-class man. If the difficulties are too great, she will have no feeling for you. She won't put up with worries or contradictions. She lets herself be loved. She will no doubt offer you physical satisfaction but will be unfaithful to you the day she has had enough, the day you no longer suffer because of her. She has no moral or metaphysical concerns, and the day you are separated you will hear no more about her. Physically, I don't know what sort of background she comes from, but she's got breed.

—   "My poor little boy," added Madame de Gastine, handing the photo back to her son.

Not only did Tristan know how true all this was, but it all came true in the future.

Soon her mother would become Biche's great friend and torture Tristan. She had forgotten all about his extraordinary judgement. It was true that his mother had never failed to make allies against her son.

His assessment of Biche must have taken on the opposite colour, and that was fatal, Tristan knew.

This stay had weakened him still further. Alone and tortured by his thoughts, without a soul to confide in.

All these trials had dissolved him.

How can we heal this tumultuous mystical impulse, this emotional tidal wave concentrated on one person, when such love directed towards God would have brought him serene peace?

Biche had returned from holiday even more beautiful. Golden blonde hair, full of sun and sea. Tristan had taken temporary accommodation, a room in the house of a hysterical old maid, full of cats and jealous of Biche's visits. This did nothing to improve the conditions for his climb out of the abyss into which he had been plunged.

The children were always in the country. Their mother was working in the business she was good at. Tristan had left her in great distress, but she was the cause. Their divorce proceedings had begun.

Years later Tristan understood. How could such situations be possible? Divorce can only happen if everything that precedes it is flawed. Neither the State, nor the Church, nor the parents, nor the non-existent spiritual and moral education, work in symbiosis to ensure that solid couples are formed and remain together in love, in the best interests of the children, who should, after the union of the couple, be the only ideal, the reality to be brought to life. The so-called freedom of the couple, like sexual freedom, is nothing but a gigantic deception that culminates in chaos and crime. If the couple were consolidated biologically, mentally and spiritually, we would not today, in the name of a sham freedom, have millions of listeners of pathogenic and criminogenic music, delinquents in droves, degenerates of all kinds, biologically and psychologically deficient, murderers of the elderly, paedophiles who murder children. All this criminal magma comes from phantom couples, divorced or whose mother works outside the home. Elementary statistics are formal, but common sense is enough to understand this without any statistics at all.

Biche was happy to be loved. Tristan was getting nothing. Biche's lack of love was overwhelming. She gave him her body, he begged for his soul. All his strength gushed into the void and dispersed.

This game challenged his whole being. Dislocated by a lifetime of superhuman effort, it was a final test.

He loved her too much, with that insatiable force of passion that loves so little that it can go so far as to destroy its object.

That evening Biche joined him at the home of the hysterical old landlady, unbalanced by a prolonged virginity for which she had no vocation. And even more so, by the lack of someone to love, as the profusion of cats proved.

Biche was harsh and brutal. The more gentle, delicate, understanding and transparent he was, the more opaque she was.

Poor love! Given what she was, Tristan was asking too much of her. For his birthday, Biche gave him a present.

She tried to be tender, but she couldn't. Tristan wasn't helping. Tristan wasn't helping: his passion for her could only suffocate Biche.

She offered herself to him.

A dizzying sensual hell, a mixture of heaven and hell that no human word can translate. Then Tristan had the incredible feeling of being a delicate whore who had slept with the caveman...

He was no longer in control of himself, no longer in control of anything. He tensed up to automatically carry out reasonable acts. The repression of the artist's self hindered his development to the point of suicide.

And this love gave him no peace. He was trying to continue his university work towards a tenure examination. He was teaching...

Every year he saw his pupils slide vertically towards the pathological, eventually reaching the hideous. In the near future, he could imagine them beating or killing teachers and classmates, murdering for a few francs. Secularism, with its religious and moral deficiencies, was making them lose a little more of their soul every year. Even their basic intellectual capacities were declining rapidly.

They were clearly becoming pure physico-chemical amalgams governed by the democratic profit and loss account and ripe for a third world butchery.

Poor kids, dumbfounded, totally atonic, plastic to all forms of fashion and collective hysteria, all forms of vulgarity. He could see them in the near future, dressed in some kind of international bullshit uniform[39] chosen 'freely', girls and boys identically dressed up by an imbecilic fashion, given over to drugs and pornography, to vile, pathogenic and criminogenic music that kills the soul and the nervous system. He saw them becoming

---

[39] This was written thirty years before the advent of **Lévis blue jeans**. Everything it says has now come true, and the horror is not even fully described.

sicker and sicker, with cancer and leukaemia. Soon viral diseases would kill millions of people unworthy of living.

In the end, exams would be abolished and no one would be able to sit them. He saw them moving towards all forms of delinquency and criminality, the most serious of which would not only be encouraged but made official. Chemical food and vitamin E deficiency would produce a profusion of impotent men, frigid women, homosexuals and paedophiles...

They would be made to vote for the clowns who run us, manipulated by the high finance of my fellow creatures...

Biche gave him no peace. He sometimes cried at night until he was exhausted. He just didn't know any more. Yet he realised the pathological nature of such outrageous love, but he could do nothing against himself, nothing against his passion.

He was guided by the thought of his two children. He loved his children, despite the storm of this mad passion. At the height of his anguish, he turned to the despairing image of his mother. It was wrong, it was wrong, he knew it. He wrote to her and she came.

Had she come to help him or like a hyena feasting on the remains of a corpse?

He lay at the bottom of the abyss, knowing that Madame de Gastine would do him nothing but harm. Yet he thirsted for her illusion, for her balm. Her balm? A tampon soaked in sulphuric acid on a gaping wound.

He handed her another photograph of Biche. He asked her to tell him more about her, to exhume a few features, a single feature that would give him hope. She told him the same things. Both were no doubt part of a typological analogy, but they were essentially different.

Tristan had invited his mother to come and soothe him. She asked about the children:

— Are you sure Patrice is yours? Besides, you're responsible for him," she added fiendishly.

A sledgehammer blow. He had told Biche about it, without comment, in all its simple horror.

— Of course," she said, "that's the first thing I would have thought of. Tristan had told her all about his past without hiding anything from her.

Tristan was alone. He went to see his little ones with their mother. It was agreed to tell them that they were both working and to visit them together as often as possible. The cruel joy of kissing them. Their thoughts were an anchor for Tristan in this ocean of fury.

Tristan met Biche's parents. Charming, restrained people, devoted to their enigmatic daughter. They exuded a reassuring calm.

Tristan moved into a room not far from Biche's parents' flat. Biche joined him in the evening.

Anything that reminded Biche that Tristan had been married and had children sent her into a state of fatal malice. She wanted Tristan all to himself, past, present and future. This attitude drove Tristan towards his children and made him acutely remorseful.

For Tristan's soul, the greatest horror was the spectacle of wickedness towards the defenceless. He preferred death to such a sight. Biche would have been happy for Tristan to abandon his children. He felt it with certainty and disgust.

His health continued to decline and his passion to tear him apart.

If my love wanted us to be happy.

There wouldn't be, darling, in you. Two beings so different.

There would only be my Biche. My darling doe

Cuddling up to my big-eyed heart.

With her sweet little rose mouth. To the sweet, sweet voice.

May it echo in my soul like a Chopin phrase. There would be you, my darling.

Hugging you to my heart. To receive caresses and kisses. Protection and love.

My darling Doe who listens to me. And loves me, but nothing more.

With confidence and devotion.

For ever who lets himself be loved. For ever and ever.

No questions asked, that's it. If my love wanted

May we be happy...

A letter from the rue Dehodencq.

He had received no news from the family since the fatal letter he had written to his *beloved Grandma* in England.

Tristan was determined to separate himself, at least in practical terms, because the mind cannot so easily cut itself off from others.

It was Aunt Denise who wanted to see him. So he went.

Her aunt took her to the Bois de Boulogne in *grandma's* Salmson, to take the poodles for a walk.

The car glided towards the edge of the wood. The aunt struck up a conversation.

—   Why did you need to write this letter to Grandma? What was the point?

—   It took me ten years, ten years of waiting, gasping and bruised, hoping for a little help before I wrote it.

—   You're selfish, you don't think about the damage you've done to Grandma and then you kill her.

There was silence for a few seconds, then she continued:

—   You're a bit crazy, my boy, and then you're stupid, I would have imposed you at home, I would have imposed you.

Another silence followed. Tristan reflected. It was true that he was a bit crazy.

This spontaneity, this sincerity, this mania for truth in all areas, this lyricism, all this was not normal. He was the opposite of them. They only acted out of permanent, Machiavellian calculation, always measuring the foolishness and weakness of others, their vanity. Tristan felt he was the antithesis of them.

The aunt added:

- Your letter shows your instincts to make demands.

Yes," thought Tristan, "like the children who worked in the mines at the beginning of Rothschild's Manchester machines: they didn't make demands, they died.

He replied to his aunt as a poodle and a perforated tube ticket danced in his mind:

- Do you know what it means, when you don't know what to do for your family, to give fifteen hundred francs to shear a poodle?

—   Yes, I understand, I understand.

—   You missed out on a few years of hard work.

—   We experienced this during the war.

—   Yes, in the Free Zone, under the protection of Pétain, like so many other Jews, and with Uncle Paul who never let you lack for anything.

The car stopped in front of *grandma's* mansion.

- What can I do for you? Says the aunt.

Tristan felt a real sense of goodwill because his aunt was stingy. But she had brought up her nephew and was much more concerned about him than his own mother. She was also much better than his mother, that definitive old camel.

Tristan felt affection and gratitude for his aunt. She had written to him to talk to him, to help him, although she was under no *legal obligation* to do so, as they said in the family.

It was a clear sign of an effort that was all the more affectionate given that not long ago she had proclaimed: "We owe you nothing".

They went in. The aunt bandaged Tristan's left arm, which had doubled in size due to a boil. He owed his aunt an astonishing balance considering what he had been through since early childhood and the abandonment that had followed. His aunt gave him one thousand five hundred francs and told him to stop working for a month. She would pay the children's board for that month: fifteen thousand francs.

That evening Tristan phoned to thank her.

— Did you buy what you needed? said her aunt.

— Yes, medicine, fruit, I've got nothing left.

— Don't spend it all, don't go overboard," she concludes.

The aunt sent Jacqueline a crossed cheque that no one could touch. Jacqueline went to rue Dehodencq to exchange the cheque for banknotes. She had the audacity to count them, but one was missing. The aunt added one more and whispered to Jacqueline:

— I've made a big effort to help Tristan, and I've had to draw on my capital.

At his aunt's instigation, he had gone to see his uncle, a senior physician at the Laennec Hospital. The latter invited him to lunch.

Tristan wanted to talk and wasn't Uncle Etienne the least inhuman of the family?

— Why did Grandma abandon us? asked Tristan.

— I know how difficult his situation is," replied his uncle.

— So why doesn't she explain it to us?

— I wouldn't allow my children to call me to account, and you didn't have to write that letter, *there are some things you just don't write*.

— I understand what separates Mum from Grandma, but we grandchildren are not responsible. It's true that I wrote this letter to Grandma, Laure has never written anything like it, and yet she's completely abandoned.

— We never see Laure, she never comes to see us.

— Do you think she has the time and inclination to come and see you in the destitution in which she lies and where you leave her?

— I can only tell you one thing," said the uncle at last, "They ate the green grapes and they will suffer for it until the Nth generation.

His uncle's nurses gave Tristan all sorts of vaccines, bacteriophages and antibiotics without achieving the slightest result in curing his atrocious furunculosis. There was no improvement.

Tristan now knew that peace of heart and soul, a healthy, moderate diet with as little meat and cooked starches as possible, plenty of vegetables and fruit, and few eggs and cheese, would have cured him completely. For centuries, people had been eating too much, in anguish, and above all anything they wanted. Since the last world war, this anarchy had worsened and people were eating everything they needed to converge on massive degeneration, with a profusion of cancers, cardiovascular and mental diseases to boot. Systematic vaccination, inflicting putrid products on the body, played a large part in the biological and mental collapse of the human race.

Despite his failing health, his engagement to Biche took place in the flat of his future sister-in-law. That day, in the Rue du Ranelagh, Tristan's nerves were on edge. A crowd of insipid bourgeois with vegetative conversations.

A kilometre from Vézelay and its Romanesque jewel, they got married.

They moved into a room opposite Biche's parents' flat.

They ate their meals as a family, which avoided many material difficulties.

Biche's brutality worsened.

He couldn't swallow anything. Every move Biche made made made his heart race. She'd leave, slamming the door, and just stand there, her face frozen, speechless. She turned the children's red-hot iron on Tristan's heart. There was an extreme fatality there. It seemed that Tristan's nature had a way of bringing out the worst in her.

There was a perpetual conflict between the peaceful, even happy, attitude he owed to his children and his foolish love, which mutilated him and made him take on Biche's own suffering.

Whichever way he looked, Tristan's heart was crushed. A kind of inordinate pride, an anguish against the human condition, grew within him.

All it took was a speck of dust to drive him mad.

A persistent fever broke out. A word from Biche was enough to increase it. His will was dead. His brain lay in effervescent chaos. He stagnated, stirring painful thoughts, dazed, almost cataleptic.

Impotent, he lay in bed. His parents-in-law phoned Uncle Etienne. Eight days passed. He arrived. He examined him, found nothing, and left a cough syrup, a common medicine.

The fever persisted.

Three weeks passed. We phoned and he didn't come. It was during the hours of extreme prostration that Biche's cruelty was amplified.

In desperation, the in-laws suggested that "maybe the nothings? No, said the uncle, there was nothing there. Uncle Jacques went to get Tristan to X-ray him: he found nothing.

Tristan left with Biche, who had accompanied him on the underground.

As he descended the hall stairs, he caught a glimpse of the white-haired, parchment-covered ghost of his *beloved grandma*.

Despite free and family prognoses, tests were carried out and found red blood cells, purulent traces and e-coli.

The in-laws informed the family of this result. Days passed without any sign of life from Uncle Etienne.

In a burst of vitality that remains in the midst of prostration, Tristan wrote a short note, the words of which he could not control in the state he was in.

He remembers that he had been whining, pathological:

"Uncle Etienne is not coming, my in-laws are revolted by your carelessness. If you want me to have any chance of getting better, don't show this letter to Uncle Etienne, because you don't know pity or love, even though you are so sensitive that a speck of dust hurts. As long as I can, I'll look after my children, and if I disappear, do for them what you didn't do for me. That will be my consolation...

Two days passed. The telephone rang. "At last", whispered the father-in-law.

No, it wasn't Tristan's health that was worrying them: Aunt Denise had shown them the letter.

He never saw them again.

Grandma died a few years later at the age of eighty-six. Tristan didn't go to the funeral. He hadn't been able to.

He had imagined her being taken to her grave, as if to the notary's, between two policemen, Uncle Jacques and Aunt Denise, for whom he was nevertheless grateful and affectionate...

Chapter XIV

> *"When we are all guilty, democracy will be achieved"* (Albert Camus)
>
> *The history of Israel is invaluable as a typical story of the distortion of natural values. The Jews have a vital interest in making humanity sick, and in overturning in a dangerous, slanderous sense, the notion of good and evil, of true and false (Nietzsche). The Jews, this handful of uprooted people, have caused the uprooting of the entire (Simone Weil).*
>
> *Who would have thought that a rite could go so far and risk destroying everything on the borders of nations. (Dominique Aubier on his book about circumcision on the 8th day).*
>
> *For 5,000 years we have been talking too much, words of death for ourselves and for others (George Steiner).*
>
> *We manipulate morons who run the masses that we have driven mad (the financier in an American film).*

They always act against someone or something. Never for anyone or anything.

Hence their unhealthy perfection. They pull, they don't give.

They uproot and mutilate nature and mankind. It's their curse.

They do not believe in themselves. So they put all their energy into the outward demonstration of a non-existent essence.

Absorbed in this negative struggle, they have nothing left to love.

The preoccupation with demonstration replaces giving, love, creation and prayer. Unable to "realise", they destroy, degrade and caricature.

So they are the opposite of human. They cut themselves off from humanity and unleash a bloody hatred against themselves: the anti-Jewishness that they have carried with them and spread everywhere for 5,000 years.

Genius and spectacular facsimiles without souls. With an outward appearance truer than the real thing, hence the universal mystification.

Doubt, uncertainty and destruction do not create love: they are poor.

Devilish weapons that allow them to achieve this satanic success outside the human, against the human, by giving the human the illusion of "for the human".

They try to penetrate the essence of things with an aggressive will, an analytical mind, not a loving one.

This is why Jewish analysis presents for all eternity a face of vertiginous despair. Illusory creations, real destruction because they violate a balance.

We feel immense pity for these beings who are eternally compelled to remain alienated from all essence, and if they wish to force it, to achieve only diabolical perfection, dazzling but...

The pastoral Church has had the immense merit of charity and monastic culture, of the splendour of Vézelay and Chartres, of the sanctity of Monsieur Vincent and François d'Assises.

But the dogmatic Church has turned history into a doctrinaire sclerosis where the fearsome notions of heresy and anathema, which ancient Paganism had ignored, have caused seas of bloodshed and tears to flow.

Dogma, a challenge to elementary intelligence and moral sense, a confection of the abstruse and contradictory, inherited from the Synagogue an exclusive, tyrannical and jealous God, the theologians' God of justice, the law of retaliation and the practice of scapegoating.

It was inevitable that this religion of doctrinaires and theophagi, which for 20 centuries has ignored the psycho-dietary rules that make man and unite him with the Transcendent, would culminate in Judeo-Cartesianism, i.e. Rothschild's atheistic speculation of liberal finance, reducing to all pollution, Einstein and the genetic attacks of nuclear power, whose waste can be stored and cannot be neutralised, Oppenheimer and his atomic bomb, Field and his hydrogen bomb, S. T. and his atomic bomb, and Einstein and the genetic attacks of nuclear power, whose waste can be stored and cannot be neutralised.T. Cohen and his neutron bomb, Freud and his pornographic abulism, Djérassi and his pathogenic and teratogenic pill, Weizenbaum and his computers that will turn men into maps, Picasso and his charnel house art.

In 5000 years of hitherto unknown racism, those who practise circumcision on the 8th day of life (the fundamental cause of a hormonal-psychic trauma that accounts for their constant particularism in time and space) have founded four revolutionary religions: Judaism, Islam, Christianity and Marxism. Marxism, an atheistic mysticism, is the final, suicidal culmination of Judeo-Cartesianism, which itself brought Judeo-Christianity to a crashing and furious end.

Surgery on the soul

The Jews are manipulated by circumcision, which is the only cause of their particularism.

This hormonal surgery is surgery on the soul. Disrupting the 21 days of the first puberty, which begins on the 8th day, it will give them an incoercible speculative-parasitic mentality. On the one hand we have the scientists and pituitary financiers and on the other the virtuoso performers and actors, the thyroid novelists. With the internal genitalia damaged, we will have a clan morality but a lack of synthesis and moral sense. *This is the inescapable reality that rules out anti-Jewishness.*

Victims of themselves, hypnotised by a religious rite of which they are unaware, they are entirely encrusted in the curse.

So the Jews see themselves as different from the others, and they are. As a result, it is inevitable that they will always be, and today more than ever, a foreign body among the nations.

They entered the nations as foreigners. They were a people among peoples, preserving their character through first-pubertal circumcision and strict, precise rites, and through laws that kept them apart and perpetuated them. They entered societies not as modest guests but as conquerors. They took over trade and finance, but not as radically and absolutely as in the year 2000. They have a spirit of superiority and a greed for money that drives them to usury, the epi-centric source of anti-Jewishness at all times and in all places. They were initially welcomed without prejudice, and were even given preferential treatment to consolidate their position. Their prestige in the wealth they acquired at the expense of those who welcomed them provoked deep aversion, and the people then expressed themselves in pogroms and expulsions from the host country. This has been the pattern of Jewish history everywhere and without exception. Today, the situation is infinitely worse, because with their total hegemony, the peoples are reduced to misery and degeneration.

In a letter to Karl Marx, Baruch Lévy wrote: "In a new organisation of humanity, the sons of Israel, scattered throughout the world, will become the leading element everywhere without encountering the slightest opposition, especially if they succeed in imposing the leadership of a Jew on the working masses".

With the victory of the proletariat, the governments of the Republic will easily pass into Jewish hands. Private property can easily be abolished by Jewish leaders who will administer public wealth. Thus will be fulfilled the promises of the Talmud that the Jews will possess the wealth of all the peoples of the world. Socialism is therefore an enormous Jewish mystification, because its aim is not the upliftment of the proletariat and the alleviation of social injustice, but Jewish world domination: this is what we call globalism in the year 2000. Two apparently antinomic parameters actually complement each other: on the one hand, Jewish money and on the other, Jewish socialism and communism. The Jews were the founders of industrial and financial capitalism and systematically collaborate in the extreme centralisation of capital which will facilitate its socialisation. On the other hand, they are Capital's fiercest adversaries. There is the gold-digging Jew and the revolutionary Jew. Rothschild versus Marx, Marx versus Rothschild, a brilliant dialectic of brotherly enemies that produces the movements of history. Starting with the Jewish revolution, not the French one, they became the masters of money and, through money, the masters of the world. Most of the masters of Bolshevism were Jews, including Lenin, whose mother was Jewish: Trotsky, Sverdloff, Zinovef, Kameneff, Ouritski, Sokolnikoff etc. In Germany, the leaders of Spartakism were Jewish: Liebknecht, Rose Luxembourg, Kurth Eisner, Eugène Lévine. In France, Léon Blum was a Jew. In Spain the absolute master of Madrid, devastated by the civil war, was Heinz Neumann, a German Jew. Contrary to what one might think, the super-capitalist mentality and the socialist mentality are in no way opposed in essence: *they are both based on an economic-materialist conception of the world.*

We need to distinguish between the owner of land or industry and the financier who lives on speculation. The revolution was fatal for the former, hence the rapid disintegration of humanity, but it made the colossal fortunes of the latter, fortunes that were artificial, gigantic and necrotic. Socialism is not the goal of revolution but a means of destruction that favours international Jewish finance. The Jews have a different fortune from that of the Goyim. They do not fear communism but profit from it. They are modern capitalists, that is to say speculators and money traffickers.

The prototype is the banker with his safe and his wallet. For Judaism the surest means of achieving world domination is social-communism which, by taking property away from the Goyim and centralising it in the hands of the Jewish-led party, will realise the Talmudic project of making the Jew king and priest of the world. Governments will thus pass into Jewish hands by means of the victory of the proletariat. Individual property can be abolished by Jewish rulers who will administer public wealth everywhere. The workers are therefore the instrument which serves the Jews, the potential masters of the world. The socialist or communist revolution is the shortest and surest route to the total concentration of capital in Jewish hands: it will be a state super-capitalism.

The prophecy of the Talmud will then be fulfilled:

"All the peoples of the earth will be chained to the throne of Israel following an atrocious world war in which three quarters of the population will be decimated. Three hundred donkeys will be needed to carry the keys to the treasure".

For the last forty years or so, everyone has been hypnotised by the 6-million-chambers-to-gas dogma. Nobody had thought about it, nobody questioned it.

The Faurisson affair broke in 1979 in the newspaper *Le Monde*.

Some people start to think. To everyone's astonishment, it became clear that the Professor did not have the right to express himself. He is entitled to heavy criminal penalties, tear gas and a failed assassination attempt. What a strange democratic system, and what a strange application of the freedom of expression enshrined in human rights!

Anyone can understand that if he were wrong he would have been allowed to express himself freely, if only to crush him in television, the press, radio and publishing in Jewish hands. Even without studying the problem, it is already clear that this is a sham, of which we have nine pieces of evidence in the form of the behaviour towards Faurisson and all the so-called 'revisionist' historians, although the term is a pleonasm because every historian is essentially a revisionist, otherwise he is nothing more than a paid propagandist.

So there you have the implacable psychological aspect of the problem: there are totalitarian, Stalinist laws to silence historians! Tristan's conclusion was peremptory before studying even the shadow of the shadow of the technical aspect of the problem.

However, curiosity led him to look into this technical aspect.

The *American Jewish Year book*, on page 666 of issue 43, states unambiguously that the number of Jews present in occupied Europe was 3,300,000!

From 1941 onwards, thousands of Jews left for the Free Zone (women and children) and Spain (men). Tristan and all his family and friends were among them.

It is absurd to cremate four million Jews on the assumption that two million died as a result of the war (which is an exaggeration), when we know how long cremation took and the number of crematoria. Moreover, advanced crematoria were not installed until the end of 1943! Before that date, cremations were technically insufficient. Under such conditions, they would have triggered typhus epidemics throughout Europe. Millions would therefore have been exterminated in around a year, which is ridiculously impossible. What's more, so many Jews left that Hitler offered to exchange a million of them to the USA for 15,000 lorries: the Jews in the USA preferred to let them die of hunger and typhus so that they could concoct the juicy Holocaust and use it for their world hegemony and the massacre of the Palestinians. Ergo, the extermination of a country like Switzerland in seven concentration camps - some of which officially never had gas chambers - is arithmetical nonsense.

Cyclon B is hydrocyanic acid. Recently, the CEO of the largest hydrocyanic acid manufacturing plant wrote to an unfortunate history teacher who had been dismissed for telling his pupils that there was a revisionist school:

- I was director of the Saint Avold plant which, with its production of forty tonnes per day of cyanide ion, was the largest in the world in 1970. Theoretically, this production would have made it possible to fatally poison 500 million human beings in one day. So I know all about the problems involved in handling hydrocyanic acid. I can confirm that all the accounts I

have read or heard about gas chambers in which 2 to 3,000 people were put are the stuff of fantasy.[40]

There's no point in going any further to see what a sham this is. But let's do it out of curiosity.

The hundreds of photographs taken by the Americans during the supposed period of the Holocaust do not reveal any of the immense piles of coal required, or any of the thick black smoke that should have been permanent for such cremations.

We all know what a hydrocyanic acid gas chamber is: that's how the Americans execute their death row inmates.

This is a room for one (maximum 2) convicts. This chamber is incredibly complex and expensive. Such a chamber for 2,000 victims would not only have been financially impossible, but would also have left considerable traces that would have been impossible to eradicate. They would have left orders, documents and archives. Raymond Aron himself said that none of this had ever been found, even though all the crematoria were still in working order. These ovens were essential in prisons and concentration camps to prevent typhus.

As for cyclon B, it has been used in Germany by the hygiene services since 1920. It was used for delousing clothes. In some camps where it is officially stated that gassing never took place, tonnes of Cyclon B have been found.

Mr Leuchter, who directs and sells everything to do with gas chambers for death row inmates, went to Germany to study the problem. His famous report concluded that such gassings were impossible. Two high-level specialists agree on the imposture. The unfortunate Leuchter paid for the honesty of his work with complete ruin. Another ninefold proof of the fraud. The democratic freedom of expression enshrined in human rights is only valid if what is said pleases the Jews. Otherwise, enslaved judges will ruin you.

A doctoral thesis on the Gerstein report (which denounced the murder of Jews in such a grotesque way that the Nuremberg tribunal could not accept his testimony, and which curiously ended in "suicide") was cancelled by

---

[40] Gérard Roubeix, CEO, Arts et Manufactures engineer.

Jewish will, against the competence of university professors, on a futile pretext.

And this dogma continues to be imposed by the Marx Merdia and the atheist Levy Zion. The world's masses have swallowed it up.

Despite these glaring realities, the comatose, hypnotic numbness of the masses, stupefied by rock, techno, football, drugs and alcohol, continues.

Big brother Rothschild Marx puts anyone who denounces the absurdity of dogma on trial. In Germany, doubt means prison.

As if all that didn't prove the imposture of a so-called democracy.

American circumcised billionaires, as red as they are circumcised, financed Bolshevism.

Hammer, with his carnivorous face, is worth twenty million dollars. During the Second World War, he alone owned as much oil as the three Axis powers. (Japan, Germany and Italy).

His telephone bill in Los Angeles exceeds one billion centimes a year. (Ten million heavy francs)

His empire is one of the most powerful on the planet. He meets heads of state all the time. From his flat opposite the White House to the one opposite the Kremlin, he travels by plane and is received like a head of state. Since 1917, he has been the Kremlin's privileged interlocutor. He has met the seven General Secretaries of the Communist Party and the thirteen Presidents of the USA.

Rockfeller (Steinhauer), another circumcised red billionaire, owns the most powerful oil company in the world. Together with Hammer, they negotiated the creation of a Soviet-American Chamber of Commerce to facilitate exports to the USSR of machine tools, without which the Soviet army, which threatened the world, would not have existed.

The circumcised bankers Kuhn, Loeb and Warburg transferred six hundred million roubles between 1918 and 1922. Hammer's father was the king of the clandestine transfer of funds for the subversive activities of the Cominterm. He was even imprisoned in Sing Sing prison in 1920 for this offence. His son Armand took over. In 1922 Hammer succeeded in convincing the anti-communist Ford to set up factories in the USSR. Communist experts came to Ford's factories to learn the ropes.

In a report to Roosevelt from the American ambassador in Moscow, we read:

"Stalin acknowledges that 2/3 of the largest Soviet companies were built with the help of American financiers.

It is understandable that Hammer should be received in Moscow like a head of state.

In 1960, he took the most powerful Western businessmen in his wake and set them on the path of East-West economic exchanges.

The vast movement towards the East that began in the early 1970s was accompanied by factory closures in the West, unemployment and tax manipulation. Communist leaders hoped that by welcoming multinationals they would consolidate their power and make up for the backwardness accumulated by their industries.

Didn't the director of the KGB at the time say:

- *We're building a communist society with your expertise, and we'll maintain our system and our rules with your help.*

Hammer's personal plane flies from his White House flat to the Kremlin without formalities.

These were trucks built by Ford on the banks of the Volga, and later used in Afghanistan.

As a symbolic example, Hammer signed the two biggest economic contracts ever negotiated between the West and the USSR. Twenty billion dollars and the supply of fertilisers to the USSR for twenty years. Eight billion dollars to supply the west coast of the USA and Japan with Siberian oil and gas exploited by Hammer's company.

Of course, for all these agreements, the USSR benefits from ridiculously low Western credits, financed by Western taxpayers.

The Iron Curtain is a transparent pane of glass for American Jewish bankers and the Goyim dragged along in their wake.

The much-vaunted "détente" was above all a period of intense economic and technological espionage.

During the Russian invasion of Afghanistan, the Hammer-Brejniev meeting ended with this statement by the billionaire:

- Afghanistan is part of the Soviet sphere of influence".

Then, by offering Pakistan to invest in oil, he arranged for promises of oil prospecting to lock down the Pakistani border, a possible crossing point for aid and supplies destined for the Afghan resistance.

No American president, from Roosevelt to Regan, was elected without Hammer's electoral contribution, Democrats and Republicans alike.

However, in 1960 a "top secret" report was submitted to the office of the President of the United States. This report had only one aim: to dissuade any President from negotiating with Hammer.

It was thanks to American billionaires circumcised on the 8th day that the USSR's industry and army existed and functioned.

There can be no Bolshevism without circumcised American capitalism.

This prototype of red billionaires is immovable and unassailable. They are the true kings of the world.

It is the absolute reign of despot-like individuals that is bolstering the so-called "democratic" world.

Hammer remains the leader of the other circumcised and some uncircumcised Red billionaires. His specially converted Boeing 727 was the only private plane to enter Soviet airspace on a permanent basis.

Lenin said: "The capitalists will sell us the rope to hang them". They also provide the gallows.

It is worth describing another Jewish billionaire, Klimrod, by way of symbolism.

It has been said that he is the richest Jewish businessman in the world along with Hammer. But that's irrelevant, because the same could be said of many Jewish financiers. He is worth billions of dollars.

In 1945 he was found in a pit full of corpses in a German concentration camp. He was alive. He then became a terrorist in Israel and an "anti-Nazi vigilante". He moved to Tangiers where he prospered from cigarette smuggling. He arrived in the USA in sneakers at the age of twenty-two, and two months later found himself at the head of sixty companies.

In 1980, he owned 1,687 companies. They covered everything that could be sold: food, restaurants, press, television, sales of all kinds of products to the USSR, including turnkey factories.

Remaining in the shadows, he dodges all the anti-trust laws and puts his own men in every government.

What does a tiny president of the United States, a peanut trader or a film actor, who is swept aside every four years, put in place by a Congress and a mob in the hands of high finance, represent in comparison with such an occult power with absolute permanence, capable of manipulating governments as it pleases?

What potential for organic, mental, ecological and moral destruction is contained in such speculative power, isolated from all the true laws of life that only the providential elites and the wise know?

It is almost impossible for the majority of human beings to become aware of the gigantic perversity of Judeo-Cartesian speculation.

They cannot grasp the destructive synthesis of financiers, Marx, Freud, Oppenheimer, S.T. Cohen, Djérassi, pathogenic and teratogenic physico-chemical medicine, materialism, the unheard-of lie of progress and democracy which is their dictatorship. Cohen, the Djérassi, pathogenic and teratogenic physico-chemical medicine, materialism, the unheard-of lie of progress and democracy, which is nothing more than their absolute dictatorship over the masses and their progressive and implacable degradation.

And yet, under the aegis of this democracy, the human rights they are full of are flouted in every country in the world, except in their own case. What's more, 2/3 of humanity is dying of hunger.

Material and spiritual misery reaches its peak under the polluting tyranny of Rothschildo-Marxist policies, exerted on bodies and souls as well as on the planet's soil, sterilised by chemicals and disturbed by deforestation.

All this is hidden from the majority of humans who have lost all synthetic intelligence and accept, in a determinism that seems absolute and cosmic, everything that goes wrong as long as it is official and publicised by the media.

Their every gesture, their mental form of expression, their objectives are strangely inhuman. They are obscene.

In a universal bath of lies, they perform an autopsy on the whole world. Their physical appearance, so prodigiously modelled on the symbolic representations of Satan in all religious traditions, is dazzling in its significance: *Mendès-France, Olivenstein, Hammer, Raymond Aron, Gainsbourg etc. perfect gargoyles. Nothing to touch up.*

Grandma and her immediate destructiveness. Hammer, Oppenheimer, Freud, Marx and their universal destruction. *Marx and hate. From Hammer and Marx to S.T. Cohen, all their analyses kill.*

Their sparkling faculties in the immediate term, their speculations that seem positive, genial to the masses, which in turn confers on them the admiration of the greatest number.

Laurent Schwarz, Trotskyist mathematician, intelligent?

S.T. Cohen, inventor of the neutron bomb, intelligent?

Hammer, the Red billionaire who is actively preparing for the Bolshevisation of the world and the Third World War, intelligent?

The ultimate mockery and mystification.

"They never have that modest attention proper to true intelligence", said Simone Weil.

True intelligence is not recognised in this way, and everything is organised to make it a sham in the eyes of a degenerate mass that can only worship its executioners.

Universal leeching and rotting.

A bloody farce of East-West antagonism, while the clique of Red billionaires spreads Bolshevism and the USSR has been supported since 1917[41] by American Jewish bankers.

They have no faith, no hope, no charity. Have we ever seen a Jewish eye containing a drop of gratuitous tenderness? Look at those eyes that are too bright, or atonal, clothed in a false gentleness from which the heart is absent.

---

[41] In reality, Jewish finance in the USA prepared the Bolshevik Revolution with financing in the 1900s. The revolution did not just break out in 1917: it took a long period of financed preparation.

Their eyes have no deep feeling, no soul. Like all neurotics, they have no heart, but they have a para-hysterical attachment to their mother. They crush everything with matter, for matter's sake. Gold loves only gold. Their speculations, however disinterested, are like a neurosis, a disease from which all human synthesis is excluded.

Why this metaphysical condemnation through the ridiculous instrument of circumcision on the 8th day?

Why can't their neurotic intelligence stop working? Why are they condemned to such fatal destruction?

Their thoughts have the face of their faces.

The exploitation of the democratic myth, the lie of progress, Capitalism, Communism, all the *isms*. The third and final world war.

The responsibility of the average man in this *enigmatic*[42] democratic mystification! nil, that's the absurdity of it...

Léon Blum versus Citroën, Marx versus Rothschild.

Tell people "I'm going to give you freedom" and enslave them, and they'll come in droves. Tell them you're going to force them and give them true freedom and they won't come, unless of course there are six million unemployed on the national territory. In the year 2000, human sluggishness is so total that even six million unemployed people will not prevent them from voting democratic! They prefer to feed on demagogy, labels, illusions, football, regressive, ignorant and pathogenic music, drugs, pornography and idiotic shows. All that's needed is for it all to shine and get agitated.

Rockefeller "The man who makes rocks fall" and doesn't care what's around.

It was the Jewish monarchy that made the revolution, for the benefit of the financiers, known as "French".

It is Jewish Socialism that is leading us to Jewish Communism and Globalism.

---

[42] *"Enaurme"* reminds us of *"King Ubu"*: "When I've taken all the money, I'll kill everyone and leave".

Satan is circumcised on the eighth day.

They are in a vicious circle from which they cannot escape and into which they drag us. They are psychopaths, they talk fast and with gestures, they talk a lot and a dialogue with them is a tour de force. They have no intellectual integrity. They seduce the masses. They flatter and exploit the stupidity, vanity, weakness and vulgarity of men and especially women. They don't sit still for a minute. They come to you... when they need you. They're not happy. They show their stubborn hatred at the drop of a hat because lying is as essential to their survival as a leaf is to a snail.

Point out to them the Jewish names of the Weimar rot, the fact that this rot disappeared with the advent of Hitler, the names of the Jewish prison and concentration camp executioners of the USSR who exterminated tens of millions of Goyim, and you will never see them again.

They can't stand any truth about themselves, but they proclaim the lies that serve them as truth, like the arithmetical-technical nonsense of 6-million-rooms-to-gas.

They lack that faculty of abstraction from themselves that allows them to look at themselves in the midst of tragedy, to find themselves metaphysically comic, to be amused by their predestination as Satan's chosen people, to fight against fate.

They sweat their "creations", their cruelty, their support, their love, their mysticism, like a sick person sweats an ominous sweat. Hyper-securitized, (Rothschild, Marx, Freud et al) never brilliant.

Everything they create destroys by synthesis and is spectacular to the blissful analyst.

No saints, no geniuses, no great Jewish artists. Mozart? Not Jewish, of course, but from a family that had left Judaism centuries earlier.

Picasso? Yes, of course: "This public clown who exploited the stupidity of his contemporaries as best he could", as he himself confessed.

As soon as they try to think, they are Freud and Marx mythomaniacs, the end points of Western Nihilism. They are closed, radically closed, to any manifestation of superior intelligence, which is essentially 'anti-Jewish', because nothing synthetic can be built in the orbit of their necrotic Judeo-Cartesian speculations.

Their dissolving analyses and the destruction of the moral sense are necessary for them to reign over an uncultured mass. Secularism inaugurates, pathogenic and criminogenic music, alcohol and drugs complete the universal destruction. The Goyim are now conditioned like slot machines. They will all vote for the necessary cretin, the mop manipulated by Israel, which pays for the elections of the American president as well as the French president and other consort presidents.

They impose their racism in the name of anti-racism. Let a single North African enter Israel, where not even Palestinians have the right to live on their own soil.

Millions of sub-human men are marching.

They have no scruples. Their infirmity is not cruelty and hatred on a scale where cruelty and hatred would be so intense as to surpass the human. Their hatred and their love are abstract, and therefore tenfold and infernal. Their love is a demonic artifice where the destruction of hundreds of millions of people appears potentially to a true thinker. Their pity can only lead to murderous humiliation in the hearts of others. Mercy and pity are strange because one unconsciously destroys the unconscious world and the other engenders a more destructive despair . They have a theoretical heart and gladly shower you with supernatural help. The family converts are ignorant of basic moral sense and would happily convert you with clubs, even though you are a billion times more 'Christian'[43] than they are.

Even if they're not intellectual converts, and in that case they're still doing a good business, they're still barred from the good things in the New Testament. Curious mystics, imitation Christians, capable of leaving their neighbours destitute and praying fervently. A converted Jew is always a living antinomy, an actor who plays false because he can't get into character. And yet they are remarkable actors, comedians, in the theatre, in the cinema, propaganda tools entirely in their hands for the global dumbing down of the masses.

Tristan could say of those famous priests who are even more Jewish than before their conversion and who never want to hear about the Jewish

---

[43] That is, endowed with a moral sense that is poorly expressed in the Gospels and better expressed in Plato and Ancient Egypt (see previous pages).

question. In fact they haven't changed at all, but there's the effect of contrast.

All these pianists with their breathtaking technique, prodigious acrobats.

No composer who surpasses the charm of Mendelssohn and Meyerbeer. Instead, it's a technical juggling act of soulless music.

They analyse, they weigh up, the important thing is that it brings in money or the neurotic satisfaction of speculation. The result is idealisms as false as capitalism, socialism and Marxism. Spinoza separated mysticism from philosophy, destroying philosophy and paving the way for suicidal modern science.

Either we live in despair, deficient, 'reduced' in the technocratic hell of the West, where our children are taking drugs and committing suicide in the midst of their multiform speculations, and Freudianism is not going to save them, because the mind gives way in the face of so much barbarism, or we are going to ask for salvation from an ideology that will plunge us into an even worse hell. The hell of elementary matricular statistical units and gulags. Our cowardice in Capitalism will precipitate us into Globalism, which will finish us off.

The great triumphant of today's "pituitary" (analytical) humanity.

They have gone as far as they can in this direction. Perhaps we should forget that they are temporarily destroying the human synthesis in order to access this revelation. They are now in over their heads and that is why they are going to exterminate us along with themselves.

They are superior involutes. They are hormonally ill.

Their psycho-physiological unity deprives them of everything that constitutes objective man: heart, intelligence, balance.

The non-existent moral sense is replaced by the morality of ostentation, self-righteousness, the sense of the tribe.

It is clear that climate, geographical location and diet determine ethnic groups. There are no fixed races. The Knowledge of the sages, like modern science, denies this vague concept.

If you look carefully at a black and white photograph of an acromegalic patient whose disease is progressing, you will see that after a while the photographs take on the appearance of a Negro. The very last photo shows a Negro without the slightest ambiguity.

A negro is therefore "a pituitary with acromegalic manifestations".

Acromegaly is a disease of the pituitary gland which confers negroid characteristics.

As the pituitary gland is highly developed in the Jews due to circumcision on the 8th day, for a long time there was talk of the Negro origins of the Jews. This is very far from the problem.

It is obvious that we will never find Negroes with the morphology of Chopin or Lamartine, who are "thyroid".

Similarly, a photograph of a myxedematous patient (pathological thyroid insufficiency) bears an incredible resemblance to that of a Pygmy: same overall morphology, same body language. This analogy shows that the Pygmy is physiologically hypothyroid.

This kind of elaboration, without which there can be no thought, is radically excluded from the university. It's the notion of identity.

No geographical or climatic influence can account for the Jewish particularity, which was constant in time and space, since they never lived in the same place for 1000 years, the time required to form an ethnic group. Their particularity is strictly due to circumcision on the 8th day, the 1st day of the first puberty, which lasts 21 days.

Jewish speculation has eradicated the moral sense, the spirit of synthesis that is the foundation of true elites. Their particularism holds the entire officialdom of the twentieth century in its grip.

Circumcision explains this often caricatured physique and these considerable speculative powers. We find them in the perversity of Freud and Marx and in all the supporters of a dishevelled liberalism that is a universal polluter. Their racism stimulates anti-racism to their advantage. Their "hyper" thyroid tendency explains their astonishing vitality, their paranoid sensitivity and their "jeremiating" psychology. Their physical sensitivity is often abnormal, as is their lack of adaptation. Their hypophyseal speculative abilities are admired by the Goyim. They use the clan to support themselves, with that hysterical tinge of mothers loving their children and children loving their mothers.

The 21 days of first puberty, which begins on the 8th day, is extremely important. It would be enough to abolish Jewish circumcision to return to traditional values and see the worldwide scourge of Jewish speculation disappear. Society cannot be built and sustained without a sense of morality and synthesis.

Western nihilism and circumcision! Cleopatra's nose!

Doctors cannot understand all this: most of them, at least, have not yet even grasped the functional anteriority of the hormonal system over the nervous system.

Why are they condemned by this ridiculous means of circumcision, which the commentaries of the Torah make even more opaque, since they say: "The effects of circumcision are beyond human understanding".

This is no longer the case.

Judeo-Cartesian rationalism will self-destruct through its inability to solve the secrets of the world and of man, through its inability to stop the martyrdom and heartbreak imposed by its incurable Rothschildo-Marxist materialism.

Man has lost confidence in this science, which is in fact nothing but black magic. He will seek the source of truth in his regenerated mind. The socialist myth cannot survive the time it takes to bring about economic and moral ruin.

It is the last mystical belief of Judeo-Christianity.

The dogmatic and sclerotic Church and socialist Masonry would have been two sides of the same coin hung around the necks of those circumcised on the 8th day after birth...

Open letter to Albert Cohen.

Dear Sir.

After seeing and hearing you on television, I was plunged into a painful meditation on our determinisms, and I wondered how a man like you could be so far removed from any fundamental awareness.

First of all, a detail from your programme: William Harvey, the English doctor who died in the middle of the 17th century and who discovered blood circulation, has nothing to do with the Swiss doctor and theologian who was burnt at the instigation of Calvin.

I've only seen ¾ of your programme and it's possible that if I'd seen and heard everything I'd have had other things to say to you than what follows, but I think that what follows is enough to shake a conscience.

You spoke of Pierre Laval's assassination with apparent compassion. Without forgetting to say that "he was a bastard who deserved a bullet in the head".

This bastard had only one aim, to save France, Europe and the world from Bolshevism with the poor cards at his disposal, an occupied France, a Marshal, aware of the Bolshevik tragedy. "I wish Germany victory", he said, "because without her the world will be Bolshevised".

When you consider the tens of millions of corpses in "Bolshevia", the 200 million victims of Marxism and the expanding tentacles of this murderous ideology, you wonder how anyone can pass such a judgment on this modern Talleyrand, who was perfectly right, as Solzhenitsyn would confirm. So he did his best to avoid such a cataclysm, even if it displeases our liberal-Marxist congeners.

Remember what the Vatican said in 1942: "Nazi Germany fights for its friends and for its enemies, because if the Eastern Front collapses, the fate of the West is sealed". Have you read *Mein Kampf* and compared it with the years since it was published in the 1920s? Then you will be able to draw the blinding conclusions that are needed.

If Hitler's policy had been followed, we would not have reached such a degree of degeneration, chaos, crime and cannibalisation of nature. An autarkic and biological policy would have been followed in Europe. A demented overpopulation of increasingly degenerate beings and the invasion of Europe by the Third World would have been impossible.

Above all, we would not be living under the dictatorship of the Red Jewish financiers, and all the countries would not be reduced to economic ruin and unpayable debts. Finally, the war of 1939 was declared by us, the Jews, to Hitler in 1933, and made inevitable by the policy of plunder established by the Treaty of Versailles, against which Hitler legitimately protested.

You should read Rabbi Reifer's article, which draws up an implacable indictment of us Jews, explaining the inevitability of Hitler's emergence.

This disastrous world policy was imposed by Jewish finance in the USA, which simultaneously financed the Allies and the Bolshevik revolution.

Then, in 1919, the Warburgs came to negotiate the peace that paved the way for the Second World War.

American newspapers report that the Jews declared war on Hitler in 1933. Documents and testimonies attest to the fact that Hitler did everything possible to avoid war. The first piece of evidence is his incredibly efficient economic system, which was totally incompatible with the very idea of war!

Hitler had reached a perfect agreement with colonel beck on the subject of Danzig, an autostrade enjoying extraterritoriality etc. It was under the influence of England, manipulated by the Jewish financier Baruch, that Beck changed his mind and made the invasion of Poland inevitable. Posnania was populated by Germans who were mistreated and sometimes massacred...

Didn't Prime Minister Chamberlain write to his sister in 1939, "It was the Jews who got us into the war"?

All these facts are realities whose evidence cannot all be destroyed by our propaganda.[44]

Thanks to courageous historians on the left, we now understand that the six-million-rooms-to-gas ratio is arithmetical and technical nonsense.

It is impossible to exterminate 4 or 6 million people, a country like Switzerland, in seven concentration camps, the majority of which officially had no gas chambers. Specialists at the highest level affirm the impossibility of gassing 2,000 people at a time with hydrocyanic acid (cyclon b).

We also realise that the Barbie affair was a set-up by the Wiessenthals and Jewish high finance. Barbie served the CIA, the Jewish-American government, to install and consolidate fascist regimes in South America. If Barbie had been French, he would have had a statue erected to

---

[44] After the death of this Jewish author, Rudolf Hess was murdered in his prison at the age of 93: it has been proven that it could not possibly have been suicide, for a number of concrete and inescapable reasons. Just imagine the worldwide explosion that his revelations could have triggered. In this age of lies, that was the last thing we needed!

commemorate his work as a soldier. Did he let a small number of Jewish children be taken away on orders? So what? Does he have exclusive rights? Who massacred thousands of Boer children in concentration camps in South Africa if not the British, who had behind them a German Jewish financier, a Portuguese Jewish financier and an English Jewish financier: Lord Rothschild, as it happens.

Did you say that *being Jewish is sublimity*?

Apart from the fact that I've never heard a more racist, megalomaniacal statement, I'd like to ask you where you get your pride from?

As a Jew from an illustrious family, I don't see any sublimity in that.

First of all, are we a race? No, because races don't exist. There are only ethnic groups that are the result of hormonal adaptation to a fixed environment for at least 1,000 years. But we have never achieved this condition. Our pathological, and brilliantly speculative, particularism comes exclusively from circumcision on the 8th day, producing a serious hormonal and psychological trauma.

This hormonally disturbed group refused the Egyptian revelation and got the carnal God they deserved. It produced a few prophets that it was quick to slaughter. It created an artificial people of fugitive slaves who destroyed by massacre the peoples whose civilisation and labour it ignored, a people of a monotheistic tribal God greedy for the blood of sacrifices.

"I have hardened their hearts so that they will not hear my word", said Isaiah, one of their rare shining lights.

Does your sublimity stem from your "hormonal" kinship?

With the red billionaires, Rothschilds, Hammer, Rockfeller, Warburg, Schiff, Sassoon, Oppenheimer et al?

With Marx and his 200 million corpses, executed by prison and concentration camp executioners like Kaganovitch, Frenkel, Yagoda, Jejoff, Abramovici, Firine, Appeter, Rappaport, etc.

Freud? And his pornography and worldwide rotting, his destruction of the family and all the tender feelings that are the essence of life, and whose smoky theory is based on nothing.

Picasso? And his aesthetic degradation, which he humbly admitted. Einstein and nuclear fission?

Oppenheimer and his atomic bomb? Field and his hydrogen bomb?

S.T. Cohen and his neutron bomb? Meyer-Lanski, godfather of the Maffia?

Flato-Sharon international swindler and electoral fraudster?

In a word, all the tyrants of the democratic dictatorship served up by well-fattened political mops from all the parties, those implacable morons who are leading us towards the worst?

No, my dear Sir, any man worthy of the name can only be ashamed to belong to this clique of major criminals who hold all the wheels of officialdom and are in the process of liquidating mankind and the planet.

Our colleague George Steiner summed it all up very well:

"For 5,000 years we have been talking too much, a word of death for ourselves and for others". Believe in my good feelings.

Chapter XV

Tristan's fever persisted. He lay in a chaos of effervescent suffering.

He was delirious.

I love to love.

That's my strength and my weakness. My enormous struggle against the impossible.

The presence of a naked heart in the face of nihilising cynicism, the death of all authentic feeling.

No more kindness, no more rigour, nothing.

Hope when there is no hope. My presence in the face of total hostility.

The aggregates see coherently in the minuscule, they easily shrink their ideas.

Nietzsche, Pascal had aphoristic tendencies.

Faced with the painful thoughts poured out by chaos, there is little room for order, and there will be less and less of it.

There are many humanoids for whom the obvious are theories, and truths are systems.

My God, give me peace. Satan, give me the peace of the lethargic happiness of a football match spectator. Millions and millions.

The absence of problems through levelling, definitive anaesthesia through the neutron bomb.

Grandma darling? Biche? I still have Chopin and the little ones.

We suffer from what is false in us. First moral, then physiological. Physiological, then moral again. And physiological again.

The downward spiral of human disintegration. Endless psychosomatic and somatopsychic illnesses. Man becomes a homunculus gesticulating to music that would make apes flee. Just look at the skull-and-crossbones faces of certain rock singers or other impostors, chanting dull, hideous beats.

A congenital defect due to our degeneration since our fall. Since the alienation of the original happiness that we perhaps had. There are peoples who know how to live, who know neither disease nor madness and only a late death at around one hundred and twenty or one hundred and fifty.[45]

If we followed the laws of life, we could experience happiness here below, a gentle and accepted death to complete a life of fulfilment.

Different climates, food that does not conform to our nature and which, in this century, is made more harmful by chemistry, are gradually degenerating us. Almost all of us are dying of cancer or cardiovascular disease, primarily because of the incongruity of our food.

When I see faces, I feel that they are not normal, often very ugly as they are, I imagine them to be beautiful, as they should be. If people regained their organic and mental balance, their faces would be glorious. God has allowed us to lose our faces along with our happiness.

He has allowed us to ignore his laws out of stupidity and ignorance. Degenerate faces. Our security was not enough for him. He wanted us to be unstable so he could watch us struggle and drown. All in all, we understood nothing about him or ourselves.

And now we are perishing under the Judeo-Cartesian scythe. And why is that? Authentic peace is non-suffering, non-joy, non-existence.

I want to go back to nothingness with my two little ones.

I was happy before I was born, I don't even remember it. Not remembering is also a form of happiness. We are all cripples: thought and genius are defects born of despair. The man in paradise looked more like a line-singer than Nietzsche.

He wasn't forced to dig through problems with his intelligence, to scream out his pain with his genius.

The actor is also a poor monster. I've seen puppets in the theatre who act out feelings and passions that don't belong to them.

---

[45] Alluding to the Hounzas in northern India. Mainly frugivores.

The actor is everything but himself: he is to be nothing.

I love to love. My darling.

Haven't we noticed that hinds always cry?

It's because they suffer. The doe would be a dancer if she were a woman, like the greyhound, the thoroughbred and the gazelle.

My doe is a woman, a doe and a bit of a cunt. She keeps quiet. She's a little monster that I want to love because she needs love and takes it beyond exhaustion. Who says we're all masochists when it comes to love? There's some truth in that.

She lets herself be loved. I love in order to love. I've given her everything, my whole heart.

All my distress. In love you choose what will demand the most of you. You choose what is most harmful to you. I chose Biche in spite of myself, knowing that perhaps she would dissolve me, annihilate me. I turned back to the past, my eyes full of tears and bewitched by my passion, I set off. I stripped myself of lives that didn't belong to me and whose security I hold dear.

I love his weakness.

I have nothing left, not even my dignity.

She's beautiful, but she can't imagine that there's anything else in the world for me other than her, just her.

- I've got a little doe's head," she told me one day, "not a big elephant's head.

Yes, she's got this adorable little Doe face that makes me suffer so much. I can't really explain it to her. But what can I do?

She was born with the gift of dance. Dance was her joy in life. Her parents couldn't see it, so she didn't become a dancer, but she will always be a dancer, just as I will always be a pianist, *essentially.*

A dancer without a dance, a pianist without a piano.

Lost in the modern world. We can't change our essence, this world of brutes can kill us, that's all.

She met my passion and she needed it. She wanted to absorb me body and soul, she wanted to be my silent idol. She won't admit anything else into my head other than herself, she can't stand my two children.

If she could discover that two children are sacred... If she could understand that these two little beings are not between her and me, between my love and her.

I can't see clearly in this doomed gloom.

Would I love her just as passionately if she were to join me in my duty as a father and artist? Or even!

Wouldn't it be implied in me in a muted way? Wouldn't we be a quiet whole? But then wouldn't we be totally different?

If I'd studied piano, I wouldn't have needed to think. I wasn't made to think. I'll always think like a child. You can only ask so much of a child's brain.

The dandy is the child par excellence. So pity us. Give him dancing, give me a piano, because I love and can't love any more.

Ma Biche, jealous of two children...

Lord, shouldn't we hate you because *you don't always tell us about the laws of life that bring happiness?*

NOËL

For the first time, for some reason, *Grandma* went to see Tristan's children. She gave the nanny a teddy bear and a small note. She said:

"What do you want, it's not because their father is a monster and an ingrate. When I think of all I've done for him! What a snake I've warmed in my bosom!"

And the people in her salon, nodding in agreement, suggested that she was a kind of saint.

Fever, always fever. Bedridden, lucid, devastated.

A few days later, he was due to sit his final licence exams.

André, his psychiatrist friend, came to see Tristan and decided it would be wiser for him to go into hospital.

The sulphonamides had eliminated the colibacilli, but the purulent traces remained.

The head doctor at the Hôtel Dieu where he was staying, son-in-law of a doctor who was a friend of his father and mother and who had given birth to Tristan, was nicknamed the "miracle professor". He had in fact cured a patient suffering from cirrhosis of the liver, cerebrospinal meningitis and other calamitous diseases. In any case, he left hospital on his own two legs, but nobody knew whether he was still alive a month later.

The doctor's attitude and physique struck Tristan strangely. He was square, athletic and had a prodigious memory, which was easy to observe when he was examining patients in the mornings with his students. The intern who followed him was exactly the same type, so much so that they could easily have been mistaken for father and son. They were two perfect pituitaries.

Tristan had noticed, as he said, the frequency of this type among the agrégés, the interns long before he gave them a 'glandular appellation'.

He was well aware that this observation would have escaped anyone else because in detail they were different, but it is precisely the detail that the ordinary man knows how to observe.

For Tristan, their resemblance was as blatant as that of Chopin, Musset, Liszt, Goethe, Disraeli and the lanky Romantics in general.

The professor observed nothing. He asked no questions. His only concern was *to find the syndrome*. Measuring instruments, material tests, x-rays of the lungs and kidneys, albumin tests, induced hyperglycaemia, various blood tests, basal metabolism...

As the purulent traces had disappeared, the professor concluded: "Physiological fever".

Tristan was given a nerve sedative that sent him into such a state of suffocation that he had to give it up.

Tristan pondered real medicine. It seemed so aberrant that he couldn't believe anyone could seriously believe in it and apply it systematically.

Only nutritional and psychological causes could lead to the origins of an illness.

Biche had come. The fever had risen. But weren't this fever, this pus, these microbes, *the physical expression of the ripping out of her soul?*

Wavering, he left the Hôtel Dieu to go to the Sorbonne for his final degree. He wrote in a semi-foggy style, passed the oral exams with flying colours and was awarded an honours degree.

He had already been teaching for ten years.

Despite this considerable seniority, many of his colleagues, who also had a degree in literature, were unable to obtain tenure: they had to pass a competitive examination, CAPES or agrégation.

Their salaries remained derisory and static. One day, a committee of non-tenured teachers got together and consulted a very important trade union. The head of the union, Mademoiselle Abraham, replied:

- We are a union for permanent teachers, so we are not interested in the problem of non-permanent teachers.

So a colleague stood up to group together and defend the interests of untenured teachers with a degree in literature. He was a communist.

No one had the choice of electing another because there was no one to defend their basic interests. The dilemma was simple: either be defended by a Communist or not be defended at all.

Was this not a fundamental aspect of the modern world? Nations whose tradition is the antithesis of Marxism end up finding only one apparent protector, Marxism.

He won't solve anything, but he's the only one.

One day it will devour the whole world, leaving Capitalism with only the financiers who will finance it, just as they financed Bolshevism in Russia: that will be globalist hell.

These university over-primaires had understood nothing of his syndrome-free agony.

Biche remained irascible and nervous, creating insane conflicts within him. The existence of children revolted her. He bled to think that those two little ones meant so little to her. He was torn between his passion and his duty.

One Thursday, he had to go and see his little ones.

Biche suffered so much. She was only mean because she was suffering. Tristan didn't take the train to the suburbs.

He stood there beside her, feeling her pain. Desperate, weakened, mad with passion and tortured.

The faces of his two children in front of him.

No, it's not love, that despicable slavery from which we die.

He could no longer want. For twenty-nine years, he had used his feeble willpower in an exhausting struggle to deny himself, to deny his vocation as a pianist, thinker and artist in order to buy, almost in spite of himself, the right to exist. Everything he had built up was collapsing because of a passion that his reason was opposed to, that he was inevitably drawn towards, and against which he could do nothing.

He felt the threat of tuberculosis and madness. The *materialistic* doctors could do nothing for him.

Providence, there's no other word for it, then put before his eyes a medical article that formulated the endocrinological translation of the four human archetypes he had observed. The ring wrestler, Stalin and Khrushchev were all *adrenals*.

Pituitary interns and associates.

Romantic artists such as Chopin, Musset, Liszt and himself were *thyroid patients*.

Dr Alexis Carrel was a perfect match for the *internal genital or interstitial* type.

He then got in touch by letter with the doctor who had written this dazzling article, whose mysteries he had immediately understood.

This Bordeaux doctor, Dr Jean Gautier, had made the most important discovery of the century in terms of our knowledge of man: *the functional anteriority of the hormonal system over the nervous system and the human being in general.*

Their first contact was a matter of urgency, and he wrote her a chaotic letter in which the wounds of his past, his marriage, his passion for Biche, his children, and his apology for the aesthete condemned to death by progress were all mixed up.

The doctor's response was swift:

My dear Sir.

Don't despair. You analyse your situation with far too much lucidity, reason and common sense not to heal and pull yourself together. You have an ideal, the piano, a duty, your children. You have everything you need to magnificently fill the life of a man with an intelligent and highly sentimental heart.

I'll help you. You've written a remarkable essay on dandyism.

Your attached photograph clearly illustrates my "thyroid" type. You have inevitably chosen a woman whose glandular type has some affinity with yours. But she lacks internal genitalia, which makes her very egotistical. They are dissatisfied, sensation-seeking and jealous.

You are like Chopin and Musset with George Sand: you show her too much that you love her. But Sand was a reproductive genitalia, which allowed her to be unfaithful, but with some kindness.

Follow the two hormone prescriptions I'm writing for you and your wife. When you've recovered, come and see me and we'll have a long talk...

Tristan and Biche took the hormones and stopped tearing each other apart.

Unfortunately, hormones were very expensive and they couldn't afford to renew them.

Then Biche, for a thousand trifles, took back her mask. He tried to bend to the enigma of her character. They looked for words to appease him. Everything displeased him. In the presence of friends he could not speak. Biche paralysed him. A single word could set her off, hurt her, flay her alive.

Tristan had said she was destroying him.

"That would suit me fine," she replied.

A letter, her son was ill.

Forty of fever. He kept his worries to himself. Biche had seen the envelope: "If you love your children, don't stay here, go and be with them", she had said.

Then to Tristan:

—   "What are you doing here?"

This scene had reduced Tristan to a daze. During lunch she would play the comedy of serenity in front of her parents. He couldn't. So she drew him aside into the living room, giving him some illusion of tenderness so that he could also act relatively happy in front of his parents.

After the meal, they found themselves alone.

—   "All we have to do is be brother and sister", she told him, "and what's more, I want to take up a modelling job that I've been offered in Switzerland". And then :

—   "I want to do what I want to do".

Finally, she added this unheard-of phrase: "I don't want to be damned alone".

She disappeared all afternoon.

He asked her where she had been. "I've been looking for a hotel", she replied. That evening, in their bedroom, he insisted that she leave.

She wanted him to leave. All he had to do was leave.

He sat on the edge of the bed, aching for them both. Their two sufferings were antagonistic: she only had hers, he was experiencing both.

So for an interminable time he talked. He explained to her that by some quirk of nature there were things she didn't understand, that she had to try, that children didn't come between him and her.

That she was a doe jealous of two children.

She had calmed down and cried in Tristan's arms. "It's not my fault" she moaned, "don't ever leave me".

Tristan knew it. Poor little hothouse flower, just the way he liked it. He had to buy more hormones, he had to, so he did.

Two weeks passed. He ventured to tell her about his plans for Switzerland. "But I don't want to be a model, why do you want me to be a model", she replied.

Biche became pregnant.

So in the weeks that followed, her little Biche started knitting some lovely things for the little fawn that was about to be born. There was a little pink coat with a hood, tiny white mittens...

How pretty it all was...

If you only knew how pretty it is to see a little Doe knitting. Her little hothouse flower...

That day, Tristan was no longer in pain. He didn't want any more pain. If it still hurt, he would tell his piano...

Chapter XVI

> *"Life is unity in variety"* (Thomas Aquinas)
> *"Suffering, the midwife of the inner man"* (Prince Paul Scortesco)

Tristan took advantage of the long summer school holidays to visit the physiologist and endocrinologist who had helped him.

This man had discovered a fundamental key to human nature: the omnipotence of the endocrine glands. He found that the "thyroid" type to which he belonged was the Apollonian of astrology and the phosphorus of homeopathy. Venusian perspectives were also part of thyroid characterology, just as Martian data was part of adrenal characterology. He felt that these data would not be perceived by a materialistic, primitive society, before the collapse of materialism.

Even the functional anteriority of the hormonal system was not understood in the twentieth century. It would take a long time for this new knowledge to penetrate the collective consciousness.

He sensed that this exchange of views was going to be a huge opening to Knowledge for him.

We had to get away from all these Judeo-Cartesian pseudo-philosophies that could only engender the nothingness of the rationalist intellect.

Synthetic intelligence and intuition had deserted man under the influence of the absolute dictatorship of a ruthless intellect given over to its exclusivity. Logically, all it had produced was materialistic stupidity and its derisory pride, leading to the suicide of bodies, souls and the planet.

The Doctor resembled Montaigne, and above all General Chiang Kai-Shek. Tristan remembered the nationalist general who, with the help of General MacArthur, was ready to prevent the advent of Mao Tse Tung and communism in China. Success was certain, but the "American" government prevented Mac Arthur from joining forces with Chiang Kai Shek and was recalled to the USA, while the nationalist general was relegated to Formosa... It is *certain* that Mac Arthur's intervention would have prevented the advent of communism in China: who *made* Chinese communism?

The scientist told Tristan that he had been a pre-Mongolian but that thanks to his understanding of hormonal man, he had managed to escape from this state. He had also succeeded time and again in turning small Mongolians into small shopkeepers and employees and giving them a physical appearance that bore only traces of Mongoloidism. When, years later, these ex-Mongolians went to see the doctor who had diagnosed their Mongolism, the latter, without exception, preferred to accuse themselves of a misdiagnosis rather than acknowledge Dr Gautier's therapeutic effectiveness.

Doctor Gautier still had an Asian vestige in his home, one that had already been mentioned, since it resembled Chiang Kai Chek.

A long, fascinating dialogue, unique in the world, was to be established between them.

— My dear Tristan, you are unusually sensitive, emotional and sentimental. You are more or less capable of understanding everything, if only by intuition. So there's nothing to stand in the way of a sort of clarification of all the general and personal problems that preoccupy and overwhelm you. First, let's talk about your marriage to the woman you call 'doe'. It's very difficult for you to adapt to your wife, let alone for her to adapt to you. Not only is she a thyroid type, but she has a mild pathological hyper-thyroid tendency. This means that it's impossible for the two of you to live together. She needs a calm, unproblematic pituitary, without an overflowing intellectual and emotional life like yours. His pathological hyperthyroid tendency is as obvious to me from a simple photograph, without any laboratory tests, as your grandmother's purplish lips, which I don't know, are to me.

Tristan was stunned.

— How can you know all this?

— It's quite simple. Your grandmother belongs to a specific type of thyroid that often appears in the sect of those circumcised on the 8th day due to a hormonal imbalance brought about by male circumcision on the 8th day . We'll talk more about this later. This detail is peculiar to him from a certain age and I can tell you that your mother, who also belongs to this type, will have these lips if she lives to a ripe old age. I might add that they both have circulation problems in their legs and a tendency to palpitations.

Tristan's curiosity was whetted by his native impatience. Chaos was rushing through his mind, a universe of questions to be asked, but the doctor continued.

—   There's a hormonal inevitability between you and your wife that there's not much you can do about, especially in the conditions we live in today. You'll have to separate before you're forced to take months off work or fall seriously ill, particularly in the case of the two of you with thyroid or lung disease.

—   But I love my wife!

—   I'm convinced of it, and even beyond measure. I'm going to help you through this difficult ordeal, first of all by explaining. We're going to take a look at humanity and try to understand what no one has yet grasped. I know that your heart rate is accelerating because your thyroid is excited by the new, oppositional aspect of everything I am explaining to you. So I'm going to explain to you some new conceptions that affect man and that nobody will understand at the moment apart from a few higher type thyroids and "interstitials". It is true these two categories of beings have practically disappeared.

—   Some mad people can't understand what "thyroid fulgurations" mean, because it's obvious that overactive thyroids are found in overactive mad people.

—   What you say is true and well observed and understood. They can sometimes understand many things, but they can't take advantage of them. The chaos of their minds is not constructive. What's more, they will tend to distort the realities we are going to expose in order to satisfy their instincts, their idiosyncrasies, their hobbies, their interests, their madness. They cannot achieve AbSTRACTION independently of their ideas, their personal feelings, their conditioning and their preferences. The genius, on the other hand, has access to the truth even if it is subjectively very unpleasant. He takes no account of his preferences, and observes only the facts and deeply considered arguments. The madman can do none of this. To understand all this, we need a minimum of thyroid and interstitial hormonal substratum.

— What is interstitial?

Tristan was drinking.

— It is a glandular part that forms part of the gonads in men and the ovaries in women. It is the counterpart to the "reproductive genitalia". The "interstitial" and "reproductive" genitalia make up the genital gland. The interstitial or "internal genital" gland is atrophied in people with dementia. This, of course, is the constant sign of madness in a normally constituted being. (Because an aberrant mental state is natural in congenitally malformed beings, such as microcephalics, anencephalics, etc.) Doesn't this suggest anything to you?

— Of course it is. The interstitial must be the gland of mental health, of moral sense, of courage, of superior intellectual capacities such as the notion of identity and synthesis - all possibilities forbidden to the insane. It is all this, together with willpower, that constitutes the true intelligence that is lacking in mad people. In popular parlance, a man without courage is said to have no testicles. Popular observation has discovered, through age-old observation, the internal genital gland without knowing it.

— The 'interstitial' is therefore a man gifted with an interstitial power that gives him mastery over his thoughts and actions.

— This gland is probably underdeveloped at present.

— No, it is meagre in today's humanity and is diminishing more and more as a result of the general conditions of modern life: hectic agitation, chemification of the soil, of food, of therapeutics, systematic vaccinations,[46] all things that are an assassination of this fundamental gland. This gland is that of human purpose. You see, Tristan, the fundamental basis of these new discoveries is that we are functionally

---

[46] Twenty or so injections of putrid products into the body containing dangerous metals such as aluminium. Vaccination causes cancer, cardiovascular disease and mental illness... In 2000, for example, vaccination against hepatitis B caused multiple sclerosis and ankylosing spondylitis...

directed by our hormonal system and not by our nervous system as the majority of doctors still believe.[47] everything in our being is affected by both the mind and the body through the hormonal system. This is why age-old techniques such as breathing, or controlled breathing, ensure that the hormonal system is perfectly controlled, making psychosomatic illnesses impossible.

I'm well aware of the importance of the hormonal system when I see the importance of the thyroid in all my reactions.

— It's natural for you to access this data directly, but there's plenty of other evidence available.

— Which ones?

— For example, certain insects whose heads have been cut off can continue their courtship! If all the nerves leading to a dog's sexual organs are cut off, this does not abolish the rut or the normal procreation of these organs. Resection of the entire sympathetic system in no way alters the vital signs, emotions or sexual activities of a dog operated on in this way. But the removal of just one of the four organic endocrine systems prevents the appearance of the sexual instinct in this animal and leads to the degeneration of the reproductive organs.

— All this has been perfectly obvious to me for a long time. I don't even understand the need for these demonstrations! If the endocrines, as Carrel said in 1937, give us our physical and mental characteristics, it is obvious that the hormonal system directs us functionally. *Our nervous system only makes us act according to what we are hormonally. It is therefore clear that our hormonal system directs our nervous system.*

— This reasoning is elementary for you, but you know enough about "agrégés" and "internes" to know that it's not at all obvious to them. We'll see later *why they can't understand.* We have four organic endocrines *adrenal, pituitary, thyroid and genital.* Each of these, when is physiologically overactive and the others are in a normal state, determines one of the four human prototypes. If you want a symbolic image, the adrenal will be a wrestler in a ring, or Stalin, the materialist type, the least evolved. His appearance is reminiscent of the orang-utan, with its mimics

---

[47] Many homeopaths and naturopaths have perfectly understood this functional anteriority.

and gestures. Everyone remembers Khrushchev tapping his desk with his shoe at a UN meeting. A large peasant from the Upper Nile is a perfect representative of the pituitary type, and General de Gaulle is a predominantly pituitary type. You represent the thyroid type perfectly, as do Chopin, Goethe, Chateaubriand and so on. A great saint would be an interstitial thyroid, you "dandy" are a less interstitial thyroid which makes you susceptible to passion. You have interstitial thyroid because otherwise you wouldn't be concerned with truth, synthesis and beauty. But it affects your brain more than your body. You can also understand Camus' phrase, "dandyism is a degraded form of asceticism". In other words, you could say that the dandy is a kind of degenerate saint, which is perfectly confirmed by endocrinology. It is not impossible for a thyroid patient to become an ascetic, as he would be in a traditional, non-pathogenic society like ours. The dandy becomes an ascetic even in our society, at least in recent centuries, because La Fontaine, a dandy before his time, and Liszt, became ascetics when they came of age. La Fontaine wore silica and Liszt became Canon Liszt. So did François d'Assises. All three were libertines. When the thyroid was tired with age, the interstitial took over, hence this evolution towards the spiritual qualities of the interstitial. Unfortunately, you're not there yet. Every charming woman puts your thyroid into a trance and exerts a kind of fatal fascination on you. All you need to cure this is vegetarian food, controlled breathing and active prayer, .e. not begging. Thyroid exacerbation leads to great use of the reproductive genitalia, which in turn reduces the activity of the internal genitalia. I'm going to tell you about a surprising phenomenon: primitive man was adrenal, he was the big brute. The one that followed was that of the Cro Magnon man, the cave artist, he was thyroid. Today's humanity is hypophyseal, analytical and ideological. But it turns out that baby man is adrenal, which enables him to hold his little arm up at right angles for three quarters of an hour, something we couldn't do. After puberty, of which there are three (and not just the second, which everyone knows and calls "puberty"), he becomes thyroid, chirps, talks, acts like a little poet and creates neologisms. Then, around the age of 18, the age of final puberty, they become interstitial, i.e. in full possession of their free will. You can understand, by the way, the need for a rigorous education to develop the interstitial and create the kind of tutors who, by acquiring the right automatisms, will help to strengthen it.

— If I understand correctly, humanity is evolving in exactly the same way as a child, and if we compare them, we would be close to our

18th birthday, our last puberty. This is what astrologers call the Age of Aquarius.

— Yes, the end of pituitary humanity is near. After our suicide, we are going to reach our last puberty: humanity will have come of age, it will have completed its eighteenth year.

— That much is clear.

— For you, Tristan, but not for a hypophysiologist who has lost all sense of the sacred, of authentic religion, of beauty, of synthesis - in a word, all the essential components of the mind that enable us to understand at this level of thought. The analytical intellect, which is the only thing to do in a suicidal officialdom, only allows us to adhere to suicidal mirages. Yet elementary analytical observation shows that science is suicidal. And yet the scientists of the time continue to be the playthings of inventive frenzy. What do you expect the pituitary glands to understand when they come up with such horrors as the Eiffel Tower, the Pompidou Centre, synthetic chemistry as a principle of health, vaccinations, and take Freud and Marx for geniuses?

Tristan remained dreamy. The doctor continued:

— You are Tristan, the direct descendant of this ancestor of the Cro-Magnon. He was tall, catlike, muscular and coquettish. He adorned his body with animal skins, colours and tattoos. He was a sorcerer and a poet He was already a visionary and a poet because of his thyroid power. It is from him that man derives the extension and breadth of his astonishing vocabulary. The Romantic period provides us with the most representative examples of this type: Chopin, Musset, Liszt, Chateaubriand, Weber, Lamartine, Disraeli, Goethe... They have that long, lanky appearance, the ovoid head, the wide-open, highly expressive and mobile eyes. Remember that pathological hyperthyroid patients have exophthalmic eyes. Their physiognomy is racy, their mobile features faithfully convey their impressions, their feelings. Their language is easy, sometimes sophisticated, and they instinctively know how to flatter. They are sentimental hermaphrodites. They are indeed men, but with something of femininity in their gestures, the gentleness of their gaze and expression. They are often more feminine than women themselves when it comes to feelings, because they are not capable of any of the meanness or pettiness that characterises female psychology. Their sensitivity is sharp and acute, and they feel the slightest sensation, the slightest injury. Even the slightest sensation makes them turn in on themselves like the slightest opposing force. They are swept along by their feelings like a torrent whose waves break on a rock and turn white with foam. Humans don't understand them, which doesn't make their marital status any easier. We don't understand humans either. We feel them, we know them, but we can't understand them because they are so far removed from our mentality. I can even say that the more we get to know them, the less we understand them. They seem to us heartless, insignificant, futile, derisory and more often than not interested in the uninteresting. This is even truer in our age of generalised stupidity and ugliness, which stupefies them. Why are we so sensitive to pain?

Well, in general, as was not the case with the strongly adrenal Goethe, they have physiologically weak adrenals. Your extremely fine hand, which chirologists call the 'psychic hand', is the antithesis of the adrenalist's big materialistic paw. The adrenals give you masculine characteristics: a relative insensitivity to pain that enables you to fight, and muscular strength that serves the same purpose. It confers a brutality that encourages the female to be forced and coerced. But whereas the adrenalian experiences pleasure bordering on masochism when subjected to pain, the thyroid dandy suffers and complains about it. He only enjoys pain because it excites his thyroid, in other words his intelligence and imagination. A thyroid with weak adrenals determines the anguish that Kierkegaard, a thyroid man, called "the thorn in the flesh".

— So that's how you explain the essential aspect of my marriage to biche?

— Yes, because you didn't just marry her because she was beautiful. It's true that she fulfilled a long-held visualisation in your mind , because it's normal for a tall, blond, slim thyroid man to fall in love with a thyroid woman of a similar type, but she provoked a passionate state of love. So what happened? A favourable psychological arousal caused thyroid arousal, the resulting secretion acted on your sexuality and the state of arousal of the latter acted on the same gland, which in turn acted on the cerebrum to produce erotic imaginative representations. The latter tended to increase sexual excitement, which once again had an impact on your thyroid: *hence this vicious functional circle*, becoming a vital element in the maintenance of oxidation, i.e. of life. So in the dandy, there is a physiological thyroid search for pain, which seems paradoxical, but which can be explained very well if we know the various functions involved. This tendency towards sadness is flagrant in Chopin's music. The polonaise in C flat is almost mournful, not a joyful dance or a dazzling march as the harmony and rhythm would seem to desire. It is certain that this functional state of excessive sensitivity, which in the ordinary, normal being transforms visual and auditory sensations into joy, is metamorphosed in the romantic dandy into a sensation which, up to a certain limit or intensity, brings joy, and beyond that a painful and then painful impression. As the Romantic seeks violent sensations to invigorate a thyroid that tires quickly because it is poorly supported by the adrenals and internal genitalia, he ends up in almost all circumstances, either by intensity or duration, with fatigue, sorrow and pain. In a traditional civilisation, vegetarianism, spiritual education and breathing would have spared him this state. He would belong to the class of priests and ruling clerics. Let's not forget that the thyroid is the gland of sexuality, which means that what doesn't come out the top comes out the bottom! Thyroid hormones are used either for high intellectuality or for sexuality. Depending on the sociological context in which he finds himself, the thyroid will basically be either highly intellectual or erotic. So the romantic evolves, undulates, varies from pleasure to pain, with the same kind of sensations, colours, music, feelings, reproductive enjoyment. He moves continually from a feeling of pleasure to a feeling of pain, in other words from the activity of his thyroid to its insufficiency. Since thyroid activity brings joy, its insufficiency brings sadness, anguish and disease, because it is important to know that it is not microbes that cause disease *but their pathogenic forms in an unhealthy environment.*[48]

It's worth noting in passing that, in addition to the numerous psychosomatic illnesses, there is the ingestion of molecules which are not specific to the human bio-type. In other words, we eat what does not suit our body. This is fundamentally pathogenic. The healing of cancers by a return to raw food and to the true instinct that returns after a few days of raw food ingestion is now a well-known phenomenon. If microbes were the cause of disease, the billions of Kock's bacilli in the Paris metro, for example, *would turn all Parisians into tuberculosis sufferers, but this is not the case.*

---

[48] Let's not forget that Pasteur died saying: "Claude Bernard is right, the microbe is nothing, the field is everything".

Such, then, is the sensitivity of the romantic dandy, exaggerated because any sensation causes him to suffer the slightest force that weighs on him, because he adapts badly. When a force acts on our being, we have to deal with it by means of the hormonal secretion that responds to it. If the force is powerful, it is the adrenals that intervene, resulting in a certain insensitivity that enables the subject to withstand violent noise, intense lighting or a heavy weight. When the force is less perceptible, such as an object that is poorly lit or located in the shade, it is the thyroid gland that must intervene to give the eye more acuity and the hearing more finesse. If a force acts for too long, the pituitary gland intervenes to provide the desired resistance. You can understand the pituitary predominance necessary for candidates in official competitive examinations such as the agrégation or internship in medicine. If danger threatens, the internal genitalia will step in to provide courage and willpower. These examples of adaptation could be multiplied ad infinitum, as they exist for every conceivable case in life.

The romantic artist does not use each of his secretions to oppose the various opposing forces. He always uses his thyroid, which becomes his all-purpose secretion. In such circumstances, suffering activates his thyroid, making him intelligent and creative. But if the suffering or opposition lasts too long, his state of physiological hyperthyroidism becomes pathological: he may go mad or commit suicide. *It's important to remember that madness is a state of hyperthyroidism*, just as neurasthenia is a state of hypothyroidism. This cannot be verified in the laboratory, hence the inability of analytical minds to realise these truths.

His egocentricity, his egotism due to his lack of adaptation and his great sensitivity, mean that he loves flattery, he loves to become a star, to distinguish himself by his artistic talents, his loquaciousness, his mimetic power or sentimental reproduction. He has an inclination for the theatre, because he is an incomparable actor. He is also an orator, a lecturer, a preacher, a great politician (absolutely not a "politician", because he cannot fit in with the amorphous herds and the nullity of regimented political parties), he has the right voice, the speed of elocution. The voice emanates not from the nervous system but from the glandular system. Anencephalics, who don't even have a protuberance, express themselves not only by gestures and emotion, but also by chirping. The voice therefore comes from the thyroid. This is why the thyroid is a good talker as soon as it feels surrounded by intelligent understanding and sympathy.

Because they are struck by the way things look, they use colourful language. Because they experience feelings to the point of suffering, they are poets first and foremost.

He has a gift for expressing his feelings in words and images. Thyroid only, he will be a more or less decadent impressionist poet. Interstitial, he tended towards classicism, i.e. painting characters common to all human beings: La Fontaine, a romantic dandy before his time, was one of these.

If you have an active reproductive genitalia, you have Alfred de Musset, and if you have a deficient interstitial genitalia, you have Oscar Wilde and his homosexuality.

Thyroid people are also excellent musicians, composers, pianists and violinists. They are intelligent, quick-witted, and understand texts and people halfway. He is an astonishing being, destined to suffer. You know that many thyroid sufferers have died of tuberculosis: Chopin, Lamartine, Keats, Schiller and others.

In fact, for thyroid sufferers, a cold or heartache can allow tuberculosis to take hold. If a chronic temperature occurs and persists, the thyroid will struggle. You have to support it, and that's what I did when you wrote to me that the doctors referred to you as having a "physiological fever", which indicates a mild state of hyperthyroidism that cannot be measured.

The disease can progress in flare-ups. When the thyroid has resources, it becomes angry, irritated and fights back with fever. In this way, the pathogenic microbes adopt a form of resistance. They remain relatively non-virulent as long as the thyroid is capable of resuming its efforts. But if a new cause weakens it, the pathogenic microbes multiply. The thyroid may still be able to fight them off, but if it becomes tired and exhausted, the infection kills the patient. This is how Keats died at the age of twenty-five, consumed by heartbreak, alas for a woman who was hardly worth the trouble. This drama is typical of our morphotype. Very pretty but mentally inadequate women are the fatal trap of the thyroid.

— Which brings me to the question of thyroid Don Juanism.

— Well, the thyroid is the gland that most frequently causes abnormalities in male sexual pleasure and desire. Thyroid sufferers have a powerful thyroid gland that is never satisfied with a normal sexual act. It tires quickly because we know that it is an endocrine gland that is stimulated by original, novel, irregular, variable and changing sensations.

It is sensations such as these that most easily activate the thyroid in life, in intellectual activity, and in everything to do with sexuality, giving a very vivid impression of pleasure and satisfaction. On the other hand, in the case of sensations which are always the same, of the same intensity, of an equal, known course, this endocrine becomes insufficient, reducing the subject to disgust, apathy, torpor which can, in the least evolved cases, lead him to drugs or alcohol. Thus it is difficult for them to perform the sexual act in a monotonous way because habit leads to a kind of impotence, a hypothyroidal chagrin depression, whereas a new woman, in appearance, manners, conversation, lifestyle restores the virility of the thyroid man by exciting his thyroid. This is what happened with your love affair with doe. On the one hand, your imaginative thyroid physiologically prevented you from having regular, ordinary conjugal relations and, on the other, your highly developed sentimental physiological functions had repercussions on your interstitial, leaving you in possession of a great moral sense, cancelled out by your passion. The encounter with biche resulted in a very sentimental, passionate state of love. We've talked about the physiological process, the functional vicious circle which, if you had lost doe, could have led to shock, hypothyroidism, suicide, madness and bronchopulmonary disease. *Passion is the insufficiency of the internal genitalia, dominated by an over-active thyroid. The thyroid, it should be noted, is the gland of temptation.* A violent conflict has therefore arisen within you between your passionate love and your love for your children, which doe didn't care about.

Isn't it metaphysically fascinating to note that this suffering has made you think, has led you to consider fundamental problems that concern all men. You have meditated on the hormonal man, totally unknown to officialdom, which has only taken analytical measurements of hormonal secretions and made purely empirical observations. A bubble of sorrow has bubbled up inside you with a fierce desire to transcend these painful ordeals.

— What do you think of my doe thyroid in terms of hormonal characterology?

— No doubt there's some doe in your wife, but your symbol is much more an illusion than reality. This kind of illusion about women is typical of the thyroid. She's much more like a cat that becomes cruel under the influence of the adrenals, or like certain high-legged felines such as the cougar or the jaguar. You noticed that she had a very pronounced thumb joint and that her feet and hands were slightly out of proportion with the rest of her body. The same disproportion can be seen in the cougar in relation to a supple, elongated body. She didn't have much heart for you or your children. She's a thyroid patient with interstitial insufficiency, and she doesn't have many feelings outside the narrow confines of her own person. I can assure you that once you're separated, she'll have nothing more to do with you. She's a *physical* thyroid, *not a sentimental* one like you. She has the ability to dance, the lightness, the suppleness, the automatisms. This is the type of Slavic dancer. There are three types of dancer: the graceful thyroid, a classical dancer, the hypophyseal, an American acrobatic dancer, and the genital, a Spanish dancer.

- Tell me about the concept of genius in terms of endocrinology.

— The genial man must possess a powerful internal or interstitial genitalia which has been the functional work of the adrenals, thyroid and pituitary glands all at once. It has the extraordinary property of provoking the activity of these three glands according to its will, because in physiology all phenomena are reversible. He is therefore strongly thyroid, artistic, sensitive, altruistic and sentimental. Thanks to the adrenals, he puts his strength and power at the service of his goodness. He is also objective and practical, because he considers phenomena as they are and not according to the whims of his personal preferences, or those of his clan or his party: he is never afraid of the truth. He is also hypophytic and analytical, making him a complete thinker. He is always a philosopher, i.e. capable of considering human problems without bias and with complete impartiality. There are no geniuses in the official world. There are only mediocre people concerned with their own immediate interests who don't even see that they are committing suicide by obeying the dictates of their all-powerful financial masters. This is why physical and moral pollution, famine, world and local wars and permanent revolutions are the end of humanity. The saint, the genius, the dandy are all thyroids with different interstitial powers. But it is not impossible for a dandy to become a genius. It depends on the discipline imposed on the interstitial by diet, breathing, spiritual work and prayer in particular.

— To conclude on this subject and to show you that I have understood you correctly, I will make two remarks: first of all, normal man is only free within a hormonal determinism. A grocer whose hormonal system is in balance will have the freedom to be a good grocer. The same goes for an artist, an intellectual, a craftsman. But it seems to me that the people of the modern world, rotten pots of hormonal, nervous and neurovegetative imbalances, are practically doomed to the absolute determinism of consumer-voters. This is obviously due to the fact that neither secularism, chemification nor systematic vaccination can develop the interstitial. As for the thyroid, I would like to translate the Camusian formula into endocrinology: "*The dandy, when he does not kill himself or go mad, makes a career and poses for posterity*". So I'll say this: "If the physiological hyper-thyroid of the superior type does not kill himself in a phase of hyper- or hypo-thyroidism, or if under the effect of too much intense suffering he does not sink into madness (frustrated forms of erotic, megalomaniac or paranoid madness) he finds in the realisation of his purpose as an artist a physiological equilibrium that makes his life possible, but more often than not it is short and painful because of the exaggerated expenditure of vital energy, his great sensitivity determined by his congenital and accentuated hyperthyroidism, the weakness of his adrenal glands, and the insufficiency of the interstitial gland which is hypotrophied by pain, the difficulties of life, sexual excesses and the lack of adaptation to circumstances.

- You've understood perfectly![49]

---

[49] This fascinating subject was dealt with in a doctorate at the Sorbonne, June 1971 under the title "*Psychophysiological study of romantic dandies* (or dandyism, physiological hyperthyroidism)". The jury was chaired by Dean Raymond Las Vergnas, and the thesis supervisor was Professor Albeaux Fernet, a well-known endocrinologist who introduced to France the famous Hans Selye, who gave us the word "stress".

Chapter XVII

> *"They never have that modest attention proper to true intelligence"* (Simone Weil)

Tristan's skull remained in such a state of effervescence that he had difficulty in expressing in a logical filament the whole synthetic globe of chaos that inhabited him. What he wanted was to understand everything he was feeling so perfectly.

—   Tristan began:

—   For years I have believed that the only common denominator that can account for Jewish particularism in time and space is circumcision on the 8th day.

You were perfectly right, that is the one and only real cause of their brilliantly speculative and parasitic particularism. But first I'm going to try your patience, because a preamble is in order. You will have noticed without difficulty that the modern world is radically deprived of geniuses because there is no working spirit of synthesis in officialdom. It would be obliged to do exactly the opposite of everything that is being done in every field. The genius would work for a qualitative and biological world. As a result, not only can no problem be solved, but they can only become radically insoluble, culminating in all forms of pollution and a third world war. The asylums are filling up with mad people, and there will be less and less space to accommodate them, especially as madness will become normative. Lucid lunatics, criminals and idiots will become writers and composers of regressive, pathogenic and criminogenic music. States are run by unbalanced people, because only primitives or graduate fools, guided by finance and Marxism, are at the visible head of states. Man is subjected to an atrocious slavery worse than that of antiquity.

—   Yes, that's indisputable.

The doctor stood up and went to a drawer, from which he took out two photographs. He handed one to Tristan:

— What do you think this is?

Tristan had been watching.

— A Negro, isn't he? But what's that got to do with the Jews who run the world and who are currently of interest to us?

— Be patient, I know you're not, but I told you I had to give you an important preamble. Well, no, he's not a nigger: he's an acromegalic after ten years of the disease. Acromegaly is a disease of the hyper-functioning pituitary gland.

The doctor showed Tristan more photographs of the patient, taken over the 10 years the disease had been progressing. The man had taken on an increasingly negroid appearance, eventually taking on the perfect appearance of a negro. The phenomenon was even more obvious in a black and white photograph.

— What do you conclude?

— It's simple, I'd say the Negro is a normal acromegalic.

— Very well understood, but badly expressed. We would say that the negro is a pituitary with acromegalic manifestations.

— I understand perfectly well and I had understood that a negro can never be a thyroid like Pericles, Chopin, Goethe, Lamartine or Chateaubriand.

— It is in fact hormonally impossible, especially near the equator. Only the Indians can have this type because their civilisation was able to produce interstitial thyroids capable of levitation. Not only can't a thyroid be born near the equator, but as an adult it couldn't live there and would die very quickly. The thyroid can only live in temperate or cold countries, without exaggeration.

— But a Negro can make a good academic specialist, an honest novelist or a jazz pianist.

— No doubt, but never a Chopin, a Pericles or a Carrel.

— It's all perfectly clear and obvious to me.

— For you, but don't think it's obvious to the pituitary gland patient we'll talk about later. Nor do you think that all this is about to penetrate the collective consciousness. It will take centuries.

The doctor produced another photograph. It showed an idiot with a protruding belly. He was in profile, with a low forehead and thick lips. He was a pathological hypo-thyroid. The doctor then took another photo and showed it to Tristan. It was very similar to the other one in its overall appearance.

— Do you know who the person in this second photo is?

— No ?

— He is a Pygmy.

— Oh, the psychological resemblance is visible in the photo: see how they both hold their left arm stupidly bent with their hand hanging down. But these two photos, so similar, were taken years apart and have nothing in common.

These new facts, so striking, forced Tristan into a moment of meditative silence, as he felt his mental effervescence grow with this realisation, the seeds of which were already within him.

— Do you know what to call the intellectual elaboration that you have just practised so naturally and without which there can be no true knowledge? It's the notion of identity. This elaboration, like synthesis, is radically excluded official intellectualism. As for those who would be capable of practising them, they are excluded by the aberrant system of technocratic competitions, which also have a pathogenic effect on the mind. These competitions leave only the analytical and the mnemonic, and are therefore veritable brainwashes. Analysis and memory are essential, of course, but they are in no way the criteria for superior intellectuality. In conclusion, the qualities of the truly elite are totally absent from officialdom.

— Obvious! But where is the question of those circumcised on the 8th day in all this?

— I'm sure you can sense that, but just wait a little longer. I'm going to tell you a symbolic anecdote that will make you understand the inevitability of our times. I receive many people here, doctors, lawyers, professors, Jews or Goyim. My office is a mess, a necessary scattering. Look on the mantelpiece.

Tristan walked over to the hearth and saw a book on Kierkegaard on the marble, with a band in red letters: "Does humanism belong to priests, saints, madmen, philosophers or dandies? This clever and comical phrase was a kind of blow to Tristan's heart. It posed an original question, both in form and substance.

On the book was a stone pistol from the fifteenth century perhaps, but he barely saw it and pushed it away with his hand to better reread the shocking question.

The doctor remained silent and continued:

- This sentence struck you, the gun was a shadow for you. Well, when I receive a circumcised person on the 8th day, even if he's just a tailor, he does what you do. The other humans, teachers, doctors even, without exception, take the gun, fiddle with it, examine it, while the sentence in red suggests nothing to them. So you see, the circumcised man thinks. Whether he thinks rightly or wrongly is not really the point. But he thinks. You see, between any synthesis, any truth and the masses, the Jew puts a "gun", an easy, insignificant little thing to capture the attention of the masses and make money on human stupidity. Think of current music, football, publishing, the press, television and radio. The official demagogic dialectic is getting down to the level of the increasingly degraded masses. The masses follow, and since the Second World War, which was radically economic, they have been rushing towards every kind of degradation and butchery. And the masses are everyone except the saints, the true geniuses, the true artists and the Jews. Only the latter have had official power since the revolution of 1789. Even the Reverend Fathers, converted Jews, cannot escape this fate. A famous Jewish father, with whom I recently had a conversation, told me that circumcision did not explain the Jews - even though he knows nothing about endocrinology, which I specialise in - that history was enough to explain them, which is absurd because the ghettos are only a few centuries old. In fact, they were at their best in many pre-Christian civilisations where anti-Semitism (or anti-Jewishness, to be more accurate) was rife. In fact, wherever they have settled, at all times in different countries and languages. He also told me that Freemasonry was a myth, which makes even the average mason laugh, and that there have never been as many great artists as in our time, that Carrel was a shallow and narrow-minded person and Simone Weil a pathological case! In other words, the Reverend Father was just repeating what any socialist-communist zombie could have told me. He is therefore incapable of listening to a specialist who has been working on endocrinology for forty years, of understanding Carrel and Simone Weil. All this with aplomb, pretentiousness and unbelievable arrogance. Simone Weil summed up this aspect of the Jewish mentality very well: "They never have that modest attention proper to true intelligence". You can see that, with these new Fathers, the Church is sinking into Marxism, into the defence of human rights that are flouted everywhere, and which are in fact only valid to protect Jewish hegemony. Despite the famous encyclicals that radically condemned liberalism and Marxism, both of which were "intrinsically perverse", the latter only existing because of the former.

We can now get down to the nitty-gritty of the most daunting of all subjects.

We know that races do not exist, only ethnic groups, which are the result of hormonal adaptation to a fixed environment for around 10 centuries. It is quite clear that it is not geographical location, nutrition or climate that can explain the Jews, who have never stayed in a fixed place for a thousand years like the Negro, the Eskimo or the Pygmy. They only stayed in Palestine for a very short time and spread throughout the world. Moreover, they take on the characteristics of the countries in which they have lived for a long time: a short, stocky Jew from South America does not resemble a tall, blond, blue-eyed Jew from Poland. They have only two aspects in common: features that are often caricatured and the object of age-old derision and, for many of them, unparalleled mnemonic and speculative skills. This is what enables them to develop the major crimes of liberalism, Marxism, Freudianism and hydrogen and neutron atomic bombs. Neither education nor Kocher food can confer such implacable particularism. The English, for example, are predominantly hypophytic: "Wait and see[50]is the formula par excellence for their empiricism. The Germans have an adrenal tendency which gives them a gregarious mentality, like the ancient Assyrians who wore the same boots as them, practised the same fifth column system and also had an aggressive tendency and tanks. In short,

---

[50] Wait and see.

Jews, whether practising or atheist, all subjected to circumcision, have been spread across the globe for thousands of years. How can a common denominator be found to account for their particularism, since no geographical location, climate or nutrition specific to that climate can account for it? Much has been said about their religious training, but this plays no role among upper middle-class Jews, who only go to Synagogue for reasons of convenience. *Circumcision on the 8th day is the only common denominator that can account for this particularism.*

This particularity is easy to define and to observe in the year 2000:

Caricatured physical traits, such as Mendès France, Raymond Aron, Serge Gainsbourg, Soros, Hamer etc. and enormous speculative possibilities to the detriment of moral sense and the spirit of synthesis.

Even materialistic science has discovered that there is an important biological moment, the first puberty, starting on the 8th day, 21 days after birth. Considerable upheaval occurs during this period.[51] Circumcision disrupts these upheavals in such a fragile little being as a newborn baby.

This practice of circumcision on the first day of puberty confers a speculative particularism that humans are incapable of conceptualising.

Circumcision is a very old practice. It was practised by the Egyptians in pre-Pharaonic times and by the Sumerians in the Tigris-Euphrates delta. The Egyptians knew about the glandular properties of the thyroid gland. They symbolised it in its anatomical location by a sun, which meant that they knew *it was the gland of life and intelligence.* They performed circumcision on the 5th day, i.e. three days before the onset of puberty. This allowed healing to take place, making the trauma inflicted on the interstitial gland, which was not yet awake, less brutal.

They did this to create a moral and intellectual elite.

But this circumcision was totally different in its effects from Jewish circumcision. The Pharaohs were baptised with water and circumcised on the 5th day after birth. They were fed wheat germ palm oil containing vitamin E (remember the importance of nutrition in bees to form their queen) and practised incestuous consanguinity to offset the disadvantages of this circumcision. In all other cases, incestuous consanguinity should be

---

[51] See my *"Secret Files of the 20th Century"*, the first part of which is devoted to Jewish circumcision.

avoided because of its serious pathogenic and degenerative effects. They received a rigorous intellectual, physical, moral and spiritual education under the aegis of the priests of Horus. For thousands of years, they succeeded one another on the Egyptian throne. Coming from a small number of families, their longevity was assured, as was their ability to reproduce. They were highly intelligent, as were the members of the priestly caste who were circumcised under the same conditions. It was their great intellectual superiority that led, among other things, to *the discovery of phonetic writing.*

Moses, an Egyptian initiate, knew much less about the glandular question than the priests of Horus. He resolved to make his people superior to all others by systematising the circumcision already prescribed by Abraham. This is why it is written in the Bible that circumcision "symbolises a pact with God and that Israel will be the people who reign on the earth".[52]

A professor of the Hebrew Bible recently told me that the prescription of circumcision is not to be found in any of the major texts of Moses, and that the term "chosen people" is a misnomer in Hebrew, the true meaning being "model people" of wisdom and virtue. All this is dubious, because why would they practise it and why this psychosis of megalomaniac superiority? Who could tell us that Rothschild, Hammer, Marx, Freud, Picasso, Oppenheimer, Field, S.T. Cohen Flato- Sharon, Djérassi, Meyer Lanski, Tordjman,[53] Bénézareff,[54] Kaganovitch,[55] Jejoff, Badinter,[56] Kouchner, Lang,[57] etc are models of wisdom and virtue?

Jewish circumcision was therefore very different from Pharaonic circumcision, and the results were also very different. As a result, the Jews

---

[52] I read in the commentaries on the Torah: "Do not try to understand the problem of circumcision, it is beyond human understanding".

[53] A rotten psychoanalyst who tells us that if we don't find pornography normal it's because we're prisoners of some backward mental clichés.

[54] King of the pornographic film.

[55] Led the USSR with Stalin and was the head of the concentration camp system that exterminated tens of millions of Russians.

[56] Jewish jurist who introduced the death penalty for the innocent and abolished it for murderers. He also tells us that a good father must be a little homosexual and a little paedophile. His wife denies the maternal instinct.

[57] The latter two tell us that children have a right to sexual pleasure... Lang was Minister of Education: poor children!

were true caricatures of the Pharaohs. They were as analytical as the Pharaohs were synthetic.

The Jews therefore believe in their racial superiority (although races do not exist and they are not an ethnic group), and moral superiority, which does not exist. *This fact, known to all, proves that they are fundamentally racist, which is comical because they champion anti-racism everywhere for their own benefit, solely to serve their own hegemonic racism. It is incredible that the Goyim are willing to fall victim to the enormity of this deception. The Jewish question can in no way be included in the myth of anti-racism that they have created.*

This sexual mutilation on the 8th day was therefore not invented by Moses but exploited by him in ignorance of hormonal reality. *This sexual mutilation on the 1st day of puberty makes the adrenals, pituitary gland, thyroid and reproductive genitalia very active, but to the detriment of the internal genitalia. That's where the drama lies.*

At this point in life, the first puberty begins. All the glands need to be activated and brought into balance to give the child the means to adapt to its new existence. In fact 3 glands, adrenal, thyroid, pituitary, at the instigation of the pituitary gland must work together to awaken the interstitial. Unfortunately, circumcision, through the wound it causes, causes the hormones secreted to flow abundantly into the external sexual parts and diverts the secretion of the internal genitalia from its essential mission: *the glandular system and the encephalon.* By prematurely attaching themselves to the external genitalia at this time, the hormones give them a high level of activity.

But the natural function of genital secretion is to affect the whole economy and, more particularly, the nervous system, to confer intellectual and moral superiority on the being. It is therefore diverted from its purpose and cannot accomplish its mission.

Instead of perfecting moral and intellectual man, it will first make him a reproducer by focusing on the sexual organs. Then, as the internal genitalia are not very efficient, it lets the other organic endocrines run wild. This is why we find among them hypoadrenalists (in small numbers, because humanity today is far removed from the adrenal humanity), many thyroidists, and quantities of pituitary specialists (finance, physics, chemistry, specialised medicine, psychoanalysis, ideologies).

But, and this is the epicentre of the drama, as they are not guided by the internal genitalia, they are carried away by their speculations in a fatal manner.

Their speculations will therefore be located at the antipodes of the human.

They produce dismasted logicians (Marx), system dreamers (Freudian erotomania) and financiers (Rothschild, Warburg). They are intelligent and alert, in the banal sense of the word, but they are totally lacking in the spirit of synthesis and are never the intellectual or artistic creators who bring life to humanity. Their only "geniuses" are two mythomaniacs: Freud and Marx. These lucid madmen led to the eroticisation of the planet and the massacre of tens of millions of human beings.

Their impulse to enjoy life, their liveliness of mind, their speculative scientific and even pituitary medical tendencies make them seem to be ahead of human evolution, but they are stuck in a state of perfection and will not be able to keep up with humanity as it moves towards the interstitial. They are already fossils or mentally deranged, and their only means of maintaining their hegemony is the power of money and demagoguery. It has to be said that some advanced Jews do not approve of the behaviour of their fellow Jews but cannot say anything. Bergson warned the Jews of Germany against their own behaviour, urging them to change it if they did not want to see the emergence of a great wave of anti-Semitism (this term makes no sense at all, because a Polish Jew who has been living in Poland for centuries is in no way Semitic: it should be anti-Jewish).

Ten years after this admonition, Nazism appeared, also announced by Rabbi Reifer. Reifer took stock of the situation in an article published in 1933, the year Hitler came to power.

—   They will become more and more unhappy, preoccupied, anxious, and pay an increasingly heavy price for madness, as the American statistics prove. Their tragedy is the lack of altruism, of 'feeling' for others (it's not a question of 'sensitivity' because they have one that borders on paranoia). Jews are always thinking of themselves, their sect, their clan, their family. They see other human beings as opportunities to be exploited, which clearly explains four or five thousand years of anti-Jewishness. All their speculations only serve them, in the final analysis. When the Jew thinks of his clan, he thinks of himself. There is a certain difference between the Jew and the Jewess. The woman is generally gifted with more qualities and it can be said that the altruism of the woman is a fundamental cause of the survival of this sect. She is more honest and courageous. Of course, the thyroid Jewess like your mother and grandmother is different. She had no heart for you, or for your children for that matter. She lacks maternal feeling. This was the case with the famous actresses Rachel and Sarah Bernard, because their interstitial function was poor.

— Your mother has most of the faults of a woman: jealousy, a tendency to commit evil and to say it to humiliate and degrade, just like your grandmother, who is of the same type. She has the characteristics of both a woman and a thyroid Jewess, the former perhaps a little more than the latter.

If Moses is largely responsible for the practice of circumcision, he made this sect of preoccupied, anguished, glandular dysregulated people, among whom we find the vast majority of neurotics in psychoanalysis. *He inculcated in them the idea of world hegemony, which they have achieved through the disappearance of the providential elites brought about by the Jewish revolution of 1789, and through the mental inferiority of the majority of human beings.*

The latter are now dazed by secularism and all that it contains, i.e. chemification of the soil, food, medicine, alcohol, pathogenic and hypnotic music, drugs, systematic vaccination, football, television, in a word finance, Freudism, Marxism. The worst horrors have become normative, since people have been conditioned from childhood to extirpate from their minds intuition, a moral sense, a sense of the sacred, an aesthetic sense - in other words, all the components of a healthy mind. The Jews can now, with the complicity of the politicians and judges who depend on them, impose the worst horrors as long as they are disseminated by the media and officialdom. All critical sense having disappeared, they can freely manipulate the masses.

— But sooner or later they will find themselves up against other glandular derangements, the Chinese, who, humanly speaking, are close to them. The Chinese have been circumcising women for thousands of years, and this practice has both speculative and moral effects similar to circumcision. It is to be feared that we will then have to endure a war or our civilisation will perish. It should be noted in passing that the bank loans that have enabled the existence of the frightening Red Army are going to open up more and more towards China, which will be able to build up an even more formidable army with American help. It would not be surprising if the USA sold China the atomic bomb.[58]

— The Jews are hypermales, the Chinese hyperfeminines. The latter can live with each other, whereas the Jews cannot and are forced to be parasites. China is the only country where Jews have not been able to penetrate, except through Marxist ideology and the beginnings of liberalism, because the Chinese are also gifted at commerce and speculation. The Chinese thrifty, frugal and enemies of material enjoyment, whereas the Jew is a man who enjoys and spends for himself and for ostentation. The financier Oppenheimer spent a whopping 150 million old francs (1.5 million new francs) on one of his evenings in South Africa.

The latter, along with Warburg, Rockfeller, Hammer, Schiff, Loeb and many other Jewish financiers, manipulate the cobwebs of international organisations such as Bilderberg, the Trilateral Commission and the C.F.R., where politicians from all parties on the right and left (excluding nationalists, who are not represented in parliaments) are 'imprisoned' (voluntarily and in their own interests).

— But Muslims also practice circumcision?

— Yes, *but not on the first day of puberty*. Their circumcision therefore has no immediate international or cosmic repercussions. Above all, their circumcision (between the ages of 8 and 12) exacerbates their reproductive genitalia. This will make them a sexual people. The other endocrines are not stimulated, on the contrary, so they will never become speculative people like the Jews, nor will they become more or less interstitial thyroid people. *The only thing that could save humanity would be the radical abolition of circumcision on the 8th day.* It seems that this would not make much difference, because it is too late: the Marxist-liberal infernal machine is being launched unmanned at high speed down a runway. It will have to finish its Sisyphean race in a global cataclysm.

— Moreover, it seems doubtful to me that the Jews can be made to understand that this practice fixes them in materialism, rationalism and pure speculation, which also lead them to self-destruction. They are aware that they have achieved world hegemony, but they do not understand that

---

[58] This was mentioned on the television news. (TF1)

this is concomitant with the general destruction caused by their *'anti-transcendence'*.⁵⁹

— And the State of Israel?

— It fits perfectly into the programme of world destruction. What can be said is that the first immigrants were the least marked by Jewish circumcision. There were many courageous men, physically beautiful, without the remarkable stigma of Jewish faces that have been the object of derision for thousands of years. He was one of the interned Jews, many of whom died of typhus and starvation. They were among the million Jews that Hitler wanted to exchange for lorries, but they preferred the lorries to their fellow Jews, who would enable them to concoct the juicy blackmail of the Holocaust. The Jewish leaders will never go to Israel: they use Israel as a bridgehead to the Middle East for oil and raw materials.

— All this is obvious to me, because I have understood it and seen it every day for decades. I'd like to ask you another question: at the turn of the century, a Jew called Otto Weininger wrote: "We are in the age of the woman and the Jew". I was struck by this sentence because it sums up my observations on modern women. It is certain that women cannot be geniuses, synthetic minds endowed with a moral sense. It is impossible to imagine a woman who somatically resembles Pericles, Goethe or Carrel. Moreover, she has proved herself to be radically incompetent when it comes to genuine non-conformism. She is incapable of abstraction: if, for example, she loves a genius, she will support him for as long as she loves him. If she separates from him, she will have nothing left of the 'emotional' awareness she had of her partner and will throw the baby out with the bathwater. A man, on the other hand, can respect and admire his opponent. Instead of relying on the centuries-old mistreatment inflicted on her to reclaim her rights as a housewife and mother of balanced children, she rushes into a hysteria of equality with the humanoids of technocracy. She has even lost the elementary aesthetic sense that the instinct for pretty clothes gave her. She has become hideous in that uniform of international silliness, the Levis blue jeans. Women have certainly integrated 'freely', through progressive conditioning, into all the conformisms created by the Jews. M.L.F., men's clothing, the pathogenic pill, generally carcinogenic and teratogenic, self-service abortion. *None of*

---

⁵⁹ Materialistic humanity without God and without a synthetic elite.

us has enough personality to dress differently from some cretinous fashion, or to say "no", what I want is a wife, a mother with a husband worthy of the name. We are not equal to men, but complementary. Our natures are different. We want children brought up according to wisdom and eternal morality". She doesn't even have enough intelligence to claim her basic purpose. For forty years I've heard her express her enslavement with this international phrase in all its stupidity: "I don't want to be your maid". It sums up their vanity, their pride and their mental inadequacy.[60] Since women have no personality, which is normal, they have become stupid because men have dumbed them down. (The man who also swallowed the idiotic myth of "the liberation of women", who became "a free object" to make pornographic films). All the female women you will meet, as long as there are any, abhor the M.L.F.

— What do you think is the metaphysical role of the Jews?

— All humanities have ended in cataclysm. The adrenal and thyroid humanity of the Cro-Magnon (and others before the appearance of man: the end of the dinosaurs, for example). Pituitary humanity must give way to interstitial humanity. The mission of the Jews seems to be to stimulate pituitary humanity by cataclysmic excess. They will be overtaken after the final duel between Rothschild and Marx, armed by Oppenheimer and S.T. Cohen. And that will be without a Sino-American war. The hyper-feminine Chinese has little beard. Due to excision, the Chinese woman can do mathematics for more than eighteen years! Through heredity, the Chinese man reaches new heights in commercial speculation.

— If there were a normal woman, what would she say?

— She would say that she cannot be as intelligent as Pericles or Rothschild. She will have thought for herself and will not be the plaything of idiotic propaganda. She will know that women have never had any transcendent initiative, even when for centuries and in different civilisations they enjoyed leisure and studied music, without ever producing a Schubert! They can, however, reach mysticism. She will tell you that she was made to complement her partner and bring up children

---

[60] There are a few women who assert their femininity, but they are increasingly rare.

who will not, as today, be doomed to drugs and delinquency, in a word, to make real men and women of them...

—   Does one exist in the West?

Chapter XVIII

> *Lévy, Homais. Homais Lévy. International vicious circle. Homais outbids them. They make him a minister, an academician, you can count on him to blindly serve his masters. He is more repugnant than Lévy, who at least has the excuse of pathological fatality, which forces him to endow the world with cretinism.*

— Are all these concepts irremediably inaccessible to our university colleagues at the Sorbonne or the Faculty of Medicine?

— You have no doubt?

— Not at all, but I would like to analyse what is for me a primary truth.

— Let's do it together. I am presenting you with knowledge expressed in 5000 pages of text that Albert Camus, in his absolute intellectual integrity, took a year to absorb.

— It doesn't matter, because I get the gist.

— Good. Have you observed the official medical world?

— Yes, I know a number of professors and doctors, and I have friends and colleagues who are hospital interns. I've even had lunch in the on-call room, with those horrible pornographic drawings on the walls, which say a lot about the level of spiritual and aesthetic evolution of the medical profession. It's hard to imagine the walls of the residences of medical priests in traditional civilisations decorated with such horrors.

— It's certainly not a place where you need to feel comfortable.

— No, but that's what I call 'my adaptation exercises'.

— What have you noticed in this environment?

—   The strange similarity of interns. Even when one is short and fat and the other tall and skinny, they *look alike*. When their general morphology is similar, I sometimes confuse them: for me, their resemblance is as flagrant as that of the Romantics of the 19th century.

—   Perfect: you've discovered the essentials. Have you ever seen one that looked like Chopin or Laennec?

—   Never.

—   Well, the type that your synthetic eye has discovered is *predominantly pituitary*.

To pass the internship, which requires great physical stamina and memory, you need to belong to this glandular type or at least have a powerful pituitary gland.

—   So a genius like Montaigne or Vigny wouldn't pass this competition?

—   Never. Their resistance is weak, their abstract memory stupid. They risk tuberculosis if they manage this physiological tour de force. Albert Camus, whose strength of thought I admired in L'homme révolté, was stopped on his way to the agrégation by tuberculosis. Montaigne always complained about his memory. Do you know the story of Semmelweis?

—   No.

—   He was a Hungarian doctor and professor, of the thyroid type, who lived in Vienna at the end of the last century. In those days, the university system was not as rigid as it is today. He discovered through a "notion of identity" that death by "puerperal fever" was inflicted on women in labour by students and doctors who did not wash their hands. *Without him, there would be no asepsis, no obstetrics and no surgery.* As a professor he was able to express himself, but he was laughed at internationally and inevitably went mad. A statue of him has since been erected in Vienna. When you study the way the medical profession behaved towards him, you are amazed at the stupidity and wickedness of mankind. Today, he wouldn't even have the chance to be ridiculed, because he wouldn't be able to hold an official position that would allow him to express himself. At most, he would be an excellent local doctor returning to basic naturopathy.[61] All researchers who do not subscribe to the Judeo-Cartesian axis of analysis are condemnable and condemned. This is all the more comical, if one dares say so, given that since official cancer research began, cancer has developed in geometric progression. Which clearly proves that the research focus is wrong. The problem of cancer is first and foremost one of chemification and stress. Any genuine research that involves the *mind and* not laboratory *weighing* is labelled "esoteric", which paralyses all research. The asphyxiation is therefore organised, politically, legally and administratively.

— In other words, there is only room for robots who allow themselves to be manipulated by the official system, which worsens the sclerosis over time. Yet pituitary surgeons are good specialists, good technicians and good surgeons.

— There is no doubt that they have these qualities. The intellectual doctor would be a mediocre technician, a deplorable surgeon because of his sentimentality. His role would be synthetic and managerial. He would avoid analytical fragmentation and keep the perspective of the global man. He would tend to keep medicine in the perspective of hygiene and natural health in general. Unfortunately, the reign of the hypophysiologists controlled by the Jews of the system is exclusive among all publishers without exception. This applies to all perspectives, not just medical. The result is that any work of synthesis that necessarily challenges the Judeo-Cartesian asphyxia is certain to be rejected everywhere. Any brilliant work will therefore be misunderstood and excluded, by Catholic publishers as much if not more than elsewhere.

— Personally, in the presence of pituitaries, I always have the feeling *that they exude minuteness.* It's like the Inspector General who has no idea how big a mind is and will report on typos left out of papers, even in higher education. People with pituitary glands show an inability to reason along more than a single logical line. They are unable to consider different levels, different aspects, a whole range of parameters once. *One gets the categorical impression that specialisation is a natural form of their mind and that they*

---

[61] There are countless discoverers in history and medicine who are heavily condemned for the crime of expressing the truth. This will make a mockery of the century (Faurisson, Garaudy, Beljanski, le Ribault, Solomidès, Hamer, to name but a few).

cannot link it to a synthesis, which is of no interest to them. They would be out of date, while false syntheses like Marxism and Freudism delight them.

— Let's imagine a spectacular little experiment. Suppose we write a very concise page on one aspect of the whole universe of new knowledge we are examining. We present this page to a pituitary. In the middle we slip in a huge blunder, for example that the sympathetic grand is not formed until the age of seventy-five. Well, our pituitary will be fascinated by this blunder. It will not try to grasp the whole picture, however brilliant it may be, whereas you, as far as you are concerned, would have perceived the whole picture and corrected the inaccuracy without attaching any importance to it other than the need for correction. At an even lower pituitary level, if you present a fascinating text, the first thing that will strike him will be the spelling mistake that you barely noticed.

— I have seen this fundamental psychology a thousand times in the approach to the pituitary gland. As I have seen, the university has excluded the true intellectual type from its benches in favour of hypophyseal and thyroid Jews (the thyroid Jew also has a solid pituitary gland). In medicine it is so spectacular as to be obscene. Moreover, education at all levels is becoming the first stage in collective dumbing down in the service of an occult totalitarianism whose sole purpose is to produce Freudo-Marxified producer-consumer specialists. The university thus becomes the agent of all kinds of materialistic, chemical, Marxist and Freudian pollution. Minds will become radically dumbed down, and will no longer be able to assimilate basic Judeo-Cartesian orthodoxy. We are going to see masses of illiterate children, baccalaureate holders unable to write three pages without a host of spelling, grammar and syntax errors.

— A fatal outcome. *But let's look at the pituitary problem in the field of medicine.* They are in the process of rotting humanity with systematic vaccination, pathogenic synthetic chemistry and teratogens. Just think: 20 to 30 injections of putrid vaccines containing dangerous metals such as aluminium and mercury increase the risk of cancer, cardiovascular disease and mental illness, not to mention paralysis, multiple sclerosis and ankylosing spondylitis. They destroy all our defences. So let's take a look at the medical pituitary gland, and you can then transpose the synthesis that emerges to all aspects of society. The pituitary gland enables the body to appreciate the physical and chemical value of human thought. Our ideas are in fact a sort of combination of hormones and vibrations from the nerve cells. *It is therefore the only thing that can tell us what a thought is.* It gives us our reason, our ability to compare ideologies. Its power to appreciate ideas gives it a certain margin of abstraction, in other words to bring an idea to bear on the objects we perceive. We see chairs of various shapes; they are seats. We see people, we count them, they are people. *This is the beginning of an abstraction, a very rudimentary abstraction, because it does not relate essentially to objectivity or to the idea under consideration, but to a number.* So the pituitary gland, with its accentuated ideological tendencies, has encouraged man to count, to make calculations, to build up the positive sciences, mathematics. Man has encountered many difficulties in arriving at mathematical symbolism. No two objects in nature are alike. Primitive people observed them with their eyesight, their hearing and their highly developed sense of touch, in their details and not in their common elements. So they multiplied signs and terms to designate everything around them. Man managed to count to 3, as some savages still do, and then after a long time to 10. The need to divide up the flooded and highly fertile land in the Nile and Euphrates valleys forced them to use length, numbers and geometry. Astronomy contributed to mathematical research. The Hindus invented numbers to replace letters. This was a clear step forward, as calculations, multiplication and division became easier and faster. Then came algebraic symbolism, which allowed letters to regain their importance. Physics went from being experimental to being increasingly mathematical. Nature offers relatively slow and usually constant changes. So scientists were able to take measurements and devise experiments that reproduced some of nature's phenomena. They have been able to discover the main forces behind them and to derive from them the applications that industry uses.

We could have understood human beings in the same way if we had been able to carry out such simple investigations on them. We can undoubtedly experiment on the material components of his body, but his emotional states remain beyond our reach and measurement. Man is in constant transformation, in perpetual variation. We can certainly conduct experiments on his blood, urine and vegetative functions, but we cannot account for the state of transformation of his spirit. *The mind, which is the manifestation of glandular phenomena, has an important influence on the general state of organic functioning.* The spectacle of a serious accident, for example, arouses a state of mind coupled with an emotion (fear, sadness, etc.) *which is simply a modification of the glandular balance, which has repercussions on all the functional metabolisms of the most diverse vegetative and nervous organs.* If the balance is not re-established, illness will follow. This alteration in the glandular balance is therefore an essential morbid potential for all the diseases seen in different types of human beings in the most diverse forms: infections, functional disorders of the heart, lungs, digestive and renal systems, and so on. Glandular disorders therefore cause damage to all the cells and organs, which is why you felt yourself becoming tubercular and schizophrenic, the two diseases of intellectuals due to their difficulty in adapting to the material world and their repression of the ego. We should also mention that illness can also be caused by the ingestion of molecules that are not specific to the human biotype. So the mind, like food, can make us ill. It has a considerable effect on the hormonal system as much as on the disturbed mind.

Let's take your example: the pituitary doctor did not find any of their listed syndromes in you. He therefore concluded: "Physiological fever", *which means absolutely nothing. He should have known that fever is a state of hyperthyroidism.* And this is true even if it cannot be measured quantitatively and even if the characteristics of your thyroid biotype are not known.

The pituitary physician has no suspicion of similar phenomena: he cannot conceive that everything in a human being is affected by both his mind and his body through his glandular system.

Allopaths have a certain superiority over homeopaths. He has succeeded in classifying illnesses, i.e. in classifying diseases, in recognising the striking symptoms of an illness and in giving it a name. He chose the essential signs and neglected the secondary ones. Homeopaths have not managed to do this, apart from a few masters such as Dr Louis Rousseau, who know that *phosphorus* is thyroid, *fluoric* is hypophyseal and *carbonic* is adrenal. But most of them are lost in a multitude of secondary symptoms which they attack, and they do not know that the various types, fluoric, carbonic, phosphoric, of which they accuse tubercular or syphilitic intoxications, correspond to glandular states. Allopaths take no account of functional, reactionary and individual states, as you were amazed to learn during your stay in hospital. They think they can solve everything with synthetic chemistry, which is a poison not only for the individual but also for his descendants. Homeopaths take account above all of individual states, but understand nothing about functional states.

Because of their mentality, pituitary doctors have been fascinated by the laboratory because they understand nothing about disease states and the possibilities of adaptation and reaction in living beings. They have run to the laboratory, they have amplified, abusively enlarged, complicated ad infinitum, the data provided to us for example in diabetes by sugar, in albuminuria by albumin. They have examined the state of our organs and cells in all liquids and secretions using chemistry and in tissues using the microscope. They have therefore observed the results in terms of more or less than normal. *In this way, urea, cholesterol and high blood pressure have become diseases when they are merely symptoms.* The notion of disease degenerates more and more as the real cause of the disease itself becomes more and more remote in the doctor's mind. To give you a spectacular example, the modern woman suffers from an extremely wide range of disorders, which require her to consult all kinds of specialists. *Yet this diversity of symptoms is part of a paradoxical hyperthyroidism syndrome. This symptom is caused not only by general chemotherapy, coffee, tobacco, alcohol and various toxic substances, but above all because modern women live against their nature.*

Thus she and her children degenerate more and more and suffer more and more from new diseases. Women are becoming uglier and losing their resemblance to the eternal feminine of all traditions, of which Botticelli's Venus remains a symbol.

Until the last war, beautiful women dressed with exquisite taste were everywhere. In the year 2000 they disappeared.

Take diabetes, for example. This is excess sugar in the urine. It results from an imbalance in glandular phenomena. The pancreas regulates the level of stored sugar. The other glands try to put it into circulation. Diabetes can be caused by the pancreas not functioning properly, or by excessive activity in the other glands. It can also have both causes. Injecting insulin does not solve the problem.

The pituitary's most serious flaw is that it can't get out of the immediate, out of what's in front of it. It's a primitive mind. It cannot refer to a wider reality that might contradict the conclusions it draws from immediate, present observation. It cannot access the true origin of phenomena.

Another vitally important observation:

*The pituitary sees a nerve that activates a muscle. He sees a man become basedowian following a psychological shock, and he concludes that it is the nervous system that directs man. **But he is the victim of an illusion supported by elementary logic!***

When we experience an emotion, all the components of our individual are involved and affected. *If we don't understand that the hormonal system is functionally superior to the nervous system*, we can't understand how the nervous system can act on all the elements, some of which, such as red blood cells, whose oxygen content varies according to the emotions, are not connected to the nervous system by the nerves!

The pituitary is riveted to the immediate present.

So he can understand nothing about man, who is nothing but evolution, transformation and variation, because of the forces which continually act on him, which condition his activity and to which he must adapt and submit. Another shortcoming of the pituitary is that it can only detect an anatomical or rhythmic cause or a lesion in the poor state of an organ, without being able to refer to the endocrine glands, their mode of action on the organs, and beyond that, to the patient's lifestyle, diet and disturbed psychology.

The functioning of the heart, lungs and digestive system depends on glandular secretions. Their action is described at length in books on endocrinology, but neither physiologists nor doctors take it into account. Why is this? Because they still think that the endocrine glands are controlled by the nervous system, which is totally false despite appearances.

They have never gone back to the source, to the functional origins of the human being, to his embryological and foetal state. They cannot understand that it is the first appearance of the organs, their age, which determines their action on the functioning of the human being. The glandular system is the first to be formed. It is therefore the one that functionally directs the being and the nervous system. I have told you that anencephalic babies, who only have a spinal cord that is usually poorly constituted, react with movements, reflexes, emotions, especially painful emotions, and a babbling that is only found later in normal children. The pituitary describes the state of the anencephalon without being able to interpret it. Not only is the pituitary, as we have just seen, incapable of true attention, but *it is impervious to true abstraction because it judges only according to its senses and measuring devices.*

It cannot free itself from sensory ideas to rise to true thought. Nor can he grasp the notion of identity and synthesis which are the higher psychological elaborations.

In short, the pituitary knows only the details, never the whole picture: he is a pure analyst. It will never occur to him that disparate, different signs may originate from the same hormonal function. In the same way, a condition manifested by similar signs can originate from opposite glandular states of the same gland or two different functional states. All this is too arduous for brains of great simplicity, even though the pituitary glands have invented mathematics, a bit of a game for their minds, but which they have complicated beyond what are usually real conceptions.

They cannot suspect that fever, mania and madness are manifestations of hyperthyroidism. That coma, syncope, melancholy, sadness, are more or less pronounced hypothyroid states. They are intellectually incapable of seeing the similarity between these states and glandular states. It is easy to see that the clinical symptoms of hypothyroidism and marked sadness are *analogous*, but this means nothing to them. In short, the pituitary cannot go beyond the analytical stage of intellectual elaboration. They are under the illusion that by searching ever more meticulously for the particularities of a phenomenon, they will end up discovering its causes. This is an enormous illusion, because only the gross signs, often visible to the naked eye, provide the basic characteristics common to a whole series of phenomena and can lead to their origin. The small distinctive signs on which pathology is based lead nowhere, except to divide our knowledge ad infinitum and to imagine, for each new sign, a chemical drug which adds to the therapeutic burden and increases iatrogenism and teratogenism. As a result, efficacy is becoming weaker and weaker, as is currently the case for antibiotics, and especially for conditions characterised by marked functional imbalances, such as glandular conditions and mental illness.

Remember a few key facts that I'm going to repeat here:

1. Some male insects continue to mate even though the female has cut off their head.

2. A headless grasshopper lives for more than ten days.

3. Sectioning all the nerves leading to the sexual organs does not abolish rutting or the normal procreative function of these organs.

4. Resection of the entire sympathetic system does not alter a dog's vital signs, emotions or sexual activities.

5. The suppression of a single organic endocrine system radically prevents the animal from developing the sexual instinct and causes degeneration of the reproductive organs.

These observations could have led to the most peremptory understanding that the nervous system plays only a very minor role in complex activities and that *the hormonal system is totally predominant functionally.*

But these obvious facts have not been understood.

It's incredible to think that before Freud it was known that removal of the thyroid resulted in the disappearance of intelligence and sexuality!

It is therefore clear that animal sexuality is controlled by the hormonal system and not the nervous system.

If the pituitary was endowed with the ability to synthesise and the notion of identity, it would have discovered that the physiological cause of madness was atrophy of the internal genital gland.

He did observe this atrophy in people with dementia, but he abandoned this constant sign in favour of looking for disparate, inconstant signs, which have nothing essential and will never teach us anything. So we examine people with normal brains who have dementia, while others with abnormal brains are perfectly normal.

So we don't know what mental illness is. The identity of madness is characterised as follows:

1. Loss of higher psychological elaborations: synthesis and notion of identity.

2. Loss of moral sense.

3. Loss of willpower.

4. Loss of voluntary attention. This is attention focused on a higher purpose, on something *that annoys us or is unpleasant.*

These are the basic characteristics of madness.

As the possession of brilliant analytical skills is perfectly compatible with a diagnosis of madness, we can make the diagnosis of :

- Psychiatry.
- Science.
- Politics.
- Medicine.
- Finance.

There is no science without a moral sense. Science of this kind can only lead to universal destruction, with the Chernobyls and unstockable, non-neutralisable nuclear waste, for example.

Our society is therefore insane and therefore suicidal.

We will now conclude this panoramic view of our present world. You are the last metaphysical dandy in the history invented by the circumcised. The dandy is in revolt against the creator and anthroposophists call him "the Luciferian". For the dandy, the Creator is responsible for the suffering of the whole of creation because God, omniscient, knew that man would fall and therefore took away from him all freedom beforehand. So God created man, knowing that his destiny would be misery and cruelty. The dandy is always oppositional by vocation. He is a human type that renews itself, comes back to life like the phoenix, develops for a time, then diminishes to the point where it seems to have disappeared. It has necessarily disappeared from all official circles devoted to mental insignificance and turpitude. You are therefore condemned to total solitude.

The degeneration of this type is represented by long-sighted homosexuals whose sexuality is not only distorted, but even impotent. They are a waste product, a glandular type of reject, generally of little interest because they are deceitful, on the fringes of what is normal and healthy. They boast of Freud, which reveals their lack of moral and intellectual value.

When the Jews dominate the world, homosexuals will have official social status because they will be invaluable auxiliaries to the Jews in their work of disintegration. They will end up totally ruining youth and fashion, and will have the right to adopt children, which is an absolute horror.

The thyroid dandy is not unbalanced: he is excessive, a being with functional variations within the human norm. He has the defects of his qualities, but a rare intellectual and emotional potential. The homosexual, on the other hand, is unbalanced in the pathological sense, while the romantic dandy is an artist who may seem unbalanced because of a normal but highly *exaggerated* glandular function.

This is what gives it its rapid intelligence, its general speed, its excellent automatisms and its impatience.

World society is collapsing, cherishing its mistakes. Insanity is taking over every aspect of official life, pseudo-knowledgeable people are making ill-considered discoveries, and genuine moral, spiritual and aesthetic values have collapsed because they are no longer supported by physiological efficiency. Man has been reduced to living only for money, sex and the preoccupation with vital security. They have been reduced to a form of slavery that is unique in human history. Criminality and madness are growing in geometric progression and cannot be contained because officialdom itself operates on criteria of madness and crime. As Carrel said in 1935: "The real criminals are not in the prisons but at the pinnacle of liberal society". He also added that "the liberal bourgeois is the elder brother of the Bolshevik". Unfortunately, these two assertions no longer need to be demonstrated in the year 2000.[62]

Secular materialistic education is spreading, and those who follow it are less and less capable of assimilating it, because it slyly hypotrophies the mind, even for the official analytical and mnemonic qualities. Pupils in the third year of secondary school are unable to carry out elementary reasoning, and the number of illiterates is growing at an alarming rate.

The plethora of knowledge oscillates between the excessive technicality to which we give the name of science, when it is only a form of application, and verbiage, the observation of facts from which we are incapable of extracting a single major idea, officialdom being radically deprived of the spirit of synthesis.

Such a world is necessarily suicidal...

Angelika

---

[62] That's why Alexis Carrel, perhaps the greatest genius of whom humanity can be proud, is being renamed everywhere. We have here the perfect symbol of all the inversions, with the abolition of the death penalty which allows the criminal to kill again from 6 to 15 times (which is not exceptional for the official press).

Chapter XIX

> Women are so stupid compared to men's abstract intelligence that they believe they can be as intelligent as men. She thinks she can become Pericles, Goethe, Chopin or Carrel! Her illusion is all the greater because she doesn't understand her own inability. The supposedly intelligent woman can only join in all the modern shams; she'll make a pill-popping minister, but never a Lao-Tseu or a Carrel.
>
> Without oblative love for a man and his children, a woman is nothing. Only the intelligent woman knows that she is not. She is a man's intuition.

Angelika

The long conversation Tristan had had with this genius of endocrinology had interested him deeply. In a way, he had nine endocrinological proof of all his observations. Isn't genius about perceiving the determinism of others through a higher determinism?

Today, when the "higher hypointerstitials"[63] reign and drive the mass of human beings increasingly mad and torn apart, isn't everything from now on entirely deterministic until the end of this hypophyseal humanity, until the third world war and general pollution? Why should we be surprised that the leaders of Communist China, organised by MacArthur's recall, were trained by the Jesuits and the Americans? Why should we be astonished to see the Pope shake hands with the highest prelate of Anglicanism when "Protestantism is the universalization of the Jewish spirit"?[64] Inanity is now universal and ecumenism can only be practised in the midst of insanity. The Rothschilds of Marx now wield totalitarian

---

[63] Hyper-pituitary, hyper-thyroid, hyper genital **physiological** reproducers, but hypointerstitutes: brilliant speculators **but a moral and a synthetic. "And the world will be ruled by monsters"** says the Apocalypse.

[64] Louis Rougier in *"La mystique démocratique"*.

power over the puppets of politics and the robots of academia who lead the panicked, zombified masses.

It was inevitable that in a world where women are disintegrated and eager for equilibrium, even artificial, even vegetative equilibrium, Tristan would be able to give them the slightest equilibrium. Women with reduced affections and decaying nervous and endocrine systems cannot have the heroism that consists in being half of an effervescence. To create today is to create dangerously, even suicidally.

For women, creation, truth, rigour and beauty are basic factors of imbalance: they can't adapt to the man who sings their praises in an ocean of lies. This ocean now feeds what remains of man and becomes the condition of survival in the world of merchants and slaves where, precisely, we are trying to survive.

Despite the advice of the learned endocrinologist, Tristan had tried to stay close to his wife. Wasn't Biche expecting a child?

But the situation did not improve, and Tristan became so exhausted that he was prescribed a three-month stay in a nursing home.

An amicable divorce was arranged by the parents-in-law. They had divorced.

They had queued up at the Palais de Justice, O mockery! Tristan had thought they would find a real judge there, to whom he could explain the inevitability of their divorce, which was necessary in such a delicate context. The judge looked like a grocer and the divorce was a serial occurrence: something like the queue for food cards during the war. A paid lawman's routine. Nothing else. Divorce was as dehumanised as marriage, which without serious foundations led to foolish divorce and the birth of tomorrow's wrecked children, drug addicts, disco customers, suicides...

The man had obviously disappeared.[65]

After three months in a rest home and inexpressible suffering, Tristan felt the desire to return to his children and their mother, despite her horrible betrayal, which he had sworn to bury in the silence of oblivion. The children were the most important thing. Jacqueline refused. Her refusal

---

[65] In 1980, a doctor told the author: "Under fifty, there are no more men". So these are the homunculi that are going to disappear.

was in line with her previous light-hearted behaviour. He had matured, he had understood. He would no longer leave his wife, not even for Venus herself.

Tristan resigned himself to renting a room from a charming elderly lady in the sixth arrondissement of Paris. He resumed teaching English at secondary school and French at a famous school for foreign adults. This school brought together the prettiest girls in the world, who came there to learn French. Tristan had many adventures there, which enchanted his Don Juan nature. How many times did he have dates during the day, and did he mix up the first names of these exquisite creatures in their twenties and thirties who slipped him love notes on his desk while others gazed at him lovingly for the duration of the course!

One day one of his pupils was having tea in the bar where he was drinking a beer.

— Ah him," said this pupil, "I wouldn't like to be your mistress!

— Why?" he retorted.

— Because I'd be the two hundred and forty-third!

— No," replied Tristan, "you'd be the two hundred and forty-third!

The pupil was away for a few days and when she returned she had to read a text that he had given to his pupils to practise diction. He lent her the book containing the text, which was called 'L'aimable voleur', and asked her to return it to him as soon as possible, as the book provided him with texts that were remarkable for their pedagogical value.

She returned it to him the next day, and Tristan put the book on his desk in his room. A fortnight later, when he needed to choose a suitable text for his students, he opened the book and found a card on which was written: "And when you have finished with the two hundred and forty third, the two hundred and forty third encore awaits its turn".

He phoned her, pretending that he had kept her waiting on purpose, and that very evening...

It was at this time that he met Hella. German, she wasn't pretty, but "better than beautiful", said a Romanian philosopher friend. Very distinguished, very well built, very elegant. Remarkably intelligent in both academic and non-academic terms, she had learnt French, which she spoke without a single accent, and had become executive secretary to the CEO of a famous printing house that had once printed Balzac. She was a perfectionist who, like happy people, has no history.

Their sexual union was of such a quality, such a 'tenth heaven', that Tristan never experienced such ecstasy with another woman. She had only one dream: marriage. Tristan had not yet passed a competitive examination that would have given him tenure, so although he had accepted the principle, he put off the deadline thanks to this alibi. When he passed the exam, Hella backed him into a corner... Tristan told her that he was willing to marry her but that he wouldn't live with her. He thought this would dissuade her, but it didn't. Tristan, from the nativity of Libra, didn't know how to say no. To please Hella, he agreed to marry her. Pleasing is often much crueler than refusing, for Hella was to pay dearly for this aberrant marriage.

He agreed, telling her that if he fell in love he would divorce her. She even agreed to that.

It's true that Tristan thought that one day he would settle down and take Hella to his heart for good.

For the time being, women, including Hella, his great friend, were no longer his goal or his problem. He was finding a physiological equilibrium in this whirlwind flirtation that left his Don Juan performances far behind. Pleasure, never pain. Until then, as soon as he had taken a woman seriously, as soon as he had given her his love, it was only to suffer martyrdom. He'd had enough, as they say, and now he was strictly by the number, not by subscription.

Never say "Fountain, I won't drink your water again".

He and Hella lived separately and he visited her at weekends. He went to pick up the children, who got on very well with her. But he was about to leave her, and she didn't have the patience to wait for Tristan, who would have returned to her for sure, so she left France, went to Germany and became seriously mentally ill.

One day when he had just finished his lesson, he spotted a young girl coming down the school's main staircase. He'd just had a good run for his money with Biche, but he was beyond redemption.

The insidious disease of passion was about to strike him down again.

He had two excuses: this twenty-two year old girl was exquisite and if he hadn't liked her, nothing would have happened. *Que sera sera.*

She wore a ravishing Bavarian dress, her long hair was as blonde as wheat, her complexion pink and clear, and her appearance was so feminine that she swore among the girls who were all, however pretty, accused of a certain masculinisation peculiar to the time. It was unthinkable to imagine her as a health minister promulgating the pill and abortion, impossible to imagine her even as a member of the Women's Liberation Movement. Real women ignore this kind of concoction, but where are they? Tristan, who was morbidly shy, felt ready for anything bold. He strode confidently towards her. He placed his fingertips gently on her arm and whispered: "That's the prettiest thing I've ever seen, Miss, could you give me a minute? She blushed pleasantly, mumbled a few words in embryonic French and said more clearly "that she would see".

Her smile had given Tristan hope. For two months she disappeared from school. She had been afraid of Tristan. She felt both attracted and frightened by him. At first, as someone else would say, she preferred to flee and take refuge with friends in England. Tristan was moping around.

Weeks went by. Suddenly he saw her coming down the grand staircase. His heart was pounding, he had to talk to her, he spoke to her. She agreed to meet him.

They were to experience months of happiness and years of unhappiness.

When he saw her again in his mind's eye, years after they had parted, with her lace bodice and her childlike charm, when he saw her marvellous naive drawings, adorable and so deliciously stylised, he felt how deeply attached his being was to her. Angelika, for that was her name, was as Venusian as Tristan. It was psychologically and astrologically obvious that Venus had brought them together.

They settled in Maisons Alfort, in a small two-room flat that they rented, and soon an adorable little Nathalie was born, who soon became her father's great love, a great love that would also become a source of pain. She was baptised at Notre Dame de Paris and, by some exception, they were granted the use of the court of honour reserved for kings and queens. Nathalie, with her golden hair and heavenly eyes, was the joy of her mum and dad.

But fate didn't want this happiness to last.

Patrice, the son of Tristan and Jacqueline, was of school age. He had a very difficult character. Born in Scorpio, he possessed the most negative qualities of this nativity. Tristan had a friend who was a remarkable astrologer and, without telling him it was his son, he asked him to draw his chart. He began as follows: "I have never seen such a profusion of bad aspects". This was followed by an analysis which, alas, was to prove true right up to the end of his unfortunate destiny, since he died at the age of thirty-nine from a cerebral haemorrhage contracted by mixing alcohol and chemical drugs. His son's difficulties made Tristan feel even more acutely that he had to do everything for him to get him out of this character-defining fate. Patrice had to pass his baccalauréat. Tristan also wanted him to pass a minimum number of exams to get into teaching. He had already sent him to a Spanish school for a year and he spoke the language perfectly. To help him in general and in English in particular, he needed to be at home more often than at his mother's house.

Unfortunately, his aggressiveness, laziness and bad tendencies made the family atmosphere precarious. Angelika, as jealous as a child of this impossible child, adopted such a painful, infantile attitude that she forced Tristan, so to speak, to take his son's side so that he didn't feel abandoned or unloved. Angelika should have stepped aside intelligently, doing her best not to add tenfold to Tristan's already crushing burden.

But this seemed impossible to a woman of this century generally deprived of any spiritual, moral and intellectual education to her measure. If they had both lived in a traditional civilisation, there would have been no divorce in the first place, then the couple's fundamental education and mutual love would have been the mainspring of everything, and everything that was opposed in their respective natures would have been channelled into a symbiosis of love and duty.

In our materialistic civilisation, everything that was different had to be opposed and become antagonistic. Defects became a source of conflict and deterministic pathologies. Such was the fate of twentieth-century couples, with their child marriages and serial divorces. What was astonishing at such a time were the marriages that lasted.

The divorce curve was rising steeply, and even cohabitation was not favoured from a tax point of view when filing a joint return.

Three years after their marriage, Angelika had shown Tristan the handwriting analysis that her father had had done in Switzerland by a

German-speaking handwriting analyst. The letter analysed had been written in English, the language in which Tristan and Angelika spoke, as Angelika did not yet know French well enough. The graphologist did not know English and her two German analyses were translated into French.

These two analyses provided an unfailing summary of what they were to experience over the next twelve years.

Tristan's analysis was as follows:

They are highly intelligent and very sensitive. He has great originality and an obvious artistic sense. He is said to have a fertile mind and the ability to work creatively because he is remarkably gifted and has a keen sense of beauty. Yet his thinking often proceeds by analysis and decomposition. He suffers from not allowing his experiences and feelings to have their integrity and from questioning them with his intelligence. Weighing up the pros and cons, reflecting, rejecting and taking up problems again are the characteristic activities of his thinking, which often put him at odds with his feelings, especially as he has a sensitive and open soul. When writing this example, the writer was in a state of heightened euphoria, in which he saw the world and his future partner in the form of an ideal image, paying too little attention to reality.

Being atmospherically dependent, it experiences disappointment and sadness as acutely as it does a momentary happy mood.

The writer is, so to speak, the prey of this cyclothymia and will find it difficult to free himself from it without outside help. It is likely that in the event of a major disagreement he will look for ways to escape from it on occasion, even in ways that would not be beneficial to him. He is sure that his partner will be able to give him a great deal of strength and help in such circumstances.

Although the scriptwriter is very attentive, the partner must be aware that her own world comes first and can only be confronted with a great deal of understanding and patience.

It would be advisable for the future partner to deepen her knowledge of this gifted and interesting man through a long engagement, so that in everyday life she can be sure of putting up with the thousand inconveniences that are the opposite of the writer's romantic conception of life.

It seemed obvious that Angelika was incapable of taking on such a companion. Her analysis confirmed it:

This is the writing of a particularly sensitive and vulnerable person who often tries in vain to solve his own problems.

This is undoubtedly due to the fact that it has exaggerated expectations of people and things. She collapses into helplessness if she doesn't achieve rapid transformation. Although quick-witted and practical, she has retained a childlike faith in the marvellous. This is why she wastes her physical and mental strength and reacts emotionally and psychologically awkwardly at critical moments. She is therefore a victim of her own feelings. She is also extremely scrupulous and her love of order is her supreme law. She has difficulty understanding that others improvise and act in fits and starts.

Her childhood must have been marked by unexpected mood swings in her immediate environment. She is unaware that this has considerably exacerbated her susceptibility. She lacks a carefree attitude and a sense of humour.

Her sense of duty and responsibility, and the effort she makes to remain patient even when she feels like "giving it all up", are all the more appreciated. She likes to be spoiled, but she also likes to spoil, and surrounds those she loves with maternal care. If she isn't paid in return, she falls into despair. However, with a little skill and psychology, those around her can obtain treasures from her. She tends to be too spontaneous. Her attempts to make amends, though well-intentioned, are not always skilful. She should take advantage of her excellent taste and artistic sensibility as well as her neglected but remarkable manual skills. She could be an interior decorator. At the time of writing, she lacks self-confidence and an external stimulus. It's crucial for her state of mind that she manages to give herself a feeling of warmth and security. She has lacked this feeling for a long time, and her attempts to acquire it are made with a feverishness that makes it difficult for those around her to understand what she wants and feels.

Her tendency to take refuge in the will to believe helped her for a while, but did not bring her any lasting moral relief.

Given the human qualities and many gifts they possess, this person should be able to bring about a turning point in their life by correcting their sickly susceptibility and proving themselves in a practical activity.

When Tristan reread his two analyses, he was stunned. Stunned by the extraordinary talent and knowledge of the graphologist, stunned because the comparison of these two analyses was a perfect synthesis of their drama. The prodigious accuracy of their revelation was unequalled. In just a few lines there was the veracity and precision of what they had lived through for twelve years.

Despite the Venusian ties that bound them together, they were about to experience martyrdom. Tristan's love for his wife and daughter was so great that he wouldn't have hesitated to give his life for her if she hadn't left him and taken their adorable little Nathalie with her.

Angelika was born in Taurus. She was its prototype. She had a face as fresh as spring, a sweet face framed by beautiful golden-blonde hair. She was sensitive and imaginative, with a hint of bovarianism. Her general appearance evoked a carnal, maternal person, with a strong tendency towards the digestive, the slow, the vegetative, all character traits that were the antithesis of Tristan, who was cerebral, intuitive, hyper-fast and idealistic.

Angelika loved nature, the countryside and the simple life, but she also loved the comforts of the city, and the complex conveniences of progress fascinated her.

Tristan was the 'thyroid Libra' we know, whose major fault was to be caught like a lark in the nets of beautiful creatures. In fact, he always preferred a pretty but morally disgraced woman to one who was less beautiful but rich in fundamental qualities, indulgence, maturity, moral strength, emotional solidity - in short, all the qualities that Tristan needed most.

Angelika was born during the Second World War, while her father, a lawyer and soldier, was away. Her mother had always been in poor psychological health, and when Tristan met her, he saw her drinking a bottle or two of champagne and liqueurs every evening, as well as smoking a lot of cigarettes. She was happily preparing herself for the cancer from which she died a few years later. It was obvious that she had never been able to give Angelika all the tenderness that this pretty Bavarian flower so badly needed.

It is therefore certain that both Angelika and Tristan suffered from a serious maternal deficiency, which could only be remedied by a *maternal* partner.

This cruel deficiency was compounded by the fact that both their mothers were alive.

So their negativity was constantly feeding their deficiency.

So they both needed a companion who would mother them to bridge this emotional chasm. But that wasn't the case.

Angelika and Tristan were drowned in a vicious sphere. Two Venusian beings, attracted to each other but incapable of mothering each other. It was a guaranteed failure, especially as Tristan, an artist and schizoid, had the greatest need of an indulgent and morally strong woman. Nothing had helped to structure either of them. When Angelika was five, bombs rained down all around her. She made her way to the shelter on her own, the shocks frightening for a small child.

Angelika's brother was an accused temperamental, a thick little adrenalian who had received even less than his sister. He was as rude in appearance as her sister was pretty and charming. Angelika had nagging memories of violent scenes involving her brother. To make matters worse, at the age of seventeen she had become secretary to her lawyer father. She had access to nightmarish divorce files, the horrors of which sowed hatred, contempt and disgust for men in her mind.

It was important for Tristan to look after his son Patrice. Admittedly, children of this generation, deprived of everything important and torn apart by divorce, are not easy. How could they be? Parents separated by the work of both members of the couple, by divorce, or by both at the same time, are no longer there to offer their children the *real* knowledge that structures their being, the constant affection, the solid education. The mother, absent from the home and on the run, can only provide her children with chemical, carcinogenic industrial food, devoid of natural vitamins,[66] minerals and trace elements. The secular influence, which conveys Marxist and Freudian influences to schoolchildren, underpins this systematic undermining of our very being.[67] So we had to be more understanding and more humane. We had to take into account all the destructive factors acting on this sacrificed generation.

Angelika, scarred by her brother's brutality, saw him in Patrice with a childish panic. Tristan, faced with this aggression that was making everything worse, had to raise a hymalaya to get his son to take the

---

[66] Synthetic vitamins have been shown to be carcinogenic.

[67] Class struggle, like sexual invasion and complexes in tremolos, was perfectly ignored and unknown under National Socialism, as it was in Ancient Egypt...

baccalauréat and learn two languages. He even managed to get him a teaching job at a private college. He was on the brink of being given tenure, because at the time he could take a competitive examination to become a college teacher without having a degree in literature. But at the age of twenty-one, when he came of age, he threw it all away and sank into chemical drugs, alcohol and tobacco, which eventually killed him at the age of thirty-nine.

Angelika's jealous and aggressive attitude meant that Tristan had to be by his son's side so that he didn't feel deprived of affection and security. Angelika's reckless behaviour left its mark on Patrice. Didn't she often say to Tristan: "You can choose between your son and me; if you choose your son, I'll leave"? Unfortunately, that's what she was going to do, because Tristan couldn't abandon his son in such distress.

When Patrice came to visit his father and stepmother, and he often came so that his father could follow him, he behaved, at least at first, in a decent manner. But things changed. He started stealing money from them, which shocked Angelika, who did nothing to stimulate the child and help him. Things got worse. Patrice would turn up haggard, staggering, with a pasty tongue and swallowed speech under the effect of chemical drugs. These unpleasant incidents sometimes prompted Angelika to go to the hotel with Nathalie when Patrice came. No doubt a son-in-law of that generation can cause problems. Tristan knew that many of the children of his own Sorbonne professors had serious problems. Recently two of them, brother and sister, children of a famous professor, had committed suicide. But how can you not have a little affection for the son of someone you claim to love? She could have taken refuge behind Tristan and let her authority and affection flow freely.

Patrice had managed to pass his baccalauréat, enrol at the Sorbonne, teach and learn three languages. But he would soon be washing dishes in London restaurants.

Angelika was suffering from a syndrome that this learned endocrinologist called "paradoxical hyperthyroidism". In the modern world, it affects a large number of women and is the cause of the birth of temperamental people with behavioural problems, and sometimes even mongoloid people. The aetiology of this syndrome lies in the fact that women live against their nature. They lose their feminine character of grace, beauty, gentleness and delicacy.

The palliative for such a syndrome is a quiet life with a maternal companion. She had various aspects of this syndrome that the pituitary gland specialists have never been able to reduce to a morbid entity: headaches, discharge, leg pain, arrhythmia, fatigue, dark thoughts. His nervous system was extremely weak and his pituitary was characteristically inadequate. This characteristic had been revealed to her by two clinical facts: on the one hand, the absence of stretch marks after childbirth, and on the other, a mental inability to distinguish between the concepts of nominative and accusative in German, her own language.

So she was not in a position to analyse the facts objectively, to fight against her own paranoid state, which is so common today. She had no sense of self-criticism. She had little capacity for voluntary attention, and showed considerable sensitivity to noises that seemed to come to her tenfold. This sign alone indicates a major thyroid disorder in the hyper sense. She was negative, demanding, aggressive and incessantly demanding. Indecisive and obsessed with insecurity, her field of consciousness was considerably narrowed.

Yet she was sometimes vaguely aware of her difficulties and showed genuine goodwill. Didn't she type in French (she barely knew the language) the entire doctoral thesis that her husband was going to defend at the Sorbonne?

She turned Nathalie against her father, so much so that the six-year-old said to him: "We've had enough, we're going to find another daddy".

That's exactly what they did later.

Angelika was cut off from her husband's world and knew nothing about it. Her field of consciousness oscillated between her daughter, whom she looked after very well in practice but to whom she certainly wouldn't give a soul. She had assimilated all the principles of health and natural medicine that Tristan had taught her. She looked after her home very well. Tristan's mistake, and what a mistake it was, was that he demanded mammoth work from a little squirrel.

Tristan had a great weakness, so well described in the graphological analysis: he needed tenderness and outpouring. He confided in intelligent acquaintances and important doctors. Angelika saw this as persecution, never as the incoercible impulse of a suffering, sentimental, frustrated husband who needed to draw strength from understanding, encouragement and consolation.

One of Tristan's friends was a famous elderly doctor, a former colleague of the great Alexis Carrel. He used to talk to him about his worries and sufferings. He began to admonish Tristan, in a fatherly way. He insisted that he should never have fallen in love with a woman who wasn't the right match for him, that he had much better things to do with his potential than waste his energy on women's problems.

Tristan let him speak without saying a word. When the doctor had finished his sermon, Tristan took a photograph of Angelika out of his wallet.

The old doctor took a long look at her and finally said:

- Ah, I understand...

Invited by Tristan to lunch and dinner at home, he was literally spoilt for choice in front of Angelika. His behaviour and his reasonable judgement were totally distorted by the feelings that Angelika had inspired in him. This simply means that if he had been forty years younger, if circumstances had wanted it, if fate had written it, he would have *fallen* exactly like Tristan...

Angelika was attracted to the elderly, which underlines her need for mothering and her childlike psychology.

Sometimes she had a painful feeling of internal coldness (a symptom of paradoxical hyperthyroidism syndrome). Then, she said, she lost all interest, even in her child. One day she banged her head against the wall shouting, "I want to be killed".

The saddest and most poignant thing is the undermining of the father that she imposed on her child. A neighbour, a friend of Angelika's, came to see Tristan one day and told him: "What your wife is doing with your daughter is criminal, the child is going to hate you".

In fact, it was worse. Nathalie became indifferent. Later, when Tristan had retired, she was in her twenties, and he had cut her pension a little, in circumstances that justified O how much, she took her father to court.

So much love poured out on people who didn't love her.

Did Tristan suspect that he was about to go through an even worse ordeal?[68]

Once there was no apparent motive, Angelika smashed the candle on the piano chandelier with the back of her hand. Worse still, she twisted a paper cutter and aimed it at the back of her neck, throwing a hysterical fit in front of the little girl, who was screaming in agony.

Nathalie totally mimicked her mother, which is normal at that age, and barked like her mother when she spoke to her father: "We're going to take all the furniture away"...

And so one day it happened. Tristan would rather have died than gone through all that.

The power of love had prevented Tristan from fleeing, from abandoning everything. Without this crazy love, he would never have had to endure so much suffering, his own, his wife's and that of the little girl for whom he could do nothing.

Tristan often tried to explain to his wife everything that concerned them, his good will, his desire to do what was best, even to accept that she would go to Bavaria to rest with her parents whenever she felt the need. Nothing helped, on the contrary. Intelligence would have been useless in these circumstances; *everything would* have had to be *on the rails of truth and nature*. Even if we understand the essentials of world geopolitics, that won't prevent the inevitability of the third world war and all the pollution, because nature never forgives.

Nobody understands, and nobody listens.

One day, while on holiday with her father in Bavaria, Angelika wrote him a letter that will remain engraved in her heart:

My love,

We thank you for your pretty roses. Yes, Christmas was sad without you, but it was better this way. Darling, I'm at the end of my rope. I don't know what I'm going to do. I'm doomed to be unhappy, my parents, you, what else is there left for me but...?

---

[68] Monique" chapter.

Forgive me if I haven't been a good wife to you. But I won't forget that I still love you and that I'll keep you in my heart forever, even if you're a long way away, yes a long way away.

I hope God will forgive me. You and the little girl too, but I can't be on this earth any more, I have to find peace, eternal peace. I've always known that. I felt that my senses and my nerves would leave me one day. Take care of our dear Nathalie and never tell her the truth. Just tell her that I loved her very, very much, and that God wanted to take her mother back. I'll save you two seats next to me. My love, do something for this poor humanity, write down everything you have to say, thinking of me and the little girl. Promise me, forgive me, forgive me, I love you. Keep me always in your heart, love me and love me by loving Nathalie.

I'd like to give you another big hug.

This letter caused Tristan immense pain. He phoned Bavaria immediately. Angelika was fine. The letter was already five days old. An even greater pain awaited him.

Angelika returns to France. She had not killed herself, as Tristan so feared. Her letter was a kind of cry for help. But what could he do? He was doing all he could with what he had. Tristan adored his wife, but he himself was in such a state of lonely depression that he would have put his head on the shoulder of any tender woman he met. Objectively speaking, Angelika had everything that was possible for reasonable happiness: a husband who loved her, a beautiful child, a comfortable flat furnished in the style of Louis XVI and English, Tristan doing up to forty hours of lessons a week, which was enormous, to make up for the lack of salary in the household where he alone worked. The little girl was brought up according to organic dietary principles and, when you looked at her at school, she looked like a little rose in a bed of thistles...

Tristan could understand everything, arrange everything, mitigate everything and his 'Libra' nature even led him to compromise and be extremely tolerant.

Angelika had known about her husband's nature long before they married, thanks to the excellent graphological analysis carried out at her father's instigation. If she had accepted her husband as he was, why make him suffer so much? Why suffer so much herself when she had such a beautiful child? Wasn't Tristan's Donjuanism deeply destroying to her? Certainly, it could play an important role. How could she take on such a flaw with a childish character when a strong woman could already put up with it so badly? Add to that the blindside of materialism, of which she was unaware, and a total spiritual and intellectual emptiness.

In the modern woman, both the body and the mind are affected. Angelika's body was splendid, but her nervous system had deteriorated. Dostoyevsky predicted in 1880 that progress applied to nutrition would destroy the nervous system. In the year 2000, this was achieved throughout the world.

The hallmark of a certain maturity and balance is to live in the present, to let the troubles of the past fade from memory, and not to wallow in negative memories, as this prevents any positive dynamism. It is essential to forget failures, to accept natural ageing and what cannot be avoided in the future.

Angelika was the opposite of all that, a kind of permanent, obsessive opposite. She lived on reproaches, ridiculous claims and negative memories, and the idea of growing old panicked her.

"What did I get out of those ten years?" she said.

Nothing: a husband who adored her and worked his fingers to the bone for her, an adorable child and a comfortable home. No, she'd had nothing.

One day Tristan, still recovering from a lung congestion, wanted to go to the university for a lecture. His car had broken down and he asked his wife to lend him hers. She refused. So Tristan took a three-hour train and metro journey from Vigneux sur Seine, where they lived, to Porte de Clignancourt, where the courses were held at Paris IV University. But he hadn't had medical permission to get out of bed.

"At such a degree of unconsciousness and selfishness", said his psychiatrist friend, who had already followed his drama with Biche, "there is no hope left".

She never mentioned all the positive things that were happening to the three of them. She saw nothing of all the energy Tristan expended on behalf of the two of them. And yet the three of them could have made an island of happiness. And to break Tristan's spirit in one fell swoop, she once said to him: "I can't give you anything, but I could to a middle-class man"...

She called it 'sincerity'. She had no idea that a brave and noble woman would have left, perhaps, but without saying such things. It's true that such a woman wouldn't have said them because she wouldn't have thought them.

This sentence had made Tristan lose all hope. He decided to repeat it to his parents-in-law. He was naive enough to think that his father-in-law, for example, would have reacted to such nonsense and taught his daughter the notions of duty and responsibility. He could also have bought them a place to live, in Angelika's name (he had the money), which would have gone a long way towards reducing Tristan's overwork. The rent was considerable.

Tristan would have asked them for the down payment, for example, and would have paid the monthly instalments. Admittedly, the rented accommodation was pleasant on the inside, but it was located in a large concrete city that was hardly conducive to the mental health of two Venusians. Suicides were frequent. Delinquency was on the increase. These factors alone undoubtedly played a part in the ruin of their household. Alas, traditional behaviour was not to be expected from parents moulded by materialism and who had already proved their worth when it came to bringing up their daughter. Their psychological and financial complicity with their daughter's dilapidated state of mind would consume their ruin.

A Jewish pharmacist who was running for parliament and who had seen Tristan as the head of an environmental movement would soon take advantage of their separation to store the furniture Angelika had removed from the flat for a fee. The departure was financed by the parents-in-law.

A few days before this desertion, a friend of Angelika's had come to the house. She told her:

—   You say your husband doesn't do little things for you, but have you gently put your arms around him to ask? You know he's a thinker and doesn't think about all those details.

Angélika made no reply. The friend continued:

—   You say that he watches the film on television at eight thirty, but you don't work, have you ever arranged for dinner to be ready at nine o'clock? Besides, your husband could have demanded it.

Angelika still didn't answer. The friend continued:

— Why didn't you lend him your car to go and do his lectures at the university, when he was still recovering from a lung congestion and his car had broken down?

Angelika remained stubbornly silent. When her friend left, she began to cry and say: "*It's a good thing I'm going to Germany, I'll never hear things like that again*".

By this time Tristan had learned the basics of astrology. He could see the extent to which human equilibrium was linked to this initiatory knowledge, radically incompatible with the materialism he called 'Judeo-Cartesian'. This ignorance would last until the suicide of this well-organised humanity since the revolution of 1789 in particular.

They were both archetypes, she of Taurus, he of Libra.

The synthesis of their relationship was perfectly expressed in this summary: "Taurus and Libra have Venusian affinities of sensitivity and kindness, but behind common tastes stand an instinctive being (Taurus) and a refined and decadent being (Libra).

The position of Tristan's moon in Angelika's Taurus implied a deep understanding of their being, which they had both experienced, but the square of Tristan's 'Scorpio' ascendant and Angelika's 'Leo' marked a radical disagreement in the order of contingencies - which they had also experienced perfectly.[69] They had lived through all this during the twelve years of their marriage.

One position in Tristan's chart was most interesting and illustrated the profound quality of all his writings. Pluto in the 8th house.

You could find it in Liszt, Hitler and de Gaulle.

This was the most dangerous position in terms of psychic balance. The "Master of the Underworld linking up with the animic forces on a karmic level" produced a state of almost permanent splitting and somnambulism. The subject is absent from mundane reality and is endowed with a magnetic force of considerable influence. Depending on the direction and

---

[69] Anyone interested in astrology knows that Leo and Scorpio are irreducible enemies. This alone would explain the tragedy of this couple.

influences of the sun, the driving force, the mystical belief in his mission on earth will make him a saint or a veritable demon.

Pluto in his general attributions concerns the masses, the people, the great currents of ideas. We are in the presence of the predestined one who must participate in or lead a great upheaval among the people. As all the planets have an opposite correspondence in terms of good or bad influences, Pluto would bring the good effects of Mars: *this explains the subject's warlike ardour in the service of a mystical psyche.*

Tristan had been experiencing this aspect of his theme for as long as he had been conscious.

But how could such a being cope with twentieth-century female psychology? Hadn't Angelika said to him:

- *You're a luxury item that nobody needs any more.*

How could a neuro-psychically half-destroyed modern woman love such an effervescent guy, when only minor preoccupations occupied her mind, or what was left of it?

Tristan had in fact been the husband of a restaurant manager's wife.

Jacqueline's husband, a polytechnician, Biche's husband, a brewery manager, Angelika's future husband...

Tristan would never be able to find a partner, because their union could only reasonably last as long as a rose grown in chemical soil. His Libra nature would still push him towards marriage, because he couldn't stand solitude, but at this moment of pain the very idea of another woman was impossible for him.

Angelika left on 20 December, a few days before Christmas. She had removed the furniture "so that Patrice wouldn't get into her furniture".

He found himself alone, shattered, in half an empty flat. He felt that everything had been ripped out of him, his whole heart. All he could think about was dying. Angelika had told him: "If you're ill, I won't come to treat you"...

Tristan lay in bed for several days, unable to swallow anything. He worked like an automaton. He wanted to die, die, die.

No letters, no telephone rings. Unbearable loneliness in a world where he found nothing to live for. His little Nathalie, whom he wanted to bring up free of materialism, whose heart they were going to dry up. Angelika had taken her away from him. He would never be able to teach her everything he knew, never make her *a woman*.

In an abyss of pain that no words could express, a prayer burst forth from his bloodied heart:

I am Lord Jesus[70] on your bent knees.
Sinful and repentant, then a sinner again.
I accept the hideousness,
I accept the beauty.
I accept the mystery of so many iniquities
I am yours,
Lord, keep me within yourself.
May my serene soul accept everything and anything.
May I remain bent beneath your divine knees...

---

[70] The author is not Catholic, for reasons explained in the preceding pages. "Jesus" here retains the meaning of divinity, the first principle of all things. He rejects Jehovah even more.

CHAPTER XX

> *The notion of karma brings peace to the soul and a certain logic to our destiny. Without it, individual life remains "a story full of noise and fury" where only injustice and absurdity reign.*
>
> *If we have problems with good and intelligent people, let's be sure that they are our problems and not theirs.*

MONIQUE, OR KARMA'S COUP DE GRÂCE

Once again Tristan survived in spite of himself. His heart, soaked in despair, wanted nothing more, and denied this century, of which he loved nothing. But there was in him this strange and miraculous super vitality that compelled him to live in spite of himself and that kept him, even at the most acute moment of despair and prostration, sexually potent. "You want to die, but you'll still have to walk", fate seemed to whisper to him. You'll still have to suffer a lot before your last breath, because nothing is finished.

Nothing was finished, and little did he know that he would still have to face some supreme trials. In extremis, the breath of fate had kept him away from the grave. He survived like an automaton, continuing his lectures at the university and marking the tests for the exams and competitions for which he was responsible. The icy solitude of the concrete city where he lived, in a flat three-quarters emptied by Angelika, was only interrupted by the Italian cleaning lady. One day, in her thick accent, she said to Tristan: "Ah sir! What a state of decay my country is in! I knew it to be prosperous and orderly in Mussolini's time. There was no Maffia at all then, but now everything is rotten here"...

A few friends and acquaintances came to see Tristan. One evening a doctor friend told him that his prostration could lead him to the worst, and that he should introduce him to a friend who ran an important marriage agency.

Tristan didn't feel like it, and what's more he knew that the physical and psychological quality of the women he met there had to be far removed from the image his Angelika had left him with his child. His loneliness was so excruciating, he was so close to suicide, that any human contact was better than this fate of living death he was suffering.

He accepted the appointment. He was welcomed by a blonde manager with a generous figure, recommended by the manager. No sooner had she seen him than she exclaimed: "What on earth are you doing here?

Two days later she crawled into bed with Tristan, who had not been able to say no to a pretty woman, and whose desperate state of mind did not render him impotent. The women she introduced him to all betrayed a distressing physical and mental state. So Tristan only stayed with them long enough to say goodbye.

One day he was ushered into a lounge where he thought it was a matter of waiting.

There was a rather small person in the room, dressed in grotesquely disfiguring extra-large green trousers, with eyes that revealed no tenderness, no feeling, and this look struck him.

He had a sort of worrying fixity. His complexion was yellowish, indicative of a bilious, aggressive, cantankerous temperament. It never occurred to Tristan for a second that he and this person had anything in common. She was the radical and absolute antithesis of the rosy blonde who had been Tristan's undoing. He thought that, like him, she was waiting.

To Tristan's amazement, a door opened and the buxom manageress said:

— How did it go? Did you get to know each other?

Tristan stammered in amazement:

— No!

Polite as he was, he exchanged a few words with this person, then, to get a better look at her, sat down with her in front of the fireplace mirror. Admittedly, the rather yellow skin, the absent expression in the eyes and the flattened chin did not augur well, as pure intuition and Lombroso's physiognomonic observation would have it.[71] The conversation was friendly, however, and although the woman's physique was far removed from Tristan's fantasies, he gave her his card. Then, thinking no more of it, he went home to sink into his thick and desperate solitude.

One evening, as usual since the departure of his wife and daughter, he remained prostrate when the telephone rang.

It was Monique, because that was the name of the person she met at the agency who was to plunge the end of her life into the most definitive despair.

She was about thirty years old.

She suggested we go out, have dinner together. In the state he was in, he knew that anything was better than the suicidal prostration he'd come to cherish, which was killing him as surely as cyanide.

Tristan went out with her. His need to express himself was so strong that he told her his tragedy. He had nothing else on his mind, nothing. He didn't hide any of his faults from her, and she responded with kindness and compassion. She fell in love. No one realises how much and how little a woman can hide when she is in love. She managed to express a character whose essence was the opposite of her own, as it would be revealed in her ordeal. She was comforting, perhaps second nature because she was a nurse. How much Tristan wanted to trust anyone who picked him up, lost in the gutter of the most absolute despair... She would be the exception of the women he met in a Parisian agency where tare was the rule. For him, shattered, she had a maternal tenderness and the sensuality of a thousand rosy blondes, often so hollow and navel-gazing. Grief demineralised him: scapulohumeral periarthritis set in, paralysing both his arms in turn. He couldn't dress, undress or comb his hair. Monique's intelligence seemed to him to be considerable; she seemed to have full access to his lucidity as a non-conformist writer and accursed philosopher.

"My God!" he said to himself, "what is pink skin and blond hair compared to this perfection of tenderness, sensuality and intelligence?

---

[71] Famous Italian psychiatrist, Jewish, who did interesting work in various fields. His book *Dégénérescence* is interesting, though too systematic.

Life had to take over again. He needed this illusion for life to regain its grip.

Monique's perfection lasted two full years. She inspired him to write this poem:

To my Monique

O I feel that my heart
Overflowing with tenderness and gratitude
For all that you are.
O my guardian angel,
O my sweet companion.
Whose tender presence is full of piety.
I know that Nathalie and her poor mother
Will never heal the wound of my torment.
And I feel that only you can, on this earth.
Bring me a little bit of the firmament with your soul.

At the beginning of this affair, Tristan had given himself up to be loved. He was too broken, too rooted in his wife and daughter to be able to love actively. But he felt a deep sense of gratitude and infinite tenderness for Monique growing inside him, a feeling that resembled love. Monique, if it wasn't for her complexion, her eyes and her chin, all clearly karmic, gave no indication of the serious mental difficulties she was experiencing. Her passionate love for Tristan masked everything and overcame her kharmic determinism. Love must be the only path beyond determinism.

Tristan's mental anguish since the departure of his family had reduced him to the worst. His paralysed shoulders that riveted his arms in an upright position, Menières syndrome after a car accident that left him with ringing in his ears, attacks of loss of balance and vomiting at night, a hearing loss in his right ear - all this, along with his grief, reduced him to an invalid, as he couldn't even take a bath on his own. This tall, handsome man was a radical wreck.

Monique, a nurse as well as a physiotherapist, looked after Tristan with tender devotion. He was her thing, totally her thing, incapable of any banal initiative. He could barely correct his papers because his state of health had led to him being appointed to the Centre National de Télé Enseignement in the higher education section. Reduced to helplessness, alone, he would undoubtedly have committed suicide, for he had no alternative at the bottom of the abyss of despair, and in a radical physical incapacity. Grief had massively demineralised him, calcium was no longer fixed, thyroid and parathyroid functioned poorly, disrupted by grief which is, as we have seen, a state of hypothyroidism.

Not only was Monique's support for his failing physical health admirable, but her moral support was equally impressive.

It was at this time that Tristan was charged by the LICRA, at the instigation of Michel Droit, for his book *"Dossiers secrets du XXIème siècle" (Secret Files of the 21st Century)*, which was not distributed but was known to an elite few. In this book, he had implacably stigmatised the actions of his global congeners of Rothschildo-Marxism, speculative, suicidal, megalomaniacally racist, disguised as anti-racism, and supported, alas, by the flaccid complicity of contemporary humanoids. In view of the author's famous Jewish name, the LICRA withdrew its complaint and the judge dismissed the case.

Michel Droit, by the first signature of the book, was unaware that its author was a Jew from a prominent family, because faux-cul-isme never takes such risks, especially if it wants to reach the Académie Française. But a Goy can indict another Goy to make himself look good...

Monique seemed Herculean. A companion morally and physically ruined, indicted by the gigantic global force of his radically totalitarian congeners... What woman today would be capable of such heroism. It took a lot of love.

Despite her precautions, Monique became pregnant. She went to see an old friend of hers who was a qualified medical doctor. Tristan never understood why she had introduced him to her. If she had felt how abnormally developed Tristan's aesthetic sense was, she wouldn't have made this mistake. She inflicted an ordeal that would remain a nightmare for the rest of her life.

She had been friends with this man! He was of average height, a Jew, and he had an ugly face. His hair was sparse and disorganised, his complexion waxy, his face emaciated and covered in such a profusion of wrinkles that he looked like an old dried-up apple. Tristan had never seen anything more horrible: he was uglier than Wiessenthal, Gainsbourg, Mendès France. How could Monique have been touched by this?

Although Monique's dream was to have a child, in the circumstances in which they found themselves, Tristan an invalid, they could not have one. Although Tristan considered abortion a crime, he considered that having a child in their situation was an even worse crime. Monique had an abortion.

Since then they've had a beautiful little boy whom they love, and when Tristan looks at him, his heart overflowing with love, he thinks that the child they killed would look like that one, and then his heart tears with horror and he asks God for forgiveness. Every time this thought occurs to him, it takes the form of a cosmic howl.

Two years had passed. He had no news of his wife and daughter and the only contact was the cheques he sent them. Monique's psychology was already changing for the worse, *but didn't the abortion she'd had have something to do with it? Is it possible to undergo such an ordeal without the somatic and psychic systems being affected?*

The answer is categorical: *abortion is a somato-psychic cataclysm.*

Monique obsessively wanted a child.

Tristan didn't want it at any price: his drama, his physical and mental health, the state of our rotting society...

But Monique wanted one so urgently that Tristan became convinced that his friend's basic equilibrium was linked to a much-desired maternity. So Tristan accepted the prospect, and even thought that all his tenderness would return, for it had been completely dulled. She needed this child who would bring back the harmony that was beginning to elude them. Tristan would have liked to be his friend's only child, but Monique wanted a child and he didn't have the courage to refuse her. He gave her this divine gift.

When Angelika found out, she demanded a divorce, but it didn't matter - she had already been living with the manager of a large German brewery for a long time.

Monique's tenderness quickly gave way to an aggressiveness, an anger that she was unable to control and of which he wondered if she was aware.

For the first two years of their marriage, when Tristan drove, Monique was impassive, relaxed and fearless. In the third year she became obnoxious when she was in the car with Tristan at the wheel. Tristan's sensitivity was so strained that he feared an accident when she was with him. Monique couldn't understand why Tristan drove differently to her. We all know we drive differently, but we overcome it. She obviously couldn't control him. Anything that didn't fit into her subjectivity as a driver seemed reckless. Tristan had the same feeling when Monique drove, but he knew how to hide it.

Three months after the birth of their son Aurélien, he was baptised in the countryside. The Jewish religion was unthinkable for Tristan, as was the Catholicism of the Conciliar Church. Catholic fundamentalism still had a moral and religious framework that could give structure to a person and not precipitate him into techno and drugs. He chose as his godfather a cultivated farmer, deeply religious and with a great quality of soul. He had known him for about ten years. Charlotte, his sister, married in America to a Frenchman, was the chosen godmother.

He hadn't seen her for about ten years, but she was his sister and she would make a good godmother because she had certain qualities.

After the ceremony in a traditional church full of people, unlike the other conciliar churches, they all gathered in a country inn that suited the occasion.

When Tristan took the little cradle basket from the car to the inn, he gazed at the angelic smile of this little creature with blue eyes, beautiful blond hair and a tender, cheeky look, and his heart suddenly swelled with love for him, a love as big as the whole blue sky. Aurélien filled her heart and made it overflow.

He would give her a heart and soul so heavy to bear at this time.

Monique and Tristan rightly felt that Paris and its suburbs were not a good place to bring up a child. Modern mega-cities had become neurotic laboratories, and generally pathogenic.

So they had to move to the provinces, even though friends had warned them about the dangers of burying a thyroid patient there.

They persisted in their plan, above all in the interests of the child, and also because Paris would soon have no future.

So they left for Berry, where they had found a house at an affordable rent. Monique had been appointed to the hospital in the main town and Tristan had resigned as a lecturer at the Paris-Sorbonne to take up a permanent post at the Centre National de Télé Enseignement. He could be anywhere in France to write his lectures and correct his DEUG and CAPES exam papers. He only had to come to Paris for a quarterly meeting.

A few weeks before they left, something happened that should have tipped Tristan off. Monique had a friend Gladys, who had gone to nursing school with her. One day she phoned Tristan with a curious message. Gladys told him: "I know that Monique is coming at three o'clock to bring me presents, so tell her that I won't be there and that she's bothering me"...

Tristan was all the more puzzled that Gladys gave no explanation or comment for this categorical ex-postulation. Tristan knew Gladys, to whom he had been introduced. She was a calm and reasonable person.

Such behaviour on his part revealed, in a nebulous way, a major anomaly in Monique's character.

Monique had a rather curious disposition: she had an incoercible impulse towards untimely devotion. She wanted to help whenever she wanted, whoever she wanted, wherever she wanted and however she wanted. Surprisingly, it was always passive people, Tristan himself in the pitiful state she had found him in (he wasn't complaining, because she had saved his life), her own mother who said nothing, old people or people seeing her for the first time who could benefit fully from an avalanche of care. This incoercible dynamism came to a screeching halt if there was the slightest opposition, criticism, questioning, embarrassment or personal opinion. The genuinely altruistic side of his approach, i.e. a function of others, was virtually absent. It seemed that the very real potential of her vocation for devotion had turned her altruistic character into a manic coloration. Once, when invited to stay with Tristan, she insisted on doing the washing-up for the lady of the house. The mistress insisted on refusing, but Monique did not give in. The hostess was forced to tell Monique,

"But Monique, I'm at home". On the other hand, Monique *didn*'t feel that you had a fundamental need for anything when you were close to her. She hadn't always been like that, on the contrary. In the period leading up to gestation, she would anticipate Tristan's slightest needs without him even having to express them.

Monique had taken maximum leave to mark the birth of Aurélien. She had to go back to work. Tristan decided that part-time was enough, because he knew how essential a mother's presence at home is to the balance of the child and the family in general.

So we had to find help at home, especially for the child.

Tristan advertised in three countries: France, Germany and England. He offered the young girl who came to him complete tuition in French, English, natural medicine, the basics of piano, and a choice of speciality to suit her through the Centre where he himself was a teacher. He received no reply. Perhaps because he had specified that he didn't want blue jeans or cigarettes.

One day, someone who lived in Vigneux came with her two daughters. One was a rather dull blonde and the other a small one with a distinctly hypothyroid bio-typological character. The mother's general appearance was distressing to the highest degree, her looks, voice and clothes.

A strange phenomenon occurred in which, especially after the years that followed, it was impossible not to see the finger of Providence with a capital P. It was obviously the pretty blonde who should have attracted Tristan in the first place. But this was not at all the case. The sister, with her slightly mongoloid face, was obviously slightly handicapped.

What's more, she was wearing trousers, which did nothing to enhance her looks. With her short hair, she could also have been mistaken for a boy.

Monique wouldn't take it. Tristan, although always attracted by beauty, especially when it came to women, *involuntarily* and *completely* forgot this particularity of his nature.

In this unattractive ensemble, he felt a tenderness, a depth, an altruistic sensitivity expressed in the eyes, revealed in the expression. He felt a perfection that would never be denied by the future.

So he agreed to take her in. He would give her a bit of pocket money, teach her, prepare her for an exam in line with her vocation, her tastes and her aspirations.

He had not been mistaken. This little girl was an angel very close to God.

Her love and competence for the child were boundless and made up for it. O how much, the slight awkwardness of her glandular typology. Beatrice's parents, as she was called, took no interest in their daughter and never showed any sentiment or gift towards her.

She was worse than an orphan, and her mother was a psycho whose worst problems could only be found in specialised institutions.

Tristan began by sending her to school himself, as she did not know the borders of France and had never heard of Napoleon.

It wasn't long before she was at school, passing her 'brevet des collèges', playing Bach's First Invention on the piano, Beethoven's Letter to Elise, Schumann's Foreign Lands and studying a book on basic naturopathy that Tristan had written.

She had taught the little boy to read and write and passed on to him the English and piano lessons that Tristan had taught him. Thanks to her, the boy played a piano piece at the local music school for two years in a row. She was an excellent teacher and Tristan himself envied her this quality, this patience that he did not possess. She also took an audio-visual typing course and began typing up all her lessons in preparation for her school-leaving certificate.

Her miracles didn't stop there: she took care of the whole house and Tristan's secretarial duties, and in his overworked state he always had a quick bite to eat when he needed it. She also looked after the garden, and Tristan had seen her carrying huge logs to put them away.

All this was shrouded in love for the child and for the three of them in general.

To say that she was astonishing does not begin to describe this unprecedented treasure, which was impossible to find in the 20th century. This kindness, this efficiency, this profound perfection enabled Tristan, by keeping an eye on her and the child, to carry out all his work as a teacher, writer and lecturer.

As long as they stayed in Vigneux, everything went well, and Béatrice went home to sleep with her parents, three hundred metres from the flat.

They soon left for the provinces, and from then on Beatrice stayed with the three of them.

For a few months, things were calm. Monique was totally cold and showed no tenderness whatsoever towards Bea, for that's what we called her. There was a very unambiguous feeling that she treated Bea as a colonist would treat a negro in the early days of colonisation. Monique was cold, without tenderness, whereas Tristan was so fond of love. His partner's sexuality had disappeared since the birth of Aurelien, and yet 'Don Juan' needed to be calmed down.

Soon, when Monique returned from work at around seven o'clock, the mood was one of anger and irritation. Instead of comforting little Bea, and showing her infinite gratitude for the treasure that she was, Monique was constantly railing against her. Instead of understanding a little awkwardness due to a slight thyroid insufficiency, so little compared to the hymalaya of qualities and love for their child that she displayed, instead of being grateful for this devotion to the house, she kept attacking her, which made the little girl's heart beat faster and rendered her speechless. Tristan tried to compensate for this despicable brutality, but to no avail:

— *You're only good for mopping,"* she said.

Tristan remembered how, as a child, his heart used to pound because of the nastiness of *his beloved grandmother*, whom his first cousin called 'cowhide'. And now he noticed the same behaviour in Monique, with the same yellowish complexion, the same look devoid of feeling that seemed to emanate from a non-biologically complete being. Tristan had never noticed Monique's generous indulgence, her basic gratitude for this marvellous being who gave them everything without counting the cost. And Tristan could only compensate her with a little pocket money and the education he gave her. Nothing compared to everything she offered them, with her open heart and the absolute gentleness that would never be denied. And such perfection for their child!

This snarling, downright sadistic, unmeasured, totally undeserved malice towards someone so good seemed to Tristan the height of monstrosity. Tristan's heart sank every time Monique attacked Bea. With his extreme sentimental sensitivity, he felt the little girl's poignant pain perfectly. He suffered for her and every time she was shocked by Monique, he was shocked too. So he tried to 'cheer her up' with all his affection.

— My little darling, it doesn't matter. You know that Monique is like that, so don't worry about it.

After Monique's brutality, she would cry for hours, sometimes days. Tristan put all his energy into countering the effects of this vile, murderous verbal abuse. It was like murder.

Tristan, who had defended his thesis "on hyper- and hypo-thyroid states", knew full well that if you attack people with a hypo tendency, you cause a serious accentuation of hypothyroidism, which can lead to tragic sadness, neurasthenia, a state of near-catatonic immobility and *hence death*.

Monique's behaviour was therefore that of a murderer. It was all the more frightening for Tristan because he had noticed that Monique had this lateral flattening of the chin, which was itself slightly recessive.

It all fitted in with the kind of impulses described by Lombroso.

Sometimes Béa, disintegrated by Monique, would remain unable to leave her bed for one or two days, so dynamic, so energetic, so tireless,[72] put into a state of shock, which we know is a state of hypothyroidism.

Tristan knew that only Monique's tenderness could do everything. He did what he could, but it was the love of the lady of the house that counted for this poor little girl, an orphan in fact, and even worse because her parents were negative. Alone to console her, he was only marginally effective.

One of those tragic days when Tristan was returning from the university's quarterly meeting in Paris, he asked on the way home:

- Did Bea eat anything or drink any broth?

Not only had the little girl taken nothing because Monique had given her nothing, but she had remained alone in her room, in her almost catatonic prostration, without a word of warmth. There was a bowl in the kitchen in front of Monique, which she had just helped herself to. Tristan took it and brought it to the poor little darling. His eyes were full of tears and he felt disgust in his heart. This murderous foetal behaviour would have been shocking if Monique had humbly accused herself of it, but as it wasn't, it was supremely despicable.

There are two kinds of suffering: that which is expressed in wickedness and inspires only disgust, and that which is expressed in kindness and arouses that supreme form of love which is compassion. This pain was Bea's. Monique was going to build this compassion into a diamond in Tristan's heart...

It's true that Monique spoke to Tristan in such a tone of voice that one day he was forced to say to her:

— I don't know of any manoeuvre that would allow their wife to speak to them in that tone of voice.

---

[72] She did, however, have strong adrenals.

A friend who had witnessed the perfect quality of the first two years of their union once said to Tristan:

— She doesn't love you any more. She gives you hateful looks, the birth of the child has destroyed everything.

Tristan explained that the birth of the child had little to do with it, as Monique's behaviour had been the same for about a year before the baby was born. But Tristan couldn't help thinking that the horrible abortion Monique had undergone had been fiercely juxtaposed with her temperamental state.

Little Aurélien, that angel of her heart, grew and learned in the calm of the day, while his father worked, covering them both. Monique would come home and make their hearts beat with her derisory and ruthless ejaculations, which little Béa put up with without a word. Only tears and frozen silences testified to the paralysis and heartbreak of her tender, generous little soul, which had given birth to the eternal, flowering tree of compassion in Tristan's heart.

Monique never made a gesture of affection, never spoke a word of kindness, never made love. She spoke harshly to Tristan and unkindly to Beatrice. What she taught Bea about housework was judicious, but she ventilated it in a way that was unacceptable, even unbearable. She was so oblivious that she didn't realise the incredible difference in tone she was using towards her son and towards Bea and Tristan. Pure honey with her son, sulphuric acid with us. More often than not, Tristan gave up talking to her because he felt she wasn't listening. You couldn't say that this was exclusive towards Tristan, because his friend Gladys had once said to Tristan: "Any conversation with Monique is like walking a tightrope". So it was all in the same vein and it would probably be an exaggeration to think that Monique reserved her behaviour for her partner and little Bea. There was a general psychopathy . When he had to talk to her because of reasonable obligations, he had to take it in his stride. He noticed that everyone gave up, even his own mother, who said to him one day:

— You know what Monique is like...

They had been in Berry for several years now and Monique was clearly getting worse and worse. Her behaviour towards Bea was childish, incoercible jealousy. Sometimes Tristan would write down all the tears he didn't shed in a notebook he kept close to him. Sometimes he would improvise bits of his heart on the piano. Monique would pass by and in a dry tone she would say:

— I'm going to sleep now.

How could Tristan's improvised melodies have kept Monique awake at night, when for months they had put their childhood love to sleep? And even if they had, how could he put it like that, without fervour, without tenderness, without respect? He felt that Monique didn't know who he was. How would their child ever know? The emotional imprint imposed on a child can paralyse intellectual understanding forever. How could he teach him everything he knew to get him out of the *Judeo-Cartesian* abyss if they didn't do it together in mutual love? Tristan was unhappy without love or respect, and with this grotesque jealousy towards little Bea who lined their home with love, patience and true culture towards their child?

We had to think of the little one and do what was best for him. He had to show his mother all the love she needed because, after all, she was ill. If she had had cancer, he would have loved her too and could have shown her that, but this mental illness was building a concrete wall between her and her partner's affection. You can't love a child if you don't love its mother. To love a child without loving your mother or father is to love only yourself. A woman who loves a child without loving her father is nothing more than a selfish woman who loves only a visceral extension of herself, and nothing else. Alas, the little boy was beginning to sound like his mother to his father. And this would continue monstrously into adulthood. The mimicry and psychological imprint of children are implacable. Monique's lack of love would be copied by the child, especially as Monique would plunge into the abyss of immorality to consolidate it, as we shall see.

Yet Tristan dreamed of raising his son to the highest heights. He wanted to teach him all his unique awareness. He had already helped little Béa to acquire what no one else had: true integrity, sound judgement, a critical mind that let nothing of the shams that engulfed us every day slip by. With patience, she taught Aurélien all the basics of nursery school: reading, writing and arithmetic, with the added bonus of soul.

Sometimes Tristan felt a cruel need for a woman worthy of the name. But that would have been a betrayal of his child. He didn't want other women, but sexual asphyxiation made him wish for adventures.

If he had been able to see Monique manifest herself as she was manifesting herself, and above all as she would manifest herself when they were separated, not only would he never have given her a child, he would never have seen her even once, just once. But now she was the mother of his beloved son. Aurélien was here now, and she had to teach him to be healthy in body and soul. To realise Tristan's living ideal in him. But Monique's recklessness was robbing her of hope.

What could he achieve in his son without Monique's love, respect and femininity? It was like trying to fill a bottomless barrel with water from Lourdes. As he looked around him in France, Germany, Spain and England, there were no more men. There were blue-jean humanoids, materialistic profiteers, and women who mimicked them in the name of the sordid and imbecilic equality of the sexes, dressed like leftovers in need of a male makeover. Politicians who were scavengers and schemers who cared about the greatness and beauty of France like they cared about their first shirt. A country penetrated by Africans to the point of complete dilution into bio-typological nothingness. If her son had to drown in this mass of asexual informality, wouldn't it be better to die with him? He wouldn't be able to do anything if Monique didn't know who he was. She would never know in her condition, because she could only love the child through her love for the father who could give him so much. Wasn't trying to bring up her son the supreme illusion that kept him alive?

O how Tristan ached for the earth...

Tristan's nerves were giving way. He hid the fact that he cried alone during the day. Beatrice's incredible gentleness, kindness and efficiency enabled him to withstand the shock, in other words Monique's psychopathy. Without Béatrice he would have collapsed. He was amazed to see little Béa doing her technical and secondary studies, studying English and piano, passing on her knowledge to Aurélien, cleaning the whole house, acting as his permanent assistant, organising reading, writing and games for the little one, all for hours on end. It was all a miracle. How could Monique not realise that they had a treasure close to them that would have been impossible to find at the end of this century?

Tristan had built Beatrice, but she had the potential that made his Pygmalion work easy. Providence had sent Béa so that Tristan could realise his spiritual ideal in his son in a world that had lost everything. She adored her son, was firm and patient, and was a miracle that Monique refused to see.

Fate's horrible sneer.

How, but how, could she not understand the marvellous harmonious complementarity of the four of them?

Didn't she understand that, even if she had had a suave character, she would never have been able, by working, to take care of the child, the house, her own mother who had come to live not far from them in town, and whose material situation was pitiful, an artist husband, all the same, he admitted, difficult to live with, because of his sensitive and aesthetic delicacy with multiple demands? But Béa, their little Béa, made it all possible, almost easy. Together they accomplished a Herculean task almost effortlessly! How could anyone be jealous of this slightly handicapped little girl whose competence, devotion and kindness gave them a home, a happy child who could, at least for the nursery school years, be isolated from secularism, the purveyor of voting-consumers, clients of pathogenic music, drugs, unemployment, potato-bellied vestimentarity with moulded buttocks, suicide which kills fifty thousand young French people a year, and terrorism. And on top of that, a husband who is already difficult to support alone...

There was in Monique a force of refusal to be happy, of destruction that was not masked by her altruistic bulldozer hysteria.

She had everything that is essential, everything that no woman could have in the second half of the twentieth century.

She didn't even kiss Tristan in the mornings and evenings any more, or reply when he spoke to her. One evening when he took a bath late - it was the only time in his life that he took a bath at that hour - she threw a fit of hysteria such that Tristan suddenly lost all confidence and hope in her.

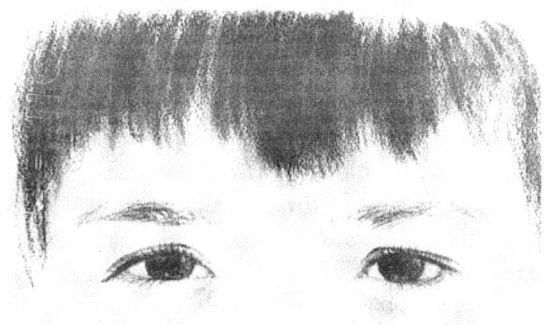

"The big-hearted servant you were jealous of".

His childish jealousy of this defenceless little cutie, so good, was only growing. Tristan could feel and see this sadistic aggression towards the little girl more and more. She was like an explosive grenade in everything she said and no amount of reasoning could change her appalling behaviour.

Tristan tried to console the poor, dear child, but Monique's destructive power was infinitely greater than the treasures of balm Tristan applied to her wounds.

When Monique's mother came to retire, Monique spent a whole month setting up the house. Béatrice and Tristan looked after the little one in the evening as well as during the day, as Monique didn't get home until late.

Béa continued to teach reading, writing, piano, English and games with her fabulous efficiency. Tristan took on his university work, writing his books and teaching Bea. Monique had never been able to stay with the child for three hours for his training and instruction. She had no vocation for it. When she wasn't working at the hospital, she had to be on the move, doing practical things, so Béa was irreplaceable: Monique was unaware of this.

Monique's jealousy was growing and so was her sadism.

So Tristan's compassion for little Bea grew even more, which led to an additional flood of jealousy and sadism from Monique. An infernal vicious circle from which he could not escape. Tristan called Béa "my little darling", just as he called his daughters Nathalie and Chantal, and he called Monique "Mummy", which is the most tender name one could give to one's companion. "My little darling" sent Monique into a frenzy. She was putting herself on the same level as this marvellous slightly handicapped girl and this provoked a certain shame on Tristan's part: how could she place herself in such a juxtaposition? The idea of jealousy was absurd. Tristan would have simply defended this lovely innocent against anyone who had done her harm, be it a close relative or a stranger. Sadly, that's what he had to do to his partner, the person closest to him, the one he loved most, the mother of his son. Such jealousy added a grotesque aspect to its pathological nature: Tristan had known a lot of pretty girls, no matter how unintelligent, none of whom would ever have been jealous of this marvellous little being marked by fate, alone, with no real parents. It was unthinkable.

For a normal woman, especially one who has a child and is forced to work, little Bea could only inspire tender gratitude, and in this case, in this century of collective suicide and decay, even distraught gratitude. Where can you find someone today who can love your child, look after him magnificently, educate him when you, the mother, are forced to work? Where? Tristan had witnessed the tragedy of children entrusted to anonymous women who, without love, do technical work for pay. Aurélien was benefiting from the impossible: *love, free devotion*, the very thing that builds a child's heart and soul. And Monique didn't understand this enormous gift of destiny? You couldn't love Aurélien without loving little Bea in the middle of the twentieth century, if you had a conscience. But soon Tristan would have nine pieces of evidence to prove Monique's lack of conscience.

Horror always has excuses, and unfortunately valid ones.

As a child, Monique had been rejected by her father and beaten up. This overall trauma clung to her and was aggravated by a fall into a well that scared her to death. All this had led to an imbalance of spirit and a frustration that could account for infantile jealousy. In fact, Monique was not strong enough to take on the job, the child, an artist husband who alone at the end of the twentieth century would have monopolised all her energies, and on top of that a mother of soft character, of weak intelligence on which Monique compensated for her father's deficiency which was, it must be said, considerable. In fact, Monique's only emotional bond was with her mother. As for her love for Aurélien, it was clearly of a *strictly biological nature*, as demonstrated by her imperative need for motherhood. If she had really loved her son she would have taken into account the *synthesis* necessary for his balance, especially with a father of quality. If the mother had had a slightly higher mental level, her firmness could have brought Monique out of her vesicosis and thus preserved her daughter's happiness. Alas, the mother had already failed twice in her marriage, so her daughter had to fail too. There was no way she could support her daughter, but she was bound to support her bladder. Any neurosis increases if it is supported by someone who is emotionally close to you. The presence of the mother would therefore precipitate everything into a void. Hadn't the mother had a hysterical fit because Tristan had dropped by to kiss her son, whom she was looking after at the time?

Despite Monique's spite towards Bea, Tristan agreed to the plan for a house that he would pay half for and that would be in Monique and Aurélien's name. He thought that Monique would be so happy to have a house that she would also understand how indispensable Bea was to them. He had the secret hope that Monique's gratitude might turn into therapy. Alas, he was an optimist and didn't gauge the seriousness of Monique's condition clinically. As soon as he had signed Monique told him in no uncertain terms that "Beatrice would never set foot in his house". He would never have signed if he had imagined the seriousness of his companion's mental state.

What's more, when the framework of the house was erected, Tristan realised that he would only be able to have a room of twenty-two square metres at his disposal! What's more, all their furniture had no chance of getting into the house. So fate had decided to separate them.

The house would be built in a few months. Monique had talked about finding a room for Bea not far from the house. Tristan found the solution acceptable, on condition that Monique showed affection for the little girl before she moved into the planned room. Under no circumstances was she to feel 'left alone' in the city, without love. Tristan accepted the solution on the sole condition that Monique would be kind to Bea over the next few months until the house was finished.

Tristan felt that his presence was not helping matters with Monique and decided to go and stay with his daughter and some friends in Spain for a few weeks. Perhaps things would be back on an even keel between Monique and Beatrice.

A little before the delicate time of the month, little Béa found herself in a nervous state, common in women in perfect health, and therefore even more understandable in Béa. All she needed was to be understood, loved, comforted and supported. Instead, Monique and her mother made a fuss about her, phoning the girl's parents (whose quality Monique knew, since she had made a number of pejorative and perfectly objective digressions about them). This had the effect of aggravating the poor girl's condition, who found herself in a moral desert populated by Monique and her crushing mother. Neither of them thought of giving the poor child a bit of tenderness. It was only much later that Tristan learned of the events from Bea's parents themselves, for Bea had said nothing to him. They said: "When Madame Monique phoned us, we thought there must be something wrong with her head". Bea's parents, though lamentable, to put it mildly, had expressed a sad truth. There were other manifestations of Monique's mental state:

Monique had two great friends, Gladys, mentioned earlier, and Simone. All three had graduated from the same nursing school in Paris. Simone had come to stay with us for a few days. When Tristan drove her back to the station, she said to him:

—   When Monique's mother and I are in the kitchen, we feel like idiots.

Even at this basic level, Monique didn't allow any initiative. Then, as they were talking about Monique's difficult character, Simone said:

—   I can't stand Monique for more than a week, even though she's my best friend.

Tristan wanted to try and have a conversation with Monique, to explain to her the heartbreaking path she was leading them all down, especially their dear child. The idea of talking to Monique was a terrible ordeal because he knew that she wasn't listening, that she was inaccessible to any reasoning, that she was incapable of understanding what was essential for the future of the little one, protected from the current situation by the calm of everyone, the tenderness of their little community. He and Beatrice were models of kindness, patience and gentleness towards her. Béa did sometimes 'talk back', but Monique had to have pushed her to the limit. Monique didn't realise how indulgent they were towards her. There was something repulsive about her cowardice towards them. It was certain that an ordinary man would have beaten her at short notice in such circumstances, or would have left her in spite of the child. Another young girl would have left, insulting Monique. This was the case with several girls who had come before Bea and who couldn't stand Monique for more than a few weeks.

Curiously, the only girl Monique had put up with was simply looking after the boy, lounging in an armchair, demanding that Tristan give her as many lessons as possible in English and naturopathy etc. She was making a comfortable living out of it. She was making a comfortable living. Then Monique overexerted herself so much that she fainted in Tristan's arms. A worried Tristan wrote to the girl's mother expressing his concern and asking her to suggest that her daughter help out around the house. The girl left a few days later on the pretext of seeing her parents and... never returned.

In a way, it was Bea and Tristan's kindness that helped them put up with Monique. She was certainly unaware of her own character. They all had to be indulgent and understand Monique's painful and complicated psychological situation. Monique was taking advantage of their intelligence and kindness towards her.

Beatrice was moved only by her love for the child and her affection for his parents. This love was so visible, so transparent, so overflowing that it brought tears to Tristan's eyes when he gazed at Beatrice and her son without appearing to do so. So many times had tears welled up in his eyes as he watched them backstage, seeing that flood of tenderness, devotion and patience. And it was on such a treasure that Monique was committing a sacrilege!

He tried again to engage Monique in a dialogue.

—   You should be aware of your character. Simone, your friend of twenty years, can't stand you for more than a week.

—   Simone told you that? I'm going to phone her to find out if it's true.

The confidence she had in what Tristan was telling her spoke volumes about the quality of his affection.

Monique telephoned:

—   Is it true, Simone, that you can't stand me for more than a week?

—   As you well know, Monique, neither does my sister when you come to visit us in Brittany. But that doesn't stop you from being my best friend.

Monique hung up and didn't see Simone again for a very long time.

This conversation didn't teach him any lessons, not even the elementary humour that would have consisted of saying: "I know I have an impossible character, protect yourself from me, don't let me do anything to you".

In fact, that's exactly what Tristan said to his girlfriends years before.

They took no notice, but there were hardly any problems.

A few days passed and Gladys, the other friend, phoned to check up. Tristan described the tragic rut they were in. He recounted Monique's phone call to Simone.

Gladys interrupted:

—   But it's not a week that I can't stand it, it's forty-eight hours.

And she repeated the phrase Tristan had heard before:

—   Every conversation with Monique is a tightrope walk.

Tristan phoned a friend who was a professor of medicine and who had worked on his doctoral thesis.

—   The most intelligent women," he tells her, "are currently involved in perversions with infantile, derisory and even grotesque fixations. It's the price of the current degeneration. I'm no more optimistic than you are, especially if it's a Cain syndrome (jealousy).

Tristan was certainly a pessimist.

Monique had betrayed her feelings, her noblest aspirations. Aurelien's future depended on Bea's miraculous efficiency, because the first years are decisive in a person's destiny, but they both had to support her. Tristan was a teacher and he could save his son from the secular school where for decades he had seen his pupils fall apart. His son had to be spared the free school, which was even more rotten than the secular one. It seemed that the Church was desperate to outdo the slide into nothingness. Monique was in the process of reducing to nothing what he had built with so much pain and so much love. What was the point of his awareness, the awareness he thought he'd given Monique and which should have been an invincible armour against his own grotesque, sadistic neurosis?

He wanted so much for Aurelian to have nothing to do with this ferocious, reductionist Christianity, this colonialism that massacred twenty thousand blacks a week for thirty years in the mines of South Africa to exploit the gold mines, these gulags that kill people by the tens of millions for their own good, this hypnotic, pathogenic, criminogenic, degrading music...

It was the end of times.

Tristan didn't know where to turn. He wanted to protect his little one. He absolutely wanted to. He had built everything up for that purpose and he couldn't let it all fall apart. He would have given his life to protect his son, to educate him according to his heart and conscience. No, it wasn't all going to be destroyed.

He wanted to die taking his little one in his arms. How great the temptation!

O that he were earth-sick!

What was this world going to offer him without the protection of his lucidity? Radical nothingness, the kind you see in the press and on television, the haunting music that kills and makes you love it through animic destruction. He would have accepted anything to raise their little one towards his ideal: for that, Monique had to love Tristan and their little one would blossom beyond destructive agents like the thirty injections of putrid vaccines that destroy our immune systems...

Tristan had a great friend, a professor of Hebrew Bible, a truly virtuous Jewess, who was so disciplined about her diet that, at the age of seventy-three, she didn't show the slightest sign of presbyopia. He wrote her his drama, Monique's Madness. The response was a shock.

> To Tristan and Monique.
>
> On the twenty-fifth of May at 8.30 p.m., my grandson Emmanuel, handsome, gifted, a poet, rejecting this society and practising none of the vices of today's youth, at the age of twenty-two with a degree in history and sociology, was out for a walk alone in a village near Orange when he was run over and killed by a motorbike crossing the road. The gendarmerie informed my

daughter, who was away in Paris. I went to Orange on my own to complete the formalities.

I found myself standing in front of the hole into which the coffin containing my beloved grandson, whom I brought up, had been lowered. Earth was thrown in and everything was consumed.

Stabat mater

In the face of this, your abracadabra conflicts seem to me to be unworthy, futile, derisory and these are just understatements. Imagine something like this happening to your son: I hope you learn a lesson from my misfortune. Don't bother writing to me. No words, nothing could soothe my pain and I will descend into the Scheal with it.

Esther

Tristan didn't need this atrocious lesson. He gave the letter to Monique. The only thing she could think of to say that gave her vesicitis its full dimension was:

— What does this have to do with me?

Tristan showed Esther's letter to Aurelian's godfather, the wise man of the land whom he had chosen for his child.

— *This is the end of times,"* he said to Tristan, showing him an image of the Virgin covered in blood, drawn by a visionary. *"The devil has not succeeded in destroying you so far. He will destroy you through the one in whom you put all your trust, the one you thought you had protected from all the impostures: woman, his constant ally. Remember what your fellow man Otto Weininger said:*

"We are in the age of the woman and the Jew".

Madame de Gastine died at the age of sixty-nine from a serious rheumatic disease, chronic progressive polyarthritis. Tristan had felt his heart reconciling with his mother and prayed the prayer he had felt overflowing from his heart when his wife and daughter left him. Unfortunately, two days after the funeral, a mutual acquaintance told him about the horrible things his mother had said about him a few days before her death.

After his mother's death, fate had decreed an eternal divorce between him and his mother...

Tristan had an old friend in Paris, but she was one of the most intelligent women of the century. Such finesse of mind, such breadth of observation of history and current affairs, were unique in the world.

He had confided his tragedy to Frédérique, as she was called, for there was no one in the world to whom such pain could be better confided. She had replied at length, thinking that reason would prevail and that Monique was simply experiencing temporary difficulties. It seemed impossible to her that such derisory jealousy could take root in Monique's heart. She had even telephoned Monique, who had said to her:

- *Everyone proves me wrong, including my mother.*

She promised Tristan that she would write to Monique and send her the text.

The perfection of the letter was unequalled on every level: *everything* was said and Tristan could never have done better than this complete synthesis.

My dear Monique.

I was dismayed to hear about the conflict over the telephone. I've thought about it and decided to write to you to help you out of the unfortunate impasse you've got yourself into.

First I would like to express my esteem for Tristan's discretion. A few weeks ago he did not breathe a word to me about your dispute, only informing me of the immense difficulties that were preventing him from writing to me.

As you know, when I met you I always made the most of you, either in my correspondence or in person, because I felt that as well as charm, you had qualities of heart and understanding, which justified Tristan's passionate nature, his hypersensitive, vulnerable nature, his thirst for tenderness, his need for protection, so common in man but to a greater degree in him, all traits worthy of compassion.

If you were a nurse, you'd know how to understand and mother a man who was forever "earth-sick" and lived only from enthusiasm to despair, never lukewarm.

You told me, Monique, that your grievance lay in the fact that he pampered with words and attentions the slightly handicapped girl in charge of caring for your little Aurélien and assisting at home and with your child's father.

How could you not rejoice, Monique, you who are all grace, at this agreement where the child disadvantaged by nature shared with Aurelien a paternal feeling naturally inclined to effusion.

Ah, Monique, you had the chance, and there was still time, to ensure a double maternity in line with Tristan's double paternity, and you would cause a triple misfortune, Aurelien's, Tristan's and yours, by rejecting the little innocent from the home. Think of the wound you would inflict on the child. Aurélien knows everything, feels everything, and the wounds imprinted on his fragile, malleable subconscious leave lifelong inhibitions that sow the seeds of serious problems in adulthood.

Out of love for this child, out of caution for this fragile human growth, out of respect for the harmony that you must teach him in an exemplary way, don't take offence at Tristan's affection-compassion, which I'm sure in no way alters the unfailing feeling he has always had for you. In reality, you have a double maternity to assume with regard to the child and the father. As you know, Monique, there is no conjugal love that does not reach maturity without the husband becoming for the wife, and this is very beautiful, the eldest child. It's the most beautiful achievement of all, and the wife so naturally becomes the mother that her husband calls her "mother".

Otherwise it is like a musical instrument that is missing a string. Don't torture your soul with the anxiety of an emotional rivalry that hides in its folds a turmoil unworthy of your incomparable charm. Don't destroy your home for the sole reason, you told me, of your intolerance of the tenderness expressed by Tristan to your little helper in words.

The fact that he pampers her like his own child is nothing to be alarmed about, nor does it detract from your priority. Open your heart wide and chase away this totalitarianism. Put your pretty smile back on Monique, "non impediat musicam" says the sacred texts: "do not prevent music". Of course, I'm not telling you anything new by saying that music is harmony, it's everything that rises from us in pleasant chords. It is the resolution of dissonances and alterations in the return to the initial tonality. It is the expression of conciliation and reconciliation in the instrument of our heart. I beg you, Monique, make peace within yourself, recreate the harmony of your home. Cherish the companion who has been skinned alive since childhood, love the precious little companion whom your Aurelian must regard as his big sister. Take a deep breath and get rid of the obsession that would be the undoing of your life. Walk up to Aurélien's father with your pretty smile and this will be the end of a collective nightmare. I make a pact with heaven to help you regain yourself and your home, in peace of heart, and I kiss you.

Frédérique

It was in the logical purpose of such a letter to perform the miracle of the spirit if it met a spirit. But it failed. Weeks later Frédérique said to Tristan, "The unfortunate woman is fundamentally wicked".

The nightmare she was going to impose on Tristan was going to take on murderous, gigantic proportions.

Everything Monique had to say in response to this letter was unspeakable:

"Frédérique dresses up like an old biddy, protects all the males in the neighbourhood and is Tristan's mistress.

Frédérique was almost eighty...

It was in destiny, in astrology, that Tristan would try to shed light on his tragedy, and above all that of his beloved son, for despite his despair, he had not lost hope...

Tristan had known a friend for years who practised the age-old art of astrology for reasons of wisdom. He had had many opportunities to observe its astonishing capacity. He had connected the endocrinological bases of biotypology with the most interesting astrological correspondences, particularly in terms of their pathological potential, which Tristan verified every day.

He wanted to know if the stars would allow him to bring up his child, in other words, in this age of total decay, to win a victory over nothingness. Such a victory was only possible with Monique's love. The problem of Monique was therefore at the epicentre of everything. So he wrote to his friend Maurice:

My dear Maurice.

You and a remarkably intelligent Parisian friend are the only people I can confide my tragedy to. That of wanting to raise my son to the level of my conscience, in this world that is practically destroyed. But Monique, whom you know well, is creating a major problem for me that I can't solve and that only she could dominate and even totally eradicate from her unconscious. But can she? That's the question I'd like to put to your astrological conscience. If I can't work for my son, nothing interests me any more. I ask you to examine our respective charts and tell me in no uncertain terms what you think.

At home, we have a little Beatrice who teaches Aurélien and helps us masterfully at home. And yet she is hypo-thyroid overall, of the glandular type, and therefore slightly handicapped. Her perfection in terms of competence is sublime. She manages to educate our child, do everything at home, study for herself with a view to her 'brevet des collèges', study piano and English, which she passes on to our child... She also takes care of my meals, secretarial work and so on. It's a miracle!

I've been teaching her for three years now, and despite her inherent glandular awkwardness, she succeeds in everything she does. She is unique and irreplaceable in this day and age, and in a providential stroke of grace, she loves Aurélien with all her heart. I know she would give her life for him! She does everything with love, and you can understand how grateful I am for this gift of Providence. She is a fundamental agent if I want to protect my child from what I call, as you remember, 'Judeo-Cartesianism'. Slightly disgraced, she was the victim of everyone. She was persecuted as a child at school - two teeth knocked out. As for her parents, they were absolute losers.

Monique, instead of being emotionally grateful for this gift from heaven that extends her with such efficiency, tenderness and patience, displays an incoercible infantile jealousy syndrome towards her that translates into the worst. Not only does she show no tenderness for the poor dear, but she never stops attacking her whatever she says or does, whereas even if Monique wasn't working, she wouldn't be able to do all that Beatrice does (patient, unbelievable, pedagogical, efficient, constant dedication).

I can't count the days that this poor child, who does everything she can and more for us, doesn't cry because of Monique's sadistic paranoia. For my part, despite my overwork as a teacher and writer, I try to compensate for Monique's brutality towards the unfortunate girl. I try to console her, to show her a little of the affection that Monique denies her. These slightly hypo-thyroid beings need much more affection than other human beings, and they know how to give it back in a way that moves the heart. I could do without this painful work because I have other things to do, but I can feel the little girl dying because Monique not only doesn't give her an iota of the affection she deserves for so much unique love and devotion, but is tragically negative towards her. Sadly, my compassion for this child increases tenfold as Monique's malice towards her increases tenfold. It's a complete vicious circle, because my intervention with the child is becoming more and more like basic therapy, but it's ineffective when you consider the trauma Monique is inflicting on her. The poor little girl sometimes cries for hours, motionless, without Monique being moved in the slightest.

I try to explain to Monique that if she gave this little Providence the love and encouragement it needs, I wouldn't have to carry out this task myself, with little success. It's no use: she continues to monologue on the premises of her vesicosis, deaf to all common sense, all reasoning, all elementary humanity.

We have a child to bring up, a house that we're buying in Monique's name, that I'm furnishing and for which I'm taking on a 50% deposit over fifteen years. But if Monique doesn't see that we've got everything and doesn't try to get better, I won't be able to do anything for my son and I won't have anything to live for. What's more, with this house we've bought, if we don't get along perfectly, we're going to descend into suicidal anarchy. That's where we are: at a dead end, and a very painful one at that. Monique doesn't understand at all that what she reproaches me for, i.e. scooping up the poor little thing every day, is her fault and hers alone!

Our friend Frédérique, who wrote her an admirable letter, told her: "You're hurling this little girl at Tristan's heart". And that's exactly what she's doing. There's no dialogue possible with Monique: she's going round in circles in her obsession and is wrecking us all, including our beloved child, which is the worst thing. I can't see any solution. And yet I tell myself that it's impossible that Monique doesn't have enough mental health to pull herself together at the last minute. What do our natal charts say?

Personally, I tell myself that everything that has intelligence, rigour and love must disappear from this world. That's why I no longer have any hope.

Three weeks later he received three studies. All these considerations shed light on, but did not resolve, the inextricable web of which Monique was the keystone.

At the start of his life, little Aurélien was destined to be tested by his mother, who would hurt him because of her disagreement with his father. His birth chart showed that his father would act stubbornly to isolate his son from the decadent world around him. Aurelian would become attached to a distant cause to which he would give all his love. He was destined to create for a wide audience in the pursuit of an ideal. He would be inclined to detach himself from earthly things, indulging in a certain renunciation, devotion, abnegation and sacrifice. He would exist in isolation, excluding notoriety. He would protect the weak, the underprivileged, care for the sick and develop supra-normal gifts.

Tristan's chart indicated that he sensed his son's destiny and tried with all his might to prepare the child for his task. It would seem that Monique and Tristan would not separate (an astrologer's error), remaining united in the perspective of love and the child's education.

Tristan's theme was one of 'over-maternal' love for his son (it was true that Tristan felt like a chicken-father).

There was a kind of noble hysteria in Tristan's theme, a desire to protect his son from the inhumanity that his heart abhorred.

Tristan would therefore have tended to impose an isolated educational system on Aurelian, but the child's chart revealed that he did not suffer from this at all, on the contrary. An agreement between Monique and Tristan concerning the child was confirmed (another and the same error by the astrologer). Aurélien would be deeply rebellious against society, but could he be more so than his father?

Aurélien was said to be gifted with a considerable amount of magnetic fluid, which could help to relieve others (Tristan had already experienced this gift in his son, who, by placing his hands on his abdomen, made stomach aches disappear in a few minutes). The child would feel as much at home with his father as with his mother. Tristan's and Monique's circumstances only served to highlight the chaotic state of their respective themes. As long as they were rowing together in the direction of a frightening lucidity and care for the afflicted, they were rowing together.

The child had thrown the rock of his presence into a water where divergent currents were in motion.

Karma imposed the full weight of their disharmony on them.

There was no hope for Monique," said Maurice. She was a serious character, stubborn and monolithic.

The first time Tristan phoned Maurice to talk about Monique's theme, before sending him a piece of written work, he told him at length about his afflicted and brutal Mars and concluded:

- I couldn't...

But who could have lived with Monique unless she had been absolutely docile for ten years, apart from Tristan? Certainly not his own mother, who had made no secret of it to Tristan.

Tristan's suicidal tendency, if he could do nothing for his son, was written into his chart.

Maurice's study of Monique was also revealing.

His ascendant was in Aries, the willful, even violent sign of Mars. The inharmonies were violent and heavy. The child would suffer from the wounds inflicted by Mars. Monique's karmic tragedy lay in the fact that she could not control her formidable Martian force, **which received no beneficial influence from Mercury (intelligence) or Venus (goodness, beauty, gentleness).** She would have had to overcome her stars, which normally "incline but do not determine".[73]

It would have been necessary for her, having become aware of the harshness of her ram's horns, to try to deflect their painful effects for others and for herself. He added a few considerations drawn from the theme of Beatrice: she was a miraculous presence for the toddler and a providence for them all. She possessed a real saving power reserved for certain beings privileged by God to help, console and save their neighbour.

---

[73] In the course of a lifetime of observation, the author can say that he has never seen anyone "dominate his stars". All the astral themes studied corresponded perfectly to the behaviour of the subject studied. So it seems that 'dominating the stars' is a rare occurrence. It is true that our decadent age has lost its free will through hypotrophy of the internal genitalia. What's more, women have been profoundly deformed by their "masculinisation".

He concluded: when you can't stand someone, your ram's horns hurt, Monique, they hurt a lot. If you love your son, it's absurd to harm this little providence, because the result can only be negative for the child, your partner and yourself. You need to overcome your instinctive impulses, which are, in this case, completely animal and which are only there to cause the greatest harm to yourself and your loved ones...

Reading Beatrice's theme turned Tristan's heart upside down. Everything about it was true both in the present and in the future, in other words, the fifteen years following the writing of this study.

Her Sun was in the 12th house, the house of trials. It represented renunciation, a spirit of sacrifice and self-denial, accomplished in isolation and in secret, confidential discretion. There was an effort to purify the conscience through voluntary sacrifices that contributed to moral progress. She had a natural inclination to care for the sick, to help and protect the weak. She would only occupy herself with work that required distance from the world. She had a tendency to seek solitude and to make self-renunciations. Her health left something to be desired, a languorous illness that would require prolonged stays in a rest home . She had an ardent desire to devote herself to the infirm, to those less fortunate.

Her feelings drove her to acts of self-sacrifice and melancholy love. Her constitution was not robust, but her sensitivity was very great, with sublime impulses towards sacrifice, charity and the desire to help her fellow human beings and her inferior brothers, the animals, for whom she felt a very special tenderness. She had an extreme sentimental sensitivity that made her infinitely sympathetic to all physical and moral distress, because all she wanted to do was soothe, relieve and console...

His judgement was clear: his life would not be long.

The life of this beloved child could not be long because of her overall hypothyroidism, and we know that the thyroid is the gland of life.

This was how Tristan had felt about the treasure that heaven had granted him for their beloved son, and which Monique was monstrously abusing with her repulsive madness.

And yet Monique sometimes had a grain of lucidity, because once, speaking of herself, she said: "In my case, Saturn is not round and Mars is not straight"...

Why had fate put Monique in Tristan's path? Of course, she had picked Tristan up from the wreck he had left behind. She had proved to be perfect, and little by little he had given her his trust and an enormous tenderness that Monique, by her behaviour, did not allow him to express.

What is a woman?

To her companion, she is an obedient being, a mother, a mistress.

What is a husband? A father to his companion, the one in charge, a lover.

Such is the human reality imposed on the wisdom of nations before all the materialistic debilities.

Was he a father to Monique? He had done everything to protect her, to give her a house, for which he assumed all the expenses, and, while he only wanted to be mothered by his companion, he had offered her a child that the world situation prevented him from wishing for. For the sake of this child and its mother, he had agreed to go to Berry, which was so out of character for him. He had built this little Beatrice, so full of heaven, so that she could help them with the work of the house, with his work as an academic and writer, and above all with the education and care of their beloved child. He was also preparing for the child's future, which was quite normal for such dedication and unprecedented competence. He had in him treasures of kindness, affection, understanding and indulgence. He was capable of running his household in accordance with the realities of a vertiginously suicidal age. He was an inexhaustible lover.

It's true that her sexual appetite was exaggerated, as is the case with 'thyroids' with sufficient adrenals and efficient reproductive genitalia, but a woman knew how to negotiate this 'defect', so as to avoid, at least relatively, carnal temptations for her partner.

And Monique.

A motherly, understanding, loving wife? Smoothing things over, diplomatic with her husband "who had to be approached with caution", as the homeopathic description of the phosphorus he was (the phosphorus of homeopathy being the thyroid of endocrinology) put it? Aware of their interest in synthesis, of the miracle represented by the presence of little Bea in their home, whom it had taken him years to educate? With gestures of tenderness? A little of that humility that is an absolute sign of mental health? An obedient companion? No, never.

How many times had Tristan heard himself speak without her listening?

Béatrice, this treasure of destiny, this well of tenderness for their child, Béatrice who helped in everything, who knew how to impart to their little one the knowledge he brought her, and she did so with that angelic patience that made Tristan's heart swell with distraught gratitude. Béa, little Béa, was treated inhumanely by Monique, who couldn't even contain herself in front of strangers. Friends and acquaintances told Tristan of their shock and indignation at Monique's behaviour towards Bea. All those marvellous things Béa brought, which relieved Monique of her unquenchable thirst for energy, meant nothing to her. The only things that mattered were a small broken thing, a hoover hose prematurely worn out by Béa's clumsiness, a misplaced object, a dusty corner of the house, while Monique's bedroom, where Béa was forbidden to clean, looked like the worst kind of souk in terms of mess and dust.

How was Aurelian going to judge his mother when he had matured, when his kindness and intelligence had grown stronger?

He was already saying at the age of six: "Why is Mum like that, we should all love each other".

He had come up with all the solutions. But it didn't suit Monique's pathology. If Aurelien's judgement became clear, she wouldn't be able to escape it. He would then do as his father had done, blaming everything on the illness and continuing to love his mother.

Monique's condition seemed too serious for Tristan to realise. It was the very state of the modern world as a whole, and that of his companion in particular. Moral sense, aesthetics and spirituality had disappeared everywhere. All that remained was formalism, and even then, animal, selfish impulses. Monique later cleared herself by marrying into the fundamentalist Church in an aberrant context that illustrated the doctrinaire formalism and dogmatism that had been the soft skeleton of two thousand years of Christianity.

The female biotype is inherently jealous. So jealousy combined with selfishness to create monstrous mentalities at the end of the century. Organic and educational deficiencies everywhere encouraged the murderous rifts that were the subject of news reports from all over the world. Secularism and general chemification had put an end to the humanity of the world. From then on, everything would be aberrant and inhuman.

Nothing would matter but childish selfishness and bestial impulses. Money would come first. How could Tristan have dreamt that his son could escape this hell? If Monique had had the slightest conscience, she would have enjoyed her unique happiness and would have had only one pain: that of the agony of the whole world.

If Monique couldn't give Bea all the indulgent and affectionate recognition she deserved, then Tristan would take a rent-controlled flat where the little girl would have her own room. He would continue to pay for Monique's house, which would one day belong to Aurélien. He would leave her the necessary furniture and the books that would one day be his son's wealth.

He was ready to keep his room in the new house. He wouldn't leave Monique, he just had to protect the little girl, whose devotion remained attentive and who didn't count the care she gave Aurelien despite his mother's behaviour.

Monique persisted in assailing Béa with her anger. She couldn't open her mouth without the little girl's heart, like Tristan's who suffered for her, starting to beat wildly. Béatrice continued to find herself in states of prostration that lasted for hours or days. Tristan's consoling tenderness was not enough to compensate for Monique's viperous behaviour.

He had to think about protecting Beatrice's physical and mental health, as well as his own. He had to remain available for the little one. Tristan's health was declining. All his problems were compounded by a stomach ulcer of psychosomatic origin. His bronchi and lungs, which were very fragile, were also beginning to give way. How could he show Monique any of the tenderness he had for the mother of his child, when he was constantly having to deal with the behaviour of a surly foetus?

It was too stupid to waste all that future that had been built with so much pain, so much love and so much sacrifice. Such a waste for such a grotesque blunder. No, Tristan couldn't resign himself.

Forty years ago, when the man was master of the household, he would have said "that's the way things are" and no madness would have prevented the normal running of things according to the reason and the heart of the captain who steered the family ship.

But today madness reigns. A demented woman with financial resources can instantly create all forms of chaos without intelligence or reason being able to intervene in any way.

Involution, degeneration, are such that this sociological inevitability now exists at the level of children whose infantilism, normal in them, is increasingly the law. The world was sinking into widespread anarchy, and Tristan had been nourished by the mad certainty that Monique, structured by her written work, would escape from everything, and in particular from herself and her vesanic, caricatured jealousy.

It was a dream. Monique had been deconstructed by an atrocious childhood whose traumas are unsurpassable, but Tristan didn't know that yet. Secularism had done its work, and his vague awareness of the phenomena of our decadence could not compensate for a distressing childhood and secularism, which combined to kill the potential for love in human beings. Yet it is love that is the key to all understanding and to the judicious struggle against oneself.

Hope, the hope that gives life and kills, drove him to write to Monique:

Of course," he wrote to her, "there are discrepancies in our astral charts, but what we have in common is a lucidity, a feeling of protection, of love for our child in a fatal situation, and the grandiose ideal we want for him.

Aren't these huge links?

The fragility of my nervous system, my incompetence in practical matters and my personal professional work mean that I can't look after Aurélien on my own. Competence is not only the knowledge we have given Beatrice, but also love and patience. And to my astonished amazement, I discovered in Beatrice these exceptional gifts of love, patience and pedagogy.

There are very few children who, at the age of five, can already read, write by syllable, play the piano a little and speak a little English. All this has only been possible thanks to Bea. All I did was give instructions and guidelines, which were wonderfully followed. A sickly sensitive character also requires a constant presence, not only for Aurélien, but for myself, who would be paralysed and sterilised without it.

When I took you on as a companion, it was certainly not to have a child in this society, but so that you would help me in my work as a thinker, so that you would see me as your child. You wanted a child, I felt how tumultuous that aspiration was, it was natural, but I gave him to you, not to me, even though I adore him now.

I built Bea so that she could help us raise Aurelien, so that she could take the strain off you at home, who work all day, so that she could help me with my work as a teacher and writer. It's easy to understand that even if your mental balance were perfect, you wouldn't be able to cope alone with your work, your home, the child and me.

It is therefore a providential opportunity that everything can be done according to the realities and not according to the aspirations of a sick subjectivity that is unaware of all the synthetic reality that concerns us.

Your work and your son, in the evening, would be enough to devour you. That's normal: you can only ask so much of a woman. That's why I don't make any more sexual demands and why it's only normal that Bea should be able to look after us, thanks to the instruction and guidance that you and I give her.

Béatrice makes up for your inevitable shortcomings and I'll never hold that against you. What would I do with my artistic temperament, my pulsating tinnitus, my vomiting and loss of balance, what would I do for the very young, for my work, without bea? I'd be totally paralysed. It's obvious, then, that we can't do anything effective for the little one without Bea's emotional, pedagogical and domestic skills, who looks after us for you.

You can even afford to stay out late, like you did for weeks to get your mother settled. Could you have done that without Bea? What could you do for the basic needs of Aurélien and myself without the daytime while you're working? I could do nothing.

Your mother is now here, three kilometres away. I've sent Bea to stay with a friend for a fortnight to help her recover from the depression you've caused her. You have entrusted Aurélien to your mother, but she will bring him nothing, absolutely nothing, of the culture and love that Bea lavishes on our son.

I have no-one to do my housework, my meals, my work, no help. I'm at a loss. Béatrice relieves you of all these contingencies, with love and competence to boot. She keeps the house in order and allows me to teach her and our child. She leaves you available for Aurélien when you come home, and she's perfection for all of us. You can understand that you owe us to Beatrice, she takes care of us, we have to be grateful to her and love her like our child's sister, because she is full of devotion, feelings and tenderness towards our little one. We need to keep her close to us, not only because without her we would panic, but also because she is part of our happiness. This beloved child has a soul.

You work all day, how can I wake you up at night when I'm having a menstrual crisis? Your overwork is too much, it's Bea who devotes herself to you.

We mustn't let madness destroy what we've worked so hard to achieve over the years, especially for you, because, as you know, I had no intention of having a child in these circumstances.

If madness is trying to destroy such a magnificent edifice, then I have no other solution than to take a flat to protect Bea and myself, so as to remain available for the little one as long as you let yourself be helped. I'll have to do it, even if it tears my heart out. Think about all this so that you can calm down and understand that you have everything and that you mustn't destroy it all...

It seemed impossible to Tristan that Monique could not understand this. It was so obvious, so clear. But was Monique capable of penetrating the mysteries of his artistic, thyroid temperament? It seemed impossible, because if she had, she would have understood that everything was perfect and that she was fulfilled...

Chapter XXI

The collapse

Throughout these years of anguish, Tristan continued to write unpublishable books in the context of all the distortions and lies in which we lived, and to teach in Higher Education where he was seconded. He thought that a post as Principal would be financially welcome, and he had all the support he needed. To do this, he would have to be appointed to a lycée in order to get back in touch with secondary education, which was becoming increasingly so!

He was appointed to a lycée a few kilometres from where he lived and drove there for his seventeen hours of lessons a week.

It had been almost twenty years since he had taught in secondary school.

It was a shock, and what a shock! A cohort of asexual blue-jeaners, real bags of shapeless starch, opposed to all forms of intelligence, wallowing with delight in everything absurd and degrading, permanently motivated by the cult of ignorant creativity, by regressive, pathogenic and criminogenic music. Colleagues who were delegated teachers in secondary schools, teachers on the cheap, leftists with unheard-of outfits, as mentally and physically unformed as their pupils. Children of twelve or thirteen smoking and kissing each other on the mouth in the playground, co-education, destructive to both sexes, with no specific teaching for either: in a word, neo-natism set up as a system and a criterion of culture. As Headmaster, he would have had to deal with this mega-deformity. So he gave up his candidacy and took early retirement.

In a few years' time, we were going to see worse things: teachers beaten up, their cars reduced to scrap metal, tyres slashed, girls 'shagging' in the corridors and giving birth in the 'shithouse', or murdering their classmates... commonplace occurrences.

This freed him from the nightmare of the Teaching and allowed him to concentrate on the nightmare Monique was forcing on him. The two nightmares at once were impossible to cope with.

The tax transition on his retirement justified a reduction in his daughter Nathalie's pension in Germany. She took him to court. The judge imposed the pension but removed the indexation.

To please Monique, to try and restore her sanity, Tristan had given her carte blanche for the house, which was almost built.

Martine, a painter friend, bore a striking resemblance to George Sand. She had drawn up the plans for her, according to her wishes.

His original paintings were a kind of diaphanous neo-romanticism, his watercolours were ravishing, and his portraits showed great talent.

Monique's mother, who had come to live near them, lived in Rabat in Morocco before retiring. Monique and Martine went to visit her in the summer when he was still there.

Martine had learned a lot about Monique's strange psychology.

Monique wanted to organise a visit to the Medina for Martine. The three of them went, including her mother. Unfortunately, that day Martine was in the critical period of the month. The Moroccan heat and Martine's typically sensitive 'thyroid' condition did nothing to improve her ordeal.

In the middle of the Medina, she was seized by an agoraphobic attack[74] and urgently wanted to leave. Instead of medically understanding such a simple situation, especially for a nurse, Monique abruptly expressed her disapproval, which further aggravated Martine's sick state and her heart palpitations.

A curious example of Monique's altruistic selfishness: Martine should have taken full advantage of the trouble she had taken to show her around the Medina. This 'altruistic' gesture automatically eliminated any shortcomings on the part of the person who was 'benefiting' from her strange devotion.

Martine, like so many people today, had serious household problems.

Monique had given him the best advice:

- Everything can be resolved with love and understanding for others".

---

[74] The agoraphobia was part of the manic diathesis, and mania is a state of hyperthyroidism. This was a classic incident in a thyroid patient.

It was sound advice that Monique should have followed herself, but in this case Martine could not.

Her husband was fat and ugly, drank a lot of whisky and cheated on her.

Monique had told Tristan about Martine's troubles. The husband was certainly not a man who, like Tristan, didn't leave the house day and night to look after and teach the two children, Aurélien and Béa.

Monique couldn't stand Martine's husband for two minutes. Good advice from Monique: irony of fate.

The house that had been built proved derisorily inadequate to accommodate Tristan and his furniture. The two thousand books had a wall bookcase, but the twenty square metres available to him were absurd.

And he had signed, thinking that Monique would take her companion's basic needs into account. That's what Martine had thought when she drew up the plans for the house, but she hadn't dared say anything.

- I didn't understand", she later told Tristan, "but as you didn't say anything, I thought you agreed, and I imagined there was a solution I didn't know about".

In fact, Monique had designed the house just for her and her child.

This architectural feature fitted in perfectly with his psychological difficulties. Tristan wouldn't be able to move in... Everything was going to separate them.

He had asked Monique to show Béa a few months of affection so that he could agree to her staying in town, without feeling "left behind".

Not only did Monique make no effort, no progress, but things got worse and tragically unravelled.

One evening Monique began to treat the poor girl in the rudest manner. To call this little "hypothyroid" girl, who had no sexuality whatsoever, who would never be a rival to any woman, a "whore" was the height of despicability.

Tristan's indignation was at its height. He was incapable of hitting a woman, and yet he summoned up all his courage and performed the most painful act of his life.

What he had done was so far removed from him that when he told his friend the astrologer, he could not help but burst out laughing. Tristan asked him why he was laughing. He replied:

- With the best will in the world I can't imagine you slapping Monique.

Indeed he did. Aurelien was in the living room where Monique had insulted little Bea, and Tristan took his companion into his own bedroom and slapped her across the face. O how deserved, how useful if the therapy had worked.

In a normal woman, with a temporary disorder, it would have worked perfectly, as a thousand examples proved, but Monique was too seriously affected for her to take stock of the situation and admit her wrongdoing. She was even more seriously affected than Tristan thought, because fifteen years later she had reached the same point. She could never accept reasonable guilt on either side because Tristan was no little Saint.

But there was worse to come, and already terrible proof of the extreme seriousness of Monique's case: to Tristan's amazement, Monique called her son.

If Tristan could even have imagined such madness, such immaturity, he would never have slapped Monique. Only a mature, reasonable woman can be properly slapped if she deserves it, and the shock always puts her right. This is impossible for a severely degenerate woman like the majority of women in the twentieth century.

Tristan's heart ached to see his little one come under such circumstances, called by his mother who would normally have kept him away. He would have preferred to die than to experience this. This is something he could never have imagined.

— Why didn't you spank Mum and not slap her? She's mean to Bea, she deserved a spanking. You spank me when I deserve it. You should have spanked Mum.

— My darling," replied Tristan, "you're right, but I haven't had time to think.

While Tristan was talking to his son, Monique came out of the room.

Two months later he learned that Monique had gone to beat the girl, who had said nothing to him for fear that Tristan would correct her further.

The next day, when Monique's bed wasn't made, Béa made it for her. Not only did Monique not thank her, but she also threw the bed away:

- I forbid Beatrice to make my bed.

There was no time to hesitate. The little girl had to be moved into a rent-controlled flat and protected.

Tristan rented the flat, his heart in tatters and his legs in cotton wool. He had to leave. His son would need little Bea too, and he had to protect her from such stupidity and sadism.

A friend helped him to move and fix up this flat in a big concrete town that Tristan hated. He set up a cosy bedroom for Béa, little Béa, she had peace and quiet.

To top it all off, she continued to look after and teach Aurélien with the same tenderness as if Monique had been kind and maternal to her: Beatrice was that.

Soon Tristan would be betrayed: Aurélien would go to primary school.

The day Tristan had slapped her, Monique had phoned Martine to come and collect her. She stayed with Martine for two days. The second day was the music school concert where Aurélien was going to play a charming little etude. Monique refused to come because Béa was also playing Bach's first prelude from the 'well-tempered harpsichord'.

For months, Martine helped Monique, helped Tristan, and facilitated relations that had become impossible since he had slapped her. Monique, mired in her mental illness, was incapable of objective reasoning: she identified Tristan with her father, who had beaten her, refused her, and subjected her to the worst abuse. Her blockages chained Monique to a Karma that broke Tristan's heart and for which he could do nothing.

He couldn't even say to her: "I love you and understand you, come into my arms". Monique's poor little cactus couldn't hear a thing.

After a few weeks, Martine decided to write a thoughtful letter to Monique. The letter of a thoughtful friend who was only looking out for the interests of both of them, for their understanding. She delivered the essential terms to Tristan, who was deeply concerned:

She told him that as a friend she had a duty to tell him sincerely what she thought. She told him about Tristan's artistic temperament, which had to be understood, about the need for Beatrice to be there to help her who was working, to look after her child and her husband who was teaching her so well to train her child, about the affection she owed to someone so touching and so full of love for their child. She reminded him of the perfect principle that she herself had taught him: "With a lot of love and understanding of others, you can achieve anything".

He also reminded her that she had a difficult character and that it was important for her to realise this.

Monique never wanted to see Martine again, like her friends Simone and Gladys, whom she saw again years later.

Monique had heard of a remark Martine had made about Monique being dictatorial even towards her own mother.

She went to show her bulldozer character in Martine's husband's workplace, so Martine said:

— She'd kill me in a week. And Beatrice said:

— Me too, if Monsieur Tristan hadn't protected me.

Tristan's dream for his son was sinking into oblivion.

It would be socialised, turned into a robot, a docile producer-consumer, perhaps a physico-chemical amalgam managed by the profit and loss account of pseudo-democracy.

Two poems sprang from the intense tears he shed before the icy tomb of his beloved son's spiritual future:

Aurélien

I remember her blue eyes on the day of her christening.
And her angelic smile that melted my heart.
I see her cradle again, her eyes, her wings.
And my distraught soul.
I could already see it, life, light, sunshine.
My flower in full bloom, in the garden of my heart.
Rose, supreme beauty, alive in my nest.
And now death has pounced on my dream.
On my rose and my heart.

I can see them both withering away.
Without hope,
O pain...
To my darling son
O my dear little one.
Wrapped in my heart.
Snuggled up against my soul.
From where streams of tenderness
Flow towards your heart.
In this world blighted by hideousness and hatred.
I think of you so much.
I'll do everything I can to ensure that you, beautiful flower.
You will blossom in the blue of heaven.
Your feet on this earth and your forehead in the sun.
I will say to the Lord.
Here, I give it to you, it has grown so beautiful
In the garden of my heart.
He is there to serve God and the universal.
He is there, O Lord!
You see, I've achieved this supreme masterpiece.
A tender, strong man.
I loved him so much,
O much more than myself.
You can forgive me for my sins and sorrows
For I offer you a treasure...

Although Aurélien bore the name of his father, who had recognised him, Monique and Tristan were not married, for tax reasons as we have seen. Their situation would have been intolerable and they could only build on the basis of a "single mother" position.

Everything converged towards their destruction. At the very moment when Monique's fixation was causing therapeutically invincible blockages, a new government had just assimilated concubines with married people.

This meant that if they had been able to afford to add a room to the house and live there together, they would have had to pay a whopping fifteen thousand francs a month in monthly payments and tax, more than Tristan's teacher's pension. The situation was absurd and insoluble.

Living apart, even paying half the rent for Monique's house, was difficult but possible. If everything had been arranged, if they had settled down in the house and been happy, they would have been devastated by the 'salary-taxes-and-drafts' situation of the house.

So we had to take this flat with Bea and also set up an institute of natural medicine and health, to save as many people as possible from the abyss of chemistry.

So there were concrete reasons for consolation: the elementary aspect of life had become possible, whereas if her ideal had been realised, if Monique had rewarded Bea for her angelic behaviour, if they had all been united in love and harmony, *they would have been destroyed from the start by the taxman.*

This was so mind-boggling to Tristan that he couldn't believe it. He had calculations done by various specialists, by a friend from the tax department, by lawyers, to get confirmation of this aberration.

It had to be said: the irreversible rift that fate was imposing on them through Monique's concrete psychic problems was saving their lives on a basic material level...

This was no consolation to Tristan, for "the heart has its reasons that reason does not know"...

Tristan's health began to fail. Bronchitis and congestion brought his temperature down to forty-five degrees. He hadn't taken a single antibiotic or chemical medicine for twenty years, because he was convinced of the fundamental satanism of chemistry in the human body.

But in such a situation, antibiotics became necessary.

A month later, there was a relapse, with the temperature rising to thirty-nine degrees. He applied a natural therapy which worked very well. Unfortunately, two months later there was another relapse, with a temperature of 40°C. He had to resort to antibiotics. This allopathic medicine is still useful in emergencies and for short periods. It is a "medical technique", not medicine. The unfortunate thing is that doctors take it for medicine because they have no critical spirit.

They don't even understand that vaccines, putrid products laced with mercury and aluminium, are cataclysms for humans. It is hygiene that has reduced epidemics. Thirty years ago, Professor Dick, a world specialist in smallpox, wrote in a newspaper: "The vaccine is more dangerous than the disease"...

On the very day that Tristan was suffering from this intense fever, Monique entrusted Aurélien to her care for three days. Thanks to little Bea, he was able to take him to the flat. Was it to please Tristan that she entrusted him with the child? Of course not, it suited him.

He later learned that she already had another man in her life. Tristan would never have thought that, believing that in the situation they would both concentrate on raising the child and protecting him from the atrocious situation. He was certain, the naive one, that she would never impose a stepfather on their child.

He was still so full of illusions about Monique that he wrote her letters, full of truth, of course, because there was no denying the facts. But he was still full of tenderness, indulgence and understanding, and he was ready to arrange everything except, of course, throwing Bea out into the street or into solitude.

Materially, the flat was the solution. The little girl was protected, Monique didn't have to put up with her presence, Tristan surrounded her with his affection, the institute was open with the sole aim of protecting open minds from all that was destroying them at the moment. True health is only possible at this price. He had kept a room in Monique's house. Financially they managed, just about, but they managed.

He wrote to her that he loved her dearly, that the child should be the goal of their lives, that Bea was nobody's rival, that they absolutely needed her because of her perfection for the child, for the house, for work, that nobody in the world could give so much love to a child while the mother had to work, teach him the basics of writing and reading, the piano and English.

In fact, he always said the same thing.

For Monique's birthday, he gave her a golden heart on a gold chain as a symbol. At Christmas, he gave her two poems and a piece of music dedicated to their son.

Nothing did. He explained that he would never have slapped her if he hadn't loved her. It must have taken a year for her to understand this therapeutic slap. He kept a copy of his letters, which could have made a thick book.

Monique had the icy heart of her time, the madness of the Iron Age.

The disease clung to him. One of his eyes took on the appearance of a tomato and cysts formed. A psychosomatic illness, like the one affecting his lungs and bronchi. In humorous medical parlance, these were called "nervous eye pregnancies".

Her heart was still speaking, against all reason:

> My Monique.
>
> When the heart speaks, you have to let it speak, and my love for you both will continue to vibrate until the day I die. After two days of antibiotics and a bruised eye, all I can think about is you. How can I tell you how much I love you? How can I make you understand that I am one of the rare men left with a heart and an intelligence full of light, beauty and sincerity?
> How can I make you understand that I love you as you are and that I understand your difficulties but that it's impossible for me to see Bea crying because you're treating her badly and that I had to do what I did, a normal act for a man worthy of the name, towards a woman worthy of the name and whom he loves?
> You see, we had achieved the heart of my writing: a small, traditional society in the midst of global chaos. The four of us were an island of diamonds, perfectly complementary. Bea loves our little one with all her heart. She even has an extraordinary authority over our child that we don't have. She makes up for my shortcomings towards you, she makes up for your shortcomings towards me. She's our guardian angel.
> As our philosopher friend C. put it so well when he came to see us a year and a half ago: "We had succeeded in creating a little society from the High Middle Ages, a unique jewel in our time, and we all functioned perfectly together".

We protected him from everything that was negative in this confused society. But for a year now, since we split up, he's had colds, bronchitis and warts. All of which points to an obvious starch overload. His physiognomy shows a tired liver and kidneys... At his age!

Thanks to béa, none of this would be possible if we were together, because the four of us combined the right care without compromise.

Our idiotic break-up will inevitably plunge him into all the compromises of necrotic current affairs. Now that I've taken early retirement, I had a lot of time to look after him. And you, at five o'clock in the evening, brought your light into our circle of love. That's true marriage.

Rumours reached me that you knew another man you wanted to marry. I didn't believe them: a marriage built on our ruins? What kind of kind-hearted man who knows our situation well could marry you? None at all. Marry you on our ruins? On an obvious and commonplace psychological disorder, so obvious that everyone can see it?

If a man of such quality could succeed me, then I would never have been anything other than a shadow in your life, and my essence would have escaped you completely.

I put myself in the place of a man worthy of the name. If you were Botticelli's Venus, in such an epic tragedy, I could do nothing but do everything I could to return you to your companion, so that your mind and your heart could heal. If I didn't, I'd feel like a vulture, a carrion-eater...

How could you replace me so quickly if you really loved me? I could never replace you because my love for the little one can never be dissociated from my love for you.

Our child needs to forge his soul by feeling, in his sleep, the presence under his roof of a loving mum and dad. Knowing that he wouldn't know it breaks my heart, and makes me cherish the thought of dying with my little one in my arms and leaving you to enjoy the madness of this decaying world.

I thought you were so intelligent! I was certain that the awareness I was giving you made all the madness I've been seeing impossible, ever since you came back from holiday in Morocco with Beatrice. Since that trip three years ago, the nightmare has begun.

But there was no way you could fall into this crude trap, which pales into insignificance in the face of the prodigious fortress that you, I and Bea had built.

You gave me the illusion that our child and I would escape all the horrors of materialism.

I thought for the first two years that you were the ideal woman, and I never believed that your sister Françoise was right when she said, referring to you whom I was praising to the skies: "We'll talk again in two years' time"...

No man worthy of the name would agree to take you as a companion if he knew about our situation, your mental difficulties, this ridiculous fixation on our little sweetheart, who is slightly disabled, and my tenderness for you.

If you've understood anything about my work, you know that only a humanoid could agree to 'make his fortune' on such ruins and, why not? To buy back my deposit on the house, on the basis of a disorder of the mind of a woman loved by her husband and whom he would certainly not marry, if she had cancer...

It's true that this mental disorder dulls all awareness, and that any modern-day jackal could take advantage of it.

Is it possible that no tears come to your eyes when you read me? Is your interstitial so deficient?

Is there no room in you for tenderness, reasoning, self-criticism or self-awareness?

I'd like to take you in my arms. I'm always here for you. Oh my silly Monique...

My Monique.

Last night I dreamt that your face was serene, and I found myself standing in front of you, so I kissed you gently all over your serene face. Then you nestled your head on my shoulder and whispered "I'm sorry". And I simply held you close to my heart without saying a word, because I had already forgiven you. I know that you can't choose your hatred over your love.

You can't possibly hate little Bea more than you love me?

My loves.

When I'm not near you both, my heart is torn, so torn that I have no words to express my suffering. Perhaps the dog who refuses to eat and lets himself die on his master's grave feels what I feel.
I couldn't have acted any differently than I did in order to cure you with a shock.
"I know of only one superiority, and that is kindness", said Beethoven.
I couldn't let you exterminate this little one, whose wickedness disintegrates more than the others because of her thyroid insufficiency. But also because I can't do anything for the little one, or for myself, or for you without this little one, a gift from heaven.
How can you not understand that?
Wake up Monique, don't make me despise you when I love you both so much.

Tristan's health was not improving.

Martine tried to comfort Tristan and Beatrice, as she had done for Monique the evening he had been forced to slap her.

Tristan's health was worrying. This corroborated the fears of the astrologer friend who had written to Monique without Tristan's knowledge. This letter had no effect on Monique, and he learned of its existence months later from Maurice himself.

Martine still wanted to intervene with Monique and took a copy of her letter to Tristan:

My dear Monique.

I'm sure you'll understand how much it costs me to write to you. But I think that sometimes you have to sit on your pride. I'm doing this for your sake and for Aurélien's.
I can see, with a certain anguish, that Tristan's morale is slipping because he realises that Aurélien no longer feels that you love his father.
I was made aware of Aurélien's comments: "Why is Mum like that, we should all love each other". If you take away all hope from Tristan I fear the worst for all of you, Aurelien and your house, which he may refuse to pay for out of desperation.

Despite all the love Tristan has for his son and for you, which even my husband finds surprising, you need to rediscover your affection for your partner. He wouldn't get over not being able to find what's essential for your child, and the worst would be to fear. I'm sure that your affection would give him back all strength he needs to look after the two of you and the house.

Beatrice and I are not enough to keep her spirits up. I'm discovering that her physical and moral fragility is much greater than I thought, and this clearly shows how indispensable Beatrice is to you.

I wrote to you eight months ago. Let me tell you that the facts prove me right about everything I said to you at that time. My letter was the cause of our falling out. I didn't understand it, because if a friend wants to help one of her friends it's obviously by enlightening her and telling her the truth. I don't think that Tristan's almost sickly kindness is inexhaustible.

May you understand before it's too late.

Tristan is worried about Bea's future if he disappears. I promised him I'd look after her.

My husband and I are going to try to get Tristan out of this H.L.M., which isn't helping his morale. Tristan would like to live in his room with you and keep the flat for all his things that will never fit in the house, and above all to protect Bea and his institute.

We cannot remain indifferent in the face of such destruction, and it is for the good of all of you that I am writing this letter. The emotion and interest I feel for you are the reason for my intervention in a painful affair in which I am in no way a stakeholder.

Please accept my warmest regards.

Martine

Charlotte, Tristan's sister, Aurélien's aunt and godmother, came every year with her husband from California to stay in the house they had built in Corrèze. She took the opportunity to see her brother, Monique and her nephew-godson. She would soon be coming to France for the summer.

Tristan had explained the tragedy that had engulfed them.

Charlotte was the last member of his family left. The very last. Charlotte's intervention would have been all the more welcome as it seemed she was the only person Monique would listen to. But in fact Monique could only accept a dialogue if no one said anything that bothered her, which was the case. Tristan, with his customary naivety, imagined that he could count on his sister to help him and influence Monique with lucid, human and reasonable arguments. Tristan was all the more convinced of this as Charlotte told him she knew him well and was well aware of Monique's characteristic stubbornness.

He left no stone unturned to inform her. She knew everything.

Curiously, Charlotte wrote strange letters to her brother, refusing to say anything to Monique. She wrote to him directly, whereas Monique had cut Tristan off from his entire family. In these preachy letters, she reproached her brother for precisely what Monique should be reproached for: lack of understanding, tenderness, indulgence, common sense... which Tristan promulgated ad infinitum in his dealings with Monique and of which Charlotte knew nothing. In short, pure *'grandmother-chérisme'*.

Martine and a well-known philosopher friend were unanimous: "Your sister is angry with you, but why? She's acting in bad faith and is particularly perverse".

It's true that there was wilful blindness, inexplicable personal resentment, bad faith and perversity in all of this: his own mother and *beloved grandmother* pure and simple.

It reminded Tristan of his painful childhood and gave him a shock that only increased his despair.

Was such stupidity and wickedness natural? What was their purpose?

Charlotte asked him to "explain many things" to her, even though she had long had all the facts about their tragedy.

He replied by sending her a letter, such as she could send to Monique, in which she would find all the information she needed.

His friends warned him: with what they had learned from Charlotte, he was sure to get nothing but a vexed refusal, full of illogic and childish self-righteousness.

He had awkwardly told his sister that he was astonished by her resentment, her bad faith, her perversity, but that *if he was wrong*, she would know how to use the elements of the letter he was sending her to compose her own.

This is what he wrote in his sister's name:

> My dear Monique.
>
> If I didn't write you this letter sooner, it's because I'm a slow thinker and it took me a long time to reflect on some complex information.
>
> I've listened to you, Tristan and your good friends like Frédérique, so I'm in any case the only human being to have so much information about your drama. I can therefore, in all humility, formulate an opinion that goes beyond the banal and superficial.
>
> Something else has prompted me to write to you: Tristan has been on antibiotics for the last 10 days, for the third bronchopulmonary attack in a few weeks, with a temperature of forty degrees, which only dropped to thirty-nine after three days of injections. I'm very worried because he was in a coma as a child with the same symptoms. For me, all this is essentially psychosomatic, which you must know better than I do, as you are familiar with his doctoral thesis on his own biotype, a thesis that I had an interesting popularisation of.
>
> Tristan has his faults. He's egocentric like all artists (but who isn't, because we all have an ego!) but he's fair and kind. He fully and honestly informed you of his nature long before you lived together. If you've accepted, you can't go back on that. It's true that women are his great danger, but didn't he live like a monk all those years with you and Aurelien, in the Berry region, spending his time on his work as an academic and writer, while teaching Beatrice and Aurelien and looking after them? He did this without taking into account any major shortcomings on your part : understanding, affection, sexuality. Everything unfolded within a framework of perfect balance, allowing Aurelien to grow in both body and spirit. Tristan couldn't bear the brutality with which you rewarded poor little Bea and I understand, O how much, that his heart bled to see her prostrate and in tears for days.
>
> He wanted to put a balm on so much pain by lavishing on the little girl a little of the tenderness that you were denying her. Your behaviour, as Frédérique wrote, 'precipitated Beatrice onto Tristan's heart': that was fatal in someone as romantic as my brother.

Tristan is the last man who would hit a woman. This is so true that your friend Maurice burst out laughing at the thought of Tristan correcting Monique. He couldn't imagine Tristan slapping Monique because that's totally out of character for him.

Beatrice, who is slightly handicapped, can't be your rival, Monique, or anyone else's, as is so obvious.

Frédérique's letter, which I have read over and over again because I was so moved by its quality, is perfect in every way and should serve as a guide to your happiness.

So when you seriously insulted little Bea, Tristan slapped you and took the child to a council flat to protect her. He acted as a man of rigour, kindness and an obvious sense of justice, in the name of a compassion that should make you love him even more.

Who in this day and age would put kindness and justice before a woman he obviously loves, because if he didn't, there would be no problem and my present letter would be useless. Tristan would not be as seriously ill as he is, his illness being merely an expression of the suffering of his soul.

Is a simple pair of slaps, deserved or not, really worth destroying your home, your child, your life?

Tristan tells me that rumours of another man in your life are spreading. If that's the case, you must not have loved my brother very much to replace him so quickly, and so infantilely break the cohesion that ensures your child's equilibrium. Who is this man who, on the pretext of a couple of slaps, which Tristan is convinced are well-founded, is going to build his happiness on a general massacre? Is he informed by you and by Tristan to assess the situation and act according to a true conscience? I doubt it.

Beatrice's practical needs are obvious. Tristan has never been a practical man, and what's more, his work takes up too much of his time, and he's not the one who, like Beatrice, is going to spend hours with your child teaching him to read and write, to play the piano, to learn English, to clean the whole house, to look after the garden, the fire in the fireplace, to cook meals, while you work all day? All this is wrapped up in a love that is so real and that Aurélien and his father measure every day. What would he do today, bedridden for days on end, for his child? This baby is a treasure trove of love and skill, that's a fact.

I know that Tristan needed a mothering companion and that he didn't want a child in the circumstances: he gave you that child all the same. So you have to accept the means to bear it! There's no doubt that Beatrice was sent by Providence. No one can be jealous of her.

Tristan had very high ideals for his son. I don't know his work, but I do know the interest shown in him by the philosophers and humanists of this century: Albert Camus, Louis Rougier, Raymond Las Vergnas, Gustave Thibon. Isn't my brother's hyper-awareness, which my nephew must benefit from, a cement that holds all of you together, a cement that makes even a couple of slaps in the face seem insignificant?

Or do you know nothing of Tristan's thinking? Which would explain your sad attitude. Faced with such a transcendent reality, there's no such thing as a couple of slaps in the face.

Have you ever caught Tristan red-handed in his lack of indulgence, generosity and kindness towards you? Didn't your mum, whom you love so much, tell Tristan that "he was the only good man she ever met"?

Whether this was an exaggeration is not the point, but she said it and I cannot believe for a moment that you doubt it.

Finally, Monique, I told you about my brother's self-centred, ladies' man character, but you also have a difficult character. You're terribly stubborn, and tyrannical even in your generosity. Even friends like Simone and Gladys have confirmed this over the phone, as Tristan told me. How can you ignore the realities about yourself? Do you think that a man can put up with a stubborn, tyrannical woman without having to react?

Doesn't life require us to be clear-headed about ourselves?

That, my dear Monique, is what I had to tell you, and which you will agree to consider if you are intelligent and fundamentally good. My brother is dying not to be able, with you, to lead your child to the cultural heights he is aiming for.

If you have to part, let it be relatively. Stay together for the little one through affection, letters and the telephone. In short, minimise the damage, because for his part, I'm sure Tristan will do his utmost. My brother has to live to be able to impart so much wealth to your child.

My love to you and my godson.

Charlotte

The response was exactly as the friends had predicted. And soon Charlotte's husband was refusing to receive little Bea.

This letter, so clear, so complete, did not shake her sister. She had no desire to prove to him "that she was not stupid, dishonest or perverse". Not only did she not do so, but *she welcomed* Monique and this man, about whom Tristan still knew nothing, *into her home*!

> Dear Tristan.
>
> I'm sorry you're ill.
> You didn't want what I was telling you and you turned against me with the same poisoned weapons. You get the same predictable results. "You can't catch flies with vinegar". If your pride didn't cloud your intelligence, you'd understand this elementary truth. If you had wanted Monique back you would have acted differently. When you want a result, you consider the means of achieving it.
> Since I've hurt you, since I'm not very intelligent, but rather perverse, and since I'm acting in bad faith, all that's left between us is a deep, brotherly affection that will last despite the inevitable physical separation. What's the point of getting closer to hurt each other or not to do each other any good? I'm no use to you and you want to use me by torturing me, so it's better to stop our correspondence or whatever.
> This doesn't stop me from praying for you, I'm even convinced that God will use all your pain to bring you closer to him.
> My way of concluding will annoy you, but I assure you that I mean what I say. Love to you,
>
> Charlotte.

The more he reread this imbecilic platitude, finished in bondieuserie, the more disgusted he became with his sister. But weren't she and Monique the product of materialism?

Didn't Otto Weininger, that Jewish thinker, write :

"We are in the age of the woman and the Jew"...

Since Tristan had moved into the council flat to protect little Bea, the post office had been forwarding the mail.

One day he received a postcard from someone he had known for two or three years. This gentleman was interested in Tristan's work and lectures. His wife was suffering from cancer, and he had referred her to an alternative medicine, which proved successful. Unfortunately, a year after her recovery, she died of pulmonary congestion.

Tristan was in no condition to answer, so he passed the card to Monique, asking her to take care of it.

A few weeks later, Tristan was surprised to find the relative in question, Lucien Furor, at Monique's house, where he was taking his son home. Tristan was delighted. If Monique had invited this relationship, it was probably a good sign. She must have invited him discreetly, without talking about his troubles, which were nothing to be proud of, especially as she was generally rather discreet about their tragedy, except for the day she had ejaculated: "My husband left with the maid"...

Those who were aware of the situation found this statement untimely, shameful and devoid of genuine and legitimate pride.

Lucien left them at the end of the weekend. Tristan wrote to him in Paris. He had helped him so much with his wife, it was only right that he should help him with his own.

He informed him of the situation, described Monique's infantile fixation as a symptom of her psychic imbalance and sent him a copy of Frédérique's marvellous letter, which was unrivalled in its objectivity, humanity and intelligence.

Tristan had once bent over her pain, he hoped he would bend over hers. He could have an excellent therapeutic effect on Monique, he could try to reason with her, to remind her of the quality of their union, of her partner's conscience, of the high education they planned for their son, which could only be achieved through emotional calm and the affection of all. He could remind her that children who were the victims of divorce were doomed to become serious temperamental individuals, some of whom would go on to become criminals, terrorists and delinquents of various kinds, as statistics had abundantly proved to those who did not understand this through pure intelligence.

Lucien seemed a calm and reasonable man.

So he was hoping for an answer like this:

"Your tragedy is impossible with an intelligent woman like Monique and a man of your stature. I'm going to do everything I can to help you, by talking to Monique, who cannot, in the circumstances, impose this destruction on your child.

He could also have seen little Bea and then convincingly shown Monique the folly of her behaviour.

All in all, he hoped that Lucien would do what any kind-hearted man would have done for a good friend in the circumstances.

The real answer was embarrassed and neutral. He did, however, allude humanely to the fact that Tristan would rather die than not get his son out of the 'Judeo-Cartesian' morass in which the world was dying.

In another letter he alluded to the 'difference' that separated him from Monique. However, Tristan had explained to him that it was an infantile fixation, an incoercible infantile jealousy, which cancelled out his field of consciousness.

The few letters he still wrote showed a distressing intellectual, sentimental and logical poverty. Didn't he write to her: "If Monique didn't want the slightly handicapped girl in the house, it was a proof of love for Tristan".

Tristan continued to pay the monthly instalments for the house. He would come to sleep with the child in the evenings, so that he could feel the presence of his father and mother under the parental roof.

One day he received a bank notice informing him that he had nothing left to pay. The house had been taken over by Lucien Furor!

Tristan was devastated. He wanted to go to the afterlife with his beloved son, not to leave him alone in this chaos, this madness, this societal rot.

But Tristan had not finished suffering this endless annihilation. One morning, as he was accompanying Bea to the market so that she didn't have to carry anything heavy, they came across a market vendor they'd known for years who said: "Your wife introduced me to her husband.

So Lucien Furor had married Monique.

Little Bea was there, with her tender, sad little eyes and her look of infinite goodness and helplessness. Tristan had the strength to explain briefly to the man the sad situation, the martyrdom of the little girl and how he had been obliged to protect her from the brutality of his companion. The little girl stood there in silence, a perfect illustration of what he had said.

The man said: "It's the folly of women, the folly of the age"...

His son was going to go through this. The wickedness towards Bea, the confiscation of his mother by a scavenger with a serious mental illness. But would he have married her if she'd had cancer? And this man belonged to a political movement that defended the couple, the family, O derision!

But it's true that Monique hadn't loved him for a long time. One of their friends, Hélène, had told her: "She doesn't love you any more, she just looks at you with hatred". And then does one have a hysterical fit because one's companion bites into a honeyed sweet? And yet he believed that she would do everything in her power to ensure that they would work together for their child, to build him beyond the nothingness of global degeneration.

One day when Aurélien was with his father and Béa, they went out to do some shopping in an organic shop. They came across Lucien, a few metres ahead of them.

Aurélien rushed over to Lucien and said in his pretty childish voice: "Lucien, this is Bea, you don't know her"...

The latter took no account of the delicacy of the little girl, of the tenderness with which she was raising Aurélien, and rushed out of the shop, saying:

— I couldn't care less.... about Beatrice.

The height of horror, stupidity and cowardice. He had married Monique's wife to please her and make his own happiness out of this heap of ruins.

A few days later Aurélien said to his father:

— Next week I'm going to Mum and Lucien's church wedding, it's going to be a party, so why don't you come with us?

Everything was consummated. And yet Tristan remembered Beatrice's remark when she had first spotted him outside the shop:

— "Look at him, he looks just like Monique".

It was striking. The same general appearance, the same roundness of the head, the same yellowish skin, the same facial morphology, the same look: there was a karmic kinship there.

Perhaps it was time to accept destiny. Not to save his son from the global chaos in which he would inevitably be immersed...

Monique had cuddled Béa's little head to her heart forever.

There was nothing left to do but wait, his heart in tatters, for the slow death of his son, crushed as he would be by all the follies of a world of selfishness, dead hearts, Marxism, Freudianism and money.

There was nothing left to do but wait for death, hands clasped, little Bea clutched to his heart.

Tristan could feel himself ageing violently as a result of this final heartbreak. He no longer wanted to live.

But Bea had to live, she had to be protected. He knew her love and her ideals for the little boy. She had a great love for him. She would not live very long, but long enough to bring him to adulthood. He would then be able to direct himself. Tristan had seen proof of Bea's human intelligence. He knew that if he and Monique disappeared, she would be there.

Since nothing could be arranged, he had to marry Bea so that she would receive a survivor's pension when he died. That would help her, and perhaps the boy.

Monique had chosen nothingness. What was essential had to be preserved.

The expression in Monique's eyes, so devoid of real feeling or tenderness, that flattened laterality, that chin, the colour of her skin, her narrow-minded stubbornness, all hinted at *an absolute determinism* that was perhaps even more characterological than pathological.

Tomorrow Lucien and Monique would be married in the traditional church.

Rather than consolidate their union by admonishing Monique, the parish priest, who knew the situation, preferred to make a *real marriage* between a vesicant and a scavenger. That was the Church of the last two thousand years: the fundamental essentials replaced by sclerotic dogmatism and doctrinaire formalism. The next pope will be a Jew.

- If Christianity triumphs", said the Emperor Julian, known as the Apostate, "in two thousand years the whole world will be Jewish".

He understood everything.

Tristan dreamed of setting off for the stars with his little Aurélien close to his heart and the cute Béa clasped in his arms.

He was alone in his council flat with little Béa, full of tenderness for him and his beloved son, now capable of a smile that had left him for years, full of moving gratitude for the tenderness Tristan showed her. With her deep gaze and gentle affection, Tristan could feel how much this little girl loved him. She knew how much Tristan cherished her, this defenceless little being of infinite goodness, ignobly martyred since childhood and who loved his son so much, this star in his firmament.

Wasn't he the only person in the world who loved Bea? Wasn't she the only one in the world who loved Tristan?

It's a strange karmic smile, this moving little darling in the path of a Don Juan thirsty for blonde sylphs...

Chapter XXII

"The truth is the only true thing."

The Will

Our destinies follow us relentlessly. Our nature, our nerve cells are on rails and it's impossible to derail. Tristan's ordeal would continue, Bea's would know no respite.

Monique was going to do everything in her destructive rage to separate Aurélien from his father. Her psychoneurosis was taking on gigantic proportions.

She began by calling him by his patronymic, which means an absolute rejection of the father and an unquenchable hatred. It was madness in the most clinical sense of the word.

They lived within five hundred metres of each other, which means that they could have lovingly collaborated on the child's upbringing through an amicable agreement that needed no legal intervention.

Tristan was perfectly suited to such an eventuality.

He and Beatrice were available, we could educate the child and avoid the communal promiscuity that led the child to criminogenic and pathogenic music and drugs.

Monique sent the child to primary school and did everything she could to prevent the father from kissing his son after school.

When she couldn't do it, she moved him to another school.

In the meantime, the scavenger recounted that "the father was a dangerous hypnotist" and that "he poisoned his snacks". Tristan couldn't accept such a huge aberration, and was summoned by a bailiff...

On another occasion, Aurélien asked his father to take him to a party at his old school. Tristan didn't refuse him, but he had no idea that everything had been prepared for the child to run away from the party and go to the police station near the school where his stepfather was waiting.

Tristan had to turn to the public prosecutor, who had Monique summoned by two uniformed policemen. He admonished her, promising to charge her if she didn't calm down. He concluded: "My God, what are we doing to this poor kid?" It had taken several days of preparation to organise this legal abduction!

The Bourges court judgement had given Tristan excellent visiting rights, so the mother took the boy to Brittany. She thought that six hundred kilometres would discourage Tristan. He loved his little one too much to give up. To obtain legitimate compensation, Tristan was forced to take his mother to court. Unfortunately, the judge, who was his mother's accomplice, withdrew his visiting rights during the week on the pretext of the distance. This was legally absurd, even in the opinion of all the legal experts he knew, but he was forced to appeal again to have his visiting rights restored. An ancient million for each appeal. To go back to appeal when you've just won it is legal ubuism. But that's how it was.

In order to have solid cars, to pay for legal actions, to come for one weekend a month, and three times the following month because of the school holidays, he had to borrow millions of years ago, which took him ten years to repay. There was also the moral stress, grief and physical fatigue of driving two thousand three hundred kilometres every two months, one month for a weekend, and the following month for the weekend, and twice for the holidays. Then there were the weekend expenses, hotel and food. All this added up to at least five thousand francs per month, not including the pension. Monique had nothing but hatred and no pity. When he asked a judge for a little help at least with travel, even though Aurélien was at the Lycée Naval in Brest at the time, where he paid nothing and received four hundred francs pocket money, the judge increased his board instead of helping him with the very modest contribution he had suggested from his mother. Everything conspired to crush him.

As for Monique, she was not frightened by the most vile methods, which were a function of the absolute zero of her moral sense.

One day Aurélien asked his father who Hitler was. Tristan told him that he was a head of state who had given bread to six million unemployed people and liberated his country from the dictatorship of high finance and Marxism. "He's a Saint", said Aurelian.

No," his father replied, "he's not a saint.

He couldn't explain any further because the child was seven years old at the time.

But he went home to his mother with this cliché in his head about "Hitler's sanctity".

The mother took advantage of this to claim at every legal hearing that Tristan had told her son that "Hitler was a saint".

In the political climate at the end of the 20th century, we can appreciate the immorality of such a procedure. It is true that, in the same vein, she had told Aurélien himself that his father wanted her to have an abortion so that he would not be born. The lie was doubly despicable. Firstly because you don't say such things to a little child, and secondly because Monique knew very well that although Tristan didn't want children at the moment, he adored his son.

All these facts underlined the seriousness of his condition.

What was serious was that Tristan couldn't educate his son when he saw him. He did everything he could, but he knew very well that if he had given him a well-deserved beating, the slouching judges would have withdrawn all visitation rights...

Lucien phoned Tristan to tell him *how much he regretted marrying Monique.*

"He would have done better to stay in Paris...". He added *that "Aurélien was awful and if he wasn't here, he'd beat his mother".* On another occasion, he told her that *"Monique was completely lax and there was nothing he could do to raise Aurélien".*

Aurélien's only quality was that he was a good pupil in class.

None of this fulfilled the ideal Tristan had forged for his son. Especially as forty years of teaching had taught him that good pupils are rarely interesting and more often than not adhere to the most degrading conformisms and fashions.[75]

Little Béa, as adorable as ever, passed her "brevet des collèges", the competitive examination for nurses' aides, and became a highly competent and appreciated nurses' aide at the hospital. Alas, she was forced by peremptory obligation to undergo the anti-hepatitis B vaccination.

Over the next few months, her back began to ache, and then little by little things got worse, and she developed ankylosing spondylitis. She stopped working, suffered horribly, especially in her back, but also in all her joints and groin, and there was no end in sight to her martyrdom. She was given morphine, which diminished her vitality to the point of causing anguish to Tristan, who feared losing the little guardian angel of his son and himself.

During all this time, fate gave him an imperial gift: the prettiest girl in town, who was very young, fell in love with Tristan, and this marvellous adventure lasted seven years. She was an oasis in the middle of hell. This marvellous little Fabienne gave him enormous fighting energy, because such a conquest, at his age, was a miracle.

Tristan, on the other hand, was becoming obnoxious towards his father, so obnoxious that Tristan could not describe his behaviour, so ashamed would he be of himself and his son.

Once, when he had crossed all the limits, he was in his first year at the Lycée Naval where he paid nothing and received pocket money, he told her that he didn't see why he should have to pay child support to a child who treated his father in such a despicable way. He had still been naive enough to believe that Monique would support him morally in a way that would shake the child up. Not only did she fail to support Tristan, which

---

[75] In the year 2000, we see excellent secondary school pupils wearing baggy trousers, accordion-fashioned over massive, caricatured shoes, their hindquarters strapped into the fabric so that we can see their arses and even the outline of their anuses: they are so well conditioned that it is freely and coquettishly that they choose the horror propelled by homosexuals supported by finance. Tomorrow they will be among the twenty-five million who voted for a president radically enslaved by high finance and Marxism. Tomorrow they will be among the twenty-five million who voted for a president radically enslaved by high finance and Marxism... All this brings to mind the phrase from the Zohar about "the Goys (*non-Jews*), that vile seed of cattle".

is a huge moral blow, but also, believing that Tristan would actually withdraw the child support, she took advantage of a few missing indexation francs to have Aurelien's child support seized...

He had nothing left to do but look after his little Bea, who was so sick and had been suffering so much for three years already, and for how much longer, my little darling?

He was going to end his ordeal with a long letter to Monique: to review everything, to make the best possible arrangements for his son and to cherish his little patient until the end of his life. His greatest wish would be to die with her and cherish her for eternity...

Tristan and Fabienne

My dear Monique.
When you have little time left on this earth, and you feel it, sincerity and truth impose themselves on the mind in a radical way, "*scripta manent*" and the signature attest to the purity of the soul and the heart. Liars and wicked people never write because they know that their own writings would pursue them beyond themselves after having plunged their noses into their own faecal matter...
The last aggressions that you imposed on me and to which I have not been able, for fifteen years, to get used to, even though I am

always ready to come to an arrangement, to engage in kind and even affectionate dialogue, which is normal with the mother of my child, have inspired me to make this final reflection and the arrangements concerning our child, after my death.

You're accusing me of not paying my son's pension last July and August, and now you're accusing me of not paying it in June! I couldn't find the bank documents for July and August. For June I found them and sent them to you.

In any case, I paid those two months, as I have always paid for the last fifteen years without the slightest default. This is shown in my account book, where I only tick off the sums that have been duly paid.

On the other hand, if my account, which was still overdrawn on the 20th of the month, had been two thousand eight hundred francs overdrawn, I would have noticed it and sorted it out immediately. But in fifteen years such a thing has never happened. If I had stopped or deducted payment, it would have been after a legal decision, since Aurélien, who had been accepted at the Lycée Naval, had paid nothing for his upkeep and lessons and received four hundred francs monthly pocket money. I've never taken such an initiative, because I know very well that, apart from appeals, judges do exactly the opposite of everything I've been told by lawyers, including famous Parisian lawyers. So I took the advice of the family court judge, who told me to go through her, whatever the merits of my request.

As for you, would you have waited a year to set yourself off and let me know that I hadn't paid two thousand eight hundred francs? That's absurd and would have provoked a legitimate reaction from both you and me. After all, with Aurélien's little account, it doesn't take a year to notice such a shortfall!

It's all deeply dishonest. The worst thing is that you didn't stop there.

Aurélien behaved towards me in a way that I would have described as horribly pejorative, but which I prefer to call Apocalyptic, since this adjective corresponds with tragic accuracy to what we read in Saint John about the children of the Apocalypse. So I wrote him this letter:

"Aurélien,

I would certainly have preferred to die before you came on the first of May, so much so that the pain you have imposed on me is worse for me than death. I certainly don't have the intelligence and sensitivity of "the sinning sailor you would have liked as a father", and of whom you told me you would be proud, whereas of me...

Alas, you have always been the light of my life. For years I fought to the point of physical, moral and financial exhaustion, committing myself to ten years of borrowing, for the illusory joy of seeing you, of loving you, of giving you an exceptional insight at a time of generalised cerebral softening.

All this despite Mum doing everything she could to separate me from you, even taking away your name, using methods that can be described as despicable without semantic inflation. All this when everything could have been settled out of court without having to ruin your stepfather, your mother's 'paying' accomplice, and myself.

When you arrived in Vierzon on the first of May and put your head on my shoulder in the car, I was in heaven, remembering the blessed moments when you slept in my arms as a little boy and I enveloped you in an almost mystical love, so much bliss you gave me. Now, not only do you no longer obey me when it comes to the basics, without which a home is anarchy, but you also want to impose pathogenic music on me. What's more, you're disrespecting me, calling me a 'moron and an idiot' about a work you don't understand, just like people like Albert Camus, Raymond Las Vergnas, Louis Rougier, Gustave Thibon, Abélio, Hans Selye, Professor Albeaux Fernet, my thesis supervisor, all people who have supported and helped me throughout this century. And I'm not talking about a famous politician who thanked me for the information I provided him over forty years.

Your judgement classifies you as an unworthy son and also as a moron. I'll never put up with your monstrous insults and lack of respect again. You are a perfect example of the children described in the Book of Revelation: selfish, disrespectful, abusive, self-righteous, incapable of meditation, proud and so on.

I can't believe that you could be so naturally monstrous towards me and it's hard not to think about Mum's conditioning. If she doesn't admonish you for such unworthy behaviour, I'll have nine pieces of evidence to prove my suspicion. How could you be so nice to your sister Nathalie and your aunt Charlotte, neither of whom suspect your behaviour. Beatrice, who brought you up and taught you for so many years and whom I adopted to compensate for the suffering that Mum imposed on her, used to say to me: "Neither Charlotte, Chantal nor Nathalie suspect his behaviour towards you, and I don't even think they would believe it".

So now that you have your education and upkeep, not to mention pocket money, at the Lycée Naval, I don't see why I should continue to pay you a pension. It's out of love for you that I've forced myself to live in a council flat, even though my street has seen three riots involving North Africans, with shops smashed up and cars burnt. You're not even aware of my suffering in this situation, let alone grateful. Wouldn't that be stupid of me? I'll give you your pension back until you're twenty-five, if you fail the competitive exams at the end of your year of special mathematics. I will do this because the law obliges me to, but there will be no show of affection on my part. If you want to see me in the meantime, I'll pay for all your trips.

If you ever disrespect me or throw a hysterical fit, you'll get a slap in the face and then do what Mum did, never speak to me again. It's impossible for me not to see the heredity in your absurd, concrete behaviour, with that mathematical gift so specific to the psychology of sociopaths.

When you have such pride and such a narrow mind, you never know when you're wrong. Pride is a specific symptom of all mental illnesses like lack of pride. I wouldn't mind, because rather than go through what you've just put me through, I'd rather not see you again. Besides, I don't believe in recovery.

What do I have to gain by listening to a son who insults me, who has no respect, who doesn't obey the elementary imperatives of a home (come to the table, put his things away so as not to turn the flat into a souk, make his bed, don't go to bed at 3am and get up at 3pm etc.)? What's more, if he thinks he's smarter than everyone else, there's nothing to gain but immense pain.

I enclose a letter I wrote to your mother for you. You haven't understood that pure intelligence has nothing to do with the analytical systematics of modern science and statistics. On the other hand, pure intelligence knows how dangerous systematic analytical-mnemonic intelligence is.

I don't think that anything will help you to love me better, because if Mum has done this work of undermining me, no argument, no feeling, not even the most tender, will have the slightest weight, but I owe it to myself to make this final effort and also to show you my affection in the midst of this harsh reality...

Letter attached:

My dear Monique.

I'm not sending this letter to Aurélien because its content will only be effective if it comes from you.

Neither Lucien, your husband from now on, nor I have the slightest influence over Aurélien. It's true that if, when he admonishes or corrects him, you say to your husband: "Leave the poor boy alone", I doubt very much that he can do anything for his education.

His mentality saddens me and often frightens me with its recklessness.

Apart from the moral problem, which I won't go into because it hurts me so much, you should teach him, before he becomes robotic, that scientism is a superstition, a totalitarian fundamentalism that believes it can solve all problems, whereas it has led to atomic, hydrogen and neutron bombs, surrogate mothers, the cancer-causing pill and all the world's pollution.

Modern pseudo-science believes that what it cannot measure, experiment with or predict does not exist. It is a suicidal cretinism that moves on the crest of equations. This hyper-reductionist positivism excludes everything that makes up life: pure intelligence, genius, love, artistic creation, faith.

The grandes écoles train sleepwalkers who believe that what is technically possible is desirable and necessary.

This reason is irrational and is in fact nothing more than the systematisation of an obsessive. I beg you to 'inoculate' our child with this awareness that he would have had if we had remained united, even if separated.

The second very important thing: Aurélien is going to Africa for a holiday with the son of a general prime minister. I am radically opposed to Aurélien going to countries that are former colonies of any socialist or left-wing dictatorial persuasion. In these countries, any white person can be murdered despite an appearance of peace

. Globalism teaches these countries to hate and slaughter white people, defending only the exploiters of raw materials supported by implacable private armies.

He has a father he won't be seeing much longer: couldn't he benefit from that? I know that if I were him, I wouldn't be able to travel 10,000 km knowing that I don't have much time left to enjoy my father.

I hope Lucien helps you for a long time, because I'm afraid you're neither conscious nor psycho-active. An engineering degree from a top school doesn't make a man. We've spoilt him too much.

Teach Aurelian what I have explained to you. For the moment he doesn't think: he speculates in analyticism like the times.

It does not understand thought, because quantitative analyticism is always opposed to fundamentally qualitative thought.

Without this, there would be no chemical therapeutics or foodstuffs, no vaccinations that destroy the immune system, and no Jewish question, because we would have understood long ago that the only common denominator to a particularism that is constant in time and space was circumcision on the eighth day.

To you, heart and light.

Since that letter I've done a lot of thinking, trying to combine reason and love. I told myself that in the psychopathic state my son was in, he would never have enough heart to come back to me and ask for forgiveness. I realised that his condition was likely to be irreversible. So I couldn't fail to make an effort to help a beloved son who was losing himself, and for whom I had to try everything, even in the ocean of despair.

During these events I had the opportunity to speak with some of the fathers, and what they told me filled me with dread.

One told me that he had to put a padlock on his fridge because his twenty-two-year-old son was emptying it with his friends. Another told me that his son had said to him: "If only you could die"...

What's up?

So I decided to write to my son:

> My little
>
> I didn't think I'd be able to write to you because my grief was so immense and my despair so absolute. But Providence decided

otherwise and that's how it should be. Since "our sad events" I've met fathers who have the same problem as me with you, and even worse!

This is clearly the apocalyptic mentality, which is a determinism engendered by the situation that I am constantly denouncing. So try the impossible, go beyond this determinism. If you realise that you are in the satanic impasse in which we all find ourselves and from which you can emerge with my help. It's true that your mother had exhaustive information that should have protected her, but she used Satan's first weapon to destroy everything: the massacre of her couple. She should have been the last person in the world to suffer that destruction. So imagine the others who know nothing and vote for the clowns of high banking and Marxism!

You come against my heart, regret it, give me your affection and I return mine with all that it implies.

I'll give you all the explanations you need for texts that you can ponder beforehand. It's normal for a mathematician son to have difficulty understanding a philosopher father, but that doesn't mean we can't love and respect each other.

I love you too much not to make a legitimate effort like this.

Following this letter, Monique, Aurélien phoned me. He apologised feebly and talked to me for an hour about the boarding house, under the pretext of not talking about it!

And what have you done, Monique?

Neither your husband nor Aurélien told me that you had admonished Aurélien in the slightest, as I would have done with great severity if the roles had been reversed. The factor of our separation would not have played a part in the slightest. It would have been the least honourable thing for me to do.

But what was your noble moral behaviour?

Although I sent the pension only a few days late, to mark the occasion, which was legitimate in such circumstances, you went and had it seized by a bailiff, claiming that a few centimes of indexation had been missed! This is all the more grotesque given that I have usually increased the pension by about a hundred francs. But what is serious, apart from the moral level of the operation, is that this garnishment means that I am barred from taking out any loans. It's also a disgrace. But what do you care, of course! To put the finishing touches to the whole thing, you're asking me for three months' unpaid rent, for which I've only been able to provide you with proof of a bank account. I had one certainty: that my little account had never been increased by the sum of two months' pension, or two thousand six hundred francs. Absolute proof, but then again, what do you care? Waiting a year to claim such a large sum! ! Nobody believes that. You would have robbed me in June if I hadn't found a bank receipt...

Of course I don't have a penny left. What little I had has been eaten up by this false debt: a teacher is not a millionaire.

"Aurélien did the right thing! I nearly lost him," you say!

Because I'm the guilty one??? This is an example of all the inversions of the time.

"Incompatible moods, you say?

With me, or with Béa, who asks him twenty times to come to the table.

Talk to your husband about it: I have very strong reasons for believing that he is clear-headed about Aurélien's character and your unconsciousness.

What a horrible attack! Aurélien's problem was painful enough for us to talk about it on the phone like two intelligent, human people. We could have colluded and pretended to cancel the pension. I could have paid it into your account without him knowing, for example.

And all the aggression I've suffered over the last twelve years - what an impact on our child's psyche!

I heard you talking about assault! That's the last straw.

I've never done anything other than fight to see and raise my son. Nothing else. For fifteen years, I thought you were intelligent and noble, proud, fair and without pride. How wrong I was. But what Herculean strength it must have taken you to play me for fifteen years! *It must have been exhausting!*

It's true that if I'd discovered your nature, as I have *since* we split up, I'd never have seen you again and our Aurélien wouldn't be here.

I was convinced that everything I thought you had in you would come out, *especially* if we were separated. What I discovered was a lady of the wine cellar. It's when you're put to the test that your qualities shine through, especially with someone as totally accommodating as me.

I've never done anything against you and it was always with great pain that the courts forced me to highlight the facts of complaints for which I never filed a civil action, knowing perfectly well that they would never be brought without this legal process.

Amicable arrangements and a supportive friendship should have contributed to our child's balance. We didn't need justice: simple papers signed between us were enough. We could have agreed on the days when I could teach Aurélien, and done us both a favour by taking one or the other of us in when necessary, as is customary.

Your assaults? My God, I know them:

Who did everything possible to separate me from my child when I had the cultural references of the most eminent people of this century, when for fifteen years you gave me the illusion of an almost heroic adherence to an awareness of a depraved era?

Who did everything to prevent me from kissing my son at school, trying to blackmail me on numerous occasions, as the school headmaster testified, even going so far as to say that I was a dangerous hypnotist and that I was poisoning my son's snacks? When your methods didn't work, and even Aurélien's teacher was outraged, you took him out of school so that I wouldn't know where he was... You even refused to give the bailiff the address of the new school, which was included in the appeal file! Assault?

Who told Aurélien "if your father gets custody of you, I'll never see you again"... aggression?

That's really the height of the traumatic horror imposed on our son. This is the etiology of a neurosis that will follow him all his life. How can we be surprised by his sociopathy, when we also think of the heredity of your brute of a father?

"Incompatible temperaments" is what you said about our child's unworthy behaviour towards me? Incompatible with Lucien? With Bea? With me? That's a lot of incompatibilities, don't you think?

To make matters worse, when Aurelien behaves in an undignified way, and I talk about taking away his pension when he's officially living on a lifestyle of thirty thousand francs a month (maintenance, lessons, pocket money, sports, shows, etc.), instead of solemnly admonishing him and telling him that he's earned it, and that any father worthy of the name would do the same, you run to the bailiff! Money, after all, is the only thing that counts: you're very much of your time. Assault?

What's more, did I take it away from him? When you separated me from my son and I threatened to take away your monthly house payment of three thousand francs, did I do it? I never did, and I paid it until your husband sold your house. Did I have any other choice to fight your madness and the false testimony you got from people who didn't even know me! Assault?

WHO made my son say that I had said that "Hitler was a saint" at a political moment when such a statement, however preposterous, could have deprived me of my son? Aggression?

Poor little boy, who, faced with such a sentence as "If your father gets custody of you, I'll never see you again", is going to feel for the rest of his life that this sentence, which can drive you mad, is ingrained in him: "If I love my father, I'll lose my mother". How can someone reach such a level of recklessness and malice? Aggression?

Poor little thing! What a shock, when I think that I can't do anything for him except put the most beautiful photo of his mother in his room so that he feels that I can't love him without loving his mother.

Is it any wonder that he finds refuge in technical obsession, as can be seen in a two-page letter in which nothing but computer manoeuvres are mentioned?

Why should we be surprised that he's closed to any self-criticism or basic altruism and wants to impose whatever he wants without bothering about other people's opinions or rights? Oh Monique, what a crime, what a ridiculous lack of awareness!

WHO forced me to spend two million old francs on legal matters alone for two appeals, when the first appeal had just been won by granting me normal access rights? Aggression!

And then, thanks to your action, a little summary judge took away all my monthly visiting rights, except for holidays, while you took away my son so as not to apply the Bourges court judgement, which was theoretically punishable under criminal law? Assault!

Here again we could have managed to adapt the new appeal judgement to the situation. We didn't need anyone. You had to prove to the judge that you were hell-bent on separating me from my son, and that didn't even work against you! Assault!

The day after the hearing at which my visiting rights had been withdrawn, after a six hundred kilometre car journey, I found myself with two almost paralysed fingers! An assault!

So another appeal to regain my visiting rights! Assault!

WHO deliberately forced me to travel 120,000 kilometres to see my son at the weekend, and to bring him back every holiday? Assault!

WHO forced me to spend two thousand francs every weekend of the month? Assault!

WHO forced me to take on these enormous burdens by accepting the help of our little Béa, whose devotion and generosity know no bounds, because all this was unaffordable on what I was earning! Aggression!

She continued to give the three of us everything, despite the ordeal you inflicted on her, poor little girl, with her miraculous work, who was "only good for mopping the floor" as you used to say, and whom your wickedness cast down forever on my heart.

By the way, I'm the one who had the pension doubled because of the trial judge's error.

WHO came to interfere with my visiting rights, making such an incredible fuss that ten people offered to give evidence for my file and you were summoned by the police? Assault!

WHO, after the first appeal judgement, refused to present my son in an incredible circus that resulted in you being summoned before the public prosecutor by two uniformed gendarmes? You suggested that he be taken to his old school's fête, while you prepared his escape to the nearby gendarmerie where you were waiting for him! This disappearance is very distressing for me, because I could never have imagined such a horror! An attack?

WHO removed my photo from my son's bedroom, while yours is right here in his room? Assault!

Who has never brought a civil action, knowing that the charges would never be brought, even after being summoned by the Public Prosecutor?

Aggression?

WHO, in a word, shamelessly attacks the other knowing perfectly well that you're lying, because you know me well enough to know that you're lying. I've always been content to plead criminal charges, but reluctantly, because I had to defend my access rights!

WHO dared to accuse me of raping his sister Françoise, as if you believed me capable of such a thing! Assault!

Françoise is a big, ugly lump who doesn't inspire me to kiss or coitus. You know the truth about your sister.

At a time of deficiency on your part and testicular effervescence on my part, I accepted his favours several times. Nothing more. At that time, if I had liked her, I could very well have given up on you and chosen her.

It turns out that I had put you on a pedestal...

But you know very well that a sister would never tell her sister that she had slept with her husband - which, by the way, she hadn't -.

Why did she lie and tell you so much? Because she hates you and wanted to hurt you. She can't forgive you for being brutally strict with her, just as strict as you are lax with our son.

She couldn't take it and saw a great opportunity for revenge.

So it's all very well for you: if you want to kill your dog, accuse it of rabies...

Knowing your sister and myself perfectly well, to take advantage of a flirtation with your sister for a slander as atrocious as rape, comes down to a moral level of the absolute zero degree... And you know it. Assault?

WHO made me spend at least twenty to twenty-five million old in twelve years and continues today under false pretences to deprive me of the few francs I had left? Aggression. And Bea, poor little darling, is suffering this ruin, because she always helped me.

"Incompatibility of moods" with me and Bea, you said. Tell that to your husband and you'll make him laugh yellow...

Béa has always been as devoted and patient as an angel with Aurélien, and she's always had much more authority over him than you or I have.

She doesn't count the expenses and outings for him. She never stops spoiling him and buying him things. I'm delighted that she's passed her A-levels, her care assistant diploma, her piano, her English and her garden, from which she grows an impressive array of fruit and vegetables.

She really has a green thumb! And I'm not even going to mention all the care she gives us - she's a treasure trove!

How could you be jealous of someone so close to God? Probably because you behave like a witch...

And what does she ask for? A little love...

Together, we could have given it to her and enabled her to take up the profession she has chosen: caring for the sick and those who are suffering.

Our son has no judgement, no respect, no modesty, no feeling. He can only be kind to strangers or to my family on holiday. With Lucien, Béa and me he is often ignominious and pretentious to the point of raving madness. Unfortunately, there's not the slightest exaggeration in what I'm saying. Unfortunately, I love him dearly, but if he persevered in this way, why would I continue to give him a pension and stay in this migratory world that is so detrimental to my age and health?

I'm not passing judgement on you, despite the horror of what happened. You have your excuses, your father. I'm simply stating the facts, just the facts, nothing but the facts, as anyone would do, including you if you were lucid. I'm afraid that you take after your father and that Aurélien takes after you.

This realisation was necessary, even though I know that I'm standing in front of a block of reinforced concrete and that you'll be incapable of taking stock of yourself and rediscovering the basic qualities that make a human being. It's pride that will paralyse you and you'll ignore pride: may I be wrong in this diagnosis.

Justice has disappeared, even at family level.

I asked the family court judge for you to give me a small contribution towards the enormous cost of travelling from Berry to Brittany and back, to see Aurélien at weekends, and to take him on and back from holidays every other month. The only expense you produced was "driving licence fees". But this was a luxury expense, because it was only sensible for him to take his driving test after his baccalauréat. Instead of granting me the small amount of help I was asking for, the judge increased my monthly pension by four hundred francs, which is enormous for a pensioner who is already struggling. This judgement was judged absurd by all the legal experts to whom I had the case notes read. Without a doubt, I should have been awarded the small amount I was asking for.

Indeed:

The expenses for the monthly weekend and the average of 2 return trips per month were overwhelming, especially for a pensioner.

My age and health had to be taken into account. The erosion of my pension was obvious. All these facts had an inescapable legal value for a judge worthy of the name and the 'accompanied' driving licence had none. What's more, as a student of higher mathematics at the Lycée Naval, Aurélien had a lifestyle valued at at least thirty thousand francs a month and pocket money from the State.

They all concluded that the female judges were arbitrary and unfair to the men. The same is true in Spain, where my son-in-law told me: "Fathers only get satisfaction on appeal, if they have the means to appeal. Otherwise they are crushed on principle. This has been true for me in France, and as in this case I don't have the means to appeal because it would cost me at least a hundred times more than what I'm asking for, I'm reduced to the effects of injustice.

But this state of affairs is not unique to Family Affairs, it's everywhere.

Political scoundrels are released, while people who overpowered a thief and handed him over to the police in handcuffs are imprisoned and convicted for false imprisonment. They should have let the thief go and filed a complaint. The complaint would, of course, never have been made or would never have been successful, as is the case with hundreds of complaints of which I am aware.

So there's no chance, even if the facts are in your favour, of getting satisfaction from a Family Affairs judge, if you're a father.

For all this, as for Bea, we could have come to an amicable arrangement, especially with a child's treasure. I was ready for any arrangement, motivated by a sense of justice and kindness. No need for a lawyer and millions spent by Lucien and myself.

As far as our tragedy in general is concerned, I will tell you, in the light of my sincerity, my age, knowledge that far exceeds a century of general dumbing down, and the sense of justice and righteousness that are the natural lot of the "Libra".

Your problem is painful and you need to try to rise above yourself. Your suffering, like all suffering, is on the road to healing or death. Choose life, choose healing, choose a new transparency full of justice and mercy.

When I first met you I told you all my faults before you even set foot in my flat.

Men with a marked personality are all thyroid patients with a hyper, but physiological, tendency.

The thyroid is the gland of intelligence, youth, sexuality and *temptation*. So they are studs all their lives, even in old age. This is true of the Romantics in my doctorate, but also of people like Saint Augustine and Saint Francis of Assisi, who only came to asceticism late in life. Even at my age, I'm still fascinated by girls with an outstanding personality. How can I resist them, especially if, quite frankly, I don't want to? It is said that there were hardly any girls at Assisi that Francis didn't know biblically.

As for writers, musicians and poets, everything has been said about them. When an elderly woman was asked if she had ever known a gentleman who matched a certain description and who had lived in the town where she lived, she replied: "Ah, yes, that pig!" and it was Goethe...

The last time I went to Spain, friends of my daughter Chantal said of me that I was a symbiosis of Don Juan and Don Quixote. Feminine perspicacity! You know all about the first, and I'll quote Dominique Aubier about the second: "Next to you, Don Quixote is a little boy"...

If you were to read a letter I received recently from a beautiful twenty-eight-year-old girl, you'd be as stunned as I was when I received it...

It's true that, as I say in my thesis: "My bio type attracts pretty girls who are a bit crazy".

I once forced you to give up a child: that was a crime. But between two crimes you have to choose the lesser. At the time, I was having a nervous breakdown because my wife and daughter had left for Germany. I was suffering from scapulohumeral periarthritis, which meant that both my arms were virtually paralysed. The financial situation wasn't great. Allowing a child to be born in such circumstances would have been even more criminal. You don't make a child to expose it to psychological and material misery.

What's more, when you see the situation of young people today, given over to music that kills, drugs, unemployment, laxity and the sanctimoniousness of tramps, there's nothing to encourage them to have children. Only the mass of colour proliferates and will deliver us a global heap of physico-chemical amalgams governed by the profit and loss account of a pseudo-democracy that is in fact nothing more than organised and planned chaos.

What's more, we're bringing them divorce, because we can't stick together for them, which for me is the absolute horror that breeds all pathologies of body and mind.

Our separation because of our little Bea, who brought us everything, will remain in my mind the major symbol of our degeneration.

It was you who aroused in me this infinite compassion for her.

This slightly handicapped girl, who would give back points to so many people considered normal... You're the one who glued my heart, more maternal than paternal, to hers.

I'll see her all my life, prostrate, silent, in her room, tears streaming down her cheeks, with nothing to eat, as I arrived from a university reunion in Paris. She who did everything for us with absolute obliviousness and who only asked for a little love...

Boundless dedication, miraculous efficiency, how could you? What an abominable waste!

This defence of Bea against your wickedness, when you and Aurelien were my treasures, should have inspired in you an enormous love for me: I sacrificed what I held dearest to my compassion.

We would then have done something for Aurélien, who is so stupid in the most essential respects, as I have seen in my best pupils over forty years of teaching. We would have made him a person of honour, honesty, respect, humility and true knowledge.

Poor little thing who was, as you said, "only good for mopping". I'm still in awe of her heart and her miraculous skill. And she doesn't hold it against you! "Monique gave me a lot", she often tells me.

Oh, if you'd had just a tiny bit of his kindness, how I would have loved you!

If I didn't marry you legally, it's still because of you. The tax study you have, carried out by a tax director friend of mine, concluded with: "Don't get married". The difference in tax was enormous for us.

When I'm gone, Béa will give Aurélien everything he deserves and can afford. Clothes, linen, jewellery, and a life insurance policy of three hundred thousand francs if Bea dies before the age of sixty. Then, as he is declared to be living with his father, everything here will belong to him.

He will have to pay the rent until he buys another home, but Bea's insurance will provide him with a substantial deposit.

Humans are so inhuman, so ugly, so cowardly, so mean, so insignificant that I'm happy to be leaving this world soon.

I thought, how naive, that you had read my book, and that you would never have added such a burden to an already gigantic suffering. Many of my friends asked me this question, knowing how you had behaved over the last fifteen years. They couldn't understand how you could have inflicted such pain on me, and all they could come up with was a psychiatric answer.

I know that you have excuses that I'm not telling you about so as not to hurt you by reminiscing about them.

I forgive you and make a lot of excuses, but you should make a little effort to set yourself and the facts straight.

Best wishes from Dad.

The biotype you describe is surely unreal.

He is too pure and too absolute to belong to the human species as such: he would be a superman with the defects of his qualities but with an intellectual and emotional potential that is rarely encountered.

(Dr Laugier, endocrinologist)

Tristan

Chapter XXIII

> *My brothers, the dandies.*
> *"The dandy is by function an oppositional".*
> *"Dandyism is a degraded form of asceticism".*
> (Albert Camus)
> *"In 1984, the most intelligent will be the least normal".*
> (Orwell).

There was no future for Tristan. He was "outside history".

Among the lethargic debris of this world, would he be able to bear the burden of his intelligence and his soul? What can you do in this heartless world where only lies, ugliness and cunning reign?

How could it suffer its true face, a symbol of solitary impotence, over the hideous atony of contemporary masks?

How could he escape the engulfing standardisation to which everyone lent themselves with flaccid complacency?

What could he do in a herd that sought freedom in a hysterical passion for servitude?

Perhaps in this robotising and robotised world, he would one day be denounced by pseudo-Christians, unconscious agents of suicidal ideologies, and then handed over to the psychiatric commissions to await the firing squad.

How could he avoid committing suicide alone in a world of suffering, despair and institutionalised ugliness, in a world where there is nothing left to say to anyone?

Would he ever find the time to technically access the liberating piano, the vertigo of Chopin?

Was he going to try to discover, among the enslaved cohorts, the new hidden guides of tomorrow's humanity, the elite who would lay the authentic foundations for the happiness of future mankind while respecting divine and natural laws?

And would Tristan, a Jew, a dormant Freemason and a baptised Catholic, show the degraded French the traditional way to the equilibrium that no-one today will ever know?

Only fate knew... But one thing was certain:

The snake never asked to be a snake! (cosmic laughter ad libitum).

Tristan's monologue

I'm a force that will...

If I'd been lucky enough to open a piano when I was five, I'd never have closed it again and I'd never have written.

I didn't want to think or write.

I'm just delivering my suffering, pure and simple.

I don't like literature, all those talents that seduce us and make us lose consciousness, those sumptuous styles, those viper's tongues in golden jewel cases...

Chopin, Schumann, Liszt, Beethoven, Mozart and Bach would have been enough for me. The dandy is aware of the forms and 'deformities' of thought.

I've been plunged into a hellish, absurd, ugly, unbearable world.

I watched it without composure, this ugliness culminating in absolute horror. That's when I got *homesick*.

I dug down to the roots of my hyper-consciousness and made my heart squeal.

I don't have a banal sense of humour, but I do have a metaphysical one. To think that I am what I am in spite of myself, marked by an implacable fatality: sometimes I wake up at night to laugh about it.

And the rest of us, the normals, who don blue jeans and ballot papers, the uniforms of international bullshit, on the edge of vegetative life, gorging ourselves on regressive, bestial music and football where we slaughter each other hysterically, doomed to total robotisation and oblivious to their hypnotic conditioning...

And all taking themselves seriously, the comatose sleepers and myself.

Nothing can be solved in a world that can only be revitalised by destruction.

Opal!

I understand the truth about opal.

It doesn't bring bad luck, it's the aesthetes who love opals. I love opals and aesthetes who lead their lives dangerously beyond good and evil are made for misfortune and they bring misfortune to opals.

Given their physiology, dandies always wear narrow shoes. This ridiculous image sums up the essential point. The ridiculous essence.

The vibrations of the outside world cause such shocks that the dandy is always in a state of nervous shaking, of physical pain.

This pain takes on metaphysical proportions and spreads its veil of shattering sadness over the whole of humanity, over the little children who never asked to come into this world.

I suffer, therefore I am.

"The dandy is nothing without his suffering" said Albert Camus. How true!

His suffering must not be pointless, it must serve a purpose. It must be purifying, grandiose, magnificent, and universal in its howl.

The dandy bears the weight of the universe; he is the idiot of the universe, the brother of the village idiot.

Dedicated, cultivated, immense, proud suffering, challenge, revolt, creation, discovery.

This suffering, barely extinguished, is followed by the anguish of the next.

Chopin! An intense, desperate cry that grows louder.

Occasionally there is an outburst of gaiety, as in certain waltzes or etudes, but this is not gaiety, it is in the manner of Harlequin and Fantasio, a kind of dandyish playfulness that is often expressed in everyday life by sudden outbursts of even fleeting buffoonery.

The Romantic is not an intellectual in the modern sense of the word, but what is less intellectual than a modern intellectual? The modern intellectual is a suicidal analytical machine for himself and for the whole world.

If feeling is distanced from intellectual elaboration, the result will be destruction and lack of knowledge. Without feeling, we cannot synthesise, because synthesis is a miracle of the heart: it is the province of providential elites.

There is no beauty, no moral sense without the heart. The puny mind of the modern homunculus could not in a single century come to terms with a single fundamental truth about Man.

A whole upside-down, false and ubiquitous world forced me to understand this basic truth.

I thought I was crazy and I discovered that the whole world was crazy. Oh my!

I feel. My universe is a feeling of acute anguish that must come out of my being, explode out of me.

It has to come out, because it's suffocating me.

The truth that does not come out poisons, like a child ready to be born that should, O how horrible, remain in the womb.

It's better to die telling the truth than to die suffocated by it.

Everything is there for the artist, the thinker. When Chopin wrote the nocturne in E flat, he didn't think: he spoke his anguish, his magical, infinite sadness. He didn't try to analyse.

Self-analysis? What could be more inartistic? The modern world has turned me into a kind of hybrid forced to analyse instead of creating and crying out beauty.

The Romantic revolts in creative sensations.

Today, for a dandy, powerless to live, to try to survive in this hostile, material, mechanised world, drowned in the "lie of progress",[76] he has to repress his ego, to try impossibly to resemble these so-called "normal" humanoids. Those who believe in and live off all the nonsense inflicted on them: cretinous politics of manipulated puppets, synthetic chemistry for

---

[76] "The lie of progress is Israel" (Simone Weil, "Gravity and Grace").

food and medicine, mind-numbing and pornographic psychoanalysis, propaganda and shrinking education, which petrifies children into the nothingness of materialism and Marxism...

Dandyism is a normal neurosis, but without a personal fortune, the man with the psychic hand is lost in this world of brutes and chaos. Matter destroys that which legitimately should dominate it, if it is given primacy. "There are ways of exercising sovereignty over matter" said a certain alchemist by the name of Eliphas Lévy.

Until the day when the matter blows up sovereignty! So suicide, madness, tuberculosis, the normal lot.

An insane world cannot preserve the superior: its fatal pathology is profitability.

How could it be otherwise if the inferior dominates?[77]

So I've put myself in a state of permanent, superhuman repression: I deny myself in order to live a basic life. Without going too far, however, so as not to descend into sheer madness.

I had to be careful not to attach too much importance to these great impulses of the soul that correspond, O humour, to glandular hypersecretions. There isn't a drop of genius, madness or philosophy that doesn't come from our endocrines.

There are two of me.

The crushed dandy, and the other who looks at the first, chuckling softly.

It was a curious experience at the end of the twentieth century. I've come to understand the calm that all the robots of this century aspire to.

I'm nostalgic for football. I love a bunch of soulless, mass-produced, inoculated, cretinised, secularised, regressive, muscular, drugged, pornographed, globalist citizens, atonic and planned.

We are slaughtering each other all over the world in the glue of liberalism and Marxism. We are lied to about everything, everywhere.

Who cares? The show goes on at twenty-one!

---

[77] The inferior is thinking of his re-election and not of a niagara of individuals from the Third World who are going to destroy his homeland.

I've sometimes wondered where this strange character, the romantic dandy, came from, as opposed to the primitive brute.

This born actor.

Even as a politician, he is an idealist. Lamartine, Hugo. Disraeli and his magnificent hat.

Politics isn't just about appearances, it's about philanthropy: it's about people in relation to social and divine injustice.

Dandies! What mistakes you made in the nineteenth century! You were, unwittingly, the worst agents of materialism.

"He who would make an angel, makes a beast"...

Primitive man acted, hunted, did not think.

With civilisation and luxury favouring leisure and culture developing the mind and sensibility, the romantic thyroid wanders on the borderline between primitive brute and pure spirit.

His soul belongs to God, but his body is tortured by matter, by Satan.

The dandies are all aristocrats or ennobled Jews. They belong to families with centuries of civilisation and culture.

Chopin was of Polish nobility. Alphonse de Lamartine, Alfred de Musset. Mendelssohn and Disraeli.

The dandy is an end product of civilisation. A product of decadent refinement, doomed to the rapid disappearance of lightning. Archaic, inappropriate, splendid, inefficient, admired for being unique and creative. A luxury item for which you pay dearly. If you don't pay him, he kills himself in the face of his radical inability to live: the psychic hand.

The dandy is a being of thought-intuition. He does not reason with the primary elements of the mind offered to human banality. He sees the whole in its chaotic, paradoxical aspect and draws synthetic conclusions from the anarchy of his suffering. His intuitive observation is extreme and dazzles the blind.

The dandy is the superior innocent, and the innocent who empties himself empties himself of the truth about the world.

He has a sense of the big picture.

Of the characteristics that make up the human personality - strength, reason, will and feeling - only the first three are necessary for material adaptation.

An angel with a weak body would only have an intelligent heart, and his ineffectiveness would lose him in ignominy. This is why, on the border between primitive man and angel, there is the romantic dandy who appears and disappears like the phoenix, the most dematerialised of beings, on the verge of the angel, of pure feeling, the only principle that remains after death.

The dandy is the closest thing to a pure spirit and is tortured by matter.

The smaller the ego, the smaller the soul. God is a giant ego: he is egocentricity par excellence. The dandy is the maximum human ego; his form of intelligence makes him inaccessible even to those closest to him, especially those closest to him.

The ordinary human being cannot understand it, and yet the dandy's revolt provides the greatest wealth of revelation emanating from a being.

The ascetic cannot reveal as much in a sensitive way because he lives in peace and metaphysical egoism.

The body is an organic and mental whole that receives the waves of the absolute, according to its degree of perfection. It picks up more or less of the waves of inaccessible total reality. This is why knowledge belongs only to saints, geniuses and dandies.

The poet is a sort of link between God, the devil and mankind.

Those who do not understand from the heart are true nonentities.[78]

Since the revolution of 1789, there has been a host of pseudo-intellectuals whose colossal logical sequences in the pure objective, result in nothingness.

---

[78] One example among a thousand: the scientists who fool around with genetics have as much analytical knowledge as those who manipulate the atom. If they all had fundamental intelligence, the intelligence of the heart, they would know not to touch anything in genetics or nuclear physics. The world's greatest physicist, who worked with Oppenheimer, resigned and went off to make pottery in her home village... True intelligence had spoken.

Heartless thinking is the quintessential product of hell.

After the ascetic, the dandy is the person who possesses the most spirituality. It is the gulf between his ideal self and his practical self that determines his poetic gift and his suicide. His body did not obey his soul, which was in love with the absolute. From great spirituality in a weak body springs the most intense human suffering. The dandy is the supreme symbol of human suffering. Unadapted to the world as it is, he strives to adapt the world to him: this tragedy corresponds to a metaphysical reality, because human purpose is spiritual.

This is why the man who thinks without loving is necessarily materialistic, and his para-altruistic logic is worse than the worst selfishness (Marxism).

Contemporary objectivity is the subjectivity of those who have no feelings, no heart.

If doctors and academics underwent training that demanded thought, feeling, meditation and synthesis as the sine qua non of authentic knowledge, they would not be assimilating robots naively believing that the ballot paper, mnemonic competitions, synthetic chemistry, Freudism and Marxism will make man happy.

I don't blame them.

The Jews ignore their lack of heart, their lack of moral sense, their ability to rot behind deceptive facades for the explorers of the immediate.

Academics are unaware of their robotic, elephantine psychology; *they don't know that they don't know that they can't know.*

That's the whole tragedy. This is the impasse.

I blame God or his shadow. So many years of suffering contemplating the sordid pain and ineptitude of the human adventure.

From generation to generation, God lets us sink into ignorance and the misery that grows with it…

The absurd is born of a-consciousness.

What we call progress is the negation of progress.

True progress is a synthesis of the material, the moral, the aesthetic and the spiritual.

It is the heart, and the heart alone, that ensures our progress.

The dandy is dying, the saint long dead. The world is dying in chaos

Despite his Luciferianism, the dandy has a very noble place in the scale of creation.

Chapter XXIV

"And this world will end in bloody anarchy.

Thorns

The truth is neither for nor against. Truth is only truth. It is against those who live on lies, who love lies, who need lies to live. It is the god of free men, as Dostoyevsky said.

I can't take the universe seriously, and so when I'm not in agony, I just enjoy the silly spectacle.

I don't have many opinions, but I do have certainties, including the absurdity of all dogmatism that excludes the laws of life and true spirituality, the functional anteriority of the hormonal system over the nervous system, the world domination and extermination of those circumcised on the 8th day, and the reality of true health through the absorption of molecules specific to the human bio-type.

I have woven truth into my suffering alone.

My soul is free. The only fatality is the weight of the body.

Nobody knows what the truth is, or at least very few people do: it's the ability to calmly force ourselves to do what's best in everything.

To reach the essence, you have to be persecuted by the essence. Hence the artist's paranoid state.

"Don't go mad", an authentic philosopher used to say to me, "because you are normal in a world of mad people".

There is no escape from transcendence, except through madness and suicide.

True intelligence is knowing how to go beyond the anti-psychological to achieve superior objectivity. You can count on your fingers the intelligent people of each generation. That's why I'm only writing for the men who will come after the 3rd World War.

Freud and Marx, suicidal global lies. True genius destroys that which does not love.

False prophets do not destroy in the short term: they undermine in time and space.

True geniuses often break with the immediate and build over time and space.

I loathe the men of this humanity, but I love man. The humanoids and homunculi of the twentieth century have nothing to do with man.

For the saint God is as obvious as for the average man the chair he sees. If you reveal to an ant the existence of the "chair synthesis" it will never be convinced because it will only ever be able to see one or two cubic millimetres of wood. In the same way, you can only believe in God if, for example, you rely on the conscience of the saint.

Some mental powers are considerable, others almost vegetative. Some will only ever see their bank account or their cup of coffee, but others can 'see' God.

The average person can only believe the true elites, just as they now blindly believe the false elites who are leading them into chaos.

The Japanese have put all their traditional qualities, once taught by true elites, at the service of Judeo-Cartesianism. Their schoolchildren are committing suicide in large numbers.

Poor little brain of man, increasingly degenerate, shaped by progress towards total destruction.[79] You reject all transcendence and you're right. You're right because you don't even know that you're rejecting it and you don't even know that you're right (even though you're wrong!).

We only know what we feel, we only feel what we love.

The gulf between dandyism and asceticism: Chopin's ravaged death mask and Pascal's calm, despite the extreme morphological analogy.

The saint is God's accomplice in the evil that exists: he is not the true innocent. The dandy is the true innocent, but he pays for his true

---

[79] "The lie of progress is Israel" (Simone Weil: *Gravity and Grace*).

innocence with his pride, and only gains access to false innocence (the true innocence) by losing his painful pride.

We are all determined, God himself, because there is at least one thing he cannot do: not be God.

A righteous man who knows the realities of these last centuries cannot accept either earth or heaven: he can only claim nothingness.

Written in 1965 and made O how true in "1984".

Before the age of twenty, every genius will go mad as soon as he begins to become conscious. Even if he does not lose his mind through collectivist suffocation, through the disappearance of truth, beauty and the moral sense, he will be considered insane by the criteria of Freudo-Marxist psychiatry and Judeo-Cartesian psychiatry in general.

A mad, cruel world, afflicted by the enormous flaw of morbid anti-transcendent rationalism: between God and man lies the opacity of Judeo-Cartesianism.

Ideologies: the metallic logic of the madman, but superior to that of the ordinary madman, who convinces the ordinary man because he adopts convincing linear reasoning: two and two make four.

We know that human knowledge is not as simple as that, and that our awareness of reality is not satisfied with so little: it's hard to be logical when you're not mad!

It is reason alone that prevents the man of today from being reasonable.

It has become a cancer that eliminates all the higher components of the mind. It has become an obsessive systematisation.

Pseudo-democracy is only possible because people are so stupid that they cannot realise its absolute impossibility. If they could, they would be much more evolved and democracy would become relatively possible because it would be transformed into an oligarchy of the most spiritualised, most disinterested beings. In every living thing there has always been an absolute master. Today, the absolute masters of "democracy" are Rothschild and Marx, followed by their criminal and suicidal elected followers.

Tell people "I'm going to give you freedom" and enslave them: they'll come in droves. Tell them you're going to force them to give them freedom and they won't come.

They prefer to feed on labels and illusions, as long as the labels are flashy and the illusions shine at least as long as you look at them.

Materialism denies the power of thought. But isn't materialism a thought?

That's certainly a worthless thought.

Descartes, exploited by the Jewish world, has become the bane of mankind. The non-existence of God would soon be proved in Cartesian fashion. It will be proved that the soul does not exist. This will be easy for those who have none. A fatal and sad evolution of false modern science, black magic.

Jahve, the first terrorist.

Jealous, intransigent, he wanted no other god but himself. If you respected his commandments, if you didn't sleep with his sister, his mother or his daughter, then this good god would help his people in their terrorist endeavours against other peoples. Seven peoples were gradually enslaved. The males were exterminated, the females enslaved, and the goods, crops, livestock and crowns of the defeated and exterminated kings were stolen.

We came home more glorious and powerful than when we left.

Nothing has changed: Dresden, Hamburg, Hiroshima, the Palestinians driven out of their land and massacred, Lebanon...

They have a god that reflects their sad mentality.

Mr Homais, an agrégé at the university and holder of the Légion d'Honneur, applies all their criteria, and will even become an anti-Semite if need be. I have never seen worse enjuivés than anti-Semites.

These beings, totally deprived of the spirit of synthesis, have built the most extraordinary, the most bewildering synthesis of destruction possible and imaginable on a planetary scale. Therein lies the unfathomable mystery of the Jewish question, which circumcision on the 8th day explains psycho-physiologically but not metaphysically.

Metaphysically, they are the fatal instrument of the end of the Dark Ages.

They are still the ones who produce the best specialised critical analytical studies of the political system they invented and of which they are the absolute masters.

Between ideological ratiocinating madness and mystical hysteria there is a via media: the harmony of heart and reason that leads to truth.

Whoever tells the truth today has everyone against him: victims and executioners. Especially the victims, who do not want to be defended, but rather anaesthetised.

They wallow in feculent, putrescent destruction.

Agrégé = petrified miniature Jew.

Sorbonne: a breeding ground for Homais and Lévy, who got on like a house on fire and joined Masonic lodges.

Channelled minds, generating little analytical currents that clash. There are no intellectuals in the walled university.

When a young intellectual has access to it, he immediately flees. He flees the extravagant rigour of the sclerotic system, the promiscuity of presumptuous people who label as fantasy, imagination, madness, what they do not understand, which is to say almost everything.

Education = first stage of collective dumbing down. Mass production of non-thinkers, in the service of an occult totalitarianism whose objective is the procreation of specialist producers-consumers-voters.

The World Bank favours secondary education: it knows what it's doing.

In "1984", these unfortunate people left public or private secondary education (no difference) knowing nothing. We deliberately forgot one little detail in education: intelligence. We now have masses of illiterates.

Internat, agrégation, intellectual sclerosis championships. These competitive examinations are necessarily psycho-pathogenic because they kill off the essence of the mind by a narrow focus on the minuscule. The news has shown us that they are indeed pathogenic: I've been shouting it for forty years.

Fundamental identity of madness: Loss of moral sense.

Loss of willpower and voluntary attention. Loss of the ability to synthesise.

Loss of the notion of identity or principle of analogy.

Unfortunately, the possession of brilliant analytical skills is perfectly compatible with a diagnosis of dementia.

We can therefore diagnose :

Psychiatry,[80] medicine, literature, official philosophy, politics and teaching.

It's hardly surprising that the number of ordinary lunatics is increasing geometrically. Our Goetheans are on the fringes or in oriental monasteries.

O the labels and magnificent principles that legitimise the collective murder of souls and bodies. O the racist genocide of humanity, in the name, supercomplete, of anti-racism.

Evil feeds on good stupidity. Soon there won't be enough good to feed the evil of the earth.

The naivety, stupidity and vanity of women and Negroes have been systematically exploited[81] to reduce them to slavery, hatred, epavism, drugs, social chaos and tuberculosis, in the name of freedom and anti-racism, to set them against each other, children against parents, women against men, Negroes against whites and all against God. This international ignominy is masterfully perpetrated by those whom the Egyptians called "the filthy".

But why are the victims so stupid?

Modern state liberalism: the international totalitarianism of Jewish gold and its Marxist epilogue.

---

[80] Psychiatry radically and absolutely ignores what mental illness is. A policeman kills 5 people. Psychiatry declares him normal. Meeting certain elementary logical criteria means nothing. "How crazy must the police be!" exclaimed Coluche!

[81] "Negrum" in Latin means black. "Negro" refers to a specific ethnic group among Africans. Black means nothing.
Some ethnic groups are black and some are not. Some pussies, for demagogic reasons, want to tamper with semantics.
Shahak teaches us that the entire slave trade from the East to Europe was perpetrated by Jews. The same goes for the Africans deported to America in atrocious conditions. More than 10 million died on the way and were thrown overboard during the entire period of the African slave trade.

The drama of flattery and stupidity, easy and convincing reasoning, apparent truth, misleading slogans, "change" (in politics) lies and deception in time and space.[82]

Modern reason becomes an indispensable means of adapting to the ignoble: it is incompatible with conscience.

In the modern world, "every action leads to crime" said Camus.

Oedipus complex? But Oedipus is a drama about fate, not incest. The Greek playwright chose this behaviour as the fatal fulfilment of the act towards which man shows the most repulsion.

Explain Freud? The Oedipus complex, of course!

Do we need symbolism to have erotic dreams?

Democracy breeds totalitarianism. If it's not too rotten, it will be Nazism or Fascism. If not, it will be the gulags of some Bolshevik.

Fifty years ago, the choice was between Nazism and Marxism.

Today, the die is cast. There's bound to be ruin and prison for the misguided, globalisation, civil wars, a world war, and murderous general pollution. Millions dead.

Here's to your good health!

Have mercy, Lord, on Israel, whom you have blinded and made all light, and who darkens us.

Hyperspeculative, never brilliant. Everything they do is spectacular to the blissful analyst. True thought is never spectacular to the blissful analyst. No Jewish saints or geniuses. All Jewish "geniuses" converge on nothingness: Rothschild, Marx, Freud, Oppenheimer, Field, S.T. Cohen, etc.

As Oppenheimer said: "We have done the devil's work".

True intelligence does not recognise itself in this way, and everything is organised to make it look like a sham and a mockery.

---

[82] There is no difference between the left and the right: the comatose zombies that make them up will always gang up against anything that might put dying France back on its feet.

Between the truth and the masses, a circumcision rises up: the truth becomes a lie and madness, and the masses laugh at this real 'ridiculousness', waving their glasses of alcohol, their cigarettes and their buttocks in a pair of Levis blue jeans.

The woman surgeon, the woman pill-popping minister, the woman taxi driver, the woman Minister for the Armed Forces (who has now disappeared, by the way), the woman policeman, and finally the 'free' woman, an apocalyptic monster, neither man nor woman, who becomes frighteningly ugly, unavailable, bloated, thick, full of tics, tobacco,[83] spongy in the face of all the nonsense and fashions of Jewish officialdom, especially when she is a professor of philosophy, liberated from man as man is liberated from God.

The circumcised professionally realise their essence by imposing on men, particularly through finance and the related industry, a "professional" image that runs counter to their essence.[84]

Go, Cartesian robot, towards your antibiotic survival.

Total enjuvenation is unconscious.

The Jewish question is part of the divine plan for humanity. They have the involutive superiority necessary for the end of the Dark Ages.

You can talk to Mr Lévy, but never to Homais. He's so stupid that it's absolutely impossible.

With Lévy it's often a dialogue of the deaf, but sometimes not completely: *a Jewish lady talked to me on the phone for five hours. She had just come out of the Birkenau camp and told me what no goy would tell me coming out of a German concentration camp: "If I were a goy, I'd be a nationalist and an anti-Semite"*.[85]

A Swiss Jew told me: "*In Israel I vote extreme right, here I vote socialist*". Isn't that a good one?

---

[83] The woman now has arteritis in her legs, which was never the case twenty years ago. This could lead to amputation.

[84] Read Simone Weil's *La condition ouvrière*.

[85] No goy would say that anywhere!

One evening, a Jewish former pupil invited me to dinner. There were seven of us Jews.

After two hours of conversation, we all agreed that Hitler had done everything necessary to liberate his country from international Jewish finance and Marxism! Never at a Goyim dinner could such a conversation and its conclusions have been possible! Why should they deprive themselves of vampirizing "this vile seed of cattle" (Zohar)?

Rothschild as Marx's brother: a brilliant dialectic of enemy brothers that produces the movements of history.

The Jewish conjuncture puts well-paid morons in apparent power. So they manipulate them perfectly, even without their knowledge. But these idiots are in the process of sawing off the branch on which they are sitting and concocting an anti-Jewishness in comparison with which the one of these four thousand years was a trifle.

The anti-Semitism of the USSR told us that all the current political regimes were Jewish.

And what about theirs?

Intelligence builds only in love; without love it destroys everything. Any work I do without love destroys me and others.

Synthetic chemistry is not a solution to health problems. It can only make humanity more and more degenerate.

The introduction of putrid products, mercury and aluminium? through vaccines is a crime of lèse-humanité.

True health has nothing to do with chemistry. Even surgery, with its spectacular advances, should have only limited applications.

TRUE HEALTH LIES IN WHAT WE INGEST WITH OUR BODY AND MIND.

Neither liberalism nor Marxism can provide health. The underlying cause of disease is the ingestion of molecules that are not specific to the human biotype.[86]

Lord, don't let me judge you.

---

[86] Burger: "The raw food war".

Life is such a sad, sad comedy that it kills you.

It's wise to have found a little ball to amuse the masses. Without it, there would have been no lions for a long time!

The modern woman oscillates between the little prick and the primitive, preferably white or black.

Jewish critics today will never find the slightest talent in a genius, especially if he has no talent.

O how many negative talents there have been over the last two centuries, how many beautiful styles aimed at deforming people's minds.

All true thought appears infantile in the eyes of an infantilised mass. Few people agree with me: that's reassuring.

How could it be otherwise when they are 'thought' by the media, without personality, without probity and incapable of informing themselves freely.

Take, for example, the myth of the 6-million-gas-chambers: it's a strictly primary myth, the stuff of arithmetic and technology. So it's easy to see how absurd it is. You can understand it in a quarter of an hour. And what's more, isn't the Gayssot law the ninth piece of evidence of this imposture?

The majority is always wrong: Vox populi, vox diaboli.

The faith of recent centuries, wrapped up in a dogmatic arsenal, could only culminate in the victory of Masonry and Marxism.

The Emperor Julian, known as the Apostate, understood it all: "If Christianity triumphs, in two thousand years the whole world will be Jewish".

A woman is always easy when she likes a man, otherwise she's a vestal virgin.

Evil will only be evil when it is done with full knowledge and will. In fact, it is only fatality, weakness, ignorance and folly.

True intelligence does not crush: it integrates. This condemns all ideologies that exclude.

Imagine Pericles campaigning and Montaigne taking the agrégation!

Crazier than a madman: a modern psychiatrist.

The stuttering critic of modern art: wee, wee, wee, wee. Exactly!

What people call intelligent is what they understand in a tiny point of time and space.

They have no idea what true intelligence is: synthesis.

Democracy: making people say, believe, think and act as a small, hidden number of people want them to, and making them believe that they are free. They'll think "I vote freely".

Yes, for a bunch of chatterboxes who won't even think of putting women back on the sacred path of their purpose! Still less will they give their children a moral and religious education, without which they will sink into delinquency, crime, drugs and suicide.

The illusion is all the greater that they will freely become Al Capone, a President of the Republic with the temperament of an accountant's assistant or a peanut merchant, who will have no real power, since Jewish finance manipulates them entirely.

How can we demand from some people an intellectual probity that would be their own suicide? The Jews can only live on lies.

How arbitrary everything seems: happy are those who perceive the harmony of the world, of beings and things.

The Venus de Milo, with arms? Ridiculous!

We live in an age when culture is the antithesis of THE culture. Goering used to say: "When people talk to me about culture, I pull out my revolver". What would he say today about the putrescent culture in which we live?

Goebbels did not want his children to live "in the atrocious world that the Jews would prepare for them". He, his wife and two children left this world together. His two daughters were movingly beautiful.

What do you think of Sartre, Sagan, Buffet, Solers et al? Who are they?

Progress has artificially created vegetative life.

"The lie of progress is Israel", said Simone Weil. We repeat this sentence because it is so obvious...

If you regard people as intelligent and speak to them with an open heart, you are insulting them because they are confusedly aware of their inadequacy. Enter into their subjectivity and flatter them, don't guide them to avoid their shortcomings, they will be delighted and you will be a man of the world.

And yet it's when you do this that you don't think much of them.

A bit of Marxism, a bit of Freudism, a "Normalien Supérieur", a structuralist, and what will be left of these pages?

There is nothing authentic that Judeo-Cartesianism cannot dissolve with its alchemy.

Access to knowledge always hurts. So what can we do?

Nothing, just play the piano, pray if you can and wait...

I aspire to the unattainable light and am plunged into darkness...

To my little one Béatrice

> *My beloved daughter, Nestled in my heart In the depths of eternity...*

Tristan is preparing to leave this world. He wants to give a final cry of suffering and love to this earth that hurts him so much...

My little Béa... She had brought up Aurélien for years with miraculous pedagogy and firmness. She had taught his entire nursery school with rare skill. She even introduced him to English and piano, which she didn't know but which she passed on to the child according to Tristan's teaching. This treasure who did everything in the house, cleaning, gardening, looking after both Monique and Tristan, even though he was overworked as a teacher and writer. But Monique, Aurélien's mother, mistreated this treasure, whose competence and dedication were astounding in their exceptional quality.

"You're only good for mopping", she used to say to this angel of devotion and perfectly unselfish competence. She didn't ask for money, so Tristan forced her to open a savings account and pay him a sum of money every month.

How could you not love such a creature, such perfection, when your mother worked at the hospital where she was a physiotherapist.

Monique's wickedness wounded Tristan's heart, and he knew how much Beatrice deserved gratitude and love for everything she did with her pure heart and absolute innocence. What love should Monique not have lavished on this angel? Everything she did for the child, for herself, for Tristan, for the house... Perfection was the child's happiness, the father's tranquillity, the mother's completeness.

OTHER TITLES

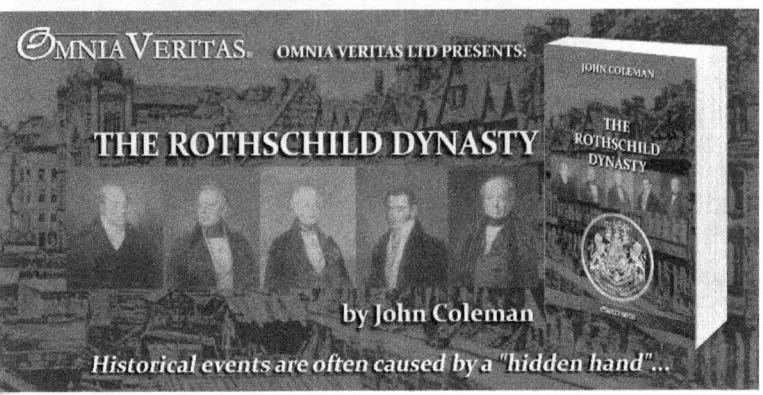

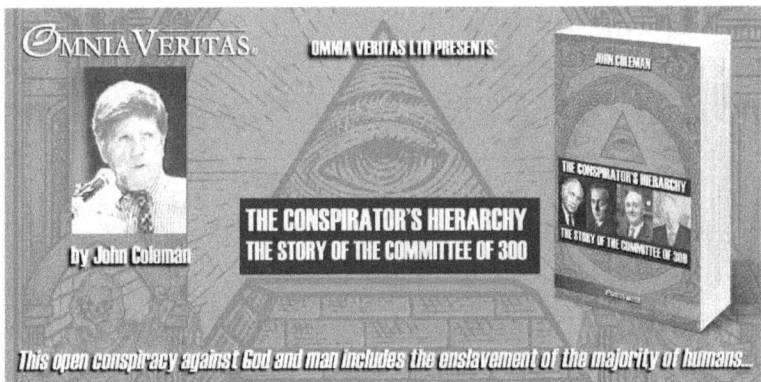

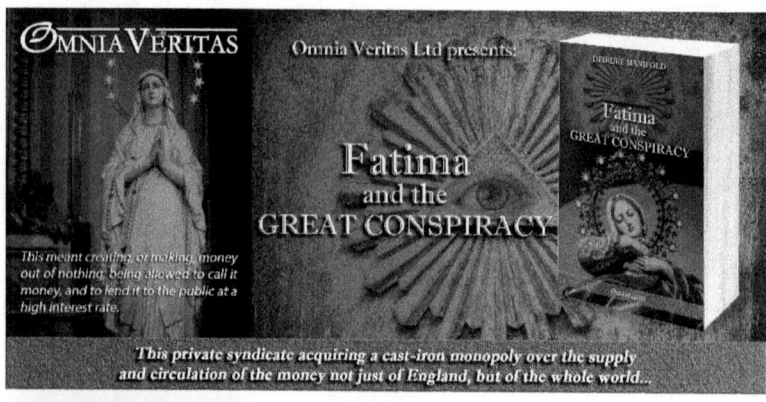

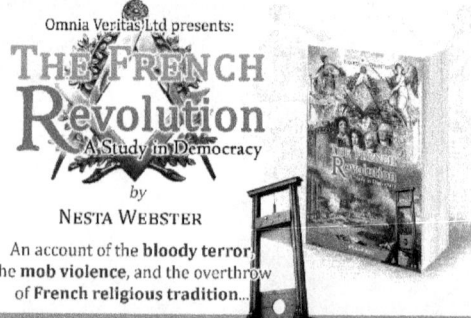

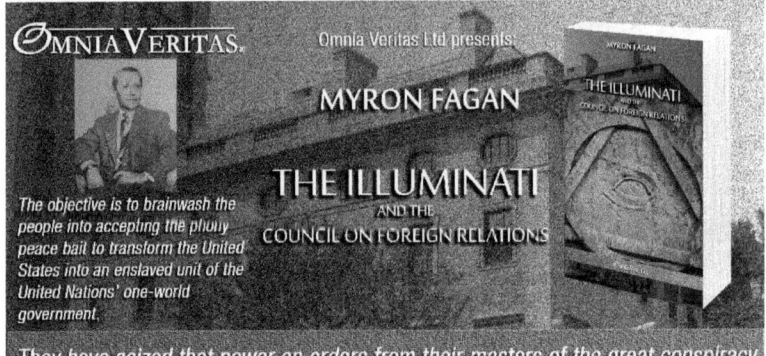

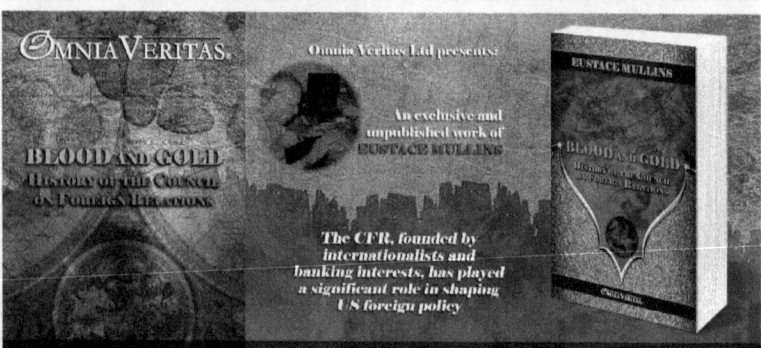

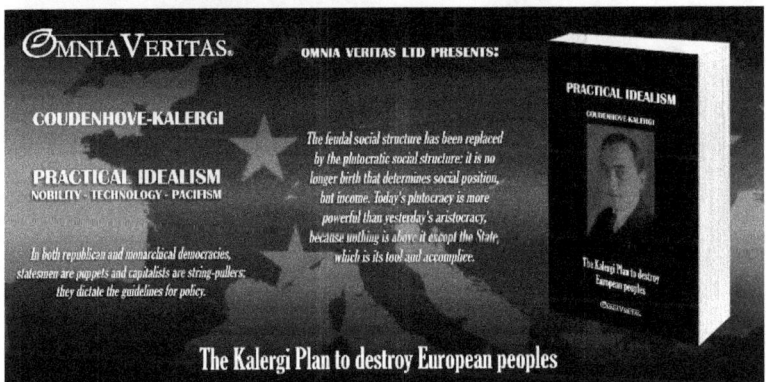

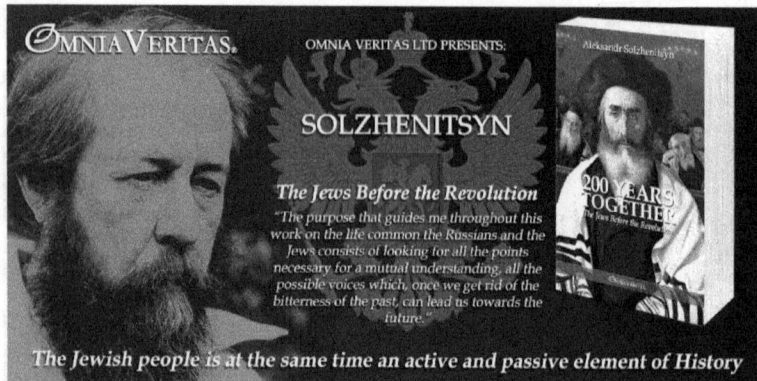
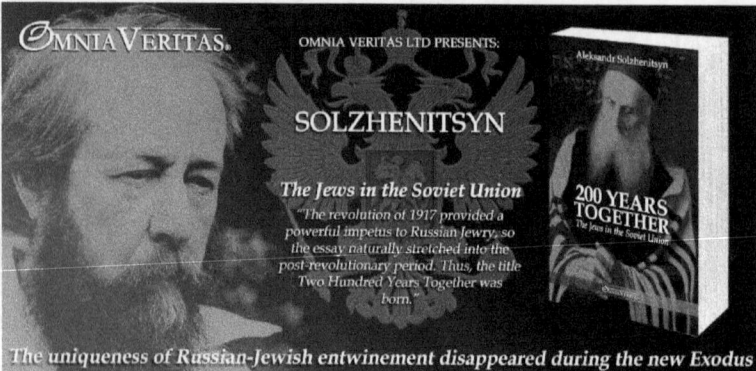

www.ingramcontent.com/pod-product-compliance
Lightning Source LLC
Chambersburg PA
CBHW071312150426
43191CB00007B/598